Enforcement of Intellectual Property Rights in Dutch, English and German Civil Procedure

KLUWER LAW INTERNATIONAL

Enforcement of Intellectual Property Rights in Dutch, English and German Civil Procedure

By

George Cumming
Mirjam Freudenthal
Ruth Janal

Wolters Kluwer
Law & Business

AUSTIN   BOSTON   CHICAGO   NEW YORK   THE NETHERLANDS

Published by:
Kluwer Law International
PO Box 316
2400 AH Alphen aan den Rijn
The Netherlands
Website: www.kluwerlaw.com

Sold and distributed in North, Central and South America by:
Aspen Publishers, Inc.
7201 McKinney Circle
Frederick, MD 21704
United States of America
Email: customer.care@aspenpubl.com

Sold and distributed in all other countries by:
Turpin Distribution Services Ltd.
Stratton Business Park
Pegasus Drive, Biggleswade
Bedfordshire SG18 8TQ
United Kingdom
Email: kluwerlaw@turpin-distribution.com

Printed on acid-free paper.

ISBN 978-90-411-2726-6

© 2008 Kluwer Law International BV, The Netherlands

Printed in Great Britain.

Table of Contents

Chapter 5
Implementation of Directive 2004/48/EC into German Civil Procedure

Preface

This book represents a modest contribution to the ongoing study, analysis and research into the field of EC harmonization of national procedure which exists in two different forms: first harmonization as lead by the European Court of Justice which evolves in the context of effectiveness, equivalence and effective judicial protection; and second harmonization by means of Community legislation, in this instance Directive 2004/48/EC[1] on the Enforcement of Intellectual Property Rights. Recital 7 of Directive 2004/48/EC (the Directive) states that the disparities between the systems of the Member States as regards the means of enforcing intellectual property rights are prejudicial to the proper functioning of the internal market, and the Directive seeks to approximate the legislative systems of the Member States and promote the level of protection within the EU.

A copy of the Directive 2004/48 EC is reproduced in this book with the kind permission of the Commission. However, the official and authentic version of the Directive remains in the paper form of the Official Journal, OJ L 157/45 30 Apr. 2004.

The focus of this book is on the analysis of the implementation of the Directive with respect to Dutch, English procedure and German national procedure in short, the fundamental question is whether or not the Directive has been or will be adequately implemented in those countries. The time which has passed since the implementation in England, Germany and the Netherlands is not long enough to determine whether the Directive has managed to achieve its aim of harmonizing the 'law in action'. Therefore, no attempt has been made to adopt a comparative legal perspective in terms of the implementation of the Directive. The primary objective is to ascertain the adequacy of a particular national implementation per se and to provide lawyers from other jurisdictions with a first access to the new legislation examined. Since the German legislation was adopted subsequent to the

---

1. A copy of the Directive 2004/48 EC is reproduced in this book with the kind permission of the Commission. However, the official and authentic version of the Directive remains in the paper form of the Official Journal, OJ L 157/45 30 Apr. 2004.

submission of manuscript, the explanations insofar refer to the government reform proposal, which however reflects the eventual act.

The task of determining the sufficiency of national implementation quite obviously depends upon the interpretation of the Directive and in particular the clarity or obscurity of its wording. It is not difficult to predict that the uncertainties in this regard are bound to evoke numerous references to the European Court of Justice pursuant to EC 234 in order to seek clarification of the exact scope and nature of the various articles of the Directive. Nonetheless, it is sincerely hoped that this book will prove to be both of use and of interest to a wide category of lawyers ranging from academics, practitioners and students of Intellectual Property Law as well as of European Law and of the respective national procedure.

Finally, an expression of thanks to Mr J. Watson of the UK Patent Office for his patient and very helpful replies to questions dealing with the English implementation of the Directive. The usual disclaimers apply in this regard. The authors are also much obliged to their editor, Mrs C. Robben of Kluwer Law International for her patience, help and encouragement.

Dr George Cumming, Paris

Dr Mirjam Freudenthal, Utrecht

Dr Ruth Janal, LL.M., Berlin

Introduction

I   OVERVIEW

Arguably, the analysis of the development of the use of national rules of procedure in order to enforce rights created by Community law may be analyzed from at least two perspectives: first, from what might be termed a teleological perspective, in the sense of the overall purpose which the use of the rules of national procedure in order to enforce Community rights is to accomplish and second, from the manner in which changes to the national rules may be effected in order to ensure that the objective or purpose is achieved. For didactic reasons[1], it might be argued that the primary purpose of the Treaty is to advance the economic, social and or political convergence of the Member States of the European and as such a critical component thereof is the creation of a legal system which has two hallmarks: namely, the uniformity and the effectiveness in the formulation and application of what might be termed Community norms. By reason notably of case law of the European Court of Justice (ECJ) the following description presented by Dougan[2] concerning the form of national civil procedure used to accomplish the aforementioned objectives would seem appropriate:

> National remedies and procedural rules are portrayed as presenting a serious problem through their tendency to offer inadequate and in any case, fragmented standards of enforcement in respect of Treaty norms. The solution is to manufacture – either by legislative of if necessary judicial means – a harmonised system of legal protection within Europe.

Accordingly, before considering the legislative means of achieving harmonizing of legal protection of Community rights notably in the form of the Directive 2004/48 European Community (EC) (the Directive), it is useful to consider what might be

---

1. M. Dougan, *National Remedies before the Court of Justice* (Oxford: Hart, 2004), generally, Introduction, Chs 1, 2 and 7 and 389.
2. Ibid.

considered, chronologically, the first method, namely, the judicial means: that is, the intervention of the ECJ and the formulation of principles as set forth in its case law.

A   HARMONIZATION THROUGH ECJ PRINCIPLES

The ECJ has consistently held in a series of cases that in the absence of Community rules, such as secondary legislation as the Directive in the instant case which deal specifically with procedure and remedies it is for the domestic legal system of each Member State to determine the procedural conditions governing actions at law intended to ensure the protection of the rights which individuals derive from Community law[3].

More generally one might describe the origin of this state of the affairs in the following manner: that is, according to the EC Treaty the actual application and enforcement of Community law is normally dependent upon the legal systems and in particularly upon the procedural systems of the Member States. This responsibility arises from what might be termed a division between on the one hand the legislative power of Community institutions and on the other the competence of Member States to enforce Community law. The responsibility of the Member States concerns specifically therefore the protection of rights which individuals derive from Community law. The protection thereof is carried out by means of the national rules of procedure and remedies where there is no applicable Community legislation in the field: that is, normally an individual with a right under Community law or an interest in its application utilises national rules of procedures and remedies in order to enforce it provided however, that no such rules are provided by Community law. Most significantly, the degree of judicial protection afforded to the individual who seeks to enforce his Community right depends upon the courts, remedies and above all procedures as provided by the Member States. Further it would appear that the system of national enforcement of Community law by means of national procedures and remedies arguably was predicated at least in some measure upon the supposition that such remedies and procedures were sufficient and adequate in order to ensure effective enforcement of the rights provided by the Community law[4]. Arguably it is the litigation which has involved the use of

---

3. *Rewe* Case No. 33/76 (1976) ECR 1989 para. 5, *Comet* Case No 45/76 (1976) ECR 2043 para. 13, *San Giorgio* Case No. 199/82 (1983) ECR 3595 para. 12, *Emmott* Case No C-208/90 (1991) ECR I 4269 para. 16, Francovich et al. Joined Cases No; C-6/90 and C-9/90 (1991) ECR I 5357 para. 43, *Stenhorst-Neerings* Case No; C-338/91 (1993) ECR I 5457 para. 15, *Johnson* Case No; C-410/92 (1994) ECR I 5483 para. 21, *Peterbroeck* Case No C-312.93 (1995) ECR I 4599 para. 12 and *van Shijndel* Joined Cases No. C-430/93 and C-431/93 (1995) ECR I-4705.
4. F. Jacobs QC 'Enforcing Community Rights and Obligations in National Courts: Striking the Balance', in *Remedies for Breach of EC Law*, eds J. Lonbay & A. Biondi (Chichester: Wiley & Sons, 1997), 25. 'It is sometimes said that the assumption made by the authors of the EC Treaty was that national legal systems based on the rule of law could be relied upon to provide an adequate level of judicial protection: it was therefore sufficient to allow Community law to be enforced by

national procedures and remedies which has demonstrated the deficiency thereof in terms of enforcement capability. Accordingly, the ECJ intervened in order to rectify the deficiencies encountered in the national procedures and remedies.[5]

B   PRINCIPLES

It is clear however, that the ECJ has developed certain principles which, as it were, serve to guide and restrict the discretion of the national courts in their use of their national rules of procedure for the enforcement of Community rights of which the following may be noted.

1   Court of National Choice

Arguably the first principle developed by the ECJ is that the Member States must ensure that there is a court with the appropriate jurisdiction in order to enforce Community rights.[6] In short, following EC Article 10, there must be a court and

---

national remedies through national courts in accordance with national procedural rules. The reality is that the authors of the Treaty had little choice but to rely on national legal systems short of undertaking immediate and extensive harmonization of rules governing the organization of courts, remedies procedures and time-limits – it was left to the Court of Justice to strike the balance between the autonomy of the Member States in these areas and the need to ensure proper application of Community law'.

5.   The ECJ also sustained its intervention and control of the national procedure and remedies by developing with respect to the EC Treaty at least the concept of a complete and coherent system of judicial protection. K. Lenaerts 'The Legal Portection of Private Parties under the EC Treaty: a Coherent and Complete System of Judicial Review' in Scrittin: GF Mancini, Vol. II, (Giudffré 1998) 591

6.   *Butter-Buying Cruises*, Case No. 158/80 (1981) ECR 1805 seem to have established that application of Community law by the national courts was not intended to created new remedies and procedures in the national courts. However, D. Curtin "Directives: the Effectiveness of Judicial Protection of Individual Rights" (1990) *CMLRev* 709 and D. Curtin, H. Schermers & T. Heukerls, *Institutional Dynamics of Euorpean Integration* (The Hague: Nijhoff, 1994), 457, with respect in particular to Factortame Case No C-213/89 (1990) ECR I 2433, argue that effectively the ECJ established an obligation on the part of the national court to create a new remedy having first found that that the initial assumption that the legal system provided sufficient means of redress was disproved. Similarly with Francovich, Joined Cases C -6/90 – C-9/90 (1991) ECR I 5357 can be presented from the point of view that a new remedy was created in so far as the national courts do not normally have power to grant damages for breaches committed by the legislature. In any event, whether or not a new remedy was created or an existing remedy was expanded it is clear that the result was that powers of the national court were substantially expanded. More recently the ECJ held in *Unibet*, Case No. C-432/05 (2007) ECR I 2271 the following which arguably clarifies the circumstances where the national court may be called upon to create new procedure and or remedies: at para. 40: 'Although the EC Treaty has made it possible in a number of instances for private persons to bring a direct action where appropriate before the Community Court, it was not intended to create new remedies in the national courts to ensure observance of Community law other than those already laid down by national law (Case 158/00 Rewe para. 44): para. 41. It would be otherwise only if it were apparent from the over all scheme of the national legal system in question that no legal remedy existed which made it possible to ensure, even indirectly, respect for individual's rights under Community law (see Case 33/76 Rewe, para. 5, Comet para. 16 and Factortame para. 19-23).'

there must be a procedure available before which and within the context of which an individual may enforce his Community rights.[7] The situation is different where the obligation to provide a specific kind of judicial protection for a specific type of Community right in favour of a particular person or category of person is established in the form Community law such as the Directive.

2   Equivalence and Effectiveness

It can be said that the ECJ has restricted the discretion of the national courts by formulating two minimum requirements which the national procedural must satisfy[8]. The first requirement may be termed the principle of equivalence[9]. This generally signifies that the substantive and procedural conditions which govern the respective actions for the enforcement of Community law must not be less favourable than those relating to similar actions of a domestic nature. The second principle is that of effectiveness and requires that the conditions are not framed in such a way as to render virtually impossible or excessively difficult the exercise of Community law rights. The ECJ established and confirmed these principles in Rewe[10], Comet[11] and San Giorgio[12]. However, the ECJ also established in San Giorgio[13] that the operation of the two principles was cumulative and not separate: that is, notably, the operation of the principle of equivalence was insufficient in order to ensure conformity of the national measures.

The requirement of non-discrimination laid down by the Court cannot be construed as justifying legislative measures intended to render any repayment of charges levied contrary to Community law virtually impossible even if the treatment is extended to tax payers who have similar claims arising from an infringement of national tax law.

It could be said that the principle of effectiveness requires no more that the proper application of Community law and that adequate remedies exist for the breach Community rights. However, the scope of this principle is not unlimited. In short, the principle of effectiveness or full application is arguably subject to that of proportionality in the sense that it must be balanced against considerations such as legal certainty, sound administration of justice and the orderly conduct of

---

7. *Foglia Novello II* Case No. 244/80 (1984) ECR 3045 and *Dorsch Consult* Case C-54/96 (1997) ECR I-4961.
8. K. Lenaerts, D. Arts & I. Maselis, *Procedural Law of the European Union*, ed. R Bray, 2nd edn (London: Sweet & Maxwell 2006) Ch. 3; F. Jacobs QC 'Enforcing Community Rights and Obligations in National Courts: Striking the Balance', in *Remedies for Breach of EC Law*, eds J. Lonbay & A. Biondi (Chichester: Wiley & Sons, 1997), 25-36.
9. S. Prechal, *Directives in EC Law*, 2nd (Oxford: OUP, 2006), 137 n. 37 interestingly observes that "Other terms such as 'non-discrimination or 'assimilation' are sometimes also used.
10. *Rewe* Case No. 158/80 (1981) ECR 1805.
11. *Comet* Case No. 45/76 (1976) ECR 2043.
12. *San Giorgio* Case No. 199/82 (1983) ECR 3595.
13. *San Giorgio* Case No. 199/82 (1983) ECR 3595 ibid. at para. 17, *Commission v. Italy* Case No. 104/86 (1988) ECR 1799, *Bianco* Joined Cases No. 331, 376 and 378/85 (1988) ECR 1099 : See however, *Edis* Case No. C-231/96 (1998) ECR I 4951.

proceedings by the court. One might say that in the absence of harmonised rules it remains in principle for Member States to strike an appropriate balance between various of the aforementioned considerations which do not constitute an finite list. Advocate General Jacobs describes what might be termed the proportional application of these principles in the following manner:

> I should like to suggest at the outset that the Court's case law can be assessed in terms of the need to achieve the appropriate balance between on the one hand the need for national courts to provide proper protection for Community rights invoked in the national courts and on the other hand, the importance of respecting within appropriate limits the procedural and indeed organization autonomy of the Member States' legal systems[14] ... the Court, in the absence of rules governing the application of Community law by the national courts, has sought – even if not invariably with success – to perform a difficult task: to achieve a proper balance between the interest in preferring the procedural and organizational autonomy of the national legal systems and that of ensuring effective protection of Community. While for the most part respecting the choices made by the Member States and merely demanding equal treatment of Community claims, the Court has on occasion been ready to intervene to secure an adequate standard of judicial protection for Community rights.[15]

Further, following San Giorgio, once it is established that one or both of the requirements of effectiveness and equivalence are not satisfied the case law would seem to indicate that the national court is thereby prevented from applying the national procedure. [16] The ECJ held as follows in San Giorgio:

---

14. F. Jacobs QC 'Enforcing Community Rights and Obligations in National Courts: Striking the Balance', in *Remedies for Breach of EC Law*, eds J. Lonbay & A. Biondi (Chichester: Wiley & Sons, 1997), 25 at 27; However in contra see R. Crauford Smith, in *The Evolution of EU Law*, eds Craig & de Burca (Oxford: OUP, 1999) '... it was suggested that three rather different interpretations of the [ECJ] case law could be detected in the academic literature: first, there has been a linear development from the requirement that national rules should to make it impossible to exercise directly enforceable rights to one 'that there should be no fetter on the provision of an effective judicial remedy'; secondly, that the case law reflects a fairly consistent application of such fundamental Community principles as supremacy and effectiveness of Community law; and thirdly, that it has been both confused and contradictory. Perhaps rather surprisingly, the above survey indicates that each of these approaches has explanatory value.'

15. F. Jacobs QC 'Enforcing Community Rights and Obligations in National Courts: Striking the Balance', in *Remedies for Breach of EC Law*, eds J. Lonbay & A. Biondi (Chichester: Wiley & Sons, 1997), ibid., 36.

16. F. Jacobs QC 'Enforcing Community Rights and Obligations in National Courts: Striking the Balance', in *Remedies for Breach of EC Law*, eds J. Lonbay & A. Biondi (Chichester: Wiley & Sons, 1997), ibid., at 26 states:

'A further misconception that conveniently be dealt with here is that the principles of the primacy and effectiveness of Community law – principles which the Court has held to be inherent in the Treaty – demand that a national court must in all circumstances set aside procedural bars to claims based on Community law'.

Once it is established that the levying of the charge is incompatible with Community law, the court must be agree to decide whether or not the burden of the charge has been passed on ... to other person.[17]

3   Supremacy[18]

In Simmenthal,[19] the ECJ established with respect to the doctrine of supremacy that a national court must:

in a case within its jurisdiction apply Community law in it is entirety and protect rights which the latter confers on individuals and must accordingly set aside any provision of national law which may conflict with it.

The ECJ went on to hold that a national court was under a duty to set aside national rules which prevented the primacy or supremacy in application of Community law, that is,

which might impair the effectiveness of Community law by withholding from the national court having jurisdiction to apply such law the power to do everything necessary at the moment of its application to set aside national legislative provisions which may prevent Community rules form having full force and effect [is] incompatible with these requirements, which are the very essence of Community law.[20]

4   Principle of Effective Judicial Protection

This principle was perhaps first established in the case of Johnston[21] which followed von Colson[22] and would appear to be a principle independent of the concept of direct effect of Community law provisions. Fundamentally one might say that the principle of effective judicial protection predicates that in the context of a

---

17. *San Giorgio* Case No. 199/82 (1983) ECR 3595 op. cit. at para. 14.
18. F. Jacobs QC refers to this as primacy in 'Enforcing Community Rights and Obligations in National Courts: Striking the Balance', in *Remedies for Breach of EC Law*, eds J. Lonbay & A. Biondi (Chichester: Wiley & Sons, 1997), op. cit. 26.
19. *Simmenthal* Case No. 106/77 (1978) ECR 629 at para. 21.
20. *Simmenthal* Case No 106/77 (1978) ECR 269 ibid. at para. 22: S. Prechal, *Directives in EC Law*, 2nd edn (Oxford: OUP, 2006), 140-141 quaeres the meaning of' having jurisdiction' in para. 22: '... the jurisdiction referred to by the Court of Justice is soley subject matter jurisdiction. Jurisdiction or power to apply the regulation at issue was lacking. Yet it is difficult to understand how direct effect and supremacy of Community law or its full effectiveness or Art. 10 of the Treaty to which the Court implicitly refers at para. 16 of Simmethal can create powers for the national courts which did not exist before. However this might be, Simmenthal remained an isolated case in this respect for the next twelve years until the judgment in Factortame was given which again raised comparable problems'
21. *Johnston* Case No. 222/84 (1986) ECR 1651.
22. *Von Colson* Case No. 14/83 (1984) ECR 1891 wherein the ECJ held that a Member State must choose a sanction which guarantees real and effective judicial protection.

Community based on the rule of law everyone must enjoy the possibility of asserting his rights before the courts.[23]

Advocate General Sharpston referred to the principle of effective judicial protection in UNIBET[24] in the following manner:

> the principle of effective legal protection itself reflects a general principle of law which underlies the constitutional traditions common to the Member States. That principle, the right to a fair trial, is enshrined in Article 6 (1) of the European Convention on Human Rights and is now recognised a general prinipcle of Community law by virtue of Article 6 (2) EU. In embodying the 'right to a court' of which the non-absolute right of access is one aspect, Article 6 (1) of the Convention impliedely requires access for the purposes of review in the control of specific cases. Limitations to such access are compatible with Article 6 (1) only where they do not impair the essence of their right where they pursue a legitimate aim and where a reasonable relationship of proportionality exists between the means employed and the aim sought to be achieved.

The ECJ in its judgement in UNIBET[25] defined the principle in the following manner:

> according to settled case law, the principle of effective judicial protection is a general principle of Community law stemming from the constitutional traditions common to the Member State which has been enshrined in Article 6 and Article 13 of the European Convention of Human Rights and Fundamental Freedoms (Case 222/84 Johnston (1986) ECR 1651, para. 18 and 19, Case 222/86 Heylens & others (1987) ECR 4097 para 14, Case 424/99 *Commission v. Austria* (2001) ECR I 9285 para. 45, Case 50/00 P Union de Peuquenos Agricultores (2002) ECR I – 6677 para. 39 and Case C-467/01 Eridrand (2003) ECR I 6471 para. 61) and which has been reaffirmed by Article 47 of the Charter of Fundamental Rights of the European Union proclaimed on 7 December 2000 in Nice.

5   Substantive Treaty Rules

It is appropriate to note that additional restraints exist on the discretion enjoyed by national courts in the use of national procedure and remedies for the enforcement of Community law rights.

In certain cases Treaty freedoms or the general prohibition on discrimination laid down in Article 12 of the Treaty among other articles may have effect on

---

23. *European Parliament v. Council* Case No C-70/88 (1990) ECR I 2041 para. 6, J. Boulouis 1988 'A propos de deux principes généraux du droit communautaire' (1988) *RFDA* 691,
24. *UNIBET* Case No C-432/05 (2007) ECR I 2271 Opinion at para. 38.
25. *UNIBET* Case No C-432/05 (2007) ECR I 2271, ibid., at para. 37.

national procedure.[26] Other articles which may have an effect are Article 28 EC on the free movement of goods, Articles 39[27], 43[28] and 49[29] dealing with the free movement of persons and Article 82 dealing with abuse of a dominant position.[30]

In short the national rules of procedure may require disapplication and modification by reason of their breaching one of the Treaty articles. However in most case, national remedies and procedural rules do not involve any direct breach of the substantive Treaty rules.

Finally, it is clear that the other eventual source for change of national procedure is to be found, as in the instant case with the Directive, in secondary Community legislation such as a directive and its interpretation of.[31]

C   EXTENT OR LEVEL OF PROTECTION OF COMMUNITY RIGHTS
               UNDER JUDICIAL HARMONIZATION

According to Advocate General Jacobs, the standard or level of protection of Community rights is or ought to be one of adequate protection. The Advocate General observes in this regard:

> It would plainly be quite another manner – and beyond the remit of the Court – to seek to derive form national law a uniform set of remedies, procedures and time-limits for actions before national courts based on Community law: instead, the Court's goal must be the more limited one of ensuring an adequate standard of judicial protection.[32]

Van Gerven[33] arguably arrives at the same result in the following manner:

> (ii) the form and the extent of the remedy are, in the absence of Community rules, a matter for the Member States; provided that the remedy made available under national law provides adequate (not just minimum) judicial protection, i.e., allows individual to obtain redress which is commensurate

---

26. *Dafeki*, Case No C-336/94 (1997) ECR I 6761, *Data Delecta* Case C-43/95 (1996) ECR I 4661, *Saldanha*, Case C-122/96 (1997) ECR I 5325 and S. Prechal Directives in EC Law (2nd ed, Oxford, OUP, 2005) p. 146, note 105.
27. *Commission v. Germany* Case C-24/97 (1998) ECR I 2133, *Sagulo*, Case 8/77 (1977) ECR 1495.
28. Skanavi Case No. C-193/94 (1996) ECR I 929, *Royer Case* No. 48/75 (1976 ECR 497, *Calfa* Case 348/96 (1999) ECI I 11, *Wijsenbeek* Case No C-378/97 (1999) ECR I 6207.
29. *Reisebüro Broed* Case No C-3/95 (1996) ECR I 6511, *Pfeiffer Grosshandel* Case No C-255/97 (1999) ECR I 2835 and *van Doren*, Case No C-244/00 (2003) ECR I 3051.
30. *Promedia* Case No. T-111/96 (1998) ECR II 2937, *Conte* Case C-221/99 (2001) ECR I 9359, *Italo Fenocchio* Case No C-412 (1999) ECR I 3845.
31. Also *Océano* Joined Cases no C-240/98 and C-244/98 (2000) ECR I 4941.
32. F. Jacobs QC 'Enforcing Community Rights and Obligations in National Courts: Striking the Balance', in *Remedies for Breach of EC Law*, eds J. Lonbay & A. Biondi (Chichester: Wiley & Sons, 1997), op. cit., 32.
33. W. Van Gerven 'Of Rights, Remedies and Procedures' (2000) *CMLRev* (37) 501 at p. 503-504.

with the nature and the degree of interference with those individual's Community rights

(iii) It is also a matter for the Member States in the absence of Community rules, to provide procedures which allow individuals to invoke the remedies before a court of law, provided that such procedural rules do not make adequate protection virtually impossible or excessively difficult (the requirement of minimum effectiveness of enforcement of Community law) and do not treat Community claims less favourable than similar national claims (the requirement of equivalence or non-discrimination.

The latter two propositions imply that the scope of application of the requirement of minimum effectiveness as defined in (iii) above is limited to the area of procedural rules whilst the area of remedial rules is to be governed by the principle of adequate judicial protection as stated under (ii).

In combination, that means that national procedural rules should not present an obstacle to adequate judicial protection.

D ADVANTAGES AND DISADVANTAGES OF JUDICIALLY LEAD HARMONIZATION

One might say that theoretically at least the primary advantage of such a system of enforcement of Community rights is that it involves a minimal amount of Community intervention in the matters such as the organization of the national administration of justice and respects thereby concepts such a procedural autonomy.[34] The use of familiar rules of national procedure and remedies may also serve to facilitate the integration of Community law into national law. However, there are arguably disadvantages: it would seem that the effectiveness of Community law may well be affected by the disparateness and the particularities of the national systems of law. Accordingly, these procedural particularities and differences may lead to enforcement disparities. Additionally, there is what might be termed something of a constitutional weakness; that is the national courts often possess sufficient ability to enforce Community law effectively and ensure effective judicial protection of Community rights. Notwithstanding it would seem that a limit on this method of enforcement may be reached when a national court is asked to effect a change in the national rules of procedure or remedies for which it simply does not possess the constitutional competence. It is in such a situation that the use of Community legislation such as a directive is useful in order to provide the necessary power.[35] Additionally, the case law which has been developed

---

34. S. Prechal *Directives in EC Law*, 2nd edn (Oxford: OUP, 2005) Ch. 7.
35. S. Prechal 'National Courts in EU Judicial Structures': 'It is argued that the jurisprudential developments amount to a direct empowerment of national courts. These should where necessary extend their existing powers or assume on the basis of Community law alone, new powers which do not exist under national law in order to fulfil effectively the tasks assigned to them

by the ECJ has in itself lead to uncertainties and thereby given rise to criticisms to either excessive intervention or on the other hand the need for legislative harmonization.[36] In some instances, the ECJ has, as it were, respected the concept of procedural autonomy and relied upon the principles of effectiveness and or equivalence. In other cases, the ECJ has invoked as in Johnston[37] the principle of effective judicial protection. Arguably this latter principle in particular has served as a basis for the introduction of new remedies into national systems of procedures and remedies culminating in the formation of the principle of State liability in Francovich.[38] Dougan[39] encapsulates some of the additional difficulties of the ECJ lead remedy of the national enforcement deficit:

> This position embraces the very real practical limitations of the Court as a lawmaking body. Legal development through the process of litigation suffers from several well known flaws, for example: the ad hoc and uncontrolled manner by which issues are presented to the courts for resolution; and the inevitable influence on the particular factual circumstances of each dispute upon the more abstract legal principles enunciated by the judges. Such flaws are exacerbated within the context of litigation before the Court of Justice: for example whether sitting in chambers of plenary session, the body is bound to speak with a single voice and thus to find some acceptable consensus between the differing opinions which must inevitably emerge between the judges, perhaps to the detriment of clear and or confident lawmaking. For such reason, many commentators have queried whether any process of remedial harmonization would not be better entrusted to the systematic consideration of the Treaty's political institutions.

> Indeed, on might ultimately feel pressed towards the conclusion that remedial harmonisation (whether based on the traditional 'integration through law' or an alternative 'secotoral' mode) is a task to which the Court is inherently unsuited[40].

---

by the Court of Justice. … National courts are (still organs of the national legal order. They still derive their authority form the State: as was already observed, the forma source of their power is national law; – see also Opinion of A-G Léger in Case C-224/01 *Köbler* (2003) ECR I-10239 at point 66.'

36. M. Hoskins, 'Tilting the Balance: Supremacy and National Procedural Rules' (1996) *ELRev* 365.
37. *Johnston* Case No. 222/84 (1986) ECR op. cit., 1651.
38. *Francovich* Joined Cases No. C-6/90 and C-90 (1991) ECR I 5357.
39. M. Dougan, *National Remedies before the Court of Justice* (Oxford: Hart, 2004) Chs 1, 2 and 7 and p. 389 see also: in favour of legislative harmonization: L. Neville-Brown, 'National Protection of Community Rights: Reconciling Autonomy and Effectiveness', in *Remedies for Breaches of EU Law*, eds J. Lonbay & A. Biondi (Chichester: Wiley & Sons, 1997), 25. R. Craufurd Smith 'Remedies for Breaches of EU Law in National Courts: Legal Variation and Selection', in *The Evolution f EU Law*, eds P. Craig & G de Burca (Oxford: OUP, 1999); C. Himsworth, 'Things Fall Apart: The Harmonisation of Community Judicial Procedural Protection Revisited' (1997) 22 *ELRev* 291.
40. M. Dougan, *National Remedies before the Court of Justice* (Oxford: Hart, 2004, op. cit).

Arguably, the Directive, in the instant case, in so far as it seeks to harmonise national procedure avoids certain of the theoretical difficulties raised notably with respect to case lead procedural harmonization of the ECJ which have been noted and in particular the lack of clarity of the legal basis to empower a national court to effect certain changes in the procedures and remedies necessary to enforce Community rights effectively. However, other difficulties arise in terms of the establishment of the degree and scope of the harmonization as established notably for the instant Directive.

E   HARMONIZATION THROUGH COMMUNITY LEGISLATION

Having, therefore, considered the judicial method of harmonization as developed and applied by the ECJ and in particular its shortcomings, it is now appropriate to consider the second method of harmonization, namely, that brought about through Community legislation notably in the form, as in the instant case of a directive. One might note, however, that there are arguably at least three legislative forms which may be utilised in order to harmonise notably the rules of procedure which are used: these are namely, regulations, directives and guidelines. It is to be observed that in the Impact Assessment Report[41] following White Paper on Actions for Damages[42] that these three possible means are discussed. In the instant case it would appear that harmonization by means of a directive which by virtue of EC Article 249 (3) obliges Member States to achieve the result prescribed within the text of the instrument was possibly chosen by reason of certain of its characteristics: generally one can say that directives respect as far as possible the sovereign powers of the Member States and in particular the position of national parliaments arguably in contrast to regulations.[43] In the instant case, the emphasis here will be placed upon the advantages of the use of a directive in order to achieve harmonization by reason of the fact that the subject of the analysis in the instant case is the Directive.

1   **Advantages: One Might Consider the**
            Following Advantages of a Directive as a Method
            of Harmonization

One notes generally that the effect upon the national procedure is specifically governed by the content of the Directive notably as regards the form and eventual changes which may require in order to ensure that the national rules of procedure may correctly implement the Directive. It may be argued that there is a certain

---

41. European Commission, *Impact Assessment Report* (Staff Working Document) SEC (2008) 405, 2 Apr. 2008 p. 29, n. 70.
42. European Commission, *White Paper on Damages Actions for Breach of the EC Anti-Trust Rules*, COM (2008) 125, 2. Apr. 2008 <europa.eu.com> in par.
43. A. Bleckman, *Europarecht*, 6th edn (Cologne: C Heymanns Verlag, 1997) generally.

amount of diversity and changeability concerning notably the rules of civil procedure involved in the enforcement of intellectual property rights. Accordingly, the
best method of enforcement in terms of the taking of the concrete decisions as it
were is left to the national institutions, the national courts, while the overall coher-
ence of the action is safeguarded by the orientation laid down in the directive.
Prechal observes in this regard:

> The limited intervention concept and the directive as a means of decentralization
> have on important feature in common: they should contribute to smooth
> achievement for the result desire by the directive within the national legal
> orders. Similarly, by virtue of these characteristics, the directive seems to go
> hand-in-glove with the principle of subsidiarity.[44]

The Member States are required to adapt or adopt law only to a certain extent,
namely as far as necessary in order to achieve the objectives set forth in a directive
and the Treaty provision which serves as its legal basis. In so far as a directive is
binding as to the results set forth in its text, that is the 'result to be achieved' the
choice of the 'form and methods' pursuant to EC 249 is left to the discretion of the
Member States. Accordingly, or at least in principle, this situation permits Member
States to introduce the Community norm by means of concepts and terminology
familiar within the national legal system.

2   Disadvantages of a Directive as a Method of Harmonization

Notwithstanding these advantages, problems do exist with directives notably in
terms of their timely and correct implementation by Member States and their
enforcement by national courts[45]. Paradoxically, it would seem that use of the
doctrine of consistent interpretation in order to remedy either inadequate or non-
implementation of a directive may in fact generate theoretically difficulties similar
to those potentially created by judicially lead harmonization: namely, what are the
limits or the scope of the national courts duty with respect to ensuring conformity
between the wording of a directive and national law where there has either been
non-implementation or mis-implementation thereof: in short does the obligation
for consistent interpretation even when based on EC Articles 249 (3) and 10 and
coupled with the doctrine of supremacy suffice to extend the interpretative powers

---

44. S. Prechal *Directives in EC Law,* 2nd edn (Oxford: OUP, 2006), op. cit., 5 and in particular n.
     27 which cites the Commission's Communication on the Principle of Subsidiarity, Bull EC
     10-1992, 123-4, and the Edinburgh Guidelines, Bull EC 12-1992, 15. See also F.Snyder 'The
     Effectiveness of European Community Law: Institutions, Processes, Tools and Tecniques'
     (1993) *MLR* 19, and D. Simon 'Le Droit communautaire et la suspension provisoire des
     mesures nationales' (1997) *RMC* 19, and D. Simon *La Directive européennne* (Paris: Dalloz,
     1997), 11-12.
45. W van Gerven «A Common Law for Europe: the Future Meeting the Past? » (2001) *European
     Review of Private Law* 343.

of national courts and change thereby their judicial functions.[46] In this regard Prechal observes.

Yet, there are also some indication that the effect of the doctrine of consistent interpretation may go in the direction of requiring national courts to stretch the boundaries of what is considered under their national law, as a matter of judicial function. [47] Yet, 'as far as possible' remains an intriguing concept in this respect. It may require to depart, to a certain extent, from national rules of construction. I may imply for the national court to 'stretch' the limits of its judicial function as it exists in the national legal system. It should, in any case, be understood as 'within the limits of the general principles of law' in particular legal certainty. In other words, although what is possible and what not lies primarily in the hands of national courts, they are not totally free, but operate under the control of – or it is perhaps better to say in the context of dialogue with – the Court of Justice, which may be quite demanding.[48]

These considerations will be examined in the course of the analysis of the implementation of the Directive. As noted earlier, the non-implementation of a directive within the time limits or inadequate implementation in the sense of partial or incorrect constitutes one of the major problems involving the use of a directive as an instrument of Community legislation. Directive 2004/48/EC as will be seen is not exempt from this situation.

3   Optimal Level of Harmonization

Arguably one of the more difficult aspects both theoretically and practically as regards the use of a directive in order to achieve harmonization is the determination of the degree of harmonization which is to be established and notably the criterion which are utilised thereby. In this regard Dougan[49] observes:

> The regulatory ideal of a Treaty-based 'level playing-field' inherent in the drive for a single market has by necessity, given way to a complex system of multi-level governance characterized by a diversity of policies across the Member States and aimed at accommodating valuable and vulnerable but often variable social interests. Nevertheless, this conceptual framework finds its limit when one attempts to define more clearly the relationship between an economic and a social Community (and thus between a uniform and differentiated normative landscape) which minimum harmonization was intended to help resolve.

One will recall that one of the criticisms of the judicially lead harmonization is that it is essentially ad hoc in nature and as such leads ipso facto to a need for harmonization through legislation.

---

46. S. Prechal *Directives in EC Law,* 2nd edn (Oxford: OUP, 2006), ibid., 203.
47. S. Prechal *Directives in EC Law,* 2nd edn (Oxford: OUP, 2006), ibid., 203 and n. 110.
48. S. Prechal *Directives in EC Law,* 2nd edn (Oxford: OUP, 2006), ibid., p. 20ç and n. 139.
49. M. Dougan « Minimum Harmonization and the Internal Market » (2000) CMLRev (37) 853 at 854-855.

Prechal observes:

> The approximation of national law by the Community is often stereotyped
> in terms of a model of 'total harmonization'. ... As such, total may be
> contrasted with minimum harmonization. In the latter case, Member States
> are permitted to maintain and often to introduce more stringent regulatory
> standards than those prescribed by Community legislation for the purposes
> of advancing a particular social or welfare interest and provided that such
> additional requirements are compatible with the Treaty. National competence
> is not completely ousted: the applicable Community legislation sets a floor,
> the Treaty itself sets a ceiling and the Member States are free to pursue an
> independent domestic policy between these two parameters.[50]

In terms of the extent of the harmonization of a directive Prechal notes further:

> The extent to which Member States may act depend also on the method [of
> harmonization] used. In the case of total harmonization the relevant field is
> exhaustively regulated with no room for independent action for the Member
> States unless provided for in the directive itself. On the other hand, where the
> Community has opted for minimum harmonization, the Member States are still
> free to maintain or adopt more stringent standards. However, the latter must
> be compatible with other Community law, in particular the Treaty. In other
> words, the Member States are free to maintain or adopt national measures
> with the directive as the floor and the Treaty as the ceiling.[51]

Dougan proposes an analysis for both for the understanding of structure of harmonization as lead by the ECJ and as evidenced in its case law and possibly to a
certain extent for the understanding of harmonization as lead by the Community
through legislation. According to the analysis of Dougan the degree of harmonization evinced at least in the case law and possibly in the legislation varies according
to the sector which is to be regulated:[52] some sectors of activity may apparently

---

50. S. Prechal, *Directives in EC Law*, 2nd edn (Oxford: OUP, 2006), ibid., 177. In general the ad
hoc approach followed by the Court – not concentrating only on the rules in the abstract but
also on the question of how they operate in context – results in dozens of procedural provisions
being submitted to the Court for scrutiny inviting it to plunge into the particularities of national
procedural law. In some case, quite some latitude is given to national courts. In other the Court
formulates precise prescriptions. As a reaction to the current situation and its inherent weakness in some quarters harmonization of national procedural law was suggested as an alternative. Others admit that indeed divergence in the remedial relief available is deplorable from the
point of view of uniformity but unavoidable.
51. S. Prechal *Directives in EC Law,* 2nd edn (Oxford: OUP, 2006), ibid., 44.
52. M. Dougan, *National Remedies before the Court of Justice* (Oxford: Hart, 2004), op. cit.,
Chs 1, 2 and 7 and p. 389 acknowledges at p. 390. That there may be some difficulties in
applying this sectoral approach with respect to Community harmonization legislation: 'While
acknowledging the limitations of this "sectoral approach" in so far as it might purport to
represent some practical legislative blueprint, one can still emphasise its strengths as a critical
conceptual tool by which to analyze the Court of Justice's volatile case law on national
remedies and procedural rules.'

by reason of their specific subject matter as well as the extent of Commission competence in relation to national competence may justify a high degree of harmonization: this in contrast to other sectors which once again because of their specific subject matter and the degree of Commission competence in relation to national competence will require only minimum harmonization. In this regard, Dougan observes as follows:

> The Treaty project is now as much about managing diversity as it is about promoting integration. Community law has a valid role in accommodating both these aims. Accordingly, the idea of some overarching principle of regulatory uniformity must be refined and with it the assumptions both that national remedies and procedures necessarily frustrate substantive Community objectives and that their harmonization would necessarily represent the most appropriate solution. What is suggested instead is a 'sectoral approach' to the enforcement deficit. The demand for uniformity at both a substantive and remedial level is purely relative, changing according to the field of Community activity in question. In some sectors (such as state aids and competition law), uniformity remains a valid goal of Treaty policy and the harmonization of domestic remedies and procedural rules might well seem justified. In other sectors (such as environmental, consumer and employee protection) the Treaty does not appear to harbour ambitions of achieving any genuine degree of regulatory uniformity and the principles of subsidiarity and proportionality suggest that we should adopt a correspondingly more restrained interpretation of the need for remedial approximation. While acknowledging the limitations of this 'sectoral approach' in so far as it might purport to represent some practical legislative blueprint one can still emphasise its strengths as a critical conceptual tool by which to analyze the Court of Justice's volatile case law on national remedies and procedural rules.[53].

In applying the analysis of Dougan in the instant case one would note the sectorial content of the Directive in terms among other things of Commission competence as opposed to national competence and as such:

The demand for uniformity at both a substantive and a remedial level is purely relative changing according to the field of Community activity in questions. ... In other sectors such as environmental, consumer and employee protection, the Treaty does not appear to harbour ambitions of achieving any genuine degree of regulatory uniformity and the principles of subsidiarity and proportionality suggest that we should adopt a correspondingly more restrained interpretation of the need for remedial approximation[54].

Dougan also observes:[55]

---

53. M. Dougan, *National Remedies before the Court of Justice* (Oxford: Hart, 2004), ibid., 389-390.
54. M. Dougan, *National Remedies before the Court of Justice* (Oxford: Hart, 2004), ibid., 133.
55. M. Dougan, *National Remedies before the Court of Justice* (Oxford: Hart 2004), ibid., 133.

Minimum harmonisation has become an increasingly common characteristic of the Community regulation. Indeed, since the Single European Act it has been 'institutionalised' through expression incorporation into the Treaty text itself. ... Even Article 95 EC contains a (much more limited) minimum harmonisation facility in respect of measures adopted under that legal basis for the completion of the Internal Market and which themselves fail to make provision for more stringent domestic standards.

Therefore, according to the analysis of Dougan as applied in the instant case, the minimal harmonization of the Directive is attributable to the type of sector which it regulates. It is the regulated legal sector as provided for and governed by the EC Treaty which establishes generally the degree of harmonization in the sense of minimal as opposed to possibly complete harmonization. However, this analysis does not per se serve to explain in detail or to justify the actual or specific degree of harmonization which is chosen notably for legislation as with the Directive, or indeed what might be the criterion for assessing what the appropriate degree of harmonization would be for a particular sector or indeed when harmonization is appropriate if at all.

In contrast, Chalmers[56] argues that in reality there exist at least two other analytical factors to be considered in addition to or possibly in place of those presented by Dougan certainly with respect to the ECJ lead harmonization as evinced in its case law. Although in principle Chalmer's analysis is directed at ECJ case lead harmonization it may be useful to endeavour to apply it to Community lead harmonization through legislation in order to try to understand the degree of harmonization to be achieved in the latter. Chalmers observes:

> First, the managerial approach.
> Attention is paid under this, in part, to the regulatory resources available. Despite being a field of exclusive competence, the administration and

---

56. D. Chalmers, Book Review (2006) *Public Law* 650. See also R. van den Bergh 'Regulatory Competition or Harmonization of Law? Guidelines for the European Regulator', in *The Economics of Harmonziation*, eds A. Marciano & J.-M Josselin (Cheltenam: Edward Elgar 2002), at 27 observes that economic analysis of regulatory competition may gives three lesses: first, that diversity in legal rules may geneal important benefits: second, when competition between legislators does not function properly because of market imperfections on the market of legislation measure coping with such economic distortions should: full harmonization should remain an ultimium remedium confided to areas of law where competition between legal rules causes custantial costs without any compensating; Third, the risk of political distortions must also be mitigated. Economic analysis of regulatory competition has convolved to a point where it is possible to created integrated step by step guidelines for decision making allowing sensible evaluation of costs and benefits of competition between legal systems. However, van den Bergh concludes at p. 45 that ultimately '... given the current lack of democracy in the European Union ... may have the effect of rejecting harmonization measures altogether' S M Smits in 'How to predict the difference in Uniformity between Different Areas of a Future European Private law? An evolution Approach', in *The Economics of Harmonization*, eds J-M Josselin & A Marciano (Cheltenam: Edward Elgard, 2002), 50 concludes at p. 66 'To predict to what extent the different areas of private law will evolve toward some uniformed system is not an easy job. If anything should have become clear ... it is that whatever way one wants to travel a strictly legal perspective does not suffice;'

enforcement of EC competition law has been devolved back to national authorities because the Commission was unable to cope on its own with the workload of exemptions generated by Article 18(3)EC. To be sure, these are guided by the principles set out in Regulation 1/2003 but as the principles, court procedures and cultures of enforcement are still predominantly national, it is impossible to argue that a partial repatriation has not taken place. The other part of this approach involves the resilience of the sector to legal correction often influencing the degree of intervention pursued in Community law. Special procedures have been put in public procurement law because observance is so patchy. Similarly, the difficulty with proving discrimination in cases involving race and sex discrimination has led to legislation reversing the burden of proof. Dougan dismisses this as a simple echoing of Court judgments but not only is this observation legally dubious but it fails to consider why the legislature sought to reinforce remedies so explicitly in these fields of existing procedures were sufficient.[57]

The second principle according to Chalmers is legal integrity:

> There is a strain of legal integrity, which pushes, however sporadically for an 'integration through law' approach. This approach may not be predominant but it is still significant and still continues to develop. The extension of the doctrine of state liability in Köbler to acts carried out by judicial actor and the doctrine of indirect effect to the third pillar in Pupino are not acts by an institution, the Court of Justice, which sees integration through law as having run its course or as there being a case for sectoral exceptionalism.[58]

Although in the instant case with the Directive, it would appear that at least initially the analysis of Dougan is helpful in understanding the establishing of the degree of harmonization through legislation it may be that the concepts of Chalmers to the extent that they are applicable to such legislation will prove more useful. Indeed, it would seem that the approach of Chalmers at least in some sense emphasises a type of empirical approach, starting with a finding in an ECJ judgment, to an enforcement inadequacy. This in turn involves an eventual finding of a procedural deficit in the following circumstances:' the resilience of the sector to legal correction often influent the degree of intervention pursued in Community law'.[59] In the instant case, with respect to the Directive, the Commission appears to commence its intervention from the position of what it interprets as an enforcement deficit in the protection of intellectual property rights by national rules of procedure. Although the Trade-Related Aspects of Intellectual Property Rights (TRIPs)[60] exists, arguably the sector of enforcement of intellectual property rights

---

57. D. Chalmers, Book Review (2006) *Public Law* ibid., 650, at 651.
58. D. Chalmers, Book Review (2006) *Public Law* ibid., 650, at 651, *Köbler* Case No. 224/01 ECR I 10239, *Pupino* Case No. C 105/03 (2005) ECR I 5285.
59. D. Chalmers, Book Review (2006) *Public Law* ibid., 650, 651.
60. The Agreement on Trade Related Aspects of Intellectual Property Rights (TRIPS), World Trade Organisation, <www.wto.org/enlgish/traop_e/trips_e/trips_e.htm>.

by rules of national procedure remains 'resilient to legal correction' in that the enforcement of the such national intellectual property rights is apparently, according to the Commission, not effective. One notes at page 20 the orientation of the Commission's consultation undertaken in the Green Paper on Combatting Counterfeiting and Piracy which arguably seeks to establish the existence of in procedural enforcement of intellectual property rights.

To enforce these intellectual property rights, right holders have at their disposal at national level a number of legal measures and procedures of both a provisions and a permanent nature which they can resort to in case of infringement. Although these measure and proceedings pursue similar objectives in all Member States bound as they are by the TRIPs agreement, the practical arrangements sometimes differ substantially from one Member State to another. While these measure and procedures are common to all Member States the details obviously differ from one Member State to another. There is therefore a need to evaluate their effectiveness in the Single Market and consider what improvements might be made for instance by extending those of these measure and procedures which have proved effective in some Member States[61].

The Commission then sets forth in a summary of its findings its conclusions on the existence of an enforcement deficit and the remedy in its Report on Responses to the Green Paper on Counterfeiting and Piracy[62]. It is perhaps here, that what Chalmer's terms' the strain of legal integrity which pushes for an "integration through law" approach ... [which] may not be predominant but it is still significant and still continues to develop' appears to apply.

Executive Summary:
1. The most striking feature of the replies to the question posed in the Green Paper is the almost universal picture of dissatisfaction with the bureaucratic complexities, delays and haphazard responses involved in the enforcement mechanism of the Member States.
2. The second most notable feature in wide spread sense of reliance and hope in the possibility of Community action, through the good officers of the European Commission, to create means to remedy the deficiencies of the national systems.
29. Conclusion
... The call for Commission action relating to harmonisation and strengthening, in conjunction with national authorities of procedures and methods was clear.
9.5 Suggested Action by the EU: Basic Points:
9.5.1 A number of respondents call for the EU, in some case through a body or a unit, to coordinate national procedures for enforcement and to obtain consistent application of law

---

61. European Commission, Green Paper, *Combatting Counterfeiting and Piracy in the Single Market*, COM (98) 0569 FINAL, 22 Oct. 1998 <www.ec.europa.eu>.
62. European Commission, *Report on Responses: Final Report on Responses to the European Commission Green Paper on Counterfeiting and Piracy*: 7 Jun. 1999 <www.ec.europa.eu>.

9.5.2 In all responses, however, it is most important to note that there is an unexpressed desire or assumption that complaints raised as to national enforcement must be taken up at EU level and common measure found for them.

9.5.5 The diversity of national measure for gather information and taking action is complained of and a uniform search and seizure procedures are required. Clearly this a call for EU action of some sort to achieve a solution. The shear diversity of national measure for gather information and taking action is complain of and clearly here again is the unwritten wish for harmonisation by the EU.

9.5.6 Clearly all of these suggestions imply at least that the Commission should take the initiative in obtaining harmonisation between Member States legal rules of procedure.

Further, in paragraph 1 of the Executive Summary of the Follow up to the Green Paper[63] the Commission refers to an enforcement deficit caused by the Member States. However the remedy proposed by the Commission is of a particular nature: namely, harmonization and of a particular kind. Arguably, expressions such as in paragraph 9.5.2 of the Report on the Responses to the Green Paper 'there is an unexpressed desire or assumption that complaints raised as to national enforcement must be taken up at European Union (EU) Level and common measures found for them'; or at paragraph 9.5.6 of the same document: 'Cleary all of these suggestion imply at least that the Commission should take the initiative in harmonization between Member States legal rules of procedure' conspicuously derive from the strain of legal integrity which pushes for an 'integration through law' noted by Chalmers. Indeed, one notes that in paragraph 9.5.1 of the Report on the Responses to the Green paper, it is noted that the respondents apparently asked for a coordination of national procedures which arguably is different from a harmonization of national procedure. Therefore, it would appear that the 'integration of law' approach noted by Chalmers in the ECJ case law is very much active as the source of the solution for what the Commission at least perceives as an enforcement deficit. However, it would appear that the Commission, having argued that an enforcement deficit exists and that the area of law in general is perhaps generally compliance resistant, nevertheless, does not provide a motivated or detailed discussion of the degree of harmonization notably for example in relation to such procedures as representative actions as provided for in Article 4 of the Directive. Arguably, a detailed description of the harmonization could have taken place in a precise and argued fashion in relation to the concept of degree of resilience to legal correction as adumbrated by Chalmers. Instead, the Commission appears to rely primarily on the 'integration through law' approach in order to justify not

---

63. European Commission: *Communication from the Commission to the Council, the Euroepan Parliament and the Economic and Social Committee: FollowUp to the Green Paper on Comabtting Counterfeiting and Piracy in the Single Market:* COM 2000/0789 FINAL 17 Apr. 2000 <www. ohim.eu.int>.

only the representative actions in Article 4 but indeed all of the content of the various articles of the Directive. Further and in contrast, the Commission could also have motivated its detailed proposals for the level of harmonization in the Directive notably in relation to Article 4 thereof in a manner analogous to that provided by the Impact Assessment Report related to the White Paper on Damages Actions for Breach of the EC antitrust rules (2008):[64] dealing with the same procedural mechanism of a representative action, the Commission endeavours to set forth reasons based upon among other things a cost benefit analysis which would justify a specific form of the representative action.

In short, assuming, which is not obvious, that the Commission has indeed in the above mentioned documents concerning the Directive established firstly, that an enforcement deficit does exist and that secondly, the solution lies within Community lead harmonization of rules of national procedure by some instrument such as a directive this by reason of the 'integration through law' stream , the actual level or extent thereof is not analyzed: Rather, the Commission having established that there is an 'unwritten' desire for Community lead harmonization then proceeds in the following manner to establish the degree of its intervention in terms of harmonization in the following manner as set for in the Follow Up to the Green Paper[65]:

Paragraph 1. In 1998 the Commission consulted the interested parties by means of a Green paper in combating counterfeiting and piracy in the Single Market in order to determine the economic import of this phenomenon on the single market to asses the effectiveness of the applicable legislation and to suggest approached that could be explored with a view to improving the situation. This consultation confirmed that counterfeiting and piracy were major problems in most economic and industrial sectors in the singled market and that the Commission and the European Union in general should take steps to strengthen and improve the fight against counterfeiting and piracy in the single market at the EU Level.

---

64. European Commission, *White Paper on Damages Actions for Breach of the EC Antitrust Rules* COM (2008) 125, 2 Apr. 2008; European Commission: *Staff Working Paper on Damages Actions for Breach of the EC Antitrust Rules* SEC (2008) 404, 2 Apr. 2008; European Commission: *Impact Assessment Report* (Staff Working Document) SEC (2008) 405, 2 Apr. 2008, at paras 78 and 83 and Table of Costs of Policy Option 1, p. 39 and Table of Costs of Policy Option 2, p.41; External Impact Study: 'Making Antitrust Damages Actions More Effective in the EU: Welfare Impact and Potential Scenarios' Final Report, CEPS, EUR and LUISS, Contract DG COMP (2006) AS/012, 21 Dec. 2007.
65. Communication from the Commission to the Council and the European Parliament and Social Committee: Follow up to the Green Paper on Combating Counterfeiting and Piracy in the Single Market, Brussels, 17 Dec. 2000 COM (2000) 789 <www.ohim.eu.int/en/mark/aspects/pdf/c_789-00.pdf> see also, Proposal for a Directive of the European Parliament and of the Council on Measure and Procedures to Ensure the Enforcement of Intellectual Property Rights: COM (2003) 46 Final, 20 Jan. 2003.

Then significantly the Commission goes on to observe concerning the level of intervention:[66]

> Paragraph 13:
> The Commission will submit a proposal for a Directive aimed at guaranteeing the smooth running of the Single Market in this respect. However, given that the TRIPS agreement provided for a minimalist approach to the means of enforcing intellectual property rights that are applied in all the Member States, the activities envisaged by the Commission in this field will only concern complementary improvement to this Agreement.

This would seem to indicate that the level of harmonization of the Directive has therefore been calculated in relation to the TRIPs agreement and that this latter has proved in terms of the degree of its harmonization to be defective or a contrario, satisfactory. There is however no mention of an examination specifically of the operation of the TRIPs agreement or more particularly methods of improving its enforcement where defective by national authorities in the aforementioned Communication. Some such as Cornish, Drexl, Hilty and Kur[67] observe:

> The Directive lies in the field that has already been provided with a plethora of ground rules by TRIPs concerning enforcement of those IPRs within that Agreement's purview. These the Member States are obliged to observes as part of their own WTO membership and within the reach of internal Community legislation on IPRs also as a matter of Community law and the Community's WTO membership. Were the Commission to be seeking to ensure that each state is respecting these TRIPs obligations, that would be an objective that could be critically examined as and for itself. (Footnote 2:
>
> Would it note be in more appropriate proportion to call for information about what was necessary and what has been done to comply with this aspect of TRIPS? If it turns out that Member States do not comply with their obligations, this could indeed justify Community legislation reinforcing the TRIPS standards. If Member States do comply, however, – as appears to be the case in the absence of any evidence to the contrary – any harmonisation measures should be confined to those areas where the standards set out in the TRIPS Agreement are considered insufficient by the Commission).

Accordingly, one might say that in applying Chalmer's lines of analysis, it becomes clear that the Commission in the aforementioned consultation documents

---

66. The Commission Staff Working Paper on Damages Actions for Breach of the EC Anti Trust Rules: SEC (2008) 4040 p. 27 n. 46 states: « Directive 2004/48/EC of the European Parliament and Council of 29 Apr. 2004 on the enforcement of intellectual property rights, OJ 2004 L 195/16. The measures on evidence adopted in the Directive are derived from the obligation of the Community and the Member States towards the World Trade Organisation under Part III of the Agreement on Trade and Related Aspects of Intellectual Property Rights of 15 Apr. 1994 »
67. W. Cornish, J. Drexl. R. Hilty & A. Kur Procedures and Remedies for Enforcing IPRs: the European Commission's Proposed Directive : (2003) *EIPR* (10) 447.

and reports endeavours to justify its intervention on the basis of the concept of enforcement deficits which it perceives to have been established in the course of the consultations. Applying its 'integretation through law' optic, the Commission decides that the remedy for such deficits is clearly harmonization of the national rules of procedure. Assuming that such a conclusion is justified, there remains however, arguably a difficulty in the analysis of the Commission: namely, that the Commission does not justify through argumentation and or empirical research the actual extent of the eventual and scope of its intervention in terms of the degree of harmonization as evidenced in the Directive beyond a reference to the TRIPs agreement providing minimum harmonization. More particularly, there is no specific argumentation dealing with the justification of the types of measures of harmonization nor their scope proposed in terms of their effectiveness in combatting the enforcement deficits. Minimum harmonization of an unmotivated type and degree are simply imposed and incorporated within the Directive on the basis of it would seem on the basis of the 'integration through law'. Accordingly, it is not clear to what extent the degree of minimum harmonization contained within the Directive and notably the manner in which it was decided can be said to provide a more rational, clear and predictable basis than ECJ lead harmonization of national procedure in general and in particular in the instant case by failing to relate deficits in national enforcement resulting from inadequacies of the application of national authorities of TRIPs. Therefore, in the instant case one would seem to be able to conclude that the manner in which question of the harmonization and in particular the level of harmonization[68] has been decided for the Directive does not serve to confer on it what have been conceived of as the advantages of harmonization through legislation in contrast to harmonization lead through the ECJ[69] notably in terms of clarity and argumented detail of the nature and scope of the harmonization.

---

68. The Commission indirectly and laconically refers to the method by which it appears to view the manner in which it decides the degree of harmonization in the Impact Assessment Report (Staff Working Document) SEC (2008) 405, 2 Apr. 2008 at p. 29, n. 70, 'The choice of the most appropriate of the possible EC legislative instruments (i.e., the choice between a regulation, a directive, or a combination of both) will ultimately depend upon (i) the exact content of the Commission proposal (ii) the legal, economic and political context at the time when the proposal is made and (iii) the degree to which a level playing-field in the EU is considered necessary or desirable'. Perhaps the most interesting section of this equation is the last consideration, namely, the 'degree to which a level playing field in the EU is considered necessary or desirable'. No indication is given by the Commission as to how it calculates the degree of such desirability or necessity or to what extent the factors in (i) and (ii) are indeed the operative factors thereon.

69. M. Dougan, *National Remedies before the Court of Justice* (Oxford: Hart, 2004), op. cit., 395, C. Himsworth, 'Things Fall Apart: The Harmonization of Community Judicial Procedural Protection Revisited (1997) 22 *ELRev* 291. L. Neville-Brown 'National Protection of Community Rights: Reconciling Autonomy and Effectiveness', in *Remedies for Breach of EC Law*, eds J. Lonbay & A. Biondi (Chichester: Wiley & Sons, 1997), 25 at 71; R. Craufurd Smith 'Remedies for Breaches of EU Law in National Courts: 'Legal Variation and Selection', in *The Evolution of EU Law*, eds P. Craig & G de Burca (Oxford: OUP, 1999), 317.

F   PROBLEMS CREATED BY THE IMPLEMENTATION OF A
                      PARTIALLY HARMONIZING DIRECTIVE

(1) As noted earlier, one of the major problems created by the use of a directive as a means of harmonization through Community legislation is that of national implementation, in terms generally of either incorrect or inadequate implementation of the obligations contained therein or non-implementation thereof: that is, more generally, in the course of this book, implementation of the Directive in the sense of the effect[70] upon the rules of the Dutch, English and German procedure will be examined in relation to what might be termed two parameters: first, in relation to the substantive and ancillary obligations which constitute the content of the component articles and recitals of the Directive therein; and second, in relation to certain principles such as, legal certainty, the principle of full effect and above all the principle of effective judicial protection. These principles serve to restrict the discretion of the national court in exercising their discretion as to the form of the implementation of the substantive obligation of a directive. The concrete application of these principles may generally very in each case according to the nature of the provisions contained by the directive and the content of the national implementing measures. More particularly, in the case of the Directive, the obligations contained therein which are directed at the Member States seek to achieve what is termed partial harmonization of the remedies, procedures and measures necessary to enforce intellectual property law: that is, the obligations provide what may be termed a minimum standard which must be fulfilled by the Member States in the course of their implementation of the Directive pursuant to EC Articles 249 (3) and 10. In this regard it may be noted that the scope and nature of certain of the substantive obligations contained within the Directive and which constitute the minimum protection may not be clear. It is submitted that in this regard the principles such as legal certainty, full effect and once again effective legal protection may well assist the national court in interpretation in addition to the normal method of reference to the ECJ pursuant to EC Article 234 in order to establish the precise meaning of the substantive obligations. Further, it would appear that it is effectively the incorporation of this principle of effective legal protection within Article 3 of the Directive which may have a very profound influence on the scope of the interpretation of the substantive obligations contained within the directive and certainly in any event upon the implementation thereof by the national court. This is notably the case with the implementation of the Articles 4 and certain aspects of Article 10, 11 and 13 of the Directive in English national procedure. It may be that a reference to the ECJ pursuant to EC Article 234 will be required in order to ascertain the scope of the substantive obligations contained by those articles particularly in relation to Articles 3 and 4 of the Directive. In so far as the national implementation notably of such articles may prove to be inadequate in relation to the principle of effective judicial protection as provided by Article 3 of

---

70.   S. Prechal, *Directives in EC Law*, 2nd edn (Oxford: OUP, 2006), op. cit., 4-5.

the Directive and as interpreted by the ECJ, the national court following the doctrine of consistent interpretation may find itself at the limits of its competence: that is, in order to ensure compliance with the wording of the Directive the national court may be called upon to effect certain changes in the national procedure. This problem of what might be termed the limits of the constitutionality as was noted earlier is characteristic of the ECJ lead harmonization. As noted, clearly, the most definitive method of resolving difficulties as to the correct interpretation of the substantive obligations of the Directive and notably their scope is through a reference to the ECJ. However, it may be that this problem could have been reduced somewhat in general in the instant case if the Community had drafted certain of the articles for example Article 4 of the Directive more clearly. Arguably, clearer drafting of the articles would assist the national courts notably with respect to the interpretation of the Directive in relation to national implementation of legislation and possibly also reduce problems attendant upon their constitutional role in relation to certain changes of national legislation which may be required in order to ensure adequate implementation of the Directive. In short, it is submitted that clear drafting of the substantive obligations in terms of the nature and the scope of the obligation can assist in facilitating the task of the national court in ensuring first, that the exercise of their constitutional function is clear and secondly and in particular that the national implementation of a directive and in the instant case of Directive 2004/48 conforms notably with the principle of effective judicial protection. This situation of unclear drafting resulting in uncertainty as to the scope and nature of certain of the substantive obligations is arguably rendered more untenable in the instant case with the Directive by reason of the fact that the actual justification of the degree of the harmonization appears not to have been established at least in a demonstrably pragmatic basis beyond stating that it should reflect that contained within the TRIPs agreement.

(2) One may note that from the point of view of practical enforcement notably by those who benefit from the rights which are conferred by the Directive, consideration will be given in the course of this book to the following matters which involve defective implementation: situations where the Directive has not been implemented at all either because the Member State believes that its current legislation is adequate or that the wording of the Directive is such that no special legislation is required as is perhaps the case of the UK with regard to certain of the articles of the Directive ; or situations where the relevant time for implementation for the Directive, in the instant case 20 April 2006, has elapsed and no specific legislation has been adopted as is the case with Germany[71]; or situations where the implementation has been inadequate because either the pre-existing legislation constitutes inadequate legislation or because the specifically adopted legislation proves, on analysis, notably by using the principle of legal certainty, to be inadequate. One might argue that what may, therefore, be generally termed defective implementation or non-implementation of the Directive is, however, susceptible to

---

71. *Commission v. Germany*, Case No. C-395/07, non-implementation of Dir. 2004/48/EC, <www. curia.europa.eu>.

three types of remedies which will be examined in more detail in subsequent chapters: first, the principle of direct effect; second the doctrine of consistent interpretation of national legislation with the Directive and third, State liability for failure to implement a directive adequately or at all. It is submitted that the Directive does not have direct effect in that various of its provisions, such as Article 4, whilst conferring rights, do not do so in a manner which is sufficiently clear that they may be invoked directly by the beneficiary: this is so by reason of the fact that arguably the rights conferred by the Directive require the Member States to exercise their discretion through the implementation process in order for them to take their individual form in the national rules of procedure. Accordingly, the doctrine of consistent interpretation[72] and State liability will be considered in terms of their offering a practical remedy for eventual litigants who may wish to use the Directive as the basis for an action to enforce their Intellectual Property (IP) rights.

(3) Briefly, it may be said that the doctrine of consistent interpretation applies in two situations: on the one hand, the national court must carry out such an interpretation even where the directive has been implemented correctly; the second situation is where the directive has been inadequately implemented: that is, inadequate implementation either through pre-existing legislation or through specially adopted legislation. Further, one notes that incorrect implementation of a directive amounts to a breach of Community law. However, there are some limits: one such limitation is to be found in the requirement that the national legislation, particularly where pre-existing legislation exists, must indeed permit a semantically consistent interpretation with the directive. In short, such national legislation must exist in default of which no consistent interpretation is possible. Moreover, it would appear that the principle of consistent interpretation may be used irrespective of whether rights are created by the directive or not and also in those situations where one private person is seeking to enforce the content of the directive against another private person. It would appear that one of the limits on the operation of consistent interpretation, in addition to the concerns of constitutionality of the national court with respect to the limits of interpretation in conformity is legal certainty in addition to general principles of Community law[73]. Where the doctrine of consistent interpretation is impossible then it would appear that it is appropriate to make recourse to the principle of State liability. In such a situation however, unlike with the principle of consistent interpretation it is necessary that a directive confer rights. As noted earlier, this is arguably the case with certain provisions of the Directive. Moreover, it is submitted that the doctrine of consistent interpretation can operate in an extremely dynamic fashion in relation to the production of eventual modifications of national rules of procedure when coupled particularly as noted earlier with the principle of effective judicial protection. This is a fortiori

---

72. *Von Colson*, Case No. (1984) ECR 1891 para. 28, *Marleasing*, Case No. C-106/89 (1990) ECR I 4135, op. cit., S. Prechal, *Directives in EC Law*, 2nd edn (Oxford: OUP, 2005), op. cit., 4-5, see generally Ch. 8 for consistent interpretation and Ch. 9 for direct effect.
73. *Kolpinghuis*, Case No. 80/86 (1987) ECR 3996 and S. Prechal, *Directives in EC Law*, 2nd edn (Oxford: OUP, 2005), 203-204.

the case when the principle of effective judicial protection is contained within a directive as is in the instant case.

Additionally, where non-implementation or incorrect implementation of a directive causes loss and damage to an individual, the appropriate remedy notably where a consistent interpretation is impossible would be an action for damages in the national court against the Member State for its breach of Community law[74]. However, three conditions which will be considered in more detail in the subsequent chapters must be fulfilled before an eventual claimant who has suffered loss and damage caused by either the non-implementation or the incorrect implementation of a directive may bring an action against the State: first, in so far as a directive is involved, it must, as is the case with Directive, confer rights on individuals. As noted earlier, it is the content of a directive in terms of its specific articles and appropriate Recitals which determines whether or not it confers rights of a specific nature on a specific category of individuals. The second condition which must be fulfilled is that the breach must be sufficiently grave and serious. In order to determine this matter the national court may consider certain factors such as the clarity and the precision of a directive, in the instant case, the Directive, which is breached and which confers rights in addition to other possible factors: the measure of discretion enjoyed by the national authorities in terms of implementation or whether the damage was voluntarily or involuntarily. The third condition which must be fulfilled is the existence of a causal link which can be established on the facts of the case between, on the one hand, the non-implementation or incorrect implementation of the Directive and the loss suffered by the applicant. Clearly the availability of this remedy is very much determined by the facts of the individual case in addition to the wording of the provision of the Directive which may be involved as well as the nature of the non-implementation or incorrect implementation once again on the facts by the Member State. These conditions when fulfilled are 'necessary and sufficient to found a right in individuals to obtain redress'.[75]

Finally, in the course of the analysis of the implementation of the Directive in the Dutch, English and German systems of civil procedure, consideration will be given to the adequacy thereof and in the case of a defective implementation, the form of remedy which is most likely to be available for an eventual litigant: in this regard the concepts of interpretation in conformity and the principle of State liability will be considered and applied with regard to elements of primarily the English implementation of the Directive, primarily the English and German implementation of the Directive.

(4) In conclusion, it is submitted that the Directive at least with respect to its implementation in English law exemplifies some of the difficulties entailed in the

---

74. *Francovich*, Joined Cases C-6/90 and C-9/90 (1991) ECR I-5357, op. cit., in particular at: para. 37: '… it is a principle of Community law that the Member States are obliged to make good loss and damage caused to individuals by breaches of Community law for which they can be held responsible;' S. Prechal, *Directives in EC Law*, 2nd edn (Oxford: OUP, 2005), op. cit., 203-204, generally Ch. 10.

75. *Brasserie du Pêcheur*, Joined Cases C-46/93 and C 48/93 (1996) ECR I-1029 para. 66.

use of a piece of Community legislation which provides for partial harmonization and where arguably the most active governing principle is that of effective judicial protection. Prechal observes:

> The main reasons for the dissatisfaction with directives are arguably no longer of a conceptual nature. More practical considerations [footnote 15 in the text: in particular the problems relating to timely and correct implementation] undoubtedly also lie behind the proposals to replace them. ... Problems encountered with respect to their implementation and in particular their enforcement by national courts have generated an impressive list of publications.

> As noted earlier, it would seem that certain of the difficulties encountered at the level of the national implementation notably in terms of the English rules could have been attenuated by clearer drafting of the substantive obligations contained by the Directive.

(5) Non-comparative analysis of the implementation of the Directive

Finally, no attempt is made to undertake a comparative law study in terms of the manner in which the Directive is or may be implemented within the Dutch, English and German systems of national procedure. The parameters of the discipline of comparative law of procedure would appear to be different from those concerned with the analysis of a directive in national procedure which is subject to the principles which govern Community law. In this regard, it would appear for example that according at least to some analysts such as Zuckerman[76] the principles and objectives which animate comparative procedural law may be articulated in the following manner:

> All systems of procedure seek to do justice. ... It is also obvious that different systems of procedure employ different methods for achieving this goal. Whether the difference between systems are small or great, a comparison is inevitably called for. .. But like any other form of assessment, this too requires

---

76. A. Zuckerman 'Justice in Crisis: Comparative Dimensions of Civil Procedure', in *Civil Justice in Crisis*, eds A. Zuckerman (Oxford: OUP, 1999), at p. 3 See also C. van Rhee (ed) *European Traditions in Civil Procedure* (Antwerp: Intersentia, 2005), 5 for whom the goal of procedure is to identify 'the nature and underlying principles' of various national systems of procedure. D. Dwyer in Book Review, of C van Rhee (ed) European Traditions in Civil Procedure (Antwerp: Intersential, 2005), (2007) MLR 342 at 344 asks why there should be an attempt to identify such principles, for example, normative: 'Do we seek something that will harmonize and ultimately replace the procedural system of individual member states or only something that fills the gaps in trans-national disputes. From an EC legal perspective, applying the principle of subsidiarity (Art. 5 EC Treaty) such a set of principles may not necessarily be expected to apply to every civil case, but perhaps only to those case where national provisions would be inadequate or inappropriate. This would be akin to the ius commune provided by the civil law in mediaeval and early modern Europe. From the perspective of Art. 6 ECHR, however, we might be looking for normative principles of general application against which to compare national provisions': and on p. 344 Dwyer asks what should be the analytical method used: historical as in van Rhee, or descriptive as in Damaska, *Faces of Justice*, (New Haven: Yale University Press, 1986) where the objective is explanatory, or functionalist and ask how 'different procedural systems have sought to implement their goals.'

some parameters, some common denominator by which we can measure and compare... .

It will be argued that justice has three dimensions by which it is measures.

Zuckerman then goes on to establish as the dimensions, first, rectitude of decisions: that is in all system of procedure doing justice involves arriving at decisions which 'give the parties before the court what is legal due to them'.[77] The other two dimensions involve the passage of time and costs.

In short:

> It is not enough to ask whether the system produces correct judgments. We have also to ask how time judgments are, because a judgment given too late may amount to a denial of justice even thought it involves a correct application of the law to the true facts. Cost too is relevant to the assessment of procedural systems. The resources available to the system will influence it global level of rectitude of decisions. Cost will affect access to justice and lastly, high litigation costs may enable rich litigants to acquire a procedural advantage against their opponents.

One might observe as follows: whilst an examination of the implementation of a directive in national procedure which is subject to Community law principles in relation to the content of a directive dealing with the partial harmonization of national procedure is different from a comparative analysis of national procedure nevertheless one might note the following: it is perhaps of use to note generally the reoccurrence of certain of the principles without seeking to establish identity in their nature or scope as they exist in the content of the Directive coupled with Community law principles on the one hand and those set forth by Zuckerman as constituting parameters for a comparative analysis of civil procedure: in this regard one notes in particular those of costs and their relationship to effective judicial protection as expressed in the Directive subject to Community law and the concept of costs as expressed at least by Zuckerman and their effect on access to justice and what he terms the rectitude of the decision. If nothing else, this apparent co-incidence might serve to justify a closer examination of certain of the substantive obligations dealing with costs in the Directive as being perhaps obligations of particular importance. Beyond that possible convergence it does not appear at least at this point possible to relate the principles involved in a comparative analysis of civil procedure at least as defined above more closely with an examination of the national implementation of a directive which involves above all its particular content notably in those instances partial harmonization of civil procedure as in the instant case for the enforcement of IP rights and governing Community law principles[78]. The question of identifying the degree of appropriate

---

77. A. Zuckerman, 'Justice in Crisis: Comparative Dimensions of Civil Procedure', in *Civil Justice in Crisis*, eds A. Zuckerman (Oxford: OUP, 1999), ibid., at p. 3.
78. D. Dwyer, Book Review: C H van Rhee (ed) *European Traditions in Civil Procedure* (Antwerp: Intersentia, 2005) (2007) MLR 342-45, op. cit.

and adequate harmonization of a directive remains to be determined, it is submitted, in an argumented and detailed manner as discussed above. Accordingly, the analysis of the implementation of the Directive in terms of Dutch, English and German national procedure has proceeded in autonomous fashion: that is, each of the national systems of procedure has been considered only in relation to the terms of the directive itself in order to ascertain more clearly to what extent the implementation thereof has been adequate. Arguably, any attempt to compare either the method of national implementation or the degree of adequacy or inadequacy thereof may have served would obscure the essential particularities of each of the three national systems in relation to the Directive.

Chapter 1
Obligations and Structure of the Directive

I   INTRODUCTION

Before analyzing the text of the Directive it is useful to consider generally what might be termed the content of a directive. More particularly pursuant to EC 249 (3), a directive imposes an objective as to the result to be achieved. The nature of this obligation may be examined from at least two points of view: as substantive obligations on the one hand and on the other, ancillary obligations.

A   SUBSTANTIVE OBLIGATIONS

The substantive obligation which is sometimes referred to as a hard core obligation defines the scope and purpose of a directive compliance and fulfilment of which is necessary in order to ensure a proper implementation thereof: that is, the substantive obligation may often describe the legal and or factual situation which the Member State must realize in order to ensure proper implementation of a directive. Furthermore, the substantive obligation or hard core rules of a directive may concern both substantive law and procedural law. In addition to the Directive, another example of directives which concern rules of procedure is Directive 91/263/EEC which deals with telecommunication terminal equipment and provides for a procedure for conformity assessment as well as Directive 98/27/EC on injunctions for the protection of consumer interests. In reality, it would seem that there is no difference between directives where the substantive obligation deals with substantive law as opposed to procedural law at least for purposes of implementation: that is, directives which deal substantive law as well as directives which deal with procedural content must both be implemented effectively. The obligations in the substantive part of a directive are addressed either to a Member State or to persons who will be concerned upon implementation of the directive,[1] as opposed to the fact that a directive as a whole considered as a Community legal instrument is addressed to exclusively to Member States. A directive may also contain provisions which provide for discretion to be exercised by a Member States permitting them thereby to derogate from its contents,[2] or to give their own interpretation of certain concepts therein.[3] It is to be noted, in this regard, that Article 4 of the Directive contains the following expressions:

> 4(a) '… in accordance with applicable law…'
>   4(b) – (d) … in so far as permitted by and in accordance with applicable law …'

It would seem that the expressions in Article 4(a)–(d) may possibly be interpreted in a manner somewhat similar to the expression 'without prejudice to the right of the Member States': that is, the Directive grants the Member State the possibility of exercising its own discretion with respect to the implementation of the form of what arguably constitutes a procedural right. In short, following this interpretation, there is no obligation on the part of the Member States to introduce such representation where it is absent from the national rules of procedure. However, it is equally submitted that following a case such as *Commission v. the UK*,[4] the Member State must exercise its discretion in a manner which is compatible both with the substantive obligations of the directive but also with Community law and its principles. In the aforementioned case, the European Court of Justice (ECJ) held that the UK had infringed its obligations under Directive 77/187/EC by failing to provide for designation of employee representatives as required by Article 6 of the Directive. UK legislation did not contain a mechanism for designation of employee representatives. Furthermore, the UK argued that by using the words: 'as provided for by the law or practises of the Member States…' the directive restricted the obligation on the part of Member States to provide such representation to those instances where such provision already existed in the national legislation. Therefore, following this interpretation the directive did not impose and obligation on the part of the UK to introduce such representation. The ECJ rejected this restrictive interpretation of the scope of the obligation for two reasons: firstly, it would deprive the directive and particularly Article 6 of its 'full effect';[5] in short

---

1. S. Prechal, *Directives in EC Law*, 2nd edn (Oxford: OUP, 2005), op cit., 42-43.
2. This possibility may be indicated by phrases such as 'does not prevent the Member States from … or that the directive is "without prejudice to the right of the Member States to" or that the "Member States may" or to giver their own interpretation', see S. Prechal, *Directives in EC Law*, 2nd edn (Oxford: OUP, 2005), 42-43 at 43.
3. Directive 77/38/EEC Art. 20 (4), or Art. 2 of Directive 74/652/EEC (road passenger transport operators) (1974).
4. *Commission v. UK*, Case No. 382/92 (1982) ECR 2601.
5. *Commission v. UK*, Case No. 382/92 (1982) ECR 2601, ibid., at para. 17. 'The interpretation proposed by the UK would allow Member States to determine the cases in which employee

'The intention of the Community legislature was not therefore to allow different national legal systems to accept a situation in which no employee representatives are designated since such designation is necessary to ensure compliance with the obligations laid down in Article 6 of the directive';[6] second, according to the ECJ, national legislation which 'makes it possible to impede protection unconditionally guaranteed to employees by a directive is contrary to Community law'.[7]

According to this line of reasoning, which arguably constitutes only one method of interpretation, it would appear that the effective implementation of Article 4 of the Directive will require the Member States, following the literal terms of thereof, and notably the expression '… shall recognise …' combined with Recital 17, 'The persons entitled to request application of such measures … should be those with a direct interest …' to ensure the following: namely, that such a procedural right of standing is effectively implemented if necessary by creation of the appropriate procedure; second, the principle of effective judicial protection may require that access to the court in terms of legal standing be ensured for all four categories provided for by Article 4 read in light of Recital 17 notably in those national systems where representative actions do not exist and thereby deny standing to categories (c) and (d).

In addition, the method of the harmonization embodied by a directive which is intimately related to the scope of the substantive obligation which it contains may affect the method of implementation which is used by the Member State. It is to be noted, in this regard, that the Directive is adopted in the context of harmonization of procedure for the internal market. Thus, total or complete harmonization may well exclude independent action by a Member State as opposed to minimum harmonization, which, as is the case with the Directive, retains the possibility for Member States to adopt more stringent measures. It is submitted that Article 2 of the Directive establishes that the scope thereof is to ensure minimum harmonization.[8]

> Without prejudice to the means which are or may be provided in Community or national legislation, in so far as those as those means may be more favourable for rights holders.

---

representatives can be informed and consulted since they can be informed and consulted only in undertakings where national law provides for the designation of employee representatives. It would thus allow Member States to deprive Art. 6 of the directive to its full effect'.

6. *Commission v. UK*, Case No. 382/92 (1982) 2601, ibid. para. 18.
7. *Commission v. UK*, Case No. 382/92 (1982) ECR 2601, ibid., at para. 18.
8. M. Dougan, 'Minimum Harmonization and the Internal Market' *CMLRev* 37 (2000): 853, and F. de Cecco 'Room to Move? Minimum Harmonization and Fundamental Rights' CMLRev 43 (2006): 9, C. Hodges 'The Americanization of European Civil Justice' Centre for Socio-Legal Studies, Oxford <www.europeanjusticeforum.org>, see for opposite view: R. Kagan 'Questioning the "Americanization" of European Law', Newsletter of the European Politics and Society Section of the American Political Science Associaton, Fall-Winter 2007, Vol. 6 No.1 <www.apsant.org/nep/newsletteropsa;_v6_no1>
C. Hodges 'The Europeanisation of Civil Justice; Trends and Issues' *Civil Justice Quarterly* 26 (2007): 96-123.

However, the exercise of this discretion must be compatible with Community law[9] and in particular various elements of the Treaty[10] as well as with the content of a directive itself.[11] In summary it is submitted that the content of the result to be achieved which is imposed upon the Member States by EC Article 249 (3) in the sense, notably, of the form of the implementing measures, is determined by the content of the substantive obligations contained with a directive. The substantive obligations contained by the Directive will be analyzed in detailed in Chapter 3.

B   ANCILLARY OBLIGATIONS

Arguably the obligations which do not fulfil the function of the substantive or hard core obligations may be considered as ancillary obligations: clearly their function is different. Such functions may involve the following as exemplified by the Directive:

(1) Period for the implementation of the directive: Article 20 (1) provides 'The Member States shall bring into force the laws, regulations and administrative provisions necessary to comply with this Directive by April 29 2006.'

(2) Adoption of laws regulations and or administrative provisions by the Member States which are necessary for compliance with the Directive. Compliance with such obligations by the Member State may be seen as compliance with their obligations pursuant to EC Article 249 (3) and the more general obligation pursuant to EC Article 10. Article 20 (1) of the Directive provides: 'Member States shall bring into force the laws, regulations and administrative provisions necessary to comply with the Directive by 29 April 2006.'

(3) Informing the Commission of measures adopted in order to comply with the directive in questions. Compliance with such a duty is required arguably by EC Article 10. Similarly the obligation may require that the

---

9. For example the principle of effective judicial protection see Ch. 2 herein.
10. S. Prechal, *Directives in EC Law*, 2nd edn (Oxford: OUP, 2005), op cit., 146. M. Dougan, National Remedies before the Court of Justice (Oxford: Hart, 2004), op. cit., Ch. 1
11. *Cremonin*, Case No. 815/79 (1980) ECR 3583 para. 6, *VNO*, Case No. 51/76(1977) ECR 113, *Commission v. Ireland*, Case No. 415/85 (1988) ECR 3097 and *Kraaijevelt*, Case No. C-72/95 (1996) ECR I 5403, *Gemeente Emmen*, Case No. C-468/93 (1996) ECR 1 1721, F. de Cecco, 'Room to Move? Minimum Harmonization and Fundamental Rights' *CMLRev* 43 (2006): 9. describes at p. 29 the control of national discretion in the context of minimum harmonization in the following terms: 'The analysis carried out in these pages has concluded that consistent interpretation applies to upwardly flexible legislation and that Community concepts bind national legislatures, in exercising the discretion flowing from minimum harmonization clauses. It has also confirmed that the absorption of measures implementing the minimum standards of a directive into non-severable stricter national legislation causes the latter to become automatically reviewable under Community law. As for the question of severable stricter legislation the duties of national courts under Art. 10 EC do not allow for the conclusion to be reached that these always fall outside the scope of application of the general principles of Community law'.

Member States communicate the text of the implementing measures to the Commission in order to facilitate the monitoring of the conformity of national measure adopted for implementation.

In this regard, Article 20 (2) provides that 'The Member States shall communicate to the Commission the texts of the provision of the national law which they adopt in the field governed by this Directive.'

(4) Informing the Commission or consulting with the Commission of the measures which the Member States have adopted in the context of the discretion which has been left to them. In this regard, Article 18 of the Directive provides that 'Three years after the date laid down in Article 20 (1) each Member State shall submit to the Commission a report on the implementation of the Directive'.

Article 20 provides: 'They shall forthwith inform the Commission thereof.'

(5) Collaboration or consultation and exchange of information between the Member States or between the Member States and the Commission. In this regard Article 19 provides: 'For the purpose of promoting cooperation including the exchange of information, among Member States and between Member States and the Commission, each Member State shall designate one or more national correspondents for any question relating to the implementation of measures provided by this directive. It shall communicate the details of the national correspondent(s) to the other Member States and the Commission.'

(6) Undertaking by the Member States of assessment studies of the implementation for evaluation by the Commission. Article 18 (1) provides: 'Three years after the date laid down in Article 20 (1) each Member State shall submit to the Commission a report on the implementation of the Directive. On the basis of these reports, the Commission shall draw up a report on the application of the Directive, including an assessment of the effectiveness of the measures taken as well as an evaluation of its impact on innovation and the development of the information society.'

(7) Submission by the Member States of regular reports on the implementation and application of the Directive to the Commission. Specifically, Article 17 (b) enjoins the Member States in the following manner: 'Member States shall encourage (b) the submission to the Commission of draft codes of conduct of national and Community level and any of the evaluations of the applications of these codes of conduct.' Article 20 (1) as noted earlier enjoins the Member States to inform the Commission of the laws which they have enacted in order to comply with the Directive.

Arguably the primary purpose of these ancillary obligations is to permit control by the Commission of the exercise of discretion enjoyed by the Member States with respect to implementation. Accordingly, the Commission intervenes in the process of implementation pursuant to EC Article 211 by means of its supervisory powers. In short, it is clear that non-compliance with the ancillary obligations may constitute an infringement of EC Article 249 (3). In short, both the substantive and the ancillary obligations form an entity of obligations which constitute the objective which the Member States are to achieve through their implementation and application of a directive.

C   SCOPE OF THE OBLIGATION TO ACHIEVE THE RESULT
                PURSUANT TO EC ARTICLE 249 (3)

Finally, it would seem that the scope of the concept of the result to be achieved pursuant to EC Article 249 (3) includes not just the implementation of the obligations both substantive and ancillary: it also includes the application of the implemented directive. In reality, it would appear that a duty subsists on the part of the Member States to ensure that the implemented directive is fully and effectively applied. This requires that a directive and its obligations both substantive and ancillary be applied and enforced in practice. One notes in this regard the statement of Mertens de Wilmars:

> 'La directive implique … l'obligation, puisque l'Etat membre a assumé une obligation de résultat de veiller à l'application efficace de la législation nationale à l'objectif communautaire'

Indeed in von Colson[12] the ECJ held that EC Article 249 (3) requires Member States to adopt all of the measures which are necessary to ensure that the provisions of the directive at issue are fully effective. Finally, according to the case of van der Tas[13] the effective implementation of a directive including in the sense of practical effect constitutes an obligation which the Member States must fulfil. It is upon this basis also that the Commission may commence infringement proceedings for non-effective implementation of a directive.[14]

II   IMPLEMENTATION

A   STRUCTURE OF THE IMPLEMENTATION

It is useful to discuss, briefly, certain aspects of the process of implementation of a directive generally before considering the specific implementation of Directive 2004/48/EC (the Directive) in Dutch, English and German civil procedure. It is recalled that EC Article 249 (3) establishes a bifurcation between the following two aspects of implementation of a directive: on the one hand, the actual content of the

---

12. *von Colson*, Case No. 14/83 (1984) ECR 1891, op cit., and *Marshall II*, Case No. C-271/91 (1993) ECR I 4367.
13. *van der Tas*, Case No. C-143/91 (1992) ECR I 5045.
14. *Commission v. Germany*, Case No. C-361/88 (1991) ECR I 2567, *Commission v. Belgium*, Case No. C-42/89 (1990) ECR I 2821.

implementing measures is to be determined by the wording of the directive itself; and on the other hand, the form and methods of the implementation are established by the Member States which process involves the use of discretion on their part.[15] Since a directive imposes upon Member States an obligation of result, the measures taken by the Member States must be such as to ensure that the directive is 'fully effective in accordance with the objective which it pursues'.[16] This means that the obligation arising from EC Article 249 (3) goes further than the actual text of the directive at issue and the mere transposition of this text into national law. It imposes certain requirements as to the nature of the implementing measures and, moreover, it requires that these measures be applied and enforced in practice in an effective manner. However, in reality, the exercise of the discretion by the Member States to implement the directives in terms of the form and methods is itself subject to certain principles in addition to the actual content of the directive itself. Thus, following the *Commission v. Germany*[17] implementation of a directive must:

> guarantee that the national authorities will in fact apply the directive fully and that, where the directive is intended to create rights for individual [their] legal position ... is sufficiently precise and clear and the persons concerned are made fully aware of their rights and, where appropriate, afforded the possibility of relying on them before the national courts.

Furthermore, for the purposes of implementation it would seem that it makes no difference whether the provisions of a directive concern substantive law or whether they related to notably the harmonization of procedural law.[18] In the case of both types of content a directive must be fully transposed into national law. It is submitted that with respect to the implementation of the Directive, the implementation of its content which concerns the partial harmonization of national civil procedure proceeds in the same manner as if the content involved harmonization of substantive law. Arguably the implementation of a directive, and notably that of Directive 2004/48/EC, concerns various fundamental principles[19] which thereby serve to restrain or control the degree of discretion which

---

15. J. Mertens de Wilmars, 'Réflexion sur le système d'articulation du droit communautaire et du droit national', in *L'Europe et le droit: Mélanges en hommage à Jean Boulouis*, (Paris: Dalloz (Ed), 1991), at 393 and *von Colson*, Case No. 14/83 (1984) ECR 1891, and C. Zoylniski, *Méthode de transposition des directives communautaires: étude à partir de l'exemple du droit d'auteur et des droits voisins* (Doctoral Thesis in Private Law, Date of Thesis Defence: 9 Dec. 2005, Université de Paris-Assas) at 9, 'La directive se définit par référence à l'articulation entre le droit communautaire et le droit national. Selon l'article 249EC 'la directive lie tout Etat membre destinataire quant au résultat à atteindre, tout en laissant aux instances nationales la compétence quant à la forme et aux moyens'. Elle s'oppose au règlement qui toujours selon l'article 249 CE 'a une porté générale', 'est obligatoire dans tous ses éléments et [...] directement applicable dans tout Etat membre'. (D. Simon, La directive européenne Dalloz, 1997).
16. *von Colson*, Case No. 14/83 (1984) ECR 1891 para. 15.
17. *Commission v. Germany*, Case No. 29/84 (1985) ECR 1661 para. 11.
18. *Commission v. Germany*, Case No. 131/88 (1991) ECR I 825 para. 61.
19. One notes that the wording of the directive itself may be through its detail restrict the discretion of the Member States in terms of implementation thereof: see S. Prechal, *Directive in EC Law*,

the Member States enjoy with respect to the implementation of directives in general. Certain of these principles are (1), legal certainty, (2) full effect[20] and (3) effective judicial or legal protection.[21] These principles in turn can be said to affect the following aspects of the process of implementation: the first involves the requirements relating to the content of the measures adopted with a view to implementation; the second relates to the requirements which concern the nature of the implementing measures and the third relates to their effective application. It is useful to consider in more detail the nature of the three aforementioned principles of legal certainty, full effect and effective judicial protection which govern the implementation process at the level of the content of the implementing measures, the nature of the implementing measures and the effective application thereof. As noted these principles apply to the implementation of a directive irrespective of whether its content involves harmonization of substantive or procedural law.

2nd edn (Oxford: OUP, 2005), op. cit., 74.

20. *Commission v. UK*, Case No. C-340/96 (1999) ECR I-2023.

21. *Commission v. Germany*, Case No. 29/84 (1985) ECR 1661; *Commission v. Sweden*, Case No. C-478/99 (2002) ECR I 4147, D. Curtin, 'The Effectiveness of Judicial Protection of Individual Rights' *CMLRev* 709 (1990), M. Ross, 'Effectiveness in the European Legal Order Beyond Supremacy to Constitutional Proportionality' *ELRev* 31 (2006): 476. With respect to Art. 6 of the Lisbon Treaty which gives legal effect to the Charter of Fundamental Rights, and which if adopted by all of the EU Member States [rejected by Ireland on 13 June 2008] will come into effect on 1 Jan. 2009, thereby, following Art. 51 thereof, applying to EU institutions and Member States when implementing EU law is subject, as regards to the UK and Poland, to Arts 1 and 2, of the Protocol on the Application of the Charter of Fundamental Rights of the European Union to Poland and the UK: that is, these articles prevent the Charter from extending the powers of any UK or ECJ court so as strike down UK legislation and from creating new justiciable rights. However, see D. Grieve MP for concerns of expansive scope of eventual ECJ judgments involving the Charter and the eventual effectiveness of the limiting Protocol and the reply in refutation of the Parliamentary Under Secretary of State for Justice both in the House of Commons Hansard Daily Debates, 5 Feb. 2008: the concern of expansive ECJ judgments is raised in the Memorandum by S. Douglas-Scott to the House of Lords Select Committee on the Constitution: Session 2002-2003, published 15 Dec. 2003 at para. 7. 'But it is still conceivable that the ECJ might take its own approach transforming some principles into directly effective rights … .' 'The question is still what is meant by Member States implementing EU Law.' <www.publications.parliament.uk/pa/con/conhansard.htm> V. Miller & C. Taylor, *Amendments to the Treaty on European Union*, House of Commons Research Paper, 08/09, 24 Jan. 2008: S. Douglas-Scott, The Charter of Rights (2004) *EHRLR* (9) 1, 37 argues consistently with previous submissions that the capacity of the Charter to effect Member States may be increased by the ECJ through judicial interpretation; R. Davies 'A Brake: The Union's New Bill of Rights' (2005) *EHRLR* 449. See generally contra this view: Lord Goldsmith The Charter of Rights (2004) *EHRLR* 474. See also, A. Dashwood, Written Evidence, House of Lords, Select Committee on the Constitution (2008), <www.publications.parliament.uk> para. 7, D. Chalmers, Written Evidence, House of Lords, Select Committee on the Constitution (2008), <www.publications.parliament.uk> para. 2; Prof A. Dashwood, 'The Charter of Fundemental Human Rights and Its Protocol: Drawing the Teeth of the Paper Tiger' Feb. 2008: paper communicated privately for which thanks are given.

B   LEGAL CERTAINTY

The principle of legal certainty must be respected, particularly, in so far as a directive concerns the creation of rights: that is the content of the implementing measures must be clear and precise particularly where the objective of a directive is to create rights for individuals.[22] Ambiguous or uncertain provisions could lead to misapplication of a directive notably by the national courts thereby potentially depriving beneficiaries of protection of their rights. In short, legal certainty and clarity are necessary in order to assist in ensuring that the national courts apply the directive correctly. It may be that the adoption of specific legislation is necessary in order to ensure adequate implementation of the directive. However, it may also be the case that pre-existing legislation can ensure adequate implementation of a directive provided that effective application of the directive may be ensured in a clear and precise manner.[23]

C   FULL EFFECT

Irrespective of whether rights are created the implementation of the measures must be effective. Indeed, the ECJ held in the *Commission v. Germany*[24] that the implementation of a directive must:

> guarantee that the national authorities will in fact apply the directive fully and that where the directive is intended to create rights for individuals [their] legal position … is sufficiently precise and clear and that persons concerned are made fully aware of their rights and where appropriate, afforded the possibility of relying on them before the national courts.

Since a directive imposes upon the Member States an obligation of result, the measures taken by the Member States must be such as to ensure that the directive is 'fully effective in accordance with the objective which it pursues'.[25] This means that the obligation arising from EC Article 249 (3) goes further than the actual text of the Directive at issue and the mere transposition of this text into national law. It imposes certain requirements as to the nature of the implementing measures and moreover it requires that these measure be applied and enforced in practice in an effective manner.

---

22. *Commission v. Germany*, Case No. C-131/88 (1991) ECR I 825, *Commission v. The Netherlands*, Case No. C-144/99 (2001) ECR I 3541.
23. *Commission v. Germany*, Case No. C-131/88 (1991) ECR I 825, ibid., Case No. C-190/90 *Commission v. The Netherlands* (1992) ECR I 3265; S. Prechal, *Directives in EC Law*, 2nd edn (Oxford: OUP, 2005), op. cit., 77 and 97.
24. *Commission v. Germany*, Case No. 361/88 (1991) ECR 1 2567 para. 18.
25. *von Colson*, Case No. 14/83 (1984) ECR 1891 para. 15, see *Munoz*, Case No. C-253/00 (2002) ECR I 7289 which was analyzed by AG Geelhoed in terms of rights of traders/competitors but decided by the Court as mainly an issued of full effectiveness of enforcement of the rules on fruit standards.

D   EFFECTIVE JUDICIAL PROTECTION

The third principle, namely effective judicial protection, would appear to constitute a free standing principle which is based upon the concept that in a Community based upon the rule of law everyone must have the opportunity to assert his rights before the courts on his own initiative.[26] The underlying rationale is the fact that in a Community based on the rule of law everyone must have the opportunity to assert his rights before the courts.[27] The protection of this right of access to the courts must be effective. Therefore, at least from this point of view, it might be considered as an expansion of the principle of effectiveness which was established in Rewe[28] and Comet[29] or as a completely separate concept as in Verholen[30] where the two principles are raised separately. One notes, in particular, the case of Johnston[31] in which the ECJ objected to an evidential rule contained in the Sex Discrimination (Northern Ireland) Order 1976 which rendered judicially incapable of review a decision of the Chief Constable of the Royal Ulster Constabulary which deprived Mrs Johnston of any remedy for review. The central provision of this part of the judgment was Article 6 of Directive 76/207/ EEC. With respect to this article the ECJ held:

> The requirement of judicial control stipulated by that article reflects a general principle of law which underlies the constitutional traditions common to the member States. That principle is also laid down in Articles 6 and 13 of the European Convention for the Protection of Human Rights and Fundamental Freedoms of 4 November 1950. As the European Parliament, Council and Commission recognized in their Joint Declaration of 5 April 1977, and as the Court has recognized in its decisions, the principles on which that Convention is based must be take into consideration in Community law. By virtue of Article 6 of Directive 76/207/EC, interpreted in the light of the general principle state above, all persons have the right to obtain an effective remedy in a competent court against measures which they consider to be contrary to the principle of equal treatment for men and women laid down in the directive. It is for the Member States to ensure effective judicial control as regards compliance with the applicable provisions of Community law and of national legislation intended to give effect to the rights for which the directives provides.'

26. *European Parliament v. Council*, Case No. C-70/88 (1990) ECR I 2041 see opinion of AG van Gerven.
27. Opinion of AG van Gerven in *European Parliament v. Council*, Case No. 70/88 (1990) ECR I 2041 para. 6. See also L. Dubouis, 'A propos de deux principes généraux du droit communautaire', *RFDA* (1998) 691
28. *Rewe*, Case No. 33/76 (1976) ECR 1989.
29. *Comet*, Case No. 45/76 (1976) ECR 2043.
30. *Verholen*, Case No. 87/90 or according to S. Prechal, *Directives in EC Law*, 2nd edn (Oxford: OUP, 2005), op. cit., 144, n. 85, wherein *Courage*, Case No. C-453/99 (2001) ECR I 3757 contains a 'mixture of both approaches'. See also, J. Jans, R. de Lange, S. Prechal & R. Widdershoven *Europeanisation of Public Law* (Groningen: Europa Law Publishing, 2007), Ch. VII, 'Judicial Protection'.
31. *Johnston*, Case No. 222/84 (1986) ECR 1651.

Advocate-General Sharpston defined the principle of effective legal protection in Unibet[32] in the following manner:

The ECJ in UNIBET in turn defined the principle as follows:

> It is to be noted at the outset that, according to settled case-law, the principle of effective judicial protection is a general principle of Community law stemming from the constitutional traditions common to the Member States, which has been enshrined in Articles 6 and 13 of the European Convention for the Protection of Human Rights and Fundamental Freedoms and which has also be reaffirmed by Article 47 of the Charter of Fundamental Rights of the European Union proclaimed on 7 December 2000 in Nice.[33]

Prechal[34] observes in this regard that the scope of the principle of effective legal protection is wider than that of Article 6 (1) European Convention on Human Rights (ECHR):

> Although for the purposes of the principles of effective judicial protection the Court may refer to the principles enshrined in Article 6 and Article 13 of the ECHR the scope of the protection required is much broader than (civil) rights.

The absence of appropriate judicial proceedings arguably would constitute a violation of Article 39 of the Treaty.[35] Although no specific mention is made of the principle within the Directive, it nevertheless applies as a general principle of Community law along with Treaty articles to the implementation of a directive.[36] Accordingly, the Member States must ensure that the rights under the national implementing measures can be asserted by judicial process by the individuals specified in the Directive. The absence of such will amount, arguably, to inadequate implementation thereof.

---

32. *UNIBET*, Case No. 432/05 (2007) ECR I 2271 13 Mar. 2007 <www.curia.europa.eu.>
33. *UNIBET*, Case No. 432/05 (2007) ECR I 2271 13 Mar. 2007. <www. curia.europa.eu>, ibid., at para. 37: the ECJ cites the following consistent case law: *Johnston*, Case No. 222/84 (1986) ECR 1651, paras 18 and 19; *Heylens*, Case No. 222/86 (1987) ECR 4097, para. 14; *Commission v. Austria*, Case No. C-424 (2001) ECR I 9285, para. 45; Case C-50/00 P *Union de Pequenos Agricultores v. Council*, Case No. C-50/00 P (2002) ECR I 6677 para. 39).
34. S. Prechal, *Directives in EC Law* (Oxford: OUP, 2005) op. cit., p. 143.
35. *Heylens*, Case No. 222/86 (1987) ECR 4097 para. 17.
36. M. Illmer, 'Lawyers' Fees and Access to Justice – The *Cipolla* and *Macrino* judgment of the ECJ: Joined Cases No. C-94/04 and C-202/04)' *CJQ*, 26 (2007) Jul. 301: Illmer noting that the principle of effective judicial protection is not specifically included within Art. 16 (1) (b) of Directive 2006/123 EU (OJ L376/28) observes: 'it seems difficult to argue that the case law justifications are not affect by the Directive. It remains to be seen whether the ECJ will interpret the Directive as restricting the grounds for justification'. He then concludes: 'The last resort would be … the fact that access to justice is recognised as a fundamental principle of EC law and in Art. 47 of the Charter of Fundamental Rights both ranking on equal footing with the freedom to provide services under Art. 49 EC'. Arguably, Illmer arrives indirectly at the same conclusion as Prechal and Dougan: namely the implementation of directives is subject to principles of Community law and articles of the Treaty.

E   TREATY ARTICLES AND COMMUNITY LAW PRINCIPLES

Fourth, it must be stressed that the implementation of directives is subject to principles in addition to legal clarity, effectiveness and effective judicial protection: that is the implementation process must also comply with the fundamental rights and primary community law notably as contained in the articles of the Treaty.[37]

F   IMPACT OF THE PRINCIPLES OF CLARITY, EFFECTIVENESS AND
                     EFFECTIVE JUDICIAL PROTECTION ON THE IMPLEMENTATION
                     PROCESS

The principles of clarity, full effect, effective judicial protection and eventually the fundamental rights and primary Community law would appear to affect the process of implementation of directives at three different levels: first, that of the content of the measures, and second that of the form or nature of the measures and third, that of the application and enforcement of the measures in practice.[38]

1   Content of the Implementing Measures

First as noted, the content of the implementing measure will be determined by the wording of a directive itself: that is the substantive obligation imposed upon the Member State by a directive may describe in a very precise manner the legal and or factual situation which the Member State is to achieve in the course of the implementation thereof. Indeed, the content of a directive as noted earlier may involve either substantive law or procedural law as is the case of the Directive. Other examples of directives which seek to harmonize procedural matters are Directive 91/263/EEC which pertains to telecommunications equipment and provides for a procedure for assessment conformity; or Article 5 of Directive 2003/86/EEC concerning family reunification establishes the procedural obligations of the Member States in relation to the submission and examination of applications for family reunification. Furthermore, it is the case that Member States may chose to implement a directive by using one of two methods: namely, through verbatim transposition or by means of national legal concepts and legislation or indeed some combination of both of the above methods. While there is no requirement that the provision be transposed literally[39] nevertheless, the content of a directive, as noted previously, must be clear and precise notably in two situations: first where

---

37.   *Wachauf*, Case No. 5/88 (1989) ECR 2609, Joined Cases *Booker Aquaculture*, Case
      No. C-20/00 and C-64/00 (2003) ECR I 7411 and *Ambry*, Case No. C-410/96 (1998) ECR I 7875 see
      S. Prechal, *Directives in EC Law*, 2nd edn (Oxford: OUP, 2005), op cit., 76, n. 22, and 146 n. 105.
38.   S. Prechal, *Directives in EC Law* 2nd edn (Oxford: OUP, 2005), op. cit., 91-92 observes that
      practically the significance of the concept of rights is that it affects the method of implementation by engaging the criterion of clarity and legal certainty.
39.   *Commission v. Germany*, Case No. 131/88 (1991) ECR 1 825, ibid.

a directive is intended to create rights and duties for individuals[40] and second even where a directive does not seek to create such rights. Clarity of the national implementing measure is necessary in order to ensure first that the beneficiaries of rights are able to both identify and enforce them; and second, where a directive does not seek to create rights clarity of implementation of the directive is necessary in order to prevent misapplication thereof by the national authorities. Furthermore, whilst specifically adopted legislation may be necessary it is possible that pre-existing legislation may also suffice provided that it ensures full application of a directive in a sufficiently clear and precise manner.[41] Indeed, in some cases the wording of a directive itself may require by reason of its lack of precision and clarity that the Member States ensure further implementation beyond mere verbatim transposition thereof. The use of case law to implement the directive or more specifically sections thereof is arguably subject to the requirement of legal certainty and clarity.

As noted earlier the creation of rights depends arguably in first instance upon the content of a directive and in particular upon the purpose as contained notably in the Recitals:[42] that is, whether a directive or one or more of its provisions creates or is intended to create individual rights and obligations is a matter of the substance of a directive and must be decided on the basis of the text of the relevant directive provisions including the Recitals of the directive. A directive may indicate that rights should be created at the national level or it may be that the rights are directly created by a directive itself.[43] More particularly, if the content of the alleged right as defined within a directive is sufficiently precise then arguably it will constitute a direct source of the rights at issue: that is, a directive may confer right without the intervention of national measures of implementation. However, even if the wording of a directive notably with respect to the definition of the category of beneficiary and the nature of the obligation which falls upon a Member State is not absolutely clear, a directive may still be intended, notably as provided in its Recitals, to confer rights. The actual creation thereof will take place at a later stage of implementation. Overall, whether a directive is intended to do this must be decided on the basis of its text and purpose. Accordingly, it would seem that directives in such a context would constitute what might be termed an indirect

---

40. *Commission v. Germany*, Case No. 131/88 (1999) ECR I 825, ibid.
41. *Commission v. Germany*, Case No. 131/88 (1999) ECR I 825, ibid., *Commission v. Germany*, Case No. 102/97 (1999) ECR I 5051.
42. S. Prechal, *Directives in EC Law*, 2nd edn (Oxford: OUP, 2005), op. cit., 111 and 106. 'As was already observed, direct effect and creation of rights may and will often coincide; the provision can thus both have direct effect and define rights although this is not always necessarily the case. The most obvious example in this respect is the Francovich case (C-6/90) In this case the directive was regarded as being designed to create rights for the benefit of individuals but the direct effect doctrine was of no avail for the individuals concerned since the provisions on the identity of the debtor were not sufficiently clear and unconditional. In other words, they did not meet the classical conditions for direct effect. Consequently for this reason and in the absence of implementing measures, the individuals could not enforce the right granted to them by Community law before national courts'. C. Plaza Martin 'Furthering the Effectiveness of EC Directives and the Judicial Protection of Individual Rights Thereunder', *ICLQ* 43 (1994): 26.
43. S. Prechal, *Directives in EC Law*, 2nd edn (Oxford: OUP, 2005), ibid., Ch. 9.

sources of rights and obligations for individuals since the rights and obligations under national law have their origin in the directive. It is submitted that in the case of the Directive, the rights are created through the implementation at the national level as opposed to being directly effective. Accordingly, the Directive would seem to constitute an indirect source of rights by reason of the fact that it seeks to achieve minimum harmonization thereby leaving substantial discretion to the Member States for the implementation of these rights albeit subject to principles of Community law:[44] that is, Recital 18 in conjunction with Article 4 of the Directive arguably establishes that the purpose of the substantive obligation contained within the latter is to create a right of standing for a category of beneficiaries who are defined in Article 4 in the following manner.

2   Standing: Locus Standi: Directive 2004/48/EC

The category of beneficiary is defined generally as one which is composed of persons who have a direct interest in Recital 18:

> Recital 18: The persons entitled to request the application of those measures, procedures and remedies should be not only the rights holders but also persons who have a direct interest.

The purpose of granting the procedural rights is to protect the substantive rights referred to in Recital 18 which belong to the category of rights holders referred to specifically therein. It is useful to consider further Recital 32:

> Recital 32: This Directive respects the fundamental rights and observes the principles recognized in particular by the Charter of Fundamental Rights of the European Union. In particular, the Directive seeks to ensure the full respect of intellectual property in accordance with art 17(2) of that Charter.

In turn the scope of category of beneficiaries of the procedural right which is namely a right to 'seek the application of the measures, procedures and remedies', that is, a right of standing, is defined in Article 4 of the Directive as follows:

> Article 4: Member States shall recognize as persons entitled to seek the application of the measures, procedures and remedies.
>
> – Holders of intellectual property rights in accordance with the provisions of the applicable law.
> – All other persons authorized to use those rights, in particular licensees, in so far as permitted and in accordance with the provisions of the applicable law.
> – Intellectual property rights management bodies which are regularly recognized as having a right to represent holders of the intellectual property

---

44. S. Prechal, *Directives in EC Law*, 2nd edn (Oxford: OUP, 2005), ibid., 313.

rights in so far as permitted and in accordance with the provisions of the applicable law.
- Professional defence bodies which are regularly recognized as having a right to represent holders of intellectual property rights in so far as permitted by and in accordance with the provisions of the applicable law.'

Whilst the essence of the right is provided in Article 4 in conjunction with Recital 18, clearly, the right is implemented by the national procedure which in turn provides the concrete basis therefore, as for example, the manner in which the representative of the class of right holders is to be designated.

3   Measures Available Which Result in Procedural Rights in Favour of the Applicant

Article 6: it is submitted that this article creates a right on a minimum level on condition of fulfilment of the requirements delineated within that paragraph for making a request for disclosure of documents from the opposite side. In short, at a minimum the applicant has the right to be able to make an application for disclosure. It is submitted, however, that the operation of this right is subject to implementation by the national judiciary by reason of the term – 'the judicial authorities "may order"'. This is mutatis mutandis the case under Articles 3, 7, 8, 9, 10, 11, 13 and 14 of the Directive in so far as they provide for 'the applicant' or in the proceedings or 'rights holder 'who is clearly one of the parties mentioned in Article 4 as being a rights holder. Each of these will be examined in more detail in the subsequent chapters dealing with the national implementation of the Directive.

4   Nature of the Implementing Measures: Legally Binding

Following the case of the *Commission v. Germany*,[45] the choice of the form and the methods of national implementation will be influenced by the content of a directive and in particular by the substantive obligation imposed thereby on the Member States. In particular, the matter of whether or not the purpose of a directive is the creation of rights is significant not only between national authorities and those directly concerned but also with respect to third parties. Normally, the ECJ requires that the implementation take the form of binding national rules as opposed to, for example, administrative circulars:[46] that is, the measure must bind the administration in relation to private individuals.[47] This requirement exists for two reasons: first, in order to ensure particularly where rights are created that the

---

45. *Commission v. Germany*, Case No. 29/84 (1985) ECR 1661 C-306/90 *Commission v. Greece*, Case No. C-306/90 (1991) ECR I 5863.
46. *Commission v. Italy*, Case No. 116/86 (1988) ECR 1323, *Commission v. Italy*, Case No. C-145/99 (2002) ECR I 2235.
47. *Commission v. Germany*, Case No. 361/88 (1991) ECR I 2567, op. cit.

beneficiaries thereof are able to ascertain them with clarity; and second so that the beneficiaries may have an enforceable legal position.

5   Implementation of Directives: Application Thereof

As was noted earlier the effective implementation of a directive involves not only the adoption of legislation but in addition the application thereof or in any event application of pre-existing legislation by the national courts. In this regard it falls to the national authority to decide which body is competent to apply the implementation of a directive. Further and conspicuously, the national body must act in conformity with the content of a directive. This process may be termed the application of a directive. It is subject to the requirements of clarity and precision in the implementing measures coupled with their legally binding which serve to prevent the misapplication of a directive, notably by the national court: that is, the application of these principles to the content and the legal nature of the implementing measures will ensure what might be termed the correct application of a directive in particular by the national courts. Arguably, insofar as implementation includes application, and notably judicial application of a directive, it is of use to advert to the duty of consistent interpretation: that is, the duty of the national authority to provide a consistent interpretation applies irrespective of whether the implementation is deficient and irrespective of whether a directive was implemented at all.[48] In short, it would appear that part of the process of judicial implementation of a directive involves the concept of consistent interpretation as established by the ECJ in von Colson.[49] There are at least two examples in this regard: the first is Case 373/90[50] which involves the transposition of Directive 84/450/EEC on misleading advertising by Article 44 of Law 73/1193 (France). The problem was not an incorrect transposition of that directive by the French law but rather the question of the construction of the expression 'new car' by the national court which could determine whether or not a particular advertisement could be considered misleading: in short, the exercise of the national court's discretion in terms of construing the national legislation in relation to Directive 84/450/EEC. The ECJ decided that the national court was obliged to interpret the expression 'new car' in the aforementioned French law in conformity both with the purpose of the directive as well as with EU law, particularly with regard to the protection of parallel imports: that is the national court was obliged to construe the expression 'new car' in a way 'that it does not preclude vehicles from being advertised as new ... when the vehicles concerned are registered solely for the purpose of important and have never been on the road ...'. Therefore, cars registered in Belgium prior to importation in France could be considered 'new cars'. A second example of what might be termed consistent interpretation in the

---

48.   S. Prechal, *Directive in EC Laws*, 2nd edn (Oxford: OUP, 2005), 187 and 190.
49.   *von Colson*, Case No. 14/83 (1984) ECR 1891.
50.   Case No. 373/90 X (1992) ECR I 131.

context of judicial implementation of a directive is that of Beets-Proper.[51] This case involved the implementation of Directive 76/207/EEC which deals with equal treatment at work. Here, Mrs Beets – Proper was dismissed at the age of 60 while her male colleagues were permitted to work until the age of 65. Her employer felt that the employment contract automatically terminated by virtue of an implied term in the employment contract at the moment that Mrs Beets-Proper became entitled to an old age pension under a pension scheme connected with the employer's pension fund. For the purpose of the pension the relevant age for women was 60 and for men 65. The question in the Dutch court was whether the implied condition of termination relied upon by the employer was compatible with Article 1637j of the Dutch Civil Code. This article read as follows at the material times:

(1) As regards the conclusion of a contract of employment, staff training, the terms of employment, promotion and the termination of the contract of employment, an employer may not make any distinction between men and women ... The terms of employment do not include benefits or entitlements under pension schemes ...

(2) Any clause which is contrary to the first sentence of paragraph 1 shall be void.

The Hoge Raad following a reference to the ECJ held that Article 1637j of the Civil Code which implemented Directive 76/207/EEC must be construed in the following manner: that is, a condition of the employment contract providing for the termination thereof on the date on which the employee attains pensionable age, must fall within the first sentence of the first paragraph of Article 1637j and not the second sentence of the first paragraph. Accordingly, the disputed implied term was covered by the second paragraph of Article 1637j and therefore was void. Therefore, Article 1637j of the Dutch Civil Code could be considered as having correctly implemented Directive 76/207/EEC and consequently, did not require any amendment.[52]

Finally, with respect to implementation of Directive 2004/48/EC, as noted earlier the content thereof concerns partial harmonization of rules of national procedure as opposed to substantive law. Accordingly, it is the content of the Directive which determines the form of the rules of procedure as opposed to the courts exercising their discretion subject to the principles of equivalence and effectiveness subject to articles of the Treaty.[53] An example in this regard in terms of English

---

51. *Beets-Proper*, Case No. 262/84 (1986) ECR 773.
52. S. Prechal, *Directives in EC Law*, 2nd edn (Oxford: OUP, 2005), op cit., 189-190.
53. S. Prechal, *Directive in EC Laws*, 2nd edn (Oxford: OUP, 2005), op cit., 135. It is submitted that where the purpose of the directive as is the case with Directive 2004/48/EC is to harmonize (partially) national procedure that judicial application of the directive concerns application of the implementation in the form of rules of civil procedure as provided for by the directive. In contrast where the directive does not provide for rules of civil procedure judicial application in terms of civil procedure involves the principle of effectiveness and equivalence coupled with Treaty articles as well as the principles of effective judicial protection and non-discrimination.

procedural law would be the requirement for English courts to interpret the grounds which can be used for granting an interlocutory injunction in such a way as to ensure correct implementation of Article 9 (3): that is, so as to ensure that the courts may '...satisfy themselves with sufficient degree of certainty ... that the applicant's right is being infringed'. Compliance with this obligation may well require the court to replace the grounds established in the case of American Cynanamid.[54] which precludes the use of criterion involving certainty based upon the merits of the substantive cause of action.

**6   Methods of Redress for Incorrectly Implemented or
            Non-implemented Directives**

In the event that a directive is incorrectly implemented or not implemented at all an individual may resort to a national court to ensure proper observance thereof. The ECJ has developed two principle methods to ensure such observance of a directive: first, the concept of consistent interpretation of national law with a directive; and second, the principle of State liability for harm caused to individuals by breaches of Community law and notably non-implementation or incorrect implementation of a directive. A third possible recourse, namely, the concept of direct effect will not be considered in the context of the Directive: that is, it would appear that the concepts of interpretation in conformity and state liability will suffice to deal with eventual problems of either incorrect implementation or non-implementation of the Directive particularly given the limitations of the use of direct effect in the context of horizontal relations or party to party as opposed to vertical or party to state relations.[55] Furthermore, certain articles of the Directive such as Article 4 (c) and (d) as well as Articles 3 and 14 particularly as they apply to costs and proportionality would seem to lack the characteristics of sufficient precision: that is the actual form that the rights are to take and their scope are not clearly defined. Accordingly, it would seem that implementation thereof requires the exercise of discretion on the part of the legislator for effective implementation.[56]

---

54. (1975) 2 WLR 316.
55. It is submitted that direct effect and the creation of rights are two separate matters: creation of rights may not always result in direct effect which is viewed as the procedural enforceability of a directive. Similarly, direct effect does not always lead to creation of rights – see generally S. Prechal, *Directives in EC Law*, 2nd edn (Oxford: OUP, 2005), op. cit., 283, S. Prechal 'Does direct effect still matter?' *CMLRev* (2000) 1047, see generally T. Hartley, *The Foundations of European Community Law*, 5th edn (Oxford: OUP, 2003), Wyatt and Dashwood, *European Union Law*, 4th edn (London: Sweet & Maxwell, 2000), A.J. Easson, 'The Direct Effect of EEC Directives' *International and Comparative Law Quarterly [ICLQ]* (1979): 319.
56. Traen, Joined Cases No. 372-74/85 (1987) ECR 2141, at para. 24-26; P. Pescatore, 'The Doctrine of Direct Effect: An Infant Disease of Community Law' *ELR* 155 (1983), S. Prechal, *Directives in EC Law*, 2nd edn (Oxford: OUP, 2005), ibid., 244-245.

7   Consistent Interpretation: Incorrectly Implemented or Non-implemented Directives

As noted earlier, in von Colson[57] the ECJ held that the national courts are under a legal duty to interpret and apply national law and in particular legislation adopted for the implementation of a directive in conformity with the latter: that is, as a matter of principle national courts are obliged to give effect to a directive through interpretation. The obligation is arguably based on the binding nature of Articles 249 (3) and 10 of the EC Treaty. The national courts are bound by EC Article 249 (3) and they are called upon to assist in achieving the result of a directive at issue. It may be, following Pfeifer,[58] that the requirement of consistent interpretation is inherent in the system of the EC Treaty. From the case law of the ECJ it appears that for the purposes of consistent interpretation it is immaterial whether the provisions which serve as standards for interpretation are directly effective or not. Furthermore, it must be pointed out that the duty of consistent interpretation is not confined to the wording of the directive. The national court must also construe national legal provision in light of the objective of the directive concerned. Following Marleasing,[59] the obligation to effect a consistent interpretation applies irrespective of 'whether the provisions in question were adopted before or after the directive'.[60] In other words, national courts are required to proceed to a purposive or teleological interpretation of national law in order to ensure that it can achieve the objective of a directive. As noted earlier in the section on rights, not only the wording but also the purpose of a directive must be taken into account. This might be termed the judicial use of consistent interpretation in contrast to the situation described earlier where a directive had been implemented correctly.[61] With respect to remedial consistent interpretation it is perhaps possible to consider non-transposed directives from two points of view: first the situation where a directive has not been transposed at all into national law although the Member States recognizes that such transposition is necessary; and second, the situation where the Member State does not admit such an obligation of transposition. In this regard the UK, following the explanation in the Accompanying Notes[62] would appear to believe that Article 4 of the Directive does not require transposition: in short, there is no need for the English legal system to provide for representative

---

57. *Von Colson*, Case No. 14/83 (1984) ECR 1891 op cit..
58. *Pfeiffer*, Case No. 397/01 – 403/01 (2004) ECR I 8835 op cit..
59. *Marleasing*, Case No. C-106/89 (1990) ECR I 4135 op cit.
60. *Tögel*, Case No. C-76/97 (1998) ECR I 5357, *Océano*, Joined Cases No. C-240/98 and C-244/98 (2000) ECR I 4941.
61. S. Prechal, *Directives in EC Law*, 2nd edn (Oxford: OUP, 2005), op. cit., 187.
62. The Patent Office, Consultation Paper, 'The UK Implementation of the Directive on the Enforcement of Intellectual Property Rights (2004/48/EC)', Annex B, Transposition Note, states for Art. 4: 'No Action Required'. It is to be noted that a consultation process concerning the implementation of Art. 4 in terms of representative actions has been undertaken with respect to Directive 2004/48/EC. See also representative Actions.

actions. In the third case, the UK has enacted some measures but they do not appear to fulfil the requirements of the Directive.

a   *Scope of the Duty of Consistent Interpretation*

Following Marleasing,[63] it would appear that the scope of the duty is wide: that is, the rules of interpretation which are to be applied would seem to be normally EU rules. As such, limitations on the application of EU law which could result from the use of national rules of interpretation are thereby avoided. These principles which could serve to limit the process of consistent interpretation would seem to include the following:[64] unjust enrichment, equity, equality, proportionality and following Kolpinghuis,[65] *nulla poena sine lege, nulum crimen sine lege*, and legal certainty including its component of contra legem. EU law determines the nature and the limits of the obligation to ensure consistent interpretation. The question of whether or not a national court is still within its judicial functions when interpreting national law is, it is submitted, ultimately a question of EU law.[66] It would appear however, that the scope of the duty does not include situations where there is no national law which governs the subject matter of the directive: that is, in such a situation simply no national law exists which can be interpreted in conformity with the directive.

b   *Limits of the Scope of Consistent Interpretation*

As noted earlier, the possible limits on the scope of the principles were established by the ECJ in Kolpinghuis:[67]

> The obligation on the national court to refer to the content of the directive when interpreting the relevant rules of its national law is limited by the general principles of law which form part of Community law and in particular the principles of legal certainty and non-retroactivity.

As noted earlier and following Timmermans[68] it is submitted that the principles are those of EU law such as legal certainty,[69] possibly proportionality, equality.

---

63. *Marleasing*, Case No. C-106/89 (1990) ECR I 4135 op cit.
64. T. Tridimas, *The General Principles of EC Law* (Oxford: OUP, 1999).
65. *Kolpinghuis*, Joined Cases No. C-74/95 and C 129/95 X (1996) ECR I 6609.
66. S. Prechal, *Directives in EC Law*, 2nd edn (Oxford: OUP, 2005), opcit., 198 notes that some such as AG Lenz in his Opinion in Case No. C-331 *Gestion Hotelera International* (1994) ECR I 1329 that in fact national rules of interpretation as opposed to Community rules are used.
67. *Kolpinghuis*, Case No. 80/86 (1987) ECR 3986.
68. C. Timmermans, 'Community Directives Revisted' *Yearbook of European Law* (YEL) 1 (1997): 23.
69. A limitation which is usually raised, for example by Y. Galmot & J.-C. Bonichot, 'La Cour de Justice des Communautés Européennes et la Transposition des Directives en Droit National' (1988) RFDA 1 is that of contra legem which is arguably part of the principle of legal certainty: that is giving the national legislation a meaning which is conspicuously different from the literal meaning. However, J. Stuyck & P. Wyntick 'Comment on Case C-106/89 Marleasing'

Thus for example, if constraints are imposed by clear language a statute cannot be interpreted in a manner which its wording will not sustain. Furthermore, in terms of effects, the most obvious with respect to consistent interpretation is that a provision of national law is given a meaning which it would not otherwise bear other that by reason of the directive. As noted earlier the concept of consistent interpretation, relates to both the national legislation and the EU legislation. An example of this would be Article 9 of the Directive concerning the grounds upon which an application for an interlocutory injunction is to be made. The use of the doctrine of consistent interpretation may ensure one of the following: namely, that the scope of the national legislation is either widened or narrowed in order to ensure the adequate implementation of the directive. The very nature of this activity consists in attributing a meaning and scope to a provision of national law which it did not have if only national law considerations were involved. The last issue to be addressed is whether a distinction is to be made where, on the one hand, an individual invokes the directive for the purposes of consistent interpretation involving another individual and on the other hand, the situation in which the State relies on the Directive for the purpose of a consistent interpretation: in the first situation it is clearly and individual who seeks to compel obedience while in the second situation it is the State which institutes proceedings. An example of the use of consistent interpretation in the context of implementation by the English courts of Article 9(3) of the Directive would be as follows: that is the courts would be obliged to exercise their discretion in such as way as to chose among competing standards the one which will ensure that an injunction is granted in conformity with Article 9(3) of the Directive.

8   State Liability

The second possible method which has been developed by the ECJ to ensure compliance with a directive is State Liability:[70] that is, if a Member State fails to comply with the obligation incumbent upon it to pursuant to Article 249 (3) of the Treaty to transpose a directive and if the result prescribed by it cannot be achieved by way of consistent interpretation of national law by the national courts, then the following will result: namely, EU law will require that a Member State compen-

---

CMLR (1991): 205 p. 211 observe that '… an interpretation in conformity with a directive, consisting in a reduction of the traditional scope of application of a provision of national law, could therefore very easily amount to an interpretation contra legem which, up until now, has been ruled out as a possible interpretation for the application of von Colson and Kamann doctrine. Opinion of AG van Gerven Case C-262/88, Douglas H Barber (1990)' and S. Prechal, *Directives in EC Law*, 2nd edn (Oxford: OUP, 2005), 207, raises the question as to whether Marleasing does not itself produce an interpretation contra legem thereby undermining at least to a certain degree this limitation including that of legal certainty.

70. T. Tridimas, 'Liability for Breach of Community Law: Growing Up and Mellowing Down'? *CMLRev* (2001) 301, S. Weatherill 'Breach of Directives and Breach of Contract Law', ELRev (2001) 177, C. Hilson 'Liability of Member States in Damages: The Place of Discretion', ICLQ (1997): 941.

sate the loss and the damage caused to individuals through its failure to transpose the directive provided that three conditions are fulfilled: first, that the result prescribed by the directive in question must entail the grant of rights to individuals; second, the breach of those rights must be sufficiently serious on the basis of the provisions of the directive and, third, there must be a causal link between the breach of the State's obligation and the damage suffered. In those circumstances, it is for the national court to enforce the right of aggrieved person such that he may obtain reparation in accordance with national law on liability.

a   *Conditions for State Liability*

i   Creation of Rights
As noted previously, following ECJ case law,[71] three conditions must be fulfilled in order in order that State liability may arise: first, the infringed Community law must be intended to confer or create rights on individuals, second, the breach must be sufficiently serious and third, there must be a direct causal link between the breach of the obligation and the damage sustained. Arguably the creation of rights is significant in that they affect not only the modalities of the implementation of the directive but also the matter of State liability. As noted previously, the creation of rights and direct effect should not be confused. It can be said that directly effective provisions may but do not necessarily confer rights.[72] There is, however, a link between direct effect and the creation of rights, namely, in the sense that rights or more precisely, their content and the beneficiaries of the rights, must be ascertainable with a sufficient degree of precision and legal clarity. It may be said that here again the test for direct effect and the identification of rights may coincide but cannot be equated. Furthermore, one must be aware that directives may intend to create rights for individuals but that the elaboration of their exact scope falls to be decided by the Member States. Moreover, a right which is declared in a directive in rudimentary form will make it impossible to determine the loss and damage incurred by the individual. A directive may therefore provide sufficient guidance in this respect. If necessary the national court may make recourse to the ECJ by means of a reference for this purpose. It is sufficient for the purposes of liability that the provisions intend to confer rights. Prechal argues that by using the term rights in the implementation context the ECJ may merely indicate that the Member State must create, through implementing measures, a legally sufficiently defined position which may be enforced in the courts if necessary.[73] In the case law involving State liability for failed or incorrect implementation of direc-

---

71. *Frankovich*, Case No. C-6/90 – C-9/90 (1991) ECR I 5357, op. cit., *Dillenkofer*, Joined Cases No. C-178/94, C-179/94, C-188/94, C-189/94 and C-190/94 (1996) ECR I 4845, *British Telecom*, Case No. 392/93 (1996) ECR I 1631 (sufficiently serious test was applied in a case of incorrect implementation of a directive) *Brasserie du Pêcheur*, Joined Cases No. C-46/93 and C-48/93 (1996) ECR I 1029.
72. S. Prechal, *Directives in EC Law*, 2nd edn (Oxford: OUP, 2005), op. cit., Ch. 6.
73. S. Prechal, *Directives in EC Law*, 2nd edn (Oxford: OUP, 2005), ibid., at 110.

tives an additional uncertainty must be considered: that is, in Francovich the ECJ held that the result of the directive must entail the grant of a right in contrast to Faccini[74] where it was held that the purpose of the directive ought to be the granting of rights. In this regard one might observe that there is a difference between the concept of purpose and that of result.

ii   Result

One might say that there is a certain gradation of precision with respect to the definition of rights: arguably the degree of certainty which is required in order to establish the existence of rights in the context of direct effect is greater than is the case with respect to rights in the context of State liability: in the context of implementation one might say that the degree of certainty required consists simply in requiring that the process of national implementation will create a sufficiently defined and enforceable position for individuals.[75]

iii   Purpose

It would seem that it is sufficient for one or more provisions where appropriate to confer or intend to confer rights. The purpose of the directive remains however an important aid for interpretation in that where directives intend to create rights they must be implemented by legally binding measures. From the case law on implementation as well as on liability it may be deduced that there are two possibilities as to whether rights are intended to be created or not, there seem to be two possibilities which correspond with the direct/indirect source scenario. The directive at issue may indicate that rights should be created at national level, that is, implementation/liability case law, or it may be that the rights are directly created by the directive namely as a result of direct effect, that is, direct effect/liability case law.

iv   Serious Breach

The ECJ held that a breach is sufficiently serious when the Member State concerned manifestly and gravely disregarded the limits on its discretion. In Dillenkofer[76] the ECJ held that if at the time of the breach the Member State concerned was not called upon to make any legislative choices and it had only considerably reduced or even no discretion, the mere infringement of Community law may be sufficient to establish the existence of a sufficiently serious breach. The ECJ also found that failure to implement a directive on time constitutes per se a sufficiently serious breach. In brief, discretion or its absence is not the decisive

---

74. *Faccini Dori*, Case No. C-91/92 (1994) ECR I 3325.
75. AG van Gerven 'Of rights, remedies and procedures', *CMLRev* 501 (2000) 507 defines rights as 'The concept of rights refers ... to a legal position which a person recognized as such by the law ... may have and which in its normal state can be enforced by that person against ... others before a court of law by means of one or more remedies ... .'
76. *Dillenkofer*, Joined Cases No. C-178.94, C-179.94, C-188/94 and C-190/94 (1996) ECR I 4845, op. cit., para. 18.

factor and neither is the capacity in which the Member State breaches Community law – legislative, administrative or judicial. In order to determine whether or not a breach is sufficiently serious in order to engage the liability of the State the ECJ notably in Dillenkofer enumerated some of the factors to be considered: they include, the clarity and precision of the rule breached, the measure of discretion left by the rule to the Member States, whether the infringement and the damage caused was intentional or involuntary, whether any error of law was excusable or inexcusable, the fact that the position taken by a Community institution may have contributed towards the omission and the adoption or retention of national measures or practises contrary to Community. One notes in this regard that in British Telecom[77] the ECJ found that Directive 90/531/EEC which deals with procurement in water, energy, transport and telecommunications section, lacked precision in drafting. Accordingly, by reason of the lack of clarity of that directive, the interpretation given thereof by the UK in good faith could not be viewed as being manifestly contrary to its wording. Therefore, the incorrect implementation of the directive did not constitute a manifestly and grave breach of EU law by the UK.

Overall it would seem that discretion or its absences is not decisive in establishing whether or not a Member State has committed a breach which is sufficiently serious so as to engage its tortious liability. Rather, it would appear that what really matters is whether the legal provision with which the Member State must comply is sufficiently clear and certain. In the more specific context of implementation of directives this means whether the legal situation to be realized by the Member State through implementation was sufficiently clear.[78]

v   Causal Link
The third condition is the existence of a direct causal link between the breach of the State's obligation and the loss and damage suffered by the injured parties. As causation is largely a question of fact, i.e., it must be assessed in the light of the facts of the case it is difficult to say in general terms what the exact content of the condition is. However, by reason of the fact that causality is one of the three EU conditions established by the ECJ, it would seem that it may be ultimately for the latter rather than the national court to determine the main elements thereof.[79] On the other hand, following Brasserie du Pêcheur, the action for damages notably as regards the issue of compensation is governed by the national rules of liability:

> The State must make reparation for the consequences of the loss and damage caused in accordance with domestic rules on liability provided that the conditions for reparation of loss and damage laid down by national law must

---

77.   *British Telecom*, Case No. C-392/93 (1996) ECR I 1631. at paras 43-44.
78.   S. Prechal, *Directives in EC Law*, 2nd edn (Oxford: OUP, 2005), op. cit., 288.
79.   *Brasserie du Pêcheur*, Case No. C-46/93 and C-48/93 (1996) ECR I 1029, and Dounias, Case No. 2-228/98 (2000) ECR I 577.

not be less favourable than those relating to similar domestic claims and must not be such as in practice to make it impossible or excessive difficult to obtain reparation.[80]

The reparation must be commensurate with the loss and damage sustained by the individual in order to ensure effective protection of their rights arising from the directive. The principles of effectiveness and equivalence apply to determine the extent of the reparation including such matters as loss of profits and exemplary damages.[81]

In conclusion, one might observe more generally that the availability of non-contractual State Liability arguably comes into play once one of the other two methods, notably, the principles of consistent interpretation and direct effect appears to be unavailable or insufficient for ensuring effective protection of rights provided by the Directive.[82]

---

80. *Brasserie du Pêcheur*, Case No. C-46/93 and C-48/93 (1996) ECR I 1029, ibid., at para. 67.
81. *Brasserie du Pêcheur*, Case No. C-46/93 and C-48/93 (1996) ECR I 1029, ibid., at paras 87-89.
82. F. Schockweiler, '*Le régime de la responsabilité extra – contractuelle du fait d'actes juridiques dans la Commuanuté européenne*' (1990) Revue Trimestrielle de Droit Européen [RTDE] 27, F. Schockweiler, '*La responsabilité de l'autorité nationale en cas de violation du droit communautaire*' (1992) RTDE 27, F. Schockweiler, '*Die Haftung der EG Mitgliedstaaten gegenüber dem einzelnen bei Verletzung des Gemeinschaftsrechts*' (1993) Europarecht 107.

Chapter 2

Structure of Directive 2004/48/EC

I   INTRODUCTION

In this chapter, the structure of Directive 2004/48/EC[1] (the Directive) will be examined in terms of the scope of the legal obligation which the Member States,[2] which includes the national courts, are obliged to implement so as to comply with their responsibility as established by European Community (EC) Article 249 (3) in conjunction with EC Article 10.[3]

---

1.   See 'Proposals for a European Parliament and Council Directive on Criminal Measures Aimed at Ensuring the Enforcement of Intellectual Property Rights', COM (2006): 168 Final; see also, R. Hilty, A. Kur & A. Peukert in 'Statement of Max Planck Institute for Intellectual Property, Competition and Tax Law on the Proposal for a Directive of the European Parliament and of the Council on Criminal Measures Aimed at Ensuring the Enforcement of Intellectual Property Rights', *IIC* 37 (2006): 436. Art. 8 of Reg. 864/2007 EC of the European Parliament and Council, adopted on 11 Jul. 2007 and coming into force on 11Jan. 2009 provides for harmonization of conflict rules concerning non-contractual obligations. Art. 8 (1) provides that the law applicable is that of the country for which protection is claimed and is to be read with Recital 27. See however the criticism of the House of Lords European Union Committee: Report on Rome II, Eight Report, Session 2003-2004, <www.publications.parliament.uk>, notably at para. 58 where the necessity of such harmonization is rejected.
2.   S. Prechal, *Directives in EC Law*, 2nd edn (Oxford: OUP, 2005) at 41 feels that the content or scope of a directive not only varies according to the subject area as for example, harmonization of the internal market will vary from those aiming at social or environmental protection but will also influence the following: namely, the implementation of a directive, the question of State liability in the event of non- or inadequate implementation of the directive and the issue of direct effect. See generally M. Dougan, *National Remedies before the Court of Justice: Issues of Harmonisation and Differentiation* (Oxford: Hart, 2004).
3.   Consolidated Version of the Treaty Establishing the European Community: Official Journal, C 325, 24 Dec. 2002: Art. 10: 'Member States shall take all appropriate measures whether general or particular to ensure fulfilment of the obligations arising out of this Treaty or resulting from action taken by institutions of the Community. They shall facilitate the achievement of the

Scope of the obligation pursuant to EC Article 249 (3):

EC Article 249 (3)[4] provides as follows:
Chapter 2: Provisions Common To Several Institutions: Article 249

(1) In order to carry out their task and in accordance with the provisions of this Treaty, the European Parliament acting jointly with the Council, the Council and the Commission shall make regulations and issue directives, take decisions, make recommendations or deliver opinions.
(3) A directive shall be binding, as to the result to be achieved, upon each Member State to which it is addressed, but shall have leave to the national authorities, the choice of the form and methods.

Accordingly, following EC Article 249 the nature and the scope of the obligation which is binding upon the Member States in relation to the Directive will be examined in this chapter. The form and methods of the implementation of this obligation which pursuant to EC Article 249 are, as noted, left to the discretion of the Member States and will therefore be examined in the chapters which deal with the national implementation of the Directive. Furthermore, the Member States have an obligation by reason of the binding nature of the directives pursuant to EC Article 249 to ensure that implementation thereof is carried out both timeously and correctly. Failure to so do could result either in infraction proceedings being initiated by the Commission against a Member State[5] or possibly a damages action being brought by an individual against a Member State for non-implementation which has resulted in personal loss.[6] The objective of the Directive is the harmonization of procedural law for enforcement of substantive intellectual property law. Harmonization may be said to representation a limited form of intervention under the EC Treaty as opposed to the introduction of uniform rules.[7] Arguably, the Directive constitutes an example of minimum as opposed to total harmonization. Accordingly, the Member States are able to either maintain or to adopt a more

---

Community's tasks. They shall abstain from any measure which could jeopardize the attainment of the objects of this Treaty.'
4. Consolidated Version of the Treaty Establishing the European Community: Official Journal C 325, 24 Dec. 2002, ibid.
5. S. Prechal, *Directives in EC Law*, 2nd edn (Oxford: OUP, 2005), op. cit., 8. 'The Court's case law relating to problems of non-implemented or (allegedly) inadequately implemented directives can be situated at two different levels; The first level is that of infringement proceedings or, to put it differently, the Community level of enforcement .... Today, these types of cases form a considerable part of Art. 226 actions brought before the Court' and at 16.
6. S. Prechal, *Directives in EC Law*, 2nd edn (Oxford: OUP, 2005), ibid., 10: 'Using the necessity of effective judicial protection as one of the two main arguments, the Court decided in 1991 that a Member State is in principle liable for harm cause to individuals by breaches of Community law, including the non-implementation of directives (Joined Cases C-6/90 and C/90 Francovich and Bonifaci (1991) ECR I 5357). It has been suggested that the Court intentionally denied direct effect of the directive at issue with a view to establishing the liability of the State as a remedy which did not depend on direct effect.'
7. S. Prechal, *Directive in EC Law*, 2nd edn (Oxford: OUP, 2005), ibid., 4; P. Slot, 'Harmonisation', *ELR* (1996) 378.

stringent standards than those which are imposed on them by the specific obligations of the Directive.[8]

II	NATURE OF THE OBLIGATION TO BE IMPLEMENTED BY THE MEMBER STATES UNDER DIRECTIVE 2004/48/EC
A	STRUCTURE: LEGAL BASIS – EC ARTICLE 95[9]

The Preamble to the Directive states:

> Having regard to the Treaty establishing the European Community and in particular, Article 95 thereof …

However, the appropriateness of this choice of EC Article 95[10] as the constitutional basis upon which to adopt the directive has been questioned:[11] that is, whether the disparities between the national procedural systems for enforcement of intellectual

---

8. In using their discretion to implement directives the Member States are therefore free to either maintain or introduce more stringent standards than those imposed by the directive provided that such comply with Community law and in particular the EC Treaty. See also S. Prechal, *Directives in EC Law*, 2nd edn (Oxford: OUP, 2005). ibid., 44.

9. M. Freudenthal, 'The Future of European Civil Procedure', *Electronic Journal of Comparative Law* 7.5 (2003), <www.ejcl.org/75/art75.6>; M. Dougan, *National Remedies before the Court of Justice* (Oxford: Hart Publishing, 2004), 14-15. Certainly, the fact that measures adopted pursuant to EC Art. 65 are not binding upon either the UK or Eire may be one of the reasons which precluded the use thereof as the basis for adoption of Directive 2004/48/EC.

10. EC Art. 95 'By way of derogation from Art. 94 and save where otherwise provided in this Treaty, the following provisions shall apply for the achievement of the objectives set out in Art. 14. The Council acting in accordance with the procedure referred to in Art. 251 and after consulting the Economic and Social Committee shall adopt measure for the approximation of the provisions laid down by law, regulation or administrative action in Member States which have as their object the establishment and functioning of the internal market.'

. EC Art. 65 provides: 'Measures in the field of judicial co-operation in civil matters having cross border implication to be taken in accordance with Art. 67 and in so far as necessary for the proper function of the internal market shall include: … (c) eliminating obstacles to the good functioning of civil proceedings if necessary by promoting the compatibility of the rules on civil procedure applicable in the Member States.' However, this article has been altered in the Treaty of Lisbon signed on 13 Dec. 2007 and to come into effect on 1 Jan. 2009 and now reads:

. 'Article 65 shall be replaced by the following: Chapter 3 Judicial Cooperation on Civil Matters and Article 65 (1) The Union shall develop judicial cooperation in civil matters having cross border implication based on the principal of mutual recognition of judgement and of decisions in extra judicial cases. Such co-operation may include the adoption of measure for the approximation of the law and regulations of the Member States. (2) For the purpose of paragraph 1, The European Parliament and Council, acting in accordance with the ordinary legislative procedure, shall adopt measures, particularly where necessary for the proper functioning of the internal market, aimed at ensuring …'

11. W. Cornish et al., 'Procedures and Remedies for Enforcing IPRS', EIPR (2003), 447 and A. Kur, 'Enforcement Directive – Rough Start, Happy Landing' *IIC* 35 (2004): 821, raise the question as to whether the necessary constitutional basis for the directive.

property rights '… are such as to obstruct the fundamental freedoms and thus have a direct effect on the functioning of the internal market'.[12] In reality, the matter turns on whether the conspicuous difference in some areas of national procedure can be said as a matter of fact to exercise a negative effect on the functioning of the internal market. However, in this regard, having observed in Recital 7 that '… despite TRIPS …' the Commission then goes on to declare in Recital 8:

> 'The disparities between the systems of the Member States as regards the means of enforcing intellectual property rights are prejudicial to the proper functioning of the Internal Market and make it impossible to ensure that intellectual property rights enjoy equivalent level of protection throughout the Community'. It may be that over all these recitals show 'clearly and unequivocally the reasons the reasons which lead the Community authority to adopt the … measure …'[13], that is, the directive[14]. If such were the case, then it would then seem that EC Article 95 would be sustainable as the legal basis for Directive 2004/48/EC.

---

12. *Commission v. Germany*, Case No. C-380/03 (2006) ECR I 11573 at para. 37.
13. *Commission v. Germany*, Case No. C-380/03 (2006) ECR I 11573, ibid., paras 107-109 and Opinion of AG LÈger at paras 175-188.
14. The meaning of the expression 'despite TRIPS' in Recital 7 is arguably not clear: in so far as the Commission may intend to signify that compliance with TRIPS by EU Member States as enforced by the ECJ has not been effective which therefore justifies intervention by the Commission EC Art. 95, this observation seems to have been contested in W. Cornish et al., 'Procedures and Remedies for Enforcing IPRS; the European Commission's Proposed Directive', *EIPR* (2003) 447, n. 2 therein, 'If it turns out that Member States do not comply with their obligations this could indeed justify Community legislation reinforcing the TRIPS Standards. If Member States do comply, however – as appears to be the case in the absence of any evidence to the contrary – any harmonization measures should be confined to those areas where the standards set out in the TRIPS agreement are considered insufficient by the Commission.' Therefore Cornish et al appear to feel that the Member States comply with Trade-Related Aspects of Intellectual Property Rights (TRIPS), i.e., 'as appears to be the case in absence of any evidence to the contrary …'. In reality however, the substantive obligations in Directive 2004/48/EC appear to 'reinforce the TRIPS standards'. Therefore the conclusion appears to be that the Commission feels that 'Member States do not comply with their obligations' without arguably identifying clearly the reason for this conclusion in the recitals given that the meaning of 'despite TRIPS' is unclear. A. Kur, 'The Enforcement Directive – Rough Start, Happy Landing'?, *IIC* 35 (2004): 821 at 825 appears to doubt that the differences in national procedure necessarily reflect legal 'deficiencies' which require Commission intervention. See also M. Dougan, *National Remedies before the Court of Justice: Issues of Harmonisation and Differentiation* (Oxford: Hart, 2004), 225 'The established "integration through law" approach to the enforcement deficit is based upon the view point which sees the Community as a singularly integrative project requiring a degree of uniformity which renders national remedies and procedural rules problematic and implies that harmonisation is the most important solution. The alternative "sectoral model" instead sees the Community as a more complex entity characterised by varying degrees of integration and differentiation across different policy fields. This means that the diversity of national remedies and procedures available in the process of decentralised enforcement should not be see as an automatic impediment to securing uniform application of Community law … It is instead proposed that the requirement of uniformity should be view in a purely relative light and this assessed at a sectoral level to determine the true nature of the Community's needs for substantive and thus remedial approximation subject to the minimum

B   OBJECTIVES: GENERAL LEGAL OBLIGATION

Directive 2004/48/EC may be said to establish, generally, a legal obligation on the part of the Member States to provide legal procedures which are to apply in the event of a breach of intellectual property rights.[15] The Directive applies in terms of scope apparently to all community and or national intellectual property rights including industrial property rights.[16] The Member States may extend the harmonization measures to acts which involve unfair competition. Further, the objective of the Directive is to provide for a degree of protection of intellectual property which is equivalent throughout the entirety of the Community by establishing a minimum degree of harmonization or minimal conditions for the protection of intellectual property. Accordingly, the Member States enjoy the discretion to establish higher standards of procedural protection.[17] Therefore, it is appropriate to consider each of the articles of the Directive in order to ascertain the precise nature and scope of the obligation which is incumbent upon the Member States pursuant to EC Article 249 (3). The presentation of the Directive will follow the structure as set forth in the text therein.

Chapter I: OBJECTIVE AND SCOPE

Article 1
Subject Matter

Article 1 of the Directive establishes its scope: the Directive concerns measure, procedure and remedies which are necessary in order to ensure the enforcement of intellectual property (IP) rights which include industrial property rights.

---

standards of Treaty control over the framework of decentralised enforcement demanded by the independent imperative of effectiveness.'

15. M. Veddern, 'The Enforcement Directive 2004/48/EC: A Further Step in the Harmonisation of IP law', IPR Help Desk Bulletin 16 (2006), Institute for Information, Telecommunication and Medial Law, Universität Münster, <www.ipr-helpdesk.org/newsletter/16/htm/ENIPRTDarticleN10AA2.htm> states: 'As regards the content, the Directive aims to transpose the provision of the TRIPS Agreement (Arts 41-50 and Art. 61) into European Law. The TRIPS (Agreement on Trade Related Aspects of Intellectual Property Rights) concluded in the context of the World Trade Organisation and approved by Council Decision 94/800/EC (OJ L 356 of 23 Dec. 1994) binds all the Member States and the Community itself.'

16. A. Kur, 'The Enforcement Directive – Rough Start, Happy Landing'?, *IIC* 35 (2004): 821 at 823, op. cit., referring to partial harmonization applying to all IP infringements: 'The latter approach reveals a dilemma which is also reflected in the present text: if it were obligatory to apply its provisions fully in each case, the directive would be highly disputable in may of its elements. However, if the national legislature and judiciary take full advantage of the built-in options for flexibility, the harmonisation effect may be severely reduced in practice.'

17. S. Prechal, *Directives in EC Law* (Oxford: OUP, 2005), op. cit., 44.

Article 2
Scope

Article 2 of the Directive establishes the scope in terms of its application in relation to the following matters:

> Article 2 (1): Minimal Harmonisation: the remedies measures and procedures
> provided for in the Directive shall apply to any infringement of intellectual
> property rights as provided either by Community and or national legislation
> of the Member States. However, such remedies procedures and measures as
> provided for by the Directive are 'without prejudice' to those provided or
> may be provided in either Community or national legislation 'in so far as
> those means may be more favourable to rights holders'. Accordingly, it is
> submitted that Article 2(1) of the Directive establishes a minimal degree of
> harmonisation[18] beyond which the Member States are free to exercise their
> discretion in order to provide for more 'favourable' protection for rights
> holders. The exercise of this discretion will however be subject to the doctrine
> of effectiveness and equivalence.[19]

However, within the parameters of IP rights in general which are not affected by
the limitations provided in subsections (2) and (3) below, according to Recital 18[20]
the Directive is designed to apply to all IP rights as covered by Community provision and or national law.[21]

Restrictions

Article 2 (2): the Directive shall 'be without prejudice' to Community legislation
on copyright and related rights notably as provided in Directive 91/250/EEC,
notably, Article 7 and Directive 2001/29/EC specifically Articles 2-6 and 8
thereof.

---

18. S. Prechal, *Directives in EC Law* (Oxford: OUP, 2005) , ibid., at p. 44.
19. The application of the doctrine of effectiveness and equivalence and the concept of national
    procedural autonomy arguably presupposes non-contravention of the substantive articles of the
    Treaty or notably European Convention on Human Rights (ECHR) Arts 6 and 13. See: Case
    432/05 Unibet London (2007) ECR I 2271 7 Mar. 2007, op.cit. <www.curia.europa.eu>,
    Opinion of AG Sharpston at para. 38; Case 453/00 Kühne Opinion of AG Léger, paras 70-72;
    also, M. Dougan, *National Remedies before the Court of Justice* (Oxford: OUP, 2004) op cit.,
    22-23 and 52-53, S. Prechal, *Directives in EC Law* (Oxford: OUP, 2005), ibid., 146 n. 105
    therein.
20. Recital 18 'It is necessary to define the scope of this Directive as widely as possible so as to
    encompass all the intellectual property rights covered by Community provisions in this field
    and/or national law of the Member State concerned.'
21. A. Kur, 'The Enforcement Directive – Rough Start, Happy Ending'?,*IIC* 35 (2004): 821 at 825,
    op. cit., observes 'Apart from the still open question of legislative competence the provision
    itself as well as the recitals fail to give an indication as to what exactly should be understood by
    "intellectual property". What about personality rights, geographical indications, trade secrets. '

Article 2 (3):

    a. the Directive shall 'not affect' Community law provisions which deal with substantive law on intellectual property such as Directive 95/46/ EC, Directive 1999/93/ EC or Directive 2000/31/EC and notably Articles 12-15 thereof;

    b. the international obligations of Member States and notably those arising from TRIPS including those relating to 'criminal procedures and penalties'

    c. any national criminal provisions which deal with infringement of intellectual property rights.

Furthermore, the Commission[22] states that at least the following (IP) rights are covered:

- copyright and rights related thereto;
- sui generic right of data base;
- rights of creators of topographies of a semi conductor;
- trademark rights;
- design rights;
- patent rights including rights derived from supplementary protection certificates;
- geographical indications;
- utility model rights;
- plant variety rights;
- trade names insofar as protected as exclusive property.

Chapter II: MEASURES, PROCEDURES AND REMEDIES

Section 1
General Provisions

Article 3
General Obligation

1. Scope of the general legal obligation: 'hard core rule':[23] Article 3 provides a general obligation on Member States to provide:

    (a) measures

---

22. State 2005/195/EC Statement by the Commission Concerning Art. 2 of Directive 2004/48/EC OJ L 94, 13 Apr. 2005, 37.
23. S. Prechal, *Directives in EC Law* (Oxford: OUP, 2005), op. cit., 41 'The "hard core" of a directive is its substantive rules spelling out the matters to which the directives relates, thus defining its scope and often indicating its purpose, thus setting the framework for implementation …. The hard core substantive rules of a directive may concern both substantive national law and procedures including those before national courts …. For purposes of implementation, it makes no difference whether the directive's provisions concern substantive law or whether they are provisions relating to procedures: Case C-131/88 *Commission v. Germany* (1991) ECR I 825, para. 61'.

    (b) procedures and
    (c) remedies

which are necessary in order to ensure the enforcement and protection of the intellectual property rights which are covered by the Directive. Following Prechal[24] this
may be termed a primary or 'hard core' or substantive obligation. However, the scope
of this 'hard core' obligation is arguably circumscribed in the following manner: that
is, the discretion of the Member States in terms of implementation of this general
obligation is restricted in that the measures, procedures and remedies adopted must
not contravene the following parameters established by Article 3 (1) of the directive:
namely that the measures and procedures utilized for implementation be:

- fair;
- equitable;
- not unnecessarily complicated;
- not unnecessarily costly;
- not entail unreasonable time limits;
- not entail unwarranted delays.

Further, Article 3 (2) requires that certain Community legal principles be respected
by the Member States in their implementation of their obligations thereunder:
namely, that the measures adopted must be:

    (i)   proportionate
    (ii) effective and
    (iii) dissuasive;
          and applied in a manner which:
    (iv) avoids creating barriers to trade
    (v) provides for safeguards against their abuse.

It is submitted that in reality, the aforementioned constitute obligations which apply
to the substantive procedural obligations which are set forth notably in the Directive
such as in Article 4 thereof. Furthermore, arguably, these procedural obligations in
Article 3 create rights notably when interpreted in relation to Article 4: that is the
purpose of the Directive and in particular, Articles 4 and 14 in conjunction with
Article 3 and Recital 18 is to ensure that rightsholders are able to enforce their substantive intellectual property rights in a manner which fulfils the obligations established in Article 3 notably with respect to cost and time effectiveness. However, the
actual form that these procedural rights may take will depend upon the national
implementation.[25] Insofar as Article 3 does create rights then the form of the implementing measures as noted earlier, must be not only clear so as to ensure that the
beneficiaries of the rights, that is the rights holders, are able to benefit from the
rights but also must conform with the principles of effectiveness and effective

---

24. S. Prechal, *Directives in EC Law* (Oxford: OUP, 2005), ibid., Ch. 3: On the content of
     Directives.
25. S. Prechal, *Directive in EC Law*, 2nd edn (Oxford: OUP, 2005), ibid., 128.

judicial protection of rights. In this regard, one notes that Article 3 (2) imposes through the words 'Those measures, procedures and remedies shall be applied in such a manner as to ... provide for safeguards against their abuse' a hard core obligation on the Member States to ensure the following: that the Member States must ensure, if necessary through adoption of special dispositions, that the implementation of the directive fulfils the obligations set forth in Article 3 (1) and (2).

Moreover, it is submitted that more generally, implementation of the Directive by the Member States may require consideration of the European Convention of Human Rights (ECHR) Article 6.1, in order to ensure effective judicial protection[26] of EC rights and in particular, following Recital 32 of the Directive,[27] of intellectual property rights.

It would seem that a clearer indication of the scope of the 'hard core' obligation may be obtained by considering certain of the recitals. Thus, Recitals 8 and 9 establish that the objective which the Directive seeks to achieve through Article 3 is the reduction of the disparity in the efficacy of national enforcement of Community and or national intellectual property rights in terms of national measures, procedures remedies. Furthermore, Recital 10 clarifies this objective by stating that the Directive is 'to approximate legal systems so as to ensure a high, equivalent and homogenous level of protection in the internal market'. It would appear that the terms 'equivalent' and 'homogenous' very much affect the scope of the hard core obligation as presented in Article 3. Finally, it would seem that Recital 10 coupled with EC law principles may require changes in the national procedure remedies and measures either in order to ensure effective enforcement of rights, even if the Directive is construed as not containing such directly effective rights, by means of the EC doctrine of consistent interpretation.[28] However,

---

26. S. Prechal, *Directives in EC Law* (Oxford: OUP, 2005), ibid., 145, and Case 50/00P Union de Pequenos Agricultores at point 38-42.
27. Recital 32: 'This Directive respects fundamental rights and observes the principles recognised in particular by the Charter of Fundamental Rights of the European Union. In particular, this Directive seeks to ensure full respect for intellectual property in accordance with Art. 17(2) of that Charter'.
28. S. Prechal, *Directives in EC Law* (Oxford: OUP, 2005), op. cit., Ch. 8 at 814: ' Scope of consistent interpretation: From the case law of the Court of Justice it appears that for the purposes of consistent interpretation it is immaterial whether the provisions which serve as standards for interpretation are directly effective or not. Yet although the precision and unconditionality required for direct effect is by no means necessary for the purposes of consistent interpretation, it should be noted that the terms of the directive must provide for a certain "minimum to hold on to" for the court concerned .... Likewise, the obligation applies irrespective of the legal relationship at issue in the main proceedings, i.e., whether there is a conflict between a private individual and the State or between two private individuals' and Ch. 9; *von Colson*, Case No. C-14/83 (1994) ECR 1891: Case 373/90 X para. 7, *Faccini Dori,* Case No. C-91/92 (1991) ECR I 3325: see consistent interpretation applied in relation to Trade-Related Aspects of Intellectual Property Rights (TRIPS) by the European Court of Justice (ECJ), *Hermes*, Case No. C-53/96 (1998) ECR I 3603, *Dior*, Case No. C-300/98 (2000) ECR I 11307, Schieving-Nijstad Case No. C-89/99 (2001) ECR I 5851 at para. 31-38; Case C-432/05 Unibet London (unreported) 13 Mar. 2007 , Opinion of AG Sharpston, 30 Nov. 2006, para. 40-42; and S. Prechal, 'Community Law in the Courts', *CMLR* 35 (1998): 681.

all of this is clearly linked to the creation of rights as set forth in Recital 18 and Articles 3 and 4 of the Directive, namely, creation of procedural rights for right-sholders in order to effectively defend their substantive intellectual property rights.

What might be termed 'ancillary obligations'[29] as opposed to the hard core or essential obligations will be considered in relation to Articles 18, 19 and 20 of the Directive.

Article 4
Scope of the General Legal Provision

(A) The hard core obligation of this article requires that legal standing be provided for four categories of claimants or legal persons such that they be able to apply for the measures, procedures and remedies covered by the directive. Effectively, Article 4 functions in the following manner:

(1) that Member States must provide legal standing: that is they must recognize as legal persons entitled to apply for the measures and remedies certain categories of persons: 'Member States shall recognize as persons entitled to seek application of the measures, procedures and remedies referred to in this chapter'.

(2) that the Member States must provide the aforementioned recognition to four groups of persons:

(B) These four categories of potential litigants are as follows:

1. 'the holders of intellectual property rights': 'in accordance with the provisions of the applicable law'
2. 'all other persons authorized to use those rights': 'in so far as permitted by and in accordance with the provisions of the applicable law'
3. intellectual property rights – management bodies 'which are regularly recognized as having the right to represent holders of intellectual property rights': 'in so far as permitted by and in accordance with the provisions of the applicable law'
4. professional defence bodies 'which are regularly recognized as having the right to represent holders of intellectual property rights': ' in so far as permitted by and in accordance with the provisions of the applicable law'

(C) Recital 18 further emphasizes the general nature of this obligation. However, the question remains as to the scope of the obligation on the Member States in Article 4 to establish representation for all of the four categories of persons even where the national rules do not provide all four categories. With respect to the so called 'hard core' obligation, it would seem that at least one possible interpretation

---

29.   S. Prechal, *Directives in EC Law* (Oxford: OUP, 2005), ibid., at p. 44..

thereof, bearing in mind that a definitive interpretation can only be rendered by the European Court of Justice (ECJ) is as follows: namely that the Member States are enjoined only to implement section (a) thereof, that is to ensure standing for rights holders and exclusive licensees of intellectual property rights. More specifically, Article 4 (b), (c) and (d) do not impose an obligation on Member States to ensure that standing be granted to categories other than rights holders or that some type of representative action exist or be introduced where such does not already exist in the national procedure. According to the provision in question, Member States shall recognize the persons authorized to use those rights as well as the representative bodies mentioned in (b), (c) and (d) as persons entitled to seek application of the relevant measures, procedures and remedies only 'insofar as permitted by and in accordance with the provisions of the applicable law'. Member States may therefore, continue to apply their own law. The result would be that these sections may serve to encourage those Member States whose national procedure does not provide for such standing to adapt their legislation in order to ensure court access to those categories of legal persons where this possibility does not yet exist.

(D) The other possible interpretation is that Article 4 is to be construed as enjoining the Member States to provide procedural legal standing, if necessary by creation, for all four categories of persons described including notably (c) and (d) therein for the following reasons: first, Article 3 of the Directive requires that the national implementation be effective;[30] second, it is submitted that the EC principle of effective legal protection[31] as developed in Johnston,[32] Heylens[33] may require that the holder of intellectual property rights be afforded effective legal protection[34] of his intellectual rights notably as provided by the directive in general[35] and in particular in Recital 32 thereof. Arguably, effective legal protection would require that

---

30. *Commission v. UK*, Case No. C-382/92 (1994) ECR I 2435. See, however, opposing view of Janal.
31. S. Prechal, *Directives in EC Law* (Oxford: OUP, 2005), op. cit., 143-144 observes that the principle of effective judicial protection is based on the rationale that in 'a Community based on the rule of law everyone must have the opportunity to assert his rights before the court and … the protection must be effective'. Furthermore, at page 144, ' the principle applies not only where a person relies directly on the provisions of a directive but also where the national law provisions implementing the directive are invoked'. See also Case No. C-432/05 Unibet London (unreported); Opinion of AG Sharpston at para. 38. '… the principle of effective legal protection reflects a general principle of law which underlines the constitution traditions common to the Member States. That principle, the right to a "fair trail" is embodied in Art. 6 (1) of the ECHR and is now recognised as a general principle of Community law by virtue of Art. 6 (2) EU.'
32. *Johnston v. Chief Constable of Ulster*, Case No. C-222/84 (1986) ECR 1651, op. cit.
33. *Unectf v. Heylens*, Case No. C-222/86 (1987) ECR 4097, op cit.
34. S. Prechal, *Directives in EC Law* (Oxford: OUP, 2005), op. cit., 142-145; M. Dougan, *National Remedies before the Court of Justice* (Oxford: Hart, 2004), Ch. 1; Case No. C-432/05 Unibet London (2007) ECR I 2271. paras 42-43 and 73 and Opinion of AG Sharptson at para. 38: Safalero Case No. C-13/01 (2003) ECR I 8679, paras 49-50 and Opinion of AG Stix-Hackl at paras 66-68.
35. Recitals 2, 3, and 32 which refers specifically to Art. 17 (2) of the Charter of Fundamental Rights of the European Union (2000/C, 364/01 OP 18 Dec. 2000): The right to intellectual

the holder of the intellectual property rights be able to enforce them either directly in personam or indirectly by means of the additional parties enumerated in Article 4 of the directive[36] which constitutes the hard core obligation of this article. Accordingly, following this interpretation of the scope of the obligations contained in Article 4 it would appear that failure to provide for representation of all four sections therein may constitute an infringement of the principle of effective judicial protection unless justifiable in terms of the European Court of Human Rights (ECtHR) case law[37] and also contravene EC Articles 249(3) and 10.[38] Therefore, following once again such an interpretation of Article 4(a)-(d) it would seem that failure to correctly implement Article 4, and notably (b), (c) and (d) could sound either in remedial action through consistent interpretation whether or not rights are created. or an action for State liability in so far as it seeks to create rights and the conditions for such liability are fulfilled which may not be obvious.

Article 5
Scope of the Provision

(1) Article 5 in conjunction with Recital 19 which refers to the Berne Convention[39] imposes an obligation on the Member States to introduce a presumption which is rebuttable as to the following matters:

---

property shall be protected; One notes also Art. 47 which guarantees a right to an effective remedy.

36. S. Prechal, *Directives in EC Law* (Oxford: OUP, 2005), op. cit., 143 'Moreover, it is similarly important to note in this context that the principle does not apply solely where a person relies directly on provisions of a directive, but also where the national law provisions implementing the directive are invoked and applied. In other words, even if a directive which, in contrast to Directive 27/207 – does note contain a provision relating to judicial protection, is as such correctly implemented in national law, the Member States must ensure that the rights under the national implementing measures can be asserted by judicial process by the individuals concerned. The absence of such a possibility will amount to inadequate implementation.'

37. Case No. C-432/05 Unibet (2007) ECR I 2271 <www.curia.europa.eu> Opinion of AG Sharpston at para. 38 who cites notably: *Golder v. UK* (1979-1980) 1 EHRR 524 at para. 36; *Klass v. Germany* (1994) 18 EHRR 305 at para. 49; *Ashingdane v. UK* (1985) 7 EHRR 528 at paras 55-57; *Lithgow v. UK* (1986) 8 EHRR 329.

38. Case No. C-382/92 *Petersen v. Council & Commission* (1994) ECR I 2435 paras 24-27.

39. Berne Convention for the Protection of Literary and Artistic Works (as amended 28 Sep. 1979): Art. 15 (1) ' In order that the author of a literary or artistic work protected by this Convention shall, in the absence of proof to the contrary, be regarded by such and consequently be entitled to institute infringement proceedings in the countries of the Union, it shall be sufficient for his name to appear on the work in the usual manner.' For legal presumptions, see A. Keane, *The Modern Law of Evidence*, 6th edn (Oxford: OUP, 2006), Ch. 22 and A. Zuckerman, *Civil Procedure* (London: LexisNexis, 2003) Ch. 21 notably at 655 'Presumptions represent techniques for distributing the risk of error by means of conditional allocation of the burden of persuasion or of the burden of adducing evidence. A presumption is a rule of law which provides that on proof of one fact (the "basic fact" by the proponent, the court is duty bound to find the existence of another fact (the "presumed fact") unless the opponent proves the contrary or as is sometimes the case, unless the opponent merely adduces evidence to the contrary'.

(a) authorship;

(b) ownership.

insofar as they relate to literary and artistic works as well as copyright and related rights.

Following Article 5 (a) the presumption which appears to be a legal in nature operates in the following manner with respect to authorship: 'for the author of a literary or artistic work … to be regarded as such … it shall be sufficient for his or her name to appear on the work in the usual manner. The party relying on this presumption bears the burden of establishing the basic facts, namely, that his or her name appears on the literary or artistic work in the usual manner'. However, Article 5 (a) indicates that this presumption is rebuttable; that is 'in absence of proof to the contrary'. Accordingly, once the purported author has produced sufficient evidence to prove this fact, his adversary then bears the legal burden of disproving the presumed fact. In the absence of rebuttal through such evidence, the presumed fact of authorship must be presumed. Article 5 (b) provides that this legal presumption and possibility of rebuttal provided for in section (a) with respect to literary or artistic works is to apply mutatis mutandis with respect to holders of rights related copyright and in particular 'with regard to their protected matter'.

The hard core obligation consists in the Member States ensuring that a legal presumption which concerns authorship and ownership of literary or artistic works and copyright which is rebuttable be introduced. However, it is submitted that the standards of proof required both to establish the initial presumption as well as its rebuttal as well as the rules governing the shifting of the burden of the rebuttal are to be determined by the national rules of procedure as a matter involving the implementation of the Directive.

Section 2
Evidence

Article 6
Evidence

1 Obtaining Evidence from Another Party: Scope of the Obligation

Article 6 of the directive imposes a hard core duty upon Member States to ensure the availability of evidence to litigants by the judicial officials in the following circumstances:

(a) on the application of a party;

(b) who has presented reasonably available evidence sufficient to support its claims;

(c) in substantiating those claims; and

(d) has specified evidence which lies in the control of the opposing party;

the competent judicial authorities may order that the opposing party present such evidence

(e) subject to the protection of confidential information.

The request for evidence may involve confidential information which is held by the opposing party in which case any order made must ensure protection of such information by the receiving party.

The obligation extends only to a situation in which a party makes such a request and therefore apparently does not require the possibility of a judicial authority to make such an order on his own motion without a request of one of the parties. Furthermore, the obligation provides only for post action commencement where the pleadings have been produced: that is, where the 'party has presented reasonably available evidence sufficient to support its claims ...'. Furthermore, it would seem that the obligation contained in Article 6 does not extend to ensuring the communication of information for what might be termed speculative requests or so-called 'fishing expeditions': that is the obligation applies only where the applying party requests information which is apparently known to exist in the control of the opposing party as opposed to information which may exist 'and has in substantiating those claims has specified evidence which lies in the control of the other party'. No specific definition is given of 'reasonably available evidence' and no mention is made of the purpose or the use which may be made of the evidence is sought from the opposing party. No specific mention is made of penalties for non-compliance by the party receiving the order by the judicial authority. Furthermore, no clarification is provided as to the eventual difference between information in the phrase 'confidential information' as opposed to 'evidence'. However 'reasonable evidence' which would seem to be different from 'reasonably available evidence' is defined as: 'For the purposes of this paragraph, Member States may provide that a reasonable sample of a substantial number of copies of copies of a work or other protected object be considered by the competent judicial authorities to constitute "reasonable evidence".'

2   Commercial Documents

Bank financial or commercial documents: here the obligation extends, mutatis mutandis with the conditions governing obtaining evidence from an opposing party, only to ensuring that a national court be able to order the communication of bank, financial or commercial documents subject to protection of commercial information in the following situation: namely, in the case of an 'infringement committed on commercial scale'. It would seem that in so far as the obligation for commercial documents exists separately from the obligation to provide evidence, the terms evidence and documents are not synonymous. Therefore at a minimum it would appear that the term evidence may refer to what might be used judicially to prove an infringement of intellectual property rights but which is not composed, necessarily, of documents. By reason of Recital 14 which defines commercial acts to be those, namely, for direct or indirect economic or commercial advantage which usually excludes end users acting in good faith. However, Member States may extend the system of disclosure of commercial documents to non-commercial documents by reason of Article 2 of the Directive.

Article 7
Measures for Preserving Evidence

Scope of the Hard Core Obligation
Article 7 (1): The general obligation falls upon Member States to ensure that judicial authorities are able to preservation of evidence by means of provisional measures in the following conditions:

Conditions

1. Time: it would seem that both pre and post action commencement applications are possible:

> Member States shall ensure that, even before the commencement of proceedings on the merits … .

2. Beneficiary: a party 'on the application of a party …' which is to be read in conjunction with Article 4.

3. Modus operandi: the obligation is to ensure that the national authorities are able to provide the necessary order to preserve the evidence in the following circumstances, namely:

   (a) on the application of a party;
   (b) who has presented reasonably available evidence to support his/her claims;
   (c) that his/her intellectual property rights have been infringed or are about to be infringed;
   (d) subject to protection of confidential information.

No explanation is given in the recitals as to why a difference exists between Article 6 'to support its claims' and Article 7 'to support his/her claims'. Moreover, as in respect of Article 6, there is no indication as to any probative level which the applicant is to achieve in order to obtain the order sought. It is clear that the 'reasonably available evidence' refers to the claim for infringement as opposed to the evidentiary standard to be achieved in the application for preservation of the evidence which is relevant to the infringement claim: that is, there is no indication of the probative value which the applicant is to achieve in order to convince the judge to grant an order to preserve the evidence relevant to the infringement claim.

4. Form of the measure: the court must be able to order a 'measure' which is:

   (a) prompt

(b) effective

(c) provisional.[40]

The scope of this measure is not defined but it may include:

(i)   a detailed description of the infringing goods with or without the following measures;

(ii)   taking samples of the infringing goods;

(iii) seizure of the infringing goods;

(iv) seizure of implements and materials used in the production and or distribution of the infringing goods; and the

(v)   seizure of documents relating thereto.

5. Purpose: no specific purpose is indicated beyond the description 'Article 7, Measures for preserving evidence'. However the obligation specifies directly: … the judicial authorities may … order prompt and effective provisions measures to preserve relevant evidence … .

6. Legal conditions

a. 'the measures may be granted' where

– 'any delay is likely to cause irreparable harm to the right holder'

– or 'where there is a demonstrable risk of evidence being destroyed'.

It is to be noted that these two conditions are singular: either one or the other is required which thereby increases, arguably, the availability of the eventual measure. On the other hand, demonstrable risk refers only to evidence being destroyed as opposed to likely to being destroyed in contrast to the property right which has been infringed or is about to be infringed.

b. Opposing party: ex parte application:

i.   the measures may be taken without the opposing party being heard

---

40. With respect to English procedure, A.A.S. Zuckerman, *Civil Procedure* (London: Sweet & Maxwell, 2003), op. cit., 265; 'It is immediately apparent that this list consists broadly speaking of two different types of interim orders which have little in common apart from the fact that they are not meant to finally determine the issues in dispute. The second type consists of measures designed to facilitate access to information or regulate the litigation process in some way. These are very different measures. There is a profound difference between an order restraining a defendant from pulling down a building to which both he and the claimant assert a right of ownership and an order directing disclosure of documents or directing a person to allow inspection of property. The former involves pre-judgment interference with substantive rights albeit on a temporary basis. Since an interim order restraining conduct may affect the very rights in dispute the court must take great care to ensure that its interim decision does not harm the very rights that it may itself endorse after trial. However, where the order is only concerned with the procedure to be followed as where the court has to decide whether to order pre-trial disclosure or inspection, it has no effect on the disputed rights or their exercises thought it may assist one or other o the parties to establish his rights. Indeed, since such order are not temporary in nature, it is hardly justified to describe them as interim. An order requiring a defendant to allow inspection of property or to disclose certain documents requires a one-off act of compliance leaving no further decision to be make on the point in final judgment.'

ii. notice must be given to the absent party at latest immediately subsequent to the execution of the measures

c. Rights of the Defence: application for discharge:
A review of the measures may be carried out upon request of the affected parties within a reasonable period of time subsequent to the notification of the measures: at that time, the review will decide whether the measures are to be modified, revoked or confirmed.

d. Type of evidence to be used in support of the application: it would appear that all evidence which is relevant to the matter of actual or potential infringement although the term relevant is not utilised. This may include confidential information which apparently may be used as evidence although the distinction between evidence and information is not provided on the condition that the confidentiality is protected. Type of evidence to which the order is directed: the order is 'relevant evidence in respect of an alleged in infringement'.

e. Procedural characteristics of the order: the obligation is on the judicial authorities to provide an order which is prompt and effective:

f. Nature of the order: the nature of the order is a provisional measure. Accordingly, the relationship between a 'provisional measure' in Article 7 and an 'interlocutory injunction' in Article 9 is not clear particularly in terms of scope.

g. Cause of action and standard of proof:
i. Article 7 (1) states ' ... to support his ... claim that his ... intellectual property right has been infringed or is about to be infringed ...'. Accordingly, it is would appear that a substantive cause of action concerning an actual or potential breach of a intellectual property right must exist. However, Article 7 does not indicate the standard of proof which must be achieved with respect to this cause of action in contradistinction to Article 9 (3) which appears to establish an evidential threshold to be achieved for an interlocutory injunction. Further, there is no indication that the applicant for the measure must lead evidence in order to establish the probability of the destruction of the relevant evidence. This is perhaps unfortunate given that subsection (4) requires compensation in the event that it is found that there was either no risk of infringement or no infringement of the intellectual property rights.

Article 7 (2) enjoins the Member States to ensure that the national courts are able to:
i. if necessary make the order for preservation of evidence subject to the 'lodging by the applicant' of either adequate security or equivalent assurance the purpose of which is

ii. to ensure compensation 'for any prejudice suffered by the defendant as provided for in paragraph 4' of Article 7. There is no distinction made between 'prejudice suffered by the defendant' directly as opposed to indirectly. However paragraph 4 thereof provides 'to provide the defendant with appropriate compensation for any injury caused by those measures'.

Article 7 (3) Rights of the Defence: this subsection provides that a defendant may apply exercise his right to apply to have the provision measures set aside either after the elapse of the period established by the court for commencement of proceedings or in default of such a date after the periods provided in subsection (3). However, it is for reasons of legal certainty the responsibility of the defendant to exercise this right.[41]

h. Rights of the Defence: an obligation enjoins Member States to provide that the judicial authorities are able to order an 'applicant' to provide the defendant with appropriate compensation for any injury caused by measures ordered by the court in the following circumstances:

i.   at the request of the defendant to the court
ii.   that the applicant / claimant provide him appropriate compensation
iii. for any injuries caused in the situations detailed below:
     – where the measures are set aside or revoked
     – where these measures lapse due to any act or omission on the part of the applicant
     – where it is found that there was either no risk of infringement or simply no infringement 7 (5) this subsection 'Member States may take measures to protect witnesses' identity' does not constitute an obligation in so far as the very 'may' is used as opposed to 'shall'.

Section 3
Right of Information

Article 8
Right of Information

Article 8.1: The hard core obligation consists in ensuring that the national judicial authorities have the discretion to make an order for what might be termed interrogatories 'in the context of proceedings concerning an infringement of intellectual property' in favour of the 'claimant'.

1. Time: it would seem that on a strict interpretation of 'in the context of proceedings' signifies post-commencement of the action even more so that the term 'claimant' is used as opposed to right holder. Therefore it is submitted that the Member States enjoy the discretion to extend this protection to interlocutory proceedings where the substantive action has not yet been commenced.

2. Beneficiary: the claimant in an intellectual property enforcement action.

---

41. Particularly in light of such cases such as *Hermes*, Case No. C-53/96 (1998) ECR I 3603, *Dior*, Case No. C-300/98 (2000) ECR I 11307, and *Schieving-Nijstad*, Case No. C-89/99 (2000) ECR I 5851.

3. Legal conditions: the request for the information must be justified and be proportionate.

No definition of justified is given. It is not clear whether the term 'justified' refers to a standard of proof which is to be achieved or whether it is to be understood in the sense of appropriate or suitable in the circumstances coupled with proportionate as related to Recital 17. Accordingly, it is not obvious whether the claimant must indicate in the drafting of his document that the request in justified in relation to a particular person because that person is believed to possess the information as opposed to may possibly possess the information. This is perhaps of significance particularly in relation to possible third party sources of information.

4. Type of information: the information deals with two categories: the origin and distribution networks of goods and or services which infringe intellectual property rights.

5. Interrogated party: The category of person against whom the order may be made consists of two categories:

(a) the infringer
(b) third party.

However, the category of the third party may consist minimally of the following persons:

(i) a person who was found to be in possession of infringing goods on a commercial scale;
(ii) a person who was found to be using the infringing services on a commercial scale;
(iii) a person who was found to be providing services on a commercial scale which were used in the infringing services;
(iv) a person identified by one of the three previous categories of persons as being a second category of third party is identified when the initial third party previously designated provides the identity of another third party who is 'involved in the production, manufacture or distribution of services or the provision of services'.

In this regard, it is not clear whether the term 'justified request' may deal with requirements imposed by the national court on the applicant concerning the probative value which the evidence lead by the applicant must achieve notably with respect to a second third party who is identified by a first third party and who is alleged to be involved in the infringement of the intellectual property rights.

Article 8.2: Scope of the information to be provided:
There are two categories of information which may be required:
Category 1: (identity of infringers) names and address of producers: manufacturers, distributors or suppliers and other previous holders of goods and services as well as intended whole sale distributors: it is not clear whether the qualification of commercial scale is also applicable.

Category 2: (quantity of infringement) information dealing with the quantity produced, manufactured delivered received or ordered, and the price obtained for the goods etc.

It would seem to be the case that the information requested here is not available or has not been obtained in normal disclosure proceedings. However, it is not clear why the obligation is restricted to post-commencement proceedings and notably why it could not be combined with a pre action use of measures which seek to prevent destruction of evidence relevant to intellectual property proceedings.

Article 8 (3): Extent of harmonization in relation to the defence rights and alternative procedures.

This section provides that the previous two subsections 'shall apply without prejudice to other statutory provisions which':

(a) grant right holders fuller information;
(b) govern the use in civil or criminal proceedings of the information provided under this article;
(c) govern the responsibility for misuse of the information;
(d) which provide for a person to refuse information which might involved admission of either his own involvement or that of a close relative in an infringement of an intellectual property right;
(e) govern the protection of confidentiality of information or the processing of personal data.

In short, the effect of Article 8(3)(a) is to establish that the obligation provided in subsections (a) and (b) are of a minimal nature. They do not preclude the Member States from adopting more favourable measures. Subsection 3 moreover allows Member States to maintain or introduce provisions which safeguard the principle of proportionality by restricting the use of the information given and by upholding the principle of *nemo tenetur se ipsum accusare*. Furthermore, following Article 8(3)(e), other statutory provisions which govern the protection of confidentiality of information or the processing of personal data remain unaffected. This subsection is of particular interest if the claimant requests that an intermediary, i.e., an internet service provider, reveal personal data of the alleged infringer or identify the alleged infringer with the help of communication traffic data. In view of Directive 2002/58/EC[42] and Directive 95/46/EC,[43] particularly Article 13(1)(g) thereof, the ECJ expounded in the decision *Promusicae* that Article 8 of Directive 2004/48/EC does not require the Member States to introduce an obligation to communicate personal data.[44] However, the Court pointed out, Community law

---

42. Directive 2002/58/EC of the European Parliament and of the Council of 12 Jul. 2002 concerning the processing of personal data and the protection of privacy in the electronic communications sector, OJ No. L 201, 31 Jul. 2002, pp. 37 et seq.
43. Directive 95/46/EC of the European Parliament and of the Council of 24 Oct. 1995 on the protection of individuals with regard to the processing of personal data and on the free movement of such data, OJ No. L 281, 23 Nov. 1995, pp. 31 et seq.
44. *Promusicae v. Telefónica de Espana*, Case No. C-275/06, 29 Jan. 2008, <curia.eu.int> at 58.

requires that, when transposing these directives, the Member States must take care to rely on an interpretation of them which allows a fair balance to be struck between the various fundamental rights protected by the Community legal order. Furthermore, when implementing the measures transposing those directives, the authorities and courts of the Member States must not only interpret their national law in a manner consistent with those directives but also make sure that they do not rely on an interpretation of them which would be in conflict with those fundamental rights or with the other general principles of Community law, such as the principle of proportionality.[45]

Section 4
Provisional and Precautionary Measures

Article 9
Provisional and Precautionary Measures

The obligation enjoins Member States to ensure that the national court may on the request of the applicant grant an interlocutory injunction against two categories of persons in order to prevent either an imminent alleged infringement or the continuation of an alleged infringement of an intellectual property right other than a copyright or related right which is covered by Directive 2001/29/EC.

Article 9 (1)
Scope of the Obligations

Article 9 (1) (a)

(1) Beneficiary: The beneficiary of this remedy is the right holder although the application for the injunction is initiated by the 'applicant'.

(2) Addressee: The scope of the addressee of the interlocutory injunction consists of the following two categories of persons: first, the alleged infringer of an intellectual property right and second, an intermediary who services are being used by a third party to infringe an intellectual property right. Article 9 (1) states with respect to the first category 'alleged infringer' whereas with the second category of infringer the term 'alleged' is absent: 'injunctions against intermediaries whose services are used by third parties to infringe an intellectual property right'.

(3) Mutatis mutandis: intermediary: 'The Directive states that the injunction against the intermediary whose services are used by third parties to infringe an intellectual property right' 'may also be issued, under the same conditions', against an intermediary as against a direct alleged infringer. No definition is provided within the directive of 'intermediary' or 'third party'. It is submitted that Article 8 (1) (b) in

---

45. Ibid., at 68. The fundamental rights referred to by the ECJ are (a) the right to property, (b) the right to an effective remedy and (c) the protection of personal data and of private life.

so far as it applies 'to any person' who is 'found to be using the infringing services on a commercial scale' could be used in relation to facilitating the bringing of an interlocutory injunction against an intermediary pursuant to Article 9.

(4) Purpose of the injunctions:[46] the Member States must ensure that the national court is able to make the following orders: issue an interlocutory injunction which can achieve the following objectives:

(a) a prohibitory interlocutory injunction to prevent an imminent infringement;
(b) a prohibitory interlocutory injunction to forbid the continuation of the alleged infringement of the intellectual property right subject;
    the prohibition is to be on a provisional basis and second, it may be subject to, where appropriate, the imposition of a 'recurrent penalty payment where this is provided for by national law':
(c) as an alternative to an interlocutory prohibitory injunction the national court must be able to permit the continuation ('or to make such continuation') of the alleged infringement but subject to the lodging of guarantees intended to ensure the compensation of the right holder;
(d) these conditions apply mutatis mutandis to intermediaries;
(e) copy right and related rights are covered by Directive 2001/29/ EC.

(5) Article 9 (1) (b): The Member States must ensure that the national judicial authorities be able to:

order the seizure or delivery up of goods which are suspected of infringing intellectual property rights
    Objective: in order to prevent the goods from either entering or moving within channels of commerce.

The types of material which may be seized are goods which are suspected infringing intellectual property rights.

(6) Article 9 (2) Member States must ensure that national judicial authorities are able to order precautionary seizure of property in the following conditions:

Condition: the national authorities must be able to make such orders
a. where the injured party demonstrates circumstances which are likely to endanger the recovery of damages.
b. the 'infringement is committed on a commercial basis'
Scope:
c. moveable property of the alleged infringer
d. immovable property of the alleged infringer

---

46. See, *Tedesco*, Case No. C-175/06 (struck out on 18 Jul. 2007) Opinion of AG Kokott, 29 Jul. 2007, paras 51 and 52 who opines that Directive 2004/48/EC should be used to interpret Regulation 1206/2001 on the collection on cooperation in the collection of evidence in civil and commercial cases.

and in particular:

e. blocking of the infringer's accounts and other assets;
f. communication of bank, financial and commercial documents or appropriate access to the relevant information. It is to be noted that the Directive states the 'competent authorities' may order the communication of such information.

(7) Article 9 (3) Legal conditions which the application must fulfil.
As noted earlier, the measure provided by Article 9 differs from that of Article 6 in that the national judicial authorities shall have the authority to request that the applicant provide them with reasonably available evidence:

Probative value: it would seem that the probative value of the evidence is significant in that it must satisfy the authorities with a sufficient degree of certainty of one of two matters:

First, that the applicant is the right holder
Second, that the applicant's right is being infringed or that such infringement is imminent. Arguably this requirement deals with the merits of the applicant's substantive cause of action.

(8) Article 9 (4) Ex parte applications
This subsection enjoins Member States to ensure that the measures provided in sections 1 (a) and (b) and 2 may be applied for on an ex parte basis, that is in the absence of the defendant, particularly in the case where delay may cause irreparable harm to the right holder. No indication is made of an obligation to provide evidence of the nature or the likelihood of the irreparable harm in the event that the application is made for this reason.

(a) Article 9 (4) review of ex parte measures: the Member States are enjoined to ensure that a review including a right to be heard may take place at the request of the defendant a reasonable time after notification of the order to the defendant. The purpose of the review would be for the judicial authorities to decide whether the measures should be modified, revoked or confirmed.

(9) Article 9 (5) Review of measures: setting aside:

(a) Scope of the obligation: the Member States are enjoined to ensure that the measures granted pursuant to Article 9 (1) and (2) may be set aside at the request of the defendant in the following conditions:
   (i) where the applicant has not commenced proceedings leading to a decision on the merits within a reasonable period of time: this period is to be reasonable:
(b) Calculation of time:
   (i) where the law of the Member State so permits, the national court is to establish the period of time after which the defendant may apply to set aside the injunction;
   or, in the absence of such judicial determination

(ii) the period is not to exceed either twenty working days or thirty-one calendar days whichever is longer upon the expiration of which the defendant may ask for the review after which the defendant may apply to set aside the injunction. It is submitted that as in the case of Article 7 (3), the review under Article 9 (3) must be activated by the defendant.

There is no indication as to why the time period for the protection of the defendant's rights is assured by a specified method for calculation of time with respect to the inter partes application for an injunction as opposed to the more general method of reasonable time which applies to ex parte applications.

(10) Article 9 (6) Scope of the obligation:
Subsection (6) provides: ' the competent judicial authorities may make the provisional measures referred to in paragraph (1) and (2) ...' would seem to establish an obligation on the part of Member States to ensure that national courts possess the procedural capacity to order, according to their discretion, measures to ensure that the claimant compensate the defendant for loss incurred as a result of an injunction granted and as provided by Article 9 (7):

(11) Article 9 (7): Scope of the obligation:
The Member States are to ensure that the competent judicial authorities have the authority to ensure that upon his request, a defendant receive 'appropriate' compensation for loss caused by measures granted under Article 9 (1) and (2) in four situations:

(a) where the measures are revoked; or
(b) where the measures lapse due to any act or omission by the defendant; or
(c) where it is subsequently found that there is no infringement; or
(d) where it is subsequently found that there is no threat of infringement.

It is clear that subsections 9 (4)-(6) provide for protection of the rights of the defendant concerning the manner in which injunction is granted by the court. However, there is no specific provision which protects such rights in the context of the enforcement of injunction granted by a court under 9 (1) (b) or (2) which involve seizure of property. Accordingly, it would seem that such protection falls within the domain of the Member States discretionary power.[47]

---

47. Arguably, the discretion of the Member States in this regard is subject on the one hand to the doctrine of effectiveness, equivalence and effective judicial protection as well as various articles dealing with substantive rights in the EC Treaty. S. Prechal, *Directives in EC Law*, 2nd edn (Oxford: OUP, 2005), op. cit., 146 fn. 105 therein: 'For the sake of clarity, it must be point out that Community law may also interfere with national procedural law through other mechanisms than the requirement of equivalence and effectiveness or effective judicial protection. In a number of cases, either the Treaty freedoms or the general prohibition of discrimination laid down in Art. 12 had implications for national procedural rules. Case C-336/94 Dafeki, op. cit., In other case, it is mainly on the basis of an interpretation of a particular directive that the Court

Section 5
Measures Resulting from a Decision on the Merits

Article 10
Corrective Measures

(1) Article 10 (1) enjoins Member States to ensure that their judicial authorities are able to provide, post-judgment, corrective measures at the request of the applicant 'appropriate measures' be taken with respect to:

 (a) goods which are found to have been infringing;
 (b) in appropriate cases, materials and implements principally used in the creation and manufacture of such goods.

The corrective measures which may be taken pursuant to this article include the following:

 (c) the measures may provide for destruction of such goods;
 (d) the recall of such goods from channels of commerce;
 (e) removal of such goods from channels of commerce.

Conditions:

 (f) the corrective measures are separate from any damages to the right holder;
 (g) without compensation of any sort.

First, this section is interpreted as meaning a claimant in legal proceedings for the following reason: it would seem that the measures are to be provided post-judgment insofar as they concern only goods which the judicial authorities have found to infringe intellectual property rights ('… that they have been found to be infringing an intellectual property right'). It is true, however, that there is no mention of legal proceedings or the 'judicial finding of infringement' being incorporated in a formal judgment. Furthermore, unlike with the orders in the preceding articles, no specific method of application for the corrective is provided and there is notably no mention of the type of evidence which may be required in order to convince the court to grant such measures taking into consideration the circumstances of the case. Notably, there is no mention as to whether the proceedings may be both inter partes or simply ex parte.

 Furthermore, in exercising its discretion, the national court must consider the principles of proportionality as well as the interests of third parties. Although the corrective measures are said to be 'without prejudice to damages to the right holder by reason of infringement …' which would seem to signify that the eventual availability of such corrective measures in a particular is not to decrease any amount of damages which might be awarded. On the other hand, it is not clear

---

reaches a result with considerable implications for national procedural law. Case C-240/98 and C-244/98 Océano, op. cit.'

that the proposition is mutatis mutandis; namely, the availability of damages might serve to diminish the need for special measures. Indeed, the obligation does not require that the applicant indicate the need or the reason for such measures.

(2) Article 10 (2) enjoins the judicial authorities to ensure that the costs effectively follow the event; that is the party against whom the order is made is to bear the costs unless there are 'particular reasons invoked' to depart from that rule. It is not clear as to whether the reasons must also be cogent or whether it suffices that they simply be 'invoked'.

(3) Article 10 (3) enjoins the judicial authorities to subject the exercise of their discretion in order the corrective measures pursuant to this article to the principle of proportionality in a specific sense: namely, balancing the gravity of the manner in which the infringement in relation to interests of third parties.[48]

Article 11
Injunctions

1. Hard core obligation: The hard core obligation consists in enjoining the Member States to ensure that the judicial authorities of the Member States are able to grant permanent injunctions.[49]

2. Scope:

    (a) Post-judgment 'where a judicial decision is taken finding an infringement against property rights'. This is taken to signify that the a finding of infringement of the intellectual property rights based upon a substantive cause of action has been entered by the national court.

---

48.   A. Kur, 'The Enforcement Directive – Rough Start, Happy Landing'?, *IIC* 35 (2004): 821 at 826, op. cit., a argues that measures such as destruction of goods and removal from the channels of commerce while appropriate for counterfeit goods released on the market are disproportionate for ordinary trade mark or patent infringement. Accordingly, it would have been appropriate to limit these remedies expressly to piracy and counterfeiting. This argument however is predicated upon insufficiency of legal control of national implementation of the directive notably on the basis of an eventual violation of Art. 10 (3) of the directive itself. It is useful to recall that the implementation by the national court in this regard would also be subject to the principle of proportionality as expressed in Art. 3 of the Directive. The question therefore is whether the level of harmonisation in light of the legal control of national implementation of Art. 10 in terms of community law is sufficiently high. It would seem that this matter could be more appropriately dealt with in terms of the pragmatic review which is provided for by Art. 18 of the Directive.

49.   Directive 2001/29/EC of the European Parliament and Council of 22 May 2000 on the harmonisation of certain aspects of copyright and related rights in the information society:

    Article 8 (3): Member States shall ensure that right holders are in a position to apply for an injunction against intermediaries whose services are used by a third party to infringe a copyright or related right.

    (b) Permanent as opposed to interlocutory injunction: 'the judicial authorities may issue against the infringer an injunction …' which contrasts with the aforementioned Article 9 of the Directive which provides for an 'interlocutory injunction'.

    (c) Purpose: ' … aimed at prohibiting the continuation of the infringement.'

3. Defendants: one notes the following:

    (a) Infringers: the instant article provides as noted, that 'where a judicial decision is taken finding an infringement of intellectual property, the judicial authorities may issue against an infringer an injunction'. Accordingly, this would seem to indicate that a substantive cause of action concerning breach of intellectual property rights must exist with regard to the infringer.

    (b) Intermediaries: the Member States are enjoined to ensure that 'right holders are in a position to apply for an injunction against intermediaries whose services are used by a third party to infringe an intellectual property right without prejudice to Article 8 (3) Directive 2001/29 EC'. Article 11 does not however use the term 'under the same conditions' which appear in Article 9 of the Directive which require that an interlocutory injunction is to be granted under the same conditions with respect to an intermediary as in relation to an infringer. However, it is submitted that the absence of the 'under the same conditions' is not in itself of significance for the following reason: first, the 'same conditions' in Article 9 refers first, to the conditions enumerated within the article itself as opposed to the national procedural requirements; second, the Directive requires that the national implementation of Article 11 particularly in relation to a permanent injunction against intermediaries, following Article 3 be effective: this is particularly case, as a noted earlier with national implementation of Article 4 in the sense of ensuring effective judicial protection of intellectual property rights. It is submitted that this requirement of effective judicial protection of a right holder's intellectual property rights applies both to interlocutory and permanent injunctions against an intermediary just as it would with respect to an infringer.

    (c) Non-compliance: Member States are enjoined to ensure that non-compliance with the injunction shall be subject to a recurring penalty payment in order to ensure compliance with the following qualifications:

        (i) where the sanction of a recurring penalty is provided for by national law;

        (ii) 'where appropriate'.

Accordingly, it is submitted that this obligation to ensure the use of a recurring penalty as a sanction for non-compliance constitutes an minimal obligation in that its application is specifically subject to the principle of proportionality: that is 'where appropriate'. In certain circumstances, therefore, its use may by definition be in appropriate.

Article 12
Alternative Measures

(1) Article 12 enjoins the Member States to ensure that the judicial authorities are able to provide alternative measures which are more proportionate in the circumstances of the case than injunctions.

(2) Legal conditions:

  (a) infringement judgement has been entered;
  (b) court may either at the initiative on its own court or on that of a person liable to be subject to one injunctive relief.

(3) Beneficiaries: defendant, or Third Party who is not a defendant or an intermediary who is not a defendant as provided for in Article 11.

(4) Grounds: pecuniary compensation may requested and or ordered in place of damage in the following conditions:

  (a) if the person liable to be subject to the measures acted unintentionally and without negligence;
  (b) if the enforcement of the injunctive relief would cause him disproportionate harm; and
  (c) if pecuniary compensation to the injured party appears reasonable satisfactory.

It would seem that these three conditions are cumulative.

Section 6
Damages and Legal Costs

Article 13
Damages

(1) Article 13 establishes an obligation on the part of the Member States to ensure that the competent judicial authorities be able to calculate the compensation of loss in two different methods according to whether or not the breach of the intellectual property right was intentional or not.

(2) Intentional breach of intellectual property rights.
Article 13 (1) establishes two different methods of compensation for breaches of intellectual property rights which may be termed intentional: that is, 'knowingly or with reasonable grounds to know'.

(3) Legal conditions: the injured party must make an application.

(4) Amount of Damages: the damages appropriate to the actual prejudice suffered by the rights holder as a result of the infringement.

(5) Intentional Breach:

  (a) First method of calculation of the damages: consideration of all the relevant factors such as the negative economic consequences such as lost profits suffered by the rights holder or unfair profits made by the infringer as a result of the infringement, non-economic factors such as the moral prejudice suffered by the rights holder as a result of the infringement.

(b) In the alternate, the second method of calculation would consist in establishing compensation as a lump sum which would represent elements such as the fees or royalties which would have been due if proper authorisation for the use of the intellectual property rights had been granted.

(6) Unintentional Breach:
The obligation requires that the Member States ensure that the judicial authorities are able to provide compensation for an unintentional breach the breach[50] where the damages would consist of the following: namely recovery of profits or the payment of damages both of which, apparently, may be pre-determined.

Article 14
Legal Costs

(1) The obligation on the Member States requires that the national courts be able to ensure that as a general rule the unsuccessful party, subject to equity, bear the legal costs and other expenses of the successful party: however these costs must be reasonable and proportionate. This rule would appear to be restricted to the in court costs of the winning party and therefore does not apply to the out of court costs incurred thereby. It would appear however, that the aforementioned Article 3, insofar as it requires that '… the measures, procedures and remedies shall not be unnecessarily costly' may apply to both in court and out of court: that is an obligation exists on the Member States to ensure that the measures, procedures and remedies used to enforce the intellectual property rights under the directive both in terms of in court legal services and out of court legal services must not be unnecessarily costly. Furthermore, pursuant to Article 3 (2) the costs must be proportionate which requirement is re-emphasized by Article 14 with respect to in court legal cost which are subject to the operation of the indemnity rule.

Section 7
Publicity Measures

Article 15
Publication of Judicial Decisions

(1) This article imposes an obligation on Member States to ensure that the judicial authorities are able to publicize the infringement decision in the following conditions:

First, the request emanates from the successful party who is the rights holder.
Second, that the costs be paid the unsuccessful party who is the infringer.

---

50. 'Where the infringer did not knowingly or with reasonable grounds know, engage … .' French version of the regulation is clearer than the English on this point: 'Lorsque le contrevenant s'est livré à une activité contrefaisante sans le savoir ou sans avoir de motifs raisonnables de le savoir …' i.e., without knowing or without having reasonable grounds to know.

The specific obligation is to ensure that the national authorities be able to take appropriate measures for the dissemination of the information concerning the decision; these measures may include:

(a) displaying the decision;
(b) publishing the decision in part or in full;
(c) other appropriate publicity measures such as prominent advertising: it may be that publication of the decision in a newspaper would fall within this category.

Chapter III: SANCTIONS BY MEMBER STATES

Article 16
Sanctions by Member States

1. Article 16: does not establish an obligation but rather simply ensures that Member States may introduce other appropriate sanctions for the infringement of intellectual property rights in addition to those provided in the directive confirming thereby the minimal harmonization of remedies. However, the exercise of the discretion of the national courts in this regard would apparently be subject to the normal restraints of the doctrine of effectiveness, equivalence and effective judicial protection on the one hand and on the other the Treaty Rights as well as properties of the Directive. Accordingly, it would seem that European Community (EC) Article 95[51] which has been chosen as a legal basis for implementation would not be appropriate for the introduction of criminal penalties.

Chapter IV: CODES OF CONDUCT AND ADMINISTRATIVE COOPERATION

Articles 17
Codes of Conduct

(A) This article details with what might be termed ancillary obligations.[52] It enjoins the Member States with respect to the following matters:

---

51. Amended Proposal for a Directive of the European Parliament and of the Council on Criminal Measures Aimed at the Enforcement of Intellectual Property Rights, COM (2006): 168.
52. S. Prechal, *Directives in EC Law* (Oxford: OUP, 2005), op. cit., 44: 'Directives also contain other types of provisions formulating obligations for the Member States. These can be designated as ancillary, as completing "hard core' provisions …. This is certainly not to suggest that they are less binding or less important (Case 274/83 *Commission v. Italy* (1985) ECR 1077: From the opinion of AG Lenz, it appears that the Italian government suggested that an obligation to notify the Commission of the implementing measures was of minor important. The Court found, however, as with respect to any other provision of the directive, that Italy had failed to fulfil its obligations'. With respect notably to obligations of notification, information or consultation, Prechal observes at page 46 that 'The implications of the obligation may differ and their non-observance may have legal effects.'

(1) Article 17 (a) the encouragement the development by trade and or professional associations and organizations of codes of conduct the purpose of which is to encourage the enforcement of intellectual property rights notably in a particular fashion: that is, by recommending the use of code placed on an optical disk which enables the identification of the place of origin of manufacture of the goods thus marked;

(2) Article 17 (b) the submission to the Commission of any draft codes of conduct on a national or Community level; and the submission to the Commission of any evaluations of the application of these codes.

Article 18
Obligations

An obligation is placed on the Member States to submit a report on the implementation of the directive three years after the period provided in Article 20 (1).[53]

National Report: the purpose of the national reports is to provide the Commission with information with which it may compile a report on the application of the directive including an assessment of the effectiveness of the measures taken as well as an evaluation of its impact on innovation and the development of the information society. The Commission is to transmit this report to the European Parliament, the Council and the European Economic and Social Council. Where necessary in light of the development of the Community order the report in relation to the development shall be accompanied by proposals for amendments of the Directive.

The article imposes a second obligation on the Member States to provide the Commission with all aid and assistance necessary in order to draw up the above report.

Article 19
Exchanged of Information and Correspondents

(A) This article deals with an ancillary obligation. It enjoins the Member States to ensure that information concerning their respective national implementation and enforcement of the directive is exchanged with other Member States and the Commission.[54]

The obligation consists in the following:

(1) in the Member States ensuring that a national correspondent or correspondents are designated for any question relating to the implementation of the directive;

---

53. S. Prechal, *Directives in EC Law* (Oxford: OUP, 2005), ibid., 45.
54. S. Prechal, *Directives in EC Law* (Oxford: OUP, 2005), ibid., 46-47.

(2) the Member States shall communicate the details of the national correspondents to both the Commission and other Member States.

(B) Objective: the purpose of the appointment of the correspondent or correspondents is to promote cooperation including the exchange of information between
the Member States themselves on the one hand and on the other hand, between the
Member States and the Commission.

(C) Recital 30 adds three matters: first, that the exchange of information is also
necessary in order to ensure the 'uniform application of the directive': and that
second, the correspondents designated by the Member States are to function in the
context of network of correspondents which in turn will assist in the uniform
application of the directive; third that regular reports are to be provided, it would
appear, by the Commission which assess the application of the directive and the
effectiveness of the measures taken and applied by the national authorities.

Article 2
Implementation

(A) This article imposes two hard core obligations on the Member States: first, to
bring into force law, regulations and administrative practices which are necessary
to comply with the Directive by 29 April 2006; second, to inform the Commission
forthwith thereof.

(B) Conditions: in implementing the Directive, the Member States must ensure
either that the measures chosen make reference to it or that they be accompanied
by such reference on the occasion of their official publication.[55]

(1) Form of the reference: the form or method of the reference is to be laid
down by the law of the Member State.

Article 21
Entry into Force

The Directive shall enter into force on twenty days following its publication in the
Official Journal of the European Parliament.

Article 22
Addressees

The Directive is addressed to Member States.

---

55. S. Prechal, *Directives in EC Law* (Oxford: OUP, 2005), ibid., 45 observes: 'The purpose of
such a reference is to make the Community origin of the implementing measures explicitly.
This will make transparent the relationship between a piece of national legislation and the
underlying directive which is of particular importance for the judicial protection of individuals
and for the control and interpretation of the implementation measures by national courts or
national authorities, where appropriate.'

Chapter 3

The Implementation of Directive 2004/48/EC in Dutch Civil Procedure

I   INTRODUCTION

The implementation of the Directive on the enforcement of intellectual property rights by the Member States had to be completed by 29 April 2006.[1] The Netherlands failed to meet this deadline. It took the Netherlands until 1 May 2007 to implement the Directive in its entirety.[2] Just some provisions of the directive were statutorily implemented in due time.[3] To realize the complete implementation of the Directive other statutes, especially the Code of Civil Procedure (CCP), had to be adapted. The full implementation was proposed by one implementation Bill.[4]

    This Bill was sent to Parliament on 29 November 2005. It is not quite clear why it took so long to propose the implementation Bill, because the government had already started consultations with interested groups at an early stage, even before the Directive was adopted. A reason for the late implementation may be found in the Directive itself, in which the descriptions of the provisions are

---

1.   Art. 20 Directive 2004/48/EC (OJ L 195/16, of 29 Apr. 2004).
2.   Staatsblad, Stbl. 2007, No. 108.
3.   See Rijksoctrooiwet 16 Feb. 2006, Stbl. 2006, No. 135 and 218. Arts 8, 9, 10, 11, 13 and 15 were implemented in this Kingdom Act, which is also applicable in the Dutch Antilles and Aruba.
4.   Kamerstukken II, 2005-2006, 30 392, Nos 1-3: Aanpassing van het Wetboek van Burgerlijke Rechtsvordering, de Auteurswet 1912, de Wet op de naburige rechten, de Databankwet, de Handelsnaamwet, de Wet van 28 oktober 1987 houdende regelen inzake de bescherming van oorspronkelijke topografieën van halfgeleiderproducten (Stb. No. 484), de Zaaizaad en plant-goedwet 2005 en de Landbouwkwaliteitswet ter uitvoering van Richtlijn nr. 2004/48/EG van het Europees Parlement en de Raad van 29 Apr. 2004 betreffende de handhaving van intellectuele-eigendomsrechten (PbEU L 195).

sometimes not quite clear. Another reason might be that, apart from the CCP, in the Dutch legislation many acts had to be amended.[5]

The late implementation of the Directive has raised the question of whether the Dutch statutory provisions on court fees and on extrajudicial costs could be interpreted in conformity with Article 14 of the Directive. The Dutch courts, in general, were of the opinion that these domestic provisions were in conformity with Article 14.[6] However, there are also non-statutory recommendations concerning court fees and extrajudicial costs which are generally applied by the Dutch courts. Dutch courts do have a discretionary power to mitigate the calculation of these non-statutory costs. In spite of these recommendations, as from 29 April 2006 the courts applied Article 14, with the consequence that in almost all court decisions on intellectual property the rather restricted maximum amount of compensation for costs as laid down in the non-statutory provisions was replaced by a more liberal compensation of costs, sometimes even full compensation for all costs. This conduct led to parliamentary questions during the implementation procedure and to an adaptation of the provision implementing Article 14.[7]

A   THE STANDPOINT ADOPTED BY LEGAL PRACTITIONERS
            CONCERNING THE PROPOSAL FOR THE DIRECTIVE

Dutch experts on intellectual property in general were of the opinion that the Directive was rather superfluous, especially for the Netherlands. One could mention the provisions on taking and preserving evidence, on provisional measures and measures resulting from the decision on the merits of the case. Compared with the existing Dutch civil procedural rules on these subjects and the Trade-Related Aspects of Intellectual Property Rights (TRIPs) Articles on the enforcement of intellectual property rights, these provisions of the Directive were considered not to be very innovative. Furthermore, these provisions were seen as very complicated, vague and difficult to understand. Take, for instance, Article 7 on 'Measures for preserving evidence', which changed so much during the European legislative process that it is not easy to identify which obligations have to be fulfilled by the national legislators to implement the Article in a satisfactory manner. Article 7 states that the Member States shall ensure, even before the commencement of proceedings on the merits, prompt and effective provisional measures to preserve evidence. What kind of measures have to be ensured is left to the Member States. For that reason it is not clear whether the French 'saisie description' or the English 'Anton Piller Order' have to be implemented or whether a less far-reaching

---

5. See above, n. 4.
6. Art. 10 EC Treaty; European Court of Justice (ECJ) 13 Nov. 1990, 'Marleasing', C-106/89, Rec. 1990, p. I-4135, NJ 1993, 163; ECJ 8 Oct. 1987, 'Kolpinghuis', 80/86, Rec. 1987, p. 3969; ECJ 10 Apr. 1984, 14/83, 'Von Colson and Kamann', Rec. 1984, p. 1891.
7. Kamerstukken I 2006-2007, 30 392, B and C. See also Sections I.A and III.G.2.

measure, like the Dutch (pre-trial) provisional examination of witnesses, suffices.[8] The same holds true for Article 14 which is drawn up in such a general way that the Dutch legislator probably does not have to make any adaptations to fulfil its obligation.[9] The Introduction (Section I) already mentions the confusion to which Article 14 has given rise in the period of transition between the date set for transposition by the Directive and the date of the entry into force of the implementation act.

Besides the unclear formulation of some of the provisions, the criticism concentrates on three more essential aspects of the Directive, namely its scope and its relationship to the principles of subsidiarity and proportionality.

As to the scope of the Directive there was doubt about the advisability that the Directive should only be applicable to infringements made for commercial purposes or to all infringements even when the defendant is acting in a bona fide manner. It might be disputed whether it is just and efficient that an applicant can dispose of a complete arsenal of procedural measures, irrespective of whether the defendant is a product pirate or a bona fide competitioner. The defendant probably cannot dispose of these measures and therefore the 'equality of arms' requirement is not sufficiently respected.[10] In the case of a bona fide competitioner this is even more problematic, because the proposed procedure to gather information is an ex parte procedure.[11]

The criticism of the principle of subsidiarity is very essential. Procedural law until recently was considered to be part of the exclusive sovereignty of the Member States. As stated in the 'Opinion' by scholars on intellectual property in the European Union (EU) 'Procedural law, civil as well as criminal, encapsulates a whole set of balances concerning fundamental freedoms of individuals when they face the operations of the justice system' […].'In large measure they apply to all types of claim, not just to particular fields, such as intellectual property, and that is a highly desirable presumption to be maintained.'[12]

Indeed, before the Treaty of Amsterdam civil procedure was not considered to be the Commission's main interest. This changed considerably after the coming into force of the Treaty of Amsterdam. Article 65 European Community (EC) now creates a legal basis for European measures in the field of judicial cooperation in civil matters having cross-border implications and in so far as is necessary for the proper functioning of the internal market.

---

8. J.L.R.A. Huydecoper, 'Nous Maintiendrons – de nieuwe "Richtlijn Handhaving"', *AMI* (2004): 117-123.
9. F.i.P.B. Hugenholtz, 'Een overbodige richtlijn', *IER* (2004): 53. The author also subscribed to the viewpoint of W.R. Cornish, a.o., 'Procedures and Remedies for Enforcing IPRs: The European Commission's Proposed Directive', *EIPR* (2003): 447-449.
10. J.L.R.A. Huydecoper (AMI 2004, see n. 8) poses the question whether Art. 6 leaves room for the defendant to take evidence himself in an infringement procedure. Actually he answers the question in a negative sense.
11. Van de brug af gezien, 'Kroniek van wetgeving, jurisprudentie en literatuur 2003', *IER* (2004): 75.
12. See n. 9, W.R. Cornish among others.

Since then, regulations on the mutual recognition of judicial decisions, the taking of evidence and the service of documents have been concluded. These regulations have led to the harmonization of related subjects of civil procedure in the EU. Of more importance for the harmonization of European civil procedure could have been the proposals for Regulations on the European order for payment and on a small claims procedure. These proposals for regulations both contained provisions for a civil procedure with quite some harmonizing elements. Initially, the scope of the proposals of these Regulations extended to cross-border as well as to internal cases. However, the Council was of the opinion that these (as far as their scope is concerned) far-reaching procedural measures could not have been based on Article 65 EC if internal cases were included. This criticism led to the decision to limit these Regulations to only cross-border cases.[13] More important was the general viewpoint behind this decision that national procedural law should not be harmonized too quickly. The exclusive sovereignty of the Member States concerning civil procedure therefore remains very strong. It is all the more surprising that the Directive on the enforcement of intellectual property rights with quite some far-reaching procedural measures could nevertheless be concluded in the way it has been. The reason might be that this instrument is based on Article 95 EC in combination with the kind of instrument (a directive instead of a regulation). A directive leaves more room and freedom for the Member States to make their own decisions as to the implementation. The harmonization of procedural law imposed by a directive is politically not very effective in general.

Also the Council had some concerns about the proportionality of the Directive. The Directive suggests that an infringement of intellectual property rights is worse than an infringement of other property rights. However, there might be some doubt as to whether the effective combating of piracy needs more procedural measures and sanctions than the existing enforcement instruments already provide.[14] Furthermore, in the Netherlands there is also some concern about the provision which introduces the common law principle of 'pre-trial' disclosure in the Directive, because 'pre-trial' disclosure will make judicial procedures, especially concerning intellectual property, too expensive and long-lasting.[15]

After the proposal was considerably amended, some Dutch experts took a more positive position.[16] Some of the criticisms have led to new provisions, like the provisions which are restricted to commercial infringements. One of the authors, Gielen, referred to the provisions and the obligations of the TRIPs agreement, which makes it necessary to implement these provisions. Although the TRIPs agreement also binds the EU Member States, it does not harmonize procedural law on intellectual property; on the contrary it promises that the national

---

13. The 'Legal Service of the Council' decided that Art. 65 EC was not an appropriate legal basis for including internal cases in the Regulation.
14. P.B. Hugenholtz (*IER* 2004), see n. 9.
15. J.L.R.A. Huydecoper (*AMI* 2004), see n. 8.
16. J.L.R.A. Huydecoper (*AMI* 2004), see n. 8.

differences should be respected.[17] As a result, for the first time the Directive will effect some harmonization on procedural measures on intellectual property rights. Although the Netherlands is not obliged to adapt its law considerably, according to Gielen some other Member States, like some southern States and the States that joined the EU in 2004, need much more extensive adaptations.[18]

II   IMPLEMENTATION

A   LEGISLATIVE PROCEDURE

Before the implementation Bill was sent to Parliament the government consulted several interested groups on the first draft of the Bill.[19] After these consultations the Bill was sent to the Council of State for advice and next to the Lower House of Parliament.[20] The Parliament and some interest groups were critical about the Bill. The central point of criticism was the position of the rightholder, which would be placed in a disadvantageous situation, because of an (in the opinion of the critics) incorrect implementation of Articles 8, 9 and 11 of the Directive, regarding cooperation between the intermediaries, especially the Internet Service Providers.[21] A year later the implementation Bill, as amended by the Lower House, was sent to the Upper House.[22] At this stage of the legislative procedure questions were raised about the compensation of costs. As mentioned in Section I, as from the date when the implementation was due, the courts in general applied, in a prospective way, the Bill's article implementing Article 14 of the Directive, an article which differs substantially from the general practice in domestic civil cases. Duly alerted, the Upper House wanted to know whether the proposed article of the Bill was in conformity with Article 14 of the Directive. Again consultations were held, this time limited to the compensation of costs. As a result, however, the Bill's Article has not been modified.[23]

---

17.   Van de brug af gezien, 'Kroniek van wetgeving, jurisprudentie en literatuur 2003', *IER* (2004): 75.
18.   C. Gielen, 'De richtlijn handhaving IE-rechten', *NTER* (2005): 6-11. The same holds true for the Member States that joined the EU in 2007.
19.   Advice was given by the Royal Society of Bailiffs, the Netherlands Bar Association, the Council for the Administration of Justice and the Royal Commission on civil procedural law.
20.   Kamerstukken II, 2005-2006, 30 292, Nos 1-3; MvT, No. 3 is the Explanatory Report (see n. 4).
21.   O. Delfos Visser & R. Brouwer, Wetsvoorstel Handhavingsrichtlijn: Nous ne maintiendrons pas!, *AMI* (2006): 77-83; the conclusion is that enforcement on the internet will be worse than without the proposed Bill, and is also in conflict with the general obligations of Art. 3, para. 1 of the Directive, because they are unnecessarily complicated. The interested parties were the enforcement organizations: Stichting Brein, Stichting SNB-REACT and Stichting STRABEL.
22.   Kamerstukken I, 2006-2007, 30 392, A, 19 Oct. 2006.
23.   Kamerstukken I, 2006-2007, 30 392, C, 9 Feb. 2007. Advice was requested from the Netherlands Bar Association and the Council for the Administration of Justice.

B IMPLEMENTATION IN GENERAL

Although in the Netherlands the enforcement of intellectual property rights can take place both by using measures of civil and criminal law, it is in the first place the decision of the claimant himself to start an action using civil procedural measures against the person who is infringing. Criminal enforcement is considered to be an *ultimum remedium*.[24] Furthermore, administrative enforcement through the customs authorities takes place at the Dutch outer boundaries of the EU.

Until now civil enforcement has taken place in conformity with some of the procedures of the Dutch CCP.[25, 26] The summary proceedings, the *kort geding*, are very useful in intellectual property cases in which provisional measures are needed. The *kort geding* offers discretionary powers to the court to order or to forbid some actions, or to hand over goods. Therefore Article 50 of the TRIPs agreement was implemented in the *kort geding* procedure.[27]

Furthermore, there are special provisions on the enforcement of intellectual property in some specific statutes.[28] The tort provision of the Civil Code (Article 6: 162 CC) has, in court decisions, led to a number of measures aimed at diminishing and preventing the damage caused or to be caused by the infringements.[29] A number of provisions of the Directive did not have to be implemented, because Dutch legislation was already in conformity with these provisions. In case implementation was necessary especially the CCP was adapted. The implementation took place by one implementation Bill.[30] The provisions in the CCP are applicable to intellectual property rights in general. Beside these general provisions, specific acts on intellectual property were adapted, e.g., the Copyright Act and the Neighbouring Rights Act.

The Directive requires minimum provisions for the civil enforcement of intellectual property rights, and does not aim at establishing harmonized rules for civil procedure (recitals 10 and 11). Therefore the Dutch legislator has implemented the Directive in a new Title 15, Articles 1019-1019i CCP, in Book 3 of the CCP called: 'Van rechtspleging in zaken betreffende rechten van intellectuele eigendom' (Proceedings Concerning Intellectual Property Rights). Creating a new Title made it possible to leave the general provisions on enforcement in the CCP undisturbed. The new Title 15 in the CCP has a supplementary character with regard to

---

24. Criminal enforcement is rarely ordered, L. Wichers Hoeth, Kort begrip van het intellectuele eigendomsrecht, eds Ch. Gielen and N. Hagemans, a.o., W.E.J. Tjeenk Willink, 2000, 477.
25. CCP is the Wetboek voor Burgerlijke Rechtsvordering (Rv).
26. Because the objective of the Directive 2004/48/EC is the approximation of rules on civil enforcement, and does not apply to criminal enforcement (Art. 2, para. 3c), this contribution will concentrate on the consequences for civil procedural law only.
27. Art. 260 CCP. This Article was repealed when the new law came into force, and was inserted in Art. 1019i CCP.
28. E.g., Art. 28 Auteurswet (Copyright Act) regulates the seizure of and claims against objects that infringe.
29. Kamerstukken II, 2005-2006, 30 392, Explanatory Report, MvT, No. 3, p. 4-5.
30. See n. 4.

all civil infringements procedures on intellectual property rights. The general provisions of the CCP are applicable as far as Title 15 does not determine differently.

Title 15 contains the following:

Article 1019 CCP: objective and scope;
Article 1019a CCP: disclosure of evidence;
Article 1019b CCP: provisional measures;
Article 1019c CCP: requirements for the seizure of evidence;
Article 1019d CCP: record of the detailed description, with or without the taking of samples;
Article 1019e CCP: interlocutory injunctions;
Article 1019f CCP: right of information;
Article 1019g CCP: damages;
Article 1019h CCP: legal costs;
Article 1019i CCP: Article 50 paragraph 1 TRIPs.

We may conclude that, by creating a new title only for intellectual property rights, the Dutch legislator found a solution to the critical remarks on the proposal of the Directive, namely that an infringement of intellectual property rights is worse than an infringement of other property rights, and needs more procedural measures and sanctions than the existing enforcement instruments already give. As a consequence, the implementation of the Directive did not only result in more procedural measures and sanctions, but also in a different regime on the compensation of costs for intellectual property cases.[31] Whether this way of implementing the Directive is satisfactory, may be disputed.[32]

C   DUTCH CIVIL PROCEDURAL LAW

To understand the implementation of the Directive in full it is necessary to give a brief description of the general provisions of the Dutch CCP which are of importance for the civil enforcement of intellectual property rights and which have been used until now, and will remain of interest as long as the new Title 15 does not stipulate otherwise. These provisions concern provisional protective measures, especially the legal system of seizure, interim injunctions and the disclosure of evidence. Before discussing these measures, attention will be given to the rules of jurisdiction and competence of Dutch courts in intellectual property rights.

---

31. See Section III.G.1.
32. R.R. Verkerk, Procesrechtelijke aspecten van het wetsvoorstel handhaving intellectuele eigendom, *TCR* (2006): 110-115; E.L. Valgaeren, L.de Gryse, Een Europese Richtlijn betreffende de handhaving van intellectuele eigendomsrechten, *SEW* (2005): 202-209.

1   Jurisdiction and Competence of the Dutch Courts

a   *Jurisdiction of Dutch Courts*

The revised CCP from 2002 includes a special section on international jurisdiction of the Dutch courts.[33] In Articles 1-14 CCP a complete system of provisions on jurisdiction is provided for, to be applied if jurisdiction cannot be based on a treaty or an EU-Regulation.

Articles 1-14 CCP are in general based on the Articles of the Brussels I Convention and the Brussels I and II Regulation and follow them. So Article 13 CCP on protective and provisional measures is in some way based on Article 24 Brussels I Convention and Article 31 Brussels I Regulation. Article 13 CCP states that the Dutch courts have jurisdiction to order provisional and protective measures, like a decision in *kort geding* even if the Dutch courts have no competence in the procedure on the merits. Although in these cases of strictly Dutch law the decisions of the European Court of Justice (ECJ) are not binding, they are nevertheless firm guidelines for the courts. In the legal practice of the past few years in international intellectual property cases – especially in patent case decisions rendered by the Hague District Court – the Dutch courts in *kort geding* used to declare themselves competent in the case of protective or provisional measures and to order domestic as well as cross-border sanctions.[34]

Since the decision of the ECJ of 1998 in the case Van Uden/Deco Line[35] the jurisdiction of the Dutch court in *kort geding* is now restricted. 'The granting of provisional or protective measures on the basis of Article 24 Brussels I Convention is conditional on, inter alia, the existence of a real connecting link between the subject-matter of the measures sought and the territorial jurisdiction of the Contracting State of the court before which those measures are sought.'[36] So, since the Van Uden decision, Dutch courts may only award provisional protective measures operational within the Netherlands if their competence is based on Articles 24 Brussels I Convention/31 Brussels I Regulation. If the competence is based on Articles 2 and 5-18 (now 24) Brussels I Convention/Brussels I Regulation, the Dutch courts may also apply cross-border measures.

The practice of the Dutch courts in *kort geding*, in which they based their jurisdiction on Article 6 paragraph 1 of the Brussels Convention, to order cross-border sanctions against several defendants, infringers of the same intellectual property right within the EU, came to an end with the decision of the ECJ in the Roche Nederland BV/Primus case.[37] The Court decided that Article 6(1) of the

---

33. Wet van 6 Dec. 2001, Stb. Nos 580 and 581. Important are also the Acts of 6 Dec. 2001, Stb. Nos 582, 583 and 584.
34. HR 24 Nov. 1989, NJ 1992, 404, Note DWFV.
35. ECJ 17 Nov. 1998, C-391/95, ECR 1998, P. I-7091.
36. No. 40. Furthermore, it was decided that interim payment of a contractual consideration does not constitute a provisional measure within the meaning of Art. 24, unless a guarantee is given.
37. ECJ of 13 Jul. 2006, C-539/03, ECR 2006, P. I-6535.

Brussels Convention must be interpreted as meaning that it does not apply in European patent infringement proceedings involving a number of companies established in various Contracting States in respect of acts committed in one or more of those States and, in particular, where those companies, which belong to the same group, have acted in an identical or similar manner in accordance with a common policy elaborated by one of them.

b   *Subject-Matter and Territorial Competence*

The court system in the Netherlands, since the revision of 2002, includes three levels, namely, first instance District Courts, Courts of Appeal and the Supreme Court.[38] The *voorzieningenrechter* in the *kort geding* procedure, or summary procedure, is a special judge within the District Court. Within the District Courts there is also a subdistrict section with competence to hear cases with a claim of under EUR 5,000 and rent and labour cases. The subdistrict section also disposes of a summary procedure, but only for cases that fall within the competence of this subdistrict section.[39]

In principle all District Courts have subject-matter competence to hear procedures on the merits in intellectual property cases. Territorial competence is normally determined by the domicile of the defendant. However, in patent and Community trademarks, The Hague District Court has exclusive competence at first instance.[40]

The subject-matter competence of the judge in *kort geding* has its own rules. In case of urgency the *voorzieningenrechter* in the *kort geding* procedure is competent to hear a case. Territorial competence is not only determined by the domicile of the defendant but also competent is the *voorzieningenrechter* of the place where the provisional measure has to take effect.

In case of pre-judgment seizure of goods the request to obtain leave has to be done to the *voorzieningenrechter* of the District Court where one of the goods is, or some of the goods are situated or, in case the seizure does not involve goods, the *voorzieningenrechter* of the domicile of the defendant is competent (Article 700 CCP). According to the case law in intellectual property cases[41] the *voorzieningenrechter* competent to give leave in case of pre-judgment seizure regarding one of the goods is also competent with regard to other seizures within the same claim and levied against the same debtor.

Another view would mean that several *voorzieningenrechters* have to give leave in the same claim. This practice is needlessly time-consuming and expensive, and may also lead to contradictory decisions.

---

38. By this revision the subdistrict courts merged with the District Courts, and became the subdistrict division of the District Courts.
39. For intellectual property cases, this summary procedure is not important.
40. Art. 80 Rijksoctrooiwet 1995.
41. Hof Amsterdam, 23 Jan. 2003, NJkort 2003, 32.

2   Pre-judgment Seizure or Attachment

In Dutch civil procedure, a distinction should be made between pre-judgment attachment or seizure and executory attachment or seizure. The executory seizure refers to the situation where the seizure creditor already disposes of an enforceable title (Articles 439-584r CCP). The ex parte pre-judgment seizure, on the other hand, is available even before a procedure has commenced and is used as a protective measure. If pre-judgment seizure is granted, the seizor is obliged to institute the procedure on the merits within a fixed time.[42] The general provisions of Articles 700-710a CCP are applicable to the different kinds of pre-judgment seizures. They refer to the requirements of pre-judgment seizures, security, costs, lifting the seizure, the pre-judgment seizure levied against the debtor entering the executory phase (Article 704 CCP), sequestration (Article 709 CCP) and administration (710 CCP).[43] It should be mentioned, that the pre-judgment seizure of immovable property levied against the debtor does not enter into the executory phase.[44]

The most important purpose of pre-judgment seizure is the freezing of assets, until an enforceable title is obtained. The judgment debtor is no longer allowed to withdraw goods from an attachment. To prevent the debtor embezzling his goods beforehand, the seizure of goods should be easy and fast. In order to achieve this goal, the court does not hear the judgment debtor on the application for leave. Open to attachment are, e.g., movables and immovable property, and attachment by garnishment. These attachments are used to recover a money claim.

Furthermore, the party who is entitled by contract – by selling or renting – to some goods can seize the goods before judgment for the purpose of surrender or delivery up (Articles 730-737 CCP).

The application of Articles 730-737 CCP is extended to intellectual property cases, too.[45] For that purpose, e.g., the copyright owner under Article 28 paragraph 4 Copyright Act, is entitled to claim the ownership of the goods, or the destruction or unusability thereof. The copyright seizure even has priority over other kinds of seizure. The general provisions of Articles 700-710a CCP, and especially the provision on sequestration of Article 709 CCP, are also applicable in intellectual property cases.

However, this provision does not cover the seizure of evidence. Although the CCP did not include a statutory rule on the seizure of evidence, in the past Article 843a CCP was already used by some lower courts as a judicial basis for the seizure

---

42. Under Art. 28 Copyright Act the procedure on the merits should be a regular procedure. A *kort geding* procedure as a procedure on the merits is no longer satisfactory: J.H. Spoor, D.W.F. Verkade & D.J.G. Visser, *Auteursrecht*, 3rd edn, (Deventer: Kluwer, 2005), 515.
43. Some provisions of Title 15 refer to the general provisions of Arts 700-710a CCP.
44. The same will apply to the pre-judgment seizure of evidence, it will not enter into the executory phase, see Subsection III.C.2.c.
45. All the different Acts on intellectual property, except the Patent Act, provide for the pre-judgment seizure of goods, especially the seizure under Arts 730-738 CCP.

of written evidence, like administration and business correspondence (see Subsections II.C.4 and III.C.1.a).

Because the judgment creditor does not yet have an enforceable title, in either of the different kinds of pre-judgment seizure, the creditor has to apply for leave to the court. The leave has to describe exactly which goods may be seized. The court will grant leave after a summary examination. Summary examination just means checking the formalities by a court clerk (Article 700 paragraph 2 CCP). The seizure of the described goods is done by the bailiff (Article 702).[46] At the request of every interested party the seizure can be lifted if it is wrongful or unnecessary or, in the case of seizure for a money claim, security has been paid (Article 705 CCP). In intellectual property cases this means that the seizure can be lifted if the interested party states that the seizure is wrongful or unnecessary. The party has to make the wrongfulness or non-necessity plausible, but does not have to provide proof. The court might therefore decide that it is not plausible that there is an infringement of in intellectual property right. The seizure might be unnecessary if one does not have to fear that the infringer will not surrender the illegal copies.[47]

3 Summary Procedures (Interim Injunctions)

In case of urgency in the Netherlands the Dutch *kort geding* is the most important summary procedure in intellectual property cases.[48] Taking into consideration the urgency and weighing the interests of the parties the court may order a provisional measure. A claim to destroy or render useless the infringed goods under Article 28 paragraph 2 Copyright Act may often not be considered urgent or will be dismissed as being too far-reaching.[49] Contrary to the pre-judgment seizure, the *kort geding* is a contradictory procedure, which means the debtor always has to be summoned for the procedure.[50] The *kort geding* procedure offers discretionary power to the court to order or forbid some actions, or to hand over goods. If an order is given the *kort geding* leads to an interim injunction. Actually, there are no procedural rules which have to be applied by the court.[51] Because of the urgency, only an oral hearing takes place.

---

46. The bailiff is the official State authority charged with seizure and the enforcement of judgments. For that reason the bailiff is now charged with the description of the infringing goods (see Subsection III.C.2.d.i).
47. A.B.E. dos Santos Gil, Bewarende'interim'-maatregelen met betrekking tot inbreukmakende goederen en documenten in auteursrechtzaken, in Molengrafica 1996, Europees Privaatrecht, Opstellen over Internationale transacties in Intellectuele eigendom (Lelystad: Koninklijke Vermande, 1996), 199-256, at 215.
48. The *kort geding* procedure has become more and more important, especially since 1932, when it became possible to impose a default fine in interlocutory proceedings.
49. C.J.J.C. Van Nispen, Verbod en bevel in het auteursrecht onder het Nieuw BW, *Informatierecht/AMI* (1992): 90-92, n. 5; A.B.E. dos Santos Gil (Molengrafica 1996), see n. 47.
50. Although the debtor is called into the procedure, this does not mean he also has to appear. If he does not appear in the procedure, the court will render a default judgment.
51. The rules of evidence do not apply in the *kort geding* procedure.

The legal basis to instigate a claim in the *kort geding* procedure is the tort provision of Article 6: 162 CC. *Kort geding* proceedings have to be brought before the so-called *voorzieningenrechter* of the District Court, an *unus judex* District Court section charged with urgent cases. The legal character of the *kort geding* procedure is that of a provisional measure. Decisions in *kort geding* are supposed to be interim measures, not final judgments. Their aim is to secure the ultimate execution of the judgment on the merits, which, in intellectual property cases is the infringement procedure. For that reason Article 50 of the TRIPs agreement was implemented in the *kort geding* procedure.[52]

The *kort geding* is exclusively lodged with the *voorzieningenrechter* of the District Court and may be entered independently of the claim on the merits. It has, however, a clear relationship to the procedure on the merits: in principle a *kort geding* proceeding should be followed by a proceeding on the merits.

4   Disclosure of Evidence

Since the revision of the Dutch Code on Civil Procedure in 2002 the disclosure of evidence has been more emphasized, both for the court as well as for the parties.[53] The competence of the court to order information from the parties or deliver some documents during the procedure has become more important (Article 22 CCP).

Before 2002 the obligation to disclose documents at the request of the parties was limited to private instruments. The revised Article 843a CCP stipulates that all kinds of documents can, at the request of a party, be ordered to be disclosed. The provision is limited to specific documents that exist, but are within the control of somebody else.[54] In earlier legal literature, Article 843a CCP was already used as a judicial basis for the seizure of evidence.[55] In the case law of the lower courts the seizure of evidence was admitted, provided that there was an obligation of delivery and the evidence could only be recovered from the other party.

In a recent intellectual property case in *kort geding*, the claimant was allowed to authorize a third party to inspect the seized digital information under the conditions set by the court for this inspection.[56] Remarkable is the case in which the court awarded a claim, which was based on Articles 6 and 7 of the Directive and Article 843a CCP, to seize evidence, even before the Directive was implemented.[57]

---

52. See also n. 27.
53. Wet van 6 Dec. 2001, Stb. Nos 580 and 581.
54. See also Subsection III.C.1.a.
55. M. Barendrecht & W.A.J.P. van den Reek, Exhibitieplicht en bewijsbeslag, *WPNR* 6155 (1994): 739; E.M. Wesseling-van Gent, To Fish or Not To Fish, That's the Question, in Het verzamelen van feiten en bewijs: begrenzing versus verruiming, een kruisbestuiving tussen civiel procesrecht en ondernemingsprocesrecht (Den Haag: Boom Juridische Uitgevers, 2006), 81-119.
56. Voorzieningenrechter Breda court, 25 Oct. 2006, LJN: AZ1374, SLC Holding/Stakenburg Beheer.
57. Voorzieningenrechter Groningen court, 8 Jun. 2007, KG ZA 07-111, Kamstra/SPI International: in this procedure, the judgment debtor requested the lifting of the seizure of evidence ordered by the court in Feb. 2007.

Due to the provisions on disclosure in the Directive on the enforcement of intellectual property rights and the proposal for the private enforcement of anti-trust rules, there is currently a serious discussion as to whether it might be useful for efficient litigation to extend the possibilities of disclosure in Dutch civil procedure in general.[58]

III   IMPLEMENTATION OF THE ARTICLES

A   INTRODUCTION

The Directive requires, on the one hand, the availability of provisional measures like attachments and interlocutory injunctions that can be affected before the procedure on the merits is initiated. On the other hand, provisions should be available to take evidence and other information concerning the infringement. In the discussion on the implementation of the Directive one has to differentiate between the articles that, in the opinion of the Dutch legislator, had to be implemented and the ones that did not need to be implemented.

The Articles or part of Articles 1, 2, 5, 6, 7, 8, 9, 10, 11, 13, 14 and 15 of the Directive have been implemented.[59] Articles 3, 4 and 12 were not implemented (see Section IV).

Before discussing the reasons for the implementation and non-implementation of the articles, an observation should be made about the scope of the Directive (Articles 1 and 2). According to recital No. 13, the scope should be defined as widely as possible in order to encompass all intellectual property rights covered by Community provisions in this field and/or by the national law of the Member State concerned. For internal purposes, the Netherlands did not make use of the possibility to implement the provisions of this Directive regarding acts involving unfair competition, including parasitic copies, or similar activities. The scope of the Directive, laid down in Articles 1 and 2, is implemented in Article 1019 CCP.

1   Article 1019 CCP

Article 1019 CCP stipulates that Title 15 applies to the enforcement of intellectual property rights pursuant to the special intellectual property rights Acts, like the Copyright Act, the Database Act, the Patents Act 1995, and the Uniform Benelux Law on Marks.[60] Although not mentioned in Article 1019 CCP, all intellectual property rights procedures based on Treaties fall within Title 15 CCP.[61]

---

58. Kamerstukken II, 2006-2007, 30 951, Herbezinning burgerlijk procesrecht, No. 1, p. 16, No. 44.
59. Implementation took place in the CCP and the different Intellectual Property Acts.
60. For the other Acts. See n. 4.
61. Kamerstukken II, 2005-2006, MvT, No. 3, p. 18.

a   *Case Law*

In the case *Synthon v. Astellas Pharma*[62] the question was raised whether a
German patent right under the European Patent Treaty 1995 could, under Article
1019 CCP, be enforced in the Netherlands. The Dutch Court was of the opinion
that the new Title 15 is not limited to Dutch intellectual property rights. This
would be contrary to the purpose and the efficiency of the Directive, namely to
harmonize the enforcement of intellectual property rights in order to combat
infringements of intellectual property rights in general and in particular the
large-scale counterfeiting and piracy, which increasingly have a cross-border
character. The Court also referred to recitals No. 7 and 8 of the Directive.
Furthermore, according to the Court, a restricted interpretation of the Dutch
Article 1019 CCP does not comply with the Brussels I Regulation, especially not
with Article 31. For that reason, the Court decided, it had jurisdiction to grant
leave for seizure and a description of the evidence under Articles 1019b, c and d
CCP, which were intended as evidence to be used in the procedure in
Germany.

B   SECTION 1: GENERAL PROVISIONS

1   **Article 5: Presumption of Authorship or Ownership**

As to the presumption of authorship determined in Article 5, this already results
from Article 6 Berne Convention and corresponds with Article 4 Copyright Act;
therefore, it was not implemented. On the other hand, the presumption of ownership of a neighbouring right was implemented in the Neighbouring Rights Act
(Article 1a). Although ownership is clear in cases of direct performance, the presumption of ownership will be relevant if the performance is recorded. For these
situations the person who is supposed to be the owner is the person who is indicated as such or, at the moment of publication, performance or distribution of the
material, was announced as the producer by the person who published, performed
or distributed the material.

Implemented in the Database Act is the presumption of which person is the
producer and therefore the party entitled to a database. The implementation of
rights that are not registered might offer a guideline to the question whether the
party is entitled to the right in question. By implementing this provision in the
Database Act the only non-registered intellectual property right is regulated in
the same way as copyrights and neighbouring rights.

---

62. Voorzieningenrechter Arnhem court, 1 Jun. 2007, LJN: BA9615.

C   Section 2: Evidence

1   Article 6: Evidence

a   Introduction

Article 6, paragraphs 1 and 2 of the Directive apply to the disclosure of evidence. Paragraph 1 provides for the general conditions under which the disclosure of evidence can be requested. Paragraph 2 refers to the same conditions, but the provision is limited to commercial infringements.

According to Article 6, paragraph 1 of the Directive, a party who wants the disclosure of specified evidence, which is under the control of the opposing party, should always on his part start to present reasonably available evidence to support his claim. This provision is implemented in Article 1019a, paragraphs 1, 2 and 3, CCP.

Article 6 paragraph 1 does not make it clear which kind of evidence, under the control of the opposing party is necessary. To answer the question one might look at paragraph 2. Article 6 paragraph 2, which does apply to commercial infringements, states that, on the application by a party, the communication of banking, financial or commercial documents under the control of the opposing party might be ordered. One might assume, under paragraph 1, that this kind of evidence cannot be requested. Therefore, the evidence under paragraph 1, probably only includes evidence to support the infringement, namely the goods or instruments used by the infringement.[63]

Article 6 paragraph 1 of the Directive is implemented in Article 1019a, paragraphs 1, 2 and 3, CCP.

Although Dutch procedural law already has different possibilities to order evidence to be presented by the opposing party, none of these possibilities completely covered Article 6 of the Directive (see Section II.C.4). Of these possibilities Article 843a CCP reflects most clearly the substance of Article 6 paragraphs 1 and 2 of the Directive. Contrary to Article 6, which limits the disclosure of evidence during the procedure, Article 843a CCP can also be used without a procedure.[64] Article 843a, paragraph 1, CCP reads:

> The party with a legitimate interest may, on his own account, claim access, a copy or an extract of specific documents[65] concerning a legal relationship between the requesting party or his predecessors, and the person in whose

---

63. C. Gielen, De richtlijn handhaving IE-rechten, NTER 2005, 6-11.
64. Art. 843a CCP, as it reads now, was implemented in the CCP, 1 Jan. 2002.
65. Documents include, besides all written documents, also computer printouts, photographs, movies, computer disks or sticks and CD-ROMS. Art. 843a, para. 1, CCP, restricts the disclosure to 'specific' documents, in order to prevent 'fishing expeditions': Parlementaire Geschiedenis, Herziening van het Burgerlijk Procesrecht, A.I.M. van Mierlo & F.M. Bart (Deventer: Kluwer, 2002) P, Art. 843a CCP, 553.

control or custody the evidence lies.[66] Documents includes also: information on data carriers.

Article 843a, paragraph 1, CCP is complemented with provisions regulating the discretionary power of the Court to determine the way in which access, a copy or extract of the documents is put forward (paragraph 2), on the privilege of non-disclosure (paragraph 3) and in case of important reasons the right to refuse disclosure of the documents or when the documents are not necessary for a fair dispensation of justice (paragraph 4). In Dutch law 'important reasons' include for instance confidential business information.

As to the costs of producing evidence, Article 14 of the Directive requires a deviation from Article 843a, paragraph 1, CCP, which stipulates that the party with a legitimate interest, may, on his own account, claim access. Article 14 of the Directive states that the reasonable and proportionate costs of access, copies and extracts of the documents incurred by the successful party shall be borne by the unsuccessful party (see Article 1019h CCP, Section III.G.2).

Not implemented is the optional provision of Article 6 paragraph 1, that a reasonable sample of a substantial number of copies of a work or any other protected object be considered by the competent judicial authorities to constitute reasonable evidence. According to the Dutch government this problem does not exist in the Netherlands. The Dutch law on evidence always allows the defendant to provide proof of the contrary (Articles 149-152 CCP).

The provision of Article 6, paragraph 2 of the Directive was not implemented, because Article 1019a CCP already includes commercial infringements.

b   *Article 1019a CCP*

i   Article 1019a paragraph 1 CCP
Article 1019a, paragraph 1, CCP refers to Article 843a CCP but extends it by codifying the rule that a legal relationship also means an obligation arising out of tort.

According to Article 6, paragraph 1 of the Directive, a party who wants the disclosure of specified evidence which is under the control of the opposing party, should always on his part start to present reasonably available evidence to support his claim. The disclosure under Article 843a CCP is more far-reaching than that required under Article 6. Article 843a CCP merely stipulates that the party needs a legitimate interest. The party does not first have to present reasonably available evidence to support his claim. Furthermore, Article 843a CCP is applicable, both when the party is not responsible for the infringement, and in the case of an action out of tort. For example, in the case of a commercial infringement.

---

66. A legal relationship includes an obligation arising out of tort: Kamerstukken II, 1999-2000, 26 855, No. 5, p. 78-79.

ii   Article 1019a paragraph 2 CCP

Article1019a, paragraph 2, CCP supplements Article 843a CCP in such a way that also other evidence may be ordered from the person who has control of the evidence or in whose custody it lies. With this extension of Article 843a CCP, also CDs, clothes, toys, perfumeries and other kinds of evidence which are of special interest in intellectual property proceedings may be ordered.

iii   Article 1019a paragraph 3 CCP

According to Article 1019a, paragraph 3, CCP, the Court will dismiss the request when the protection of confidential information cannot be guaranteed.[67]

In Dutch literature the question is raised whether, based on the new provision of Article 1019a, paragraph 3, CCP, the Court will still be able to balance the interests of both parties in order to decide whether confidential information should be disclosed.[68]

According to Article 843a, paragraph 4 CCP, an article which does not apply in the case of Article 1019a, paragraph 3, CCP, courts have discretionary power to decide on the request, balancing the interests of both parties. Over the last five years the case law now shows that Article 843a CCP is interpreted by the courts in quite a broad sense. For instance, concerning an obligation of secrecy concerning competitively sensitive documents, the court decided that the documents should be disclosed, on condition that both parties agreed and only the court could have access to the documents.[69] To guarantee the confidentiality of information, in Dutch practice in procedures on intellectual property, only the client's attorney receives the competitively sensitive documents, and he is not allowed to show them to his client. If necessary, the court can order the parties to adhere to an obligation of secrecy (Article 29 CCP). On the other hand, at the moment of initiating a procedure, to determine whether there is an infringement, due to the principle of fair trial under Article 6 European Convention on Human Rights (ECHR) it is common practice that, besides the court and the attorney, the interested party receives the information. Therefore Article 1019a CCP can, in practice, more often lead to the situation where the court has to decline a request for disclosure.

The Dutch government is of the opinion that the courts can still balance the interests of both parties when deciding whether the documents are necessary for a fair dispensation of justice. And, finally, it should be prevented that the measures will lead to 'fishing expeditions', in which the creditor has the opportunity to delve into the affairs of the company of the opposing party by requesting all kinds

---

67. Art. 843a, para. 3, CCP, already determines the strict confidentiality of persons in their function as public servants or within their profession. This rule will also be applicable.
68. R.R. Verkerk, Procesrechtelijke aspecten van het wetsvoorstel handhaving intellectuele eigendom, *TCR* (2006): 110-115.
69. HR 20 Dec. 2002, NJ 2004 (Lightning Casino/Antillen), J. Ekelmans, De exhibitieplicht in de praktijk: de ruime mogelijkheden tot opvragen van bescheiden, *TCR* (2005): 59-68.

of 'evidence'.[70] This is even more important in the case of Article 6, paragraph 2 of the Directive, which refers to commercial infringements.

2   Article 7: Measures for Preserving Evidence

a   Introduction

Article 7 provides rules on measures for preserving evidence at the unilateral request of the interested party. However, contrary to Article 6 of the Directive, which limits the disclosure of evidence during the procedure, Article 7, paragraph 1 of the Directive relates to provisional measures taken before the commencement of proceedings on the merits. As for Article 6, according to Article 7 the party who wants to request provisional measures for preserving evidence to support his claim always has to present reasonably available evidence that his intellectual property right has been infringed or is about to be infringed. The court will grant leave after a summary examination, in other words checking the formalities to see whether the underlying claim does not seem unfounded and balancing the interests of both parties. Although it was feared that the new provisional measures might cause 'fishing expeditions', the government was of the opinion that because of the examination by the court, there was no reason for such trepidation, and reproduced this part of Article 7 in Article 1019b CCP.[71]

Article 7 paragraph 1 creates the opportunity to introduce several kinds of provisional measures. The Netherlands has only implemented these measures in Article 1019b CCP. In compliance with the Directive, the detailed report of findings, with or without the taking of samples, has been implemented.

Article 1019b CCP is the basic article on provisional measures in intellectual property cases. In Article 1019c CCP the Dutch legislator introduced rules according to which the 'seizure of evidence' has to take place. Article 1019d CCP provides rules on the detailed report of findings and the taking of samples. The other provisional measures of Article 7 paragraph 1 did not need implementation. Dutch civil procedure already has of a variety of provisions on provisional seizure (Articles 700-770c CCP, Section II.C.2). As already mentioned, the pre-judgment seizure for the purpose of the surrendering goods is applicable in intellectual property cases, too.[72] The government was of the opinion that the new provisions on the seizure of evidence and the report of findings under Article 1019b CCP, which are lighter variations of the ruling in Article 730 CCP, should be sufficient to replace the pre-judgment seizure for the purpose of surrendering goods in the future.[73]

---

70. Kamerstukken II, 2005-2006, 30 392, MvT, No. 3, p. 19-20.
71. Kamerstukken II, 2005-2006, 30 392, No. 6, p. 6.
72. See Subsection II.C.2.
73. Kamerstukken II, 2005-2006, 30 392, No. 6, p. 6. In my opinion, it is difficult to say, as yet, whether the seizure of evidence and the description compared to the seizure for the purpose of surrender or delivery of goods are lighter variations. Anyway, the seizure under Art. 730 CCP has not been used very often, and the seizure of evidence in the short period since May 2007 is already quite popular.

Therefore it was not necessary to implement the rule on physical seizure, because the corresponding judicial sequestration is regulated in Article 709 CCP.

Article 7 paragraph 2 requires adequate security or assurance to ensure compensation for any prejudice suffered by the defendant. This requirement is already regulated in Article 701 CCP.

Regulated too are, according to Article 7 paragraph 3, the remedies of revocation and a review of the provisional measures to preserve evidence if the applicant does not instigate, within a reasonable period, proceedings leading to a decision on the merits of the case; see the former Article 260 CCP. Article 260 CCP was the implementation of Article 50, paragraph 6 TRIPs. With the implementation of this Directive, Article 260 CCP has been replaced by Article 1019i CCP.

Article 7 paragraph 4, which contains a provision for appropriate compensation for any damage caused by those provisional measures, was implemented in Article 1019g CCP.

Article 1019g CCP is the general article on compensation of costs for all the situations contained in the Directive.

The optional provision of Article 7 paragraph 5, to protect witnesses' identity, was not implemented either, because Dutch civil law does not provide for this kind of protection. This kind of protection is only known in criminal cases. So, if a criminal organization engages in intellectual property infringements, criminal law should be applied instead of civil law.

b	*Article 1019b CCP*

i	Article 1019b paragraph 1 CCP

Because Dutch civil procedure was not acquainted with the seizure of evidence, Article 7, paragraph 1 of the Directive had to be implemented. Article 1019b paragraph 1 CCP reads that the '*voorzieningenrechter*'[74] is competent to grant permission for effective provisional measures to preserve evidence, upon an application by a party who, to support his claim, has shown that it is likely or plausible that his intellectual property right has been infringed or is about to the infringed. According to Article 7 paragraph 1 the *voorzieningenrechter* has a discretionary power to grant such provisional measures (The Article reads: the judicial authorities *may*). Because the *voorzieningenrechter* in the Dutch the *kort geding* procedure has this discretionary power, and because in *kort geding* conclusive evidence does not have to be adduced, it is enough that the applicant has sufficiently made a reasonable case.[75]

Such provisional measures may include, apart from the provisional measures already regulated in other provisions of the CCP, the seizure of evidence, the

---

74. The '*voorzieningenrechter*' is a special judge who hears the summary proceedings (*kort geding*).
75. The text of Art. 1019b CCP seems different from the text of Art. 6 of the Directive. The Dutch text was proposed by the Council for the Administration of Justice, because these words were already used in intellectual property procedures and in general in *kort geding* procedures.

detailed report of finding, or the taking of samples of the alleged infringing movables, and the materials, tools and documents which are used for the production of the infringing movables. Because the seizure of evidence is regulated in Article 1019b CCP, the seizure of evidence is now only possible in intellectual property cases.

Article 1019b paragraph 1 CCP presents a number of optional provisional measures, but the list of measures mentioned is not exhaustive. The regular provisional measures, mentioned in other parts of the CCP can also be requested in intellectual property cases. These measures are, for instance, the provisional hearing of witnesses (Article 186 et seq. CCP)[76] and of experts (Article 202 et seq. CCP).

The provisional measures taken in a special case should comply with the principles of proportionality and subsidiarity. Therefore, the court can decide whether the provisional measure requested does comply with these principles. The Dutch government is of the opinion that the physical seizure of the infringing goods is a far-reaching measure and for that reason it has implemented two less far-reaching provisional measures, namely the report of findings and the taking of samples.[77] The pre-trial seizure of the infringing goods can result in closing the business down, whereas with the description or the taking of samples the same evidence can be gathered without closing the business down.

ii   Case Law

In a Dutch decision of July 2007[78] an indication is given as to the scope of the provision 'on application by a party who has presented reasonably available evidence to support his/her claims that his/her intellectual property right [...] is about to be infringed'. The court considered that the threshold to order a seizure of evidence should be an easy one. Otherwise it would be almost impossible to grant these provisional measures. Following the seizure of evidence, in the *kort geding* procedure the applicant has to show that it is likely that his intellectual property right is about to the infringed. In this case the applicant did not produce any information to make it sufficiently plausible that his intellectual property right was about to be infringed and as a consequence the seizure of evidence was lifted.

iii   Article 1019b paragraph 2 CCP

According to Article 1019b paragraph 2 CCP the court may determine the report of findings, or the taking of samples as regulated in Article 1019d, has to take place and decide what happens with the samples afterwards. The bailiff has to follow the instructions of the court.

---

76. See: LJN: BA7783, Gerechtshof 's-Hertogenbosch, 21 Mar. 2007, in which the Court of Appeal allowed the provisional hearing of witnesses in a patent case.
77. The requirements for seizure of evidence, the description and the taking of samples are regulated in Arts 1019c and 1019d CCP.
78. Voorzieningenrechter 's-Gravenhage court, 25 Jul. 2007, LJN: BB2652, KG ZA 07-623, Abbott/Teva.

iv   Article 1019b paragraph 3 CCP

Article 1019b paragraph 3 CCP introduces the rule that provisional measures can be taken, if necessary without the other party having been heard, especially if it is likely that any delay will cause irreparable damage or in case there is a clear danger of embezzlement or loss of evidence. Although the ex parte seizure has already been regulated in Dutch civil procedure (Article 700, paragraph 2 CCP), this provision is explicitly included because, besides the seizure of movables, other provisional measures may exist in which it is less obvious that the other party might not be heard. Because the principle of equality of arms is not upheld in these provisional measures the court should exercise caution in allowing such measures. Although the Dutch law of seizure determines, even in ex parte decisions, that the court has competence to inform the judgment debtor beforehand about the seizure, unless there are very special circumstances of urgency, in legal practice this rule is no longer upheld because it involves the courts in a great deal of bureaucracy. All the more remarkable is the decision of The Hague court to reintroduce the possibility that a party can, beforehand, inform the court about his objections against provisional measures under the Articles 1019b and 1019e CCP.[79] Mention should be made of the fact that The Hague court has exclusive competence in patent and Community trademarks.

The way of notifying any provisional measures taken, and the possibility of a review, including the right to be heard under Article 7 second paragraph of the Directive, were not implemented because the CCP already provides for these. Under Article 702 paragraph 2 CCP the application and judicial leave together with the bailiff's notification are served on the judgment debtor. The possibility of a review is regulated in Article 705 CCP. The *voorzieningenrechter* who gave leave for the seizure can subsequently lift this order, e.g., if the seizure is invalid or if the seizure proves to be unnecessary.

v   Article 1019b paragraph 4 CCP

Finally, Article 1019b paragraph 4 CCP stipulates that leave for a provisional measure will not be given when the protection of secret information cannot be guaranteed.

The court has some discretionary power to grant leave. For instance, the court may decide in case of confidential information that the procedure will take place behind closed doors.[80] Another solution may be that the confidential information is placed with a third independent party, like a notary. Subsequently, an independent expert can decide which materials are relevant and can be disclosed.

---

79. <http://www.rechtspraak.nl/Gerechten/Rechtbanken/s-Gravenhage>. This experiment started on the day of the implementation of the directive in the Netherlands, 1 May 2007 is still operative. The objections have to be in writing, but might also be sent by electronic means: A.I.M. van Mierlo, Hoe zwart kan zwart zijn? Kleur in het recht, *WPNR* 6718 (2007): 611-612. See also Section III.C.2.c.i.

80. Kamerstukken II, 2005-2006, 30 392, No. 4, p. 3 and Arts 27 and 29 CCP.

c   *Article 1019c CCP: Requirements for the Seizure of Evidence*

The new provision 'seizure of evidence' is, according to Dutch procedural law, qualified as a protective measure. The seizure merely serves to protect any evidence needed to prove the infringement. But the seizure of evidence does deviate from the general system, namely that the pre-judgment seizure does not enter into the executory phase. As a consequence, after the decision is delivered in the procedure on the merits and this decision has become final and conclusive, the seizure is *ipso jure* lifted. The procedure on the merits is, as a rule, a request to order the halting the threatening infringement. If the court wants to view, in the procedure on the merits, the seized goods or one of the parties wants to put forward the seized goods as evidence, Dutch civil procedure has several alternatives. The court may, for instance, make an official visit to the spot (Article 201 CCP), or order an expert opinion (Article 194 CCP).

Although the seizure merely serves to protect any evidence needed to prove an infringement, in today's legal practice the seizor often asks the court to give permission to the sequestrator to investigate the goods to be seized. It is expressly noted that since the pre-judgment debtor is not heard, the courts do not have the competence to allow the request to have the seized goods investigated. If the seizor wants to investigate the seized evidence, he has to institute a separate procedure in *kort geding*. Another possibility mentioned is that if the request for seizure is granted, this may be subject to the condition that the procedure on the merits by which the evidence can be disclosed under Articles 843a and 1019a CCP will be instigated within fourteen days.[81]

i   Article 1019c paragraph 1 CCP

Article 1019c paragraph 1 CCP stipulates that the pre-judgment seizure of evidence takes place according to the general rules of seizure under Articles 700-710a CCP, except for Article 709, paragraph 3 CCP.[82] Article 709, paragraph 3 CCP determines that the court has competence to inform the judgment debtor beforehand about the seizure, unless there are very special circumstances of urgency. Contrary to Article 1019c paragraph 1, CCP, The Hague court recently decided to reintroduce the possibility that a party can, beforehand, inform the court about his objections against provisional measures under the Articles 1019b and 1019e CCP.[83]

---

81. De Beslagsyllabus, May 2007: internal rules for the courts on attachments or seizures, <www.rechtspraak.nl>.
82. The Directive obliges the seizure of evidence, irrespective where the evidence is located. In general the provisions on seizure are applicable to the infringing party himself, even when the infringing goods are situated with a third person. Only when the third person objects, are the provisions on garnishment applicable.
83. See Subsections III.C.2.b.iii and II.C.1.b.

ii   Article 1019c paragraph 2 CCP

Article 1019c paragraph 2 CCP refers to the situation in which the decision is given in the procedure on the merits and this decision has become final and conclusive. As a consequence, the seizure is *ipso jure* lifted. In case the seized goods were held in sequestration, the sequestrator has to return the goods to the judgment debtor, unless the court decides otherwise, at the request of the creditor. For instance, when the infringer is ordered to make a minor change to the infringing goods so that the infringement is lifted and the infringer can go on selling them.

The seized goods mentioned in Article 1019b CCP not only include the goods seized as evidence, but also other goods mentioned in Article 1019b CCP, namely the materials, tools and documents which were used for the production of the infringing movables.[84] What will happen to the seizure if the claim is rejected, is not regulated. One may assume, that the seizure is lifted *ipso jure* also, and the seizor will become liable for damages. The court can, at the request of the parties or ex officio, provide further instructions.[85]

d   *Article 1019d CCP: Report of Findings*

The detailed report of findings concerning the infringing goods, the materials and the instruments used in the production and/or distribution of these goods and the documents relating thereto, as well as the taking of samples are new to Dutch law. The report of findings might be used as evidence in the infringement procedure. The way in which this report is compiled is regulated in Article 1019d paragraph 1 CCP. The taking of samples is regulated in the second paragraph of the Article. The report of findings has to mention the courts' leave for this to be made.

i   Article 1019d paragraph 1 CCP

The description of the infringing goods, referred to in Article 1019b CCP, is done by the bailiff at the place where the goods are situated. The bailiff has to report immediately and precisely about the *alleged* infringing external characteristics, especially the amount, weight, and their nature. The report of findings concerning these characteristics is of importance regarding infringing goods. The description of materials and implements used in the production and/or distribution of these goods and the documents relating thereto, will be of a more general nature. One can think about the production and manufacturing processes, and the production number of goods by unit. Because in intellectual property cases one deals mainly with external characteristics, the description can also be done by photographic evidence or tape recording, and copies of technical drawings added to the report of findings. Not allowed is copying the administration or other documents regarding the infringement. A description is not the same as copying on a one-to-one base. If a complete text is necessary, the creditor has to request the seizure of that text.

---

84. Kamerstukken II, 2005-2006, 30 392, MvT, No. 3, p. 22.
85. For a corresponding provision see Art. 1019d para. 3 CCP, Section III.C.2.d.iii.

It is important to note that the report of findings not only concerns the infringing characteristics but also the *alleged* infringing characteristics. This results in not only the description of similarities, but also of the differences in the goods protected by the intellectual property right. The government was of the opinion that a description of both the similarities and the differences was necessary to be able to answer the principal question in the infringement procedure, namely, whether there is an infringement at all.[86]

Because of the special position of the bailiff in the report of findings procedure, some general provisions that refer to the duties of the bailiff are applicable mutatis mutandis. These provisions relate to the requirements concerning the seizure, the description of the seized goods, entry to every place necessary, and the obligation to cooperate by third persons (Articles 440 paragraph 2, 443, 444, 444a and 444b CCP). Pursuant to these Articles, the bailiff may be joined by an expert. On the other hand, the party requesting the report of findings is not allowed to be present, unless the bailiff is of the opinion that the presence of this person is necessary (Article 443 paragraph 2 CCP). If the bailiff has to enter a closed place, he can request the help of the police to secure entry. The same holds true if the alleged infringing goods are held at the place of a third person. If that third person does not cooperate with the bailiff he can be fined.

ii   Article 1019d paragraph 2 CCP

The taking of samples by the bailiff is regulated in Article 1019d paragraph 2 CCP. The Articles on pre-judgment seizure are applicable mutatis mutandis, especially the provision concerning sequestration (Articles 700-710a).[87]

Sequestration in this sense means the taking of the goods to a place under the control of the sequestrator. The bailiff will not take more than three samples of each kind of goods, and hand these over to the sequestrator who is appointed by the court. If the court wants to see the samples, it may, if it so desires or at the request of one of the parties, summon the sequestrator to show the samples at the hearing.

iii   Article 1019d paragraph 3 CCP

Article 1019d paragraph 3 CCP refers to the situation in which the decision is given in the procedure on the merits and this decision has become final and conclusive. Then the sequestrator has to return the samples to the judgment debtor, unless the court decides otherwise, at the request of the creditor. The court may, ex officio, or at the request of each party, give further instructions. It can order that the handing over of the goods, and therefore also of the samples, has to be done in a particular way, e.g., by handing over the packaging without its contents.

---

86. Kamerstukken II, 2005-2006, 30 392, MvT, No. 3, p. 22.
87. The sequestrator is always a bailiff appointed for that purpose. Kamerstukken II, 2005-2006, 30 392, No. 6, p. 8.
      Art. 709 para. 3 CCP is not applicable. This means the seizure debtor will not be heard before the samples are taken.

Or the court can order that the infringing party shall slightly change the infringing goods, so that there is no longer any infringement and the assumed infringing party may carry on selling the goods; in that case the samples should be changed in the same way.

iv   Article 1019g CCP

Article 1019g CCP is a general article on compensation. It is at the same time the implementation of Articles 7 paragraph 4 and 9 paragraph 7 of the Directive, when compensation has to be paid for a wrongful seizure or the lifting of the seizure or where it is subsequently found that there has been no infringement of or a threat of infringing an intellectual property right (or measures to preserve evidence).

The Article concerns all the provisional measures under the new Title 15 CCP and under all the different intellectual property right Acts. Compensation can also be claimed under this Article for an injunction granted in *kort geding* regarding a real or future (threatened) infringement or for an injunction granted in *kort geding* against an intermediary who was found to be providing services used in infringing activities. If it is clear in the procedure on the merits that there was no infringement, the persons who had been earlier subjected to an injunction or other measure may claim compensation.

The Directive, in general, places the holders of an intellectual property right in a better position. The provision on compensation is meant to prevent these persons from taking too much advantage of their position at the expense of competitors.[88]

v   Case Law

In the Dutch case Synthon v. Astellas[89] in May 2007 the court granted leave for the seizure of, for preserving and for a report of findings concerning evidence under Articles 1019b, 1019c paragraph 1 and 1019d CCP. The court determined that the seized documents had to be transferred to a bailiff, who was appointed as the sequestrator. The sequestrator was allowed to make copies of the documents *for the benefit* of Astellas, the seizor, and furthermore the documents themselves had to be returned to the judgment debtor within seven days. According to the facts of the case, the bailiff submitted all the documents to the lawyer and patent agent of Astellas. The lawyer and patent agent made a report on the information, by making copies of the documents. This report was adduced as evidence in a German procedure. In the procedure of June 2007, the lifting of the seizure and the order to preserve and to compile a report of findings concerning the evidence was requested by Synthon. The court considered that it was too general, but the seizor had abused this leave by making copies of all the information. The seizure of evidence is meant to preserve the evidence, and not to enable the seizor to acquaint himself with all the industrial information. The leave to seize evidence does not automatically mean the right of inspection. On this

---

88. Kamerstukken II, 2005-2006, 30 392, MvT, No. 3, p. 25.
89. See under n. 62.

point, the leave was too general, and the court reviewed the decision under Article 1019e paragraph 3 CCP.

This judgment, which was delivered shortly after the implementation of the Directive, gave rise to a discussion in legal practice about the character of the seizure for the purpose of preserving evidence. Does it only mean preserving the evidence or also the right of inspection?

Probably a middle course will be adopted as mentioned under Section III.C.2.c. If the seizor wants to investigate the seized evidence, he has to institute a separate procedure in *kort geding* or the request for seizure has to state that the evidence should be disclosed on condition that the procedure on the merits by which the evidence can be disclosed under Articles 843a and 1019a CCP is instituted within fourteen days.

D   SECTION 3: RIGHT OF INFORMATION[90]

1   Article 8: Right of Information

a   Introduction

The right of information in Article 8 is already known in several intellectual property laws as far as this information concerns the origin of the goods which infringe an intellectual property right, and this information can be obtained from the infringing party. As far as this provision had not yet been incorporated in intellectual property laws, the provision is indeed now implemented.[91] However, Article 8 of the Directive states that the existing right of information is extended as regards the right of information about the origin of the goods and the distribution networks.[92] The Member State's obligation to introduce the right to request information about the distribution networks of the goods or services which infringe an intellectual property right, is also implemented in the different Dutch intellectual property laws.

Furthermore, in the opinion of the government, a provision had to be introduced to request information from third persons, who are not yet involved in a procedure.[93] This procedural provision is implemented in Article 1019f CCP.

---

90.   J.L.R.A. Huydecoper, 2004, see n. 8, is critical about the title 'Right of information', whereas Art. 8 of the Directive, merely concerns obligations to provide information.
91.   See Art. 28 para. 9 Copyright Act, which also includes the provision under Art. 8 para. 3(d) on declining to provide evidence. The same holds true for Art. 17 para. 6 Act on neighbouring rights; Art. 5c para. 5 Databases Act; Art. 18 para. 8 Act on topography and semiconductor products; Art. 70 para. 11, Seeds and Planting Materials Act and Art. 13a Agricultural Quality Act.
92.   See already the Supreme Court in 2005 on providing information by other chains in the distribution network: HR 25 Nov. 2005, RvdW 2005, 133, LJN: AU4019 (Lycos/Pessers).
93.   Kamerstukken II, 2005-2006, 30 392, MvT, No. 3, p. 12.

The Explanatory Report mentions that a third person, who possesses infringing goods or uses infringing services on a commercial scale, has to provide information about the origin of the goods and the distribution networks. According to the government, in this case one should distinguish between a third person in possession of the infringing goods or who uses the infringing services on a commercial scale, and by doing so, generally infringes the intellectual property right himself and a third person indicated by the person who is infringing as being involved in the production, manufacture or distribution of the goods or the provision of the services and who is providing services on a commercial scale, used in infringing activities, but is not involved in the infringement itself.[94]

The possibility of gathering information from every third party who is not yet involved in the procedure has been implemented in Article 1019f CCP. The right of information as regulated in Article 8 paragraph 3 of the Directive shall apply without prejudice to other statutory provisions which protect third parties against self-incrimination or protect the confidentiality of the information. Since the legislator does not refer to this provision in Article 1019f CCP, it will be up to the court to balance the claimant's right of information against the confidentiality of the information.[95]

b   *Article 1019f CCP: Right of Information*

Due to critical remarks from the Lower House of Parliament, the original proposal for a provision on the right of information was amended.[96] Originally, the right of information, as provided in Article 1019f CCP, concerned provisions on procedural law and substantive law. There was no clear division between them. The competence of the party entitled to claim information from a third party, who is not yet involved in a procedure, is now regulated in the different intellectual property laws.

Article 1019f CCP is limited to procedural rules. Implementation was considered to be necessary because procedural rules should be provided in the special situation in which a third party becomes involved in a procedure without proving evidence in this procedure. Until the implementation of the Directive, Dutch civil

---

94. Kamerstukken II, 2005-2006, 30 392, MvT, No. 3, p. 24. O. Delfos Visser & R. Brouwer, Wetsvoorstel Handhavingsrichtlijn: Nous ne maintiendrons pas!, *AMI* (2006): 77-83, are critical concerning the point of view of the government, which is later denied by the government itself. Because of this distinction, according to critics, the claimant cannot obtain information when the third person is not himself infringing. This might not have been the intention of the government because Art. 1019f CCP no longer makes this distinction.

95. The original proposal of Art. 1019f CCP included a paragraph on self-incrimination. Why this paragraph was deleted is not clear. However, the Explanatory Memorandum makes clear that the third person only has to provide information about the infringement concerning the distribution network and not about his own involvement (Kamerstukken II, 2005-2006, 30 392, MvT, No. 3, p. 25).

96. Kamerstukken II, 2005-2006, 30 392, No. 6, p. 7.

procedure only had a provision to hear witnesses.[97] Article 1019f includes paragraphs 1 and 2 CCP, in which the third party is indicated as being a witness.[98]

i   Article 1019f paragraph 1 CCP
Article 1019f paragraph 1 CCP stipulates:

> In the case where a claimant in an (infringement) procedure wants to obtain
> information from a third party, who was found to be in possession of, or
> using the infringing goods on a commercial scale, or was found to be using
> the infringing services on a commercial scale, or was indicated by one of the
> persons as being involved in the production, manufacture or distribution of the
> goods or the provision of the services, the court may, in response to a justified
> and proportionate request from the claimant, order a witness hearing, in which
> the third party has to give all the information, known to him, about the origin
> and distribution networks of the infringing goods or services. This hearing
> concerns only the information mentioned in para. 1 of this Article.

The party entitled under Article 1019f paragraph 1 CCP may involve every third
party who meets the requirements of Article 1019f paragraph 1 CCP in the procedure.[99] The third party might be a carrier or transporter. Furthermore, critical
remarks in the legal literature state that the purpose of the Directive is to make it
possible to obtain information especially from third parties like Internet Service
Providers who do not themselves disclose and are therefore not infringing the copyright. This is also in conformity with European and international regulations.[100]

The Dutch government is of the opinion that Article 8 of the Directive as well
as Article 1019f CCP offers the possibility to request information from intermediaries. But the request has to be made, according to Article 8 of the Directive: 'in
the context of proceedings concerning an infringement of an intellectual property
right'.[101]

There are different procedural ways of instituting a procedure against the
infringer and a third party. There will be no procedural obstacles if both parties,
the infringer and the third party, whose names are known, are involved in the
procedure at the same time. In this procedure, the court has to examine whether an
infringement has taken place and, if so, will subsequently allow the claim.

Article 1019f CCP does not make clarify in which way the claimant has to
call a third party who is not yet involved in the (infringement) procedure. Mention
is merely made that the third party has to be called to a provisional witness
hearing. The Explanatory Memorandum to the Act mentions that the claimant has

---

97. Kamerstukken II, 2005-2006, 30 392, MvT, No. 3, p. 13.
98. It is important to know whether somebody is a witness, because his testimony, according to
     civil procedural law, can be used as evidence (Art. 163 CCP).
99. Some members of Parliament were of the opinion that third persons, being Internet providers,
     were excluded from the obligation to provide information. Contrary to this point of view, Art.
     1019f CCP applies to all third persons, Kamerstukken II, 2005-2006, 30 392, No. 6, p. 6.
100. O. Delfos Visser and R. Brouwer, (AMI 2006), see n. 94.
101. Kamerstukken II, 2005-2006, 30 392, No. 6, p. 7.

to state his request for a provisional witness hearing in the summons and as a consequence the alleged infringer or the third party, not being an infringer, must be known.[102] The third party will be known if he is indicated by the person who is infringing as being involved in the production, manufacturing or distribution of the goods or the provision of the services.

However, it is not mentioned how the claimant has to summon a third party who is unknown. In Dutch civil procedure it is not possible to summon an unknown person.[103] The Explanatory Memorandum states that Article 1019f CCP is not intended to summon an Internet Service Provider merely to gather information concerning the owners of websites. To gather this kind of information the claimant has to start a *kort geding* procedure or a procedure on the merits. Critics are of the opinion that the implementation of Article 8 of the Directive is incorrect. The Dutch government should have taken into account a recent decision of the Supreme Court.[104] In the proper perspective of this decision, in an intellectual property case the existence of a preceding judgment should not be required. The Supreme Court decided that even when information is published on a website, and this information is not unmistakeably unlawful but might be unlawful, a service provider could be acting unlawfully if he does not, at the request of the claimant, provide information about the name and address or other kind of identity of the website owner.[105] The decision of the Supreme Court is further-reaching then the *lex specialis* of Article 1019f CCP. The consequence of the decision of the Supreme Court may be that, in intellectual property cases there might be more possibilities to obtain information than provided by the Directive.

The legal practice on intellectual property is not satisfied with the fact that only the provisional witness hearing may be followed to obtain information. Witness hearings can be lengthy and the claimant has to know exactly beforehand which person can provide the information needed. This might be a problem, especially concerning large-scale Internet providers.

Furthermore, infringements on the Internet almost always require urgent action. The hearing of a provisional witness will in that case take too much time, and is also quite expensive. For that reason, Article 1019f paragraph 2 CCP provides for an alternative to the provisional witness hearing.

ii   Article 1019f paragraph 2 CCP

For legal practice the provision of Article 1019f paragraph 2 is much more important. As an alternative to the provisional witness hearing, the witness may deliver

---

102. Kamerstukken II, 2005-2006, 30 392, MvT, No. 3, p. 24.
103. R.D. Chavannes, Effectief procederen tegen anonieme internetgebruikers, *NJB* (2007): 1816-1823, a Dutch 'John Doe procedure' is proposed in the case of an anonymous website owner.
104. HR 25 Nov. 2005, HR 25 Nov. 2005, RvdW 2005, 133, LJN: AU4019, Lycos/Pessers. Commentary by J.J.C. Kabel, IER 2006, No. 1, p. 1-3.
105. The Supreme Court considered that such an act was not unlawful if special conditions were met, e.g., the claimant could recover this information by other means.

the information meant in paragraph 2 in writing. This might be done together with or without a witness hearing.

E   SECTION 4: PROVISIONAL AND PRECAUTIONARY MEASURES

1   **Article 9: Provisional and Precautionary Measures**

a   *Introduction*

The greater part of Article 9 of the Directive did not need to be implemented. As mentioned earlier, the summary procedure, the *kort geding*, has proved to be very useful in intellectual property cases in which provisional measures are needed and meets almost all the requirements of Article 9 paragraph 1(a) of the Directive regarding the alleged infringer.[106] In *kort geding* a party may request an injunction and may always claim a penalty payment when the injunction is not adhered to (Article 611a-611i CCP).

However, the provision that, at the request of the applicant, the continuation of the alleged infringement could be made subject to the lodging of guarantees intended to ensure compensation for the rightholder, had to be implemented.[107] As far as the obligation exists to institute provisional measures against an intermediary whose services are used in committing the infringements, this obligation was not implemented in the Dutch CCP. This part of Article 9 paragraph 1 (a) of the Directive is formulated, in the opinion of the Dutch government, as a provisional measure, and therefore it was considered not to be necessary to restrict these claims to provisional measures. After all, urgent claims can always be instituted in a *kort geding* procedure. The claim against an intermediary was generally implemented according to Article 11 of the Directive, a provision which concerns both the procedure on the merits and the *kort geding* procedure. The same paragraph of Article 9 paragraph 1 (a) requires the introduction of a possibility to order an interlocutory injunction against an intermediary so as to prevent an alleged infringement or to forbid the continuation thereof or to subject the continuation of the alleged infringement to the lodging of guarantees intended to ensure the compensation of the rightholder. As far as Directive 2001/29/EC (on the harmonization of certain aspects of copyright and related rights in the information society) did not yet cover these requirements, this part of Article 9 paragraph 1 (a) was also implemented.[108] Pursuant to Directive 2001/29/EC,

---

106. Arts 254-259 CCP.
107. Provisions on compensation are regulated in Art. 1019g CCP and in different intellectual property right acts.
108. Regarding the implementation of provisions against intermediaries, the measures of Arts 9 and 11 Directive were, as far as necessary, implemented in the different Acts on intellectual property. Due to Directive 2001/29/EC the provision regarding guarantees by intermediaries was not implemented in the Copyright Act, the Neighbouring Rights Act or the Databases Act.

according to Article 6: 196c CC the rightholder can order internet service providers to delete information or block the website.

The seizure of goods suspected of infringing an intellectual property right, as provided for in Article 9 paragraph 1(b) of the Directive, is already regulated in Articles 700-710a and 730-737 CCP and in combination with the special Articles in the Acts on intellectual property which are in accordance with Article 9 paragraph 1(b), (see Subsections II.C.2 and III.C.2.a).[109]

Article 9 paragraph 2 allows for the precautionary seizure of the movable and immovable property of the alleged infringer, including the blocking of his/her bank accounts and other assets. To that end, the competent authorities may order the communication of bank, financial or commercial documents. There are several precautionary or pre-judgment forms of seizure to recover damages if it is likely that the debtor endangers the recovery of these documents in Dutch civil procedure, especially attachment by garnishment. Dutch civil procedure does not limit these forms of seizure to commercial parties, but they also apply to private parties. Implementation is therefore not necessary. However, according to the provisions of the Articles 718-723 and 475-479a CCP I doubt whether a bank is allowed to give the information mentioned in Article 9 paragraph 2 of the Directive.[110]

Article 9 paragraph 3 of the Directive stipulates that the applicant has to provide any reasonably available evidence that he is the rightholder and that his right is being infringed. This requirement is already regulated in the different intellectual property right Acts. The general principle of evidence is laid down in Article 150 CCP. Therefore the implementation of this provision is not necessary.

Article 9, paragraph 4 of the Directive was implemented in article 1019e CCP, because the *kort geding*, as regulated in Articles 254-259 CCP did not provide an answer to Article 9 paragraph 4. The *kort geding* is a contradictory procedure, which means that the debtor should always be summoned for an oral hearing. Article 1019e CCP now provides for the situation where the defendant is not heard. With regard to pre-judgment seizure, implementation is not necessary because in general the judgment debtor is not heard in the Netherlands (see for an exception Subsection III.C.2.b.iv). In the same way it is not necessary to implement the last sentence of paragraph 4: 'In that event, the parties shall be so informed without delay after the execution of the measures at the latest.' Dutch civil procedure stipulates under Article 430, paragraph 3 CCP that a decision against a debtor cannot be enforced before the decision is served on the debtor.

---

109. See e.g., Art. 28 Copyright Act.
110. The judgment creditor can only attach a bank account of the debtor if he has details of that bank account. At the moment of attachment he is usually not acquainted with the balance on the account. The bank will not inform the judgment creditor or the competent authorities (the bailiffs) about the balance of the account at the moment of garnishment. Within four weeks the bank has to inform the bailiff of the funds which, at the moment of garnishment, were available for attachment.

According to Article 9, paragraph 5 of the Directive provisional measures have to be revoked or otherwise cease to have effect, upon the request of the defendant, if the procedure on the merits is not instituted within a reasonable period. According to the former Article 260 CCP, which implemented Article 50 paragraph 1 TRIPs, and which was replaced by Article 1019i CCP, this is already provided.

The lodging of security as mentioned in Article 9 paragraph 6 is provided for in Article 701 CCP in the case of pre-judgment seizure. Although, in principle, the lodging of security may, according to Article 235 CCP, be requested in the *kort geding* procedure, this provision will also be implemented in Article 1019e paragraph 2 CCP.[111]

Article 9 paragraph 7 of the Directive is also implemented in article 1019g CCP which provides rules on damages.

b   *Article 1019e CCP*

i   Article 1019e paragraph 1 CCP
As already mentioned, of the provisional and precautionary measures mentioned in Article 9 paragraph (a) and (b), only the provisional measure in which the defendant does not have to be heard had to be implemented.

Article 1019e CCP provides for the procedural rules which have to be followed in this so-called ex parte *kort geding*.[112]
Article1019e CCP reads:

> In urgent cases, especially if a delay would cause irreparable harm for the holder of the intellectual property right, the *voorzieningenrechter* on request[113] has competence to render an immediate provisionally enforceable decision against the alleged infringer and to issue an order to prevent a threatening infringement of the holder's intellectual property right without calling the alleged infringer.

The Explanatory Memorandum mentions that it is not quite clear what has to be understood by 'irreparable harm'. It may be that the Court of Justice will in the future have to decide what the words 'irreparable harm' mean in the case of an imminent infringement of an intellectual property right.

Article 1019e CCP procedure will commence upon request and will be instituted with the *voorzieningenrechter* of the District Court. The start of this procedure by a request deviates from the start of the *kort geding* procedure in general, and therefore from the interlocutory injunction as mentioned in Article 9 paragraph 1(a) of the Directive. In the *kort geding* procedure, as a general interlocutory

---

111. In legal practice, security in *kort geding* is not often ordered by the court.
112. If the *lex specialis* of Art. 1019e CCP does not suffice, the general provisions on *kort geding* will apply.
113. 'On request' means: by request, contrary to the summons in the general (*kort geding*) contradictory procedure.

injunction in which the defendant is heard, the defendant has to be summoned by the bailiff. The content of the request is limited to a restraining order. The claims that can normally be requested in *kort geding*, or in a procedure on the merits, are left to one side because the defendant cannot defend himself. If the request is dismissed, the applicant can appeal against the dismissal, or can still commence the general *kort geding* procedure by having the bailiff serve a summons. Even if the case is urgent, the dismissal does not have to lead to real problems, because the *voorzieningenrechter* can already set a date for the new procedure.

ii   Article 1019e paragraph 2 CCP
Article 1019e paragraph 2 CCP explicitly states that the *voorzieningenrechter* can allow the request subject to the condition that security is paid. The amount of the security will be determined by the court.

iii   Article 1019e paragraph 3 CCP
After the decision has been served on the defendant (by the bailiff), the alleged infringer can require that the decision be reviewed. A review must take place in a *kort geding* procedure, which is comparable with the lifting of an attachment in a *kort geding* procedure under Article 705 CCP (see Subsection II.C.2)

iv   Case Law
Several decisions have been delivered under Article 1019e CCP. The applicant has to state and present the necessary information to justify that any delay would cause irreparable harm. In the case of Paletti, the court order was given on the same day as the request was made.[114] The order also stated the period within which the procedure on the merits according to Article 1019i CCP and Article 50 paragraph 6 TRIPs had to be instituted. Remarkable is the fact that the court imposed a penalty payment in case of non-compliance. Since Article 1019e CCP does not mention otherwise, the legislator is of the opinion that the court may only allow the order, and no other claims could be allowed.[115] Legal practice, however, is uncertain whether a penalty payment can be requested.

Recently, in a Community trademark case The Hague Court made an order under Article 1019e CCP which seems to be the general practice in the Hague court nowadays.[116] It does not mean that other courts in the Netherlands follow the same practice when giving orders under Article 1019e CCP. In this case the order was issued subject to the following conditions.

As has already been mentioned above the order stated the period within which the procedure on the merits according to Article 1019i CCP and Article 50 paragraph 6 TRIPs had to be instituted and also imposed a penalty payment of

---

114.   Voorzieningenrechter The Hague Court, 7 Jun. 2007 <www.Boek9.nl>.
115.   Kamerstukken II, 2005-2006, 30 392, MvT, No. 3, p. 23.
116.   Voorzieningenrechter The Hague Court, 14 Feb. 2008, KG RK 08/0243, Westland Kaas-Groep BV/Roos. The Hague Court has exclusive competence in patent and Community trademark cases, see Section II.C.1.b.

300 Euros for each infringing product (cheese) in case of non-compliance. Furthermore, the court decided that the order, together with the request, should be served on the other party no later than 16 February 2008. The order also mentioned that the court (voorzieningenrechter) had already set a date and an hour for the review (on 20 February, at 2 pm) if the infringing party wished to have the order reviewed. This is a new practice which has never been previously used. If the infringing party wanted a review, it had to serve the writ on the requesting party on 19 February, at 2 pm at the latest.

F   SECTION 5: MEASURES RESULTING FROM A DECISION ON THE MERITS OF THE CASE

1   **Article 10: Corrective Measures**

a   *Introduction*

Article 10 paragraph 1 of the Directive requires that at the request of the applicant, appropriate measures should be taken with regard to infringing goods and in appropriate cases goods used in the creation or manufacturing of these goods.

Such measures may include the recall of the infringing goods from the distribution channels, the definite removal of these distribution channels or the destruction of these goods.

According to Article 10 paragraph 2, the measures taken under Article 10 paragraph 1 are to be carried out at the expense of the infringer, unless there are particular reasons for deciding otherwise.

After all, Article 10 paragraph 3, requires proportionality between the seriousness of the infringement and the remedies ordered as well as taking the interest of third parties into consideration.

b   *Implementation in Intellectual Property Acts*

The corrective measures listed in Article 10, paragraphs 1, 2 and 3 of the Directive with regard to the goods already exist in most of the Dutch intellectual property Acts. The different intellectual property Acts were supplemented with the provisions mentioned in Article 10. Article 28 paragraph 1 Copyright Act, for instance, was extended with the provision that corrective measures can also be taken with regard to the materials and implements principally used in the creation or manufacturing of the goods in question. The corrective measures include the recall of the goods as well as their definitive removal from distribution channels,[117]

---

117. The Supreme Court in Hameco, 23 Feb. 1990, NJ 1990, 664, with a note by DWFV, accepted the recall of infringing goods. It should be mentioned that it might be problematic to recall goods that have already been sold. As an option, the infringer, possible by mail, must inform buyers that, if they do not return the goods, the rightholder will take action against them.

measures which are already mentioned in Article 28 paragraph 1. Whether the removal of the goods from distribution channels is definitive or temporary depends on the claim, the judgment, and the intention of the rightholder, because it is the rightholder himself who may decide what will be done with the claimed infringing goods.

Article 28 paragraph 5 Copyright Act, which stipulated that the applicant had to pay for the handing over of the goods, had to be deleted since Article 10 of the Directive determines that the corrective measures should be taken without prejudice to any damages due to the rightholder by reason of the infringement, and without compensation of any sort. The provision regulating the costs of these corrective measures is now implemented in Article 28 paragraph 4 of this Act.

Therefore, Article 28 paragraph 4 Copyright Act now implements Article 10 paragraph 2 of the Directive: the measures mentioned in paragraph 1 will be carried out at the expense of the infringer, unless there are particular reasons for not doing. By calculating the legal costs under Article 1019h CCP the court has to consider whether there are particular reasons in the sense of Article 28 paragraph 4 CCP to do so.

Article 10 paragraph 3 was eventually implemented in Article 28 paragraph 8 Copyright Act: in considering a request from the rightholder or his agent for corrective measures, as mentioned in the paragraphs 1, 2 and 7, the court shall take into account the need for proportionality between the seriousness of the infringements and the remedies ordered as well as the interests of third parties.[118]

Article 10 paragraphs 1, 2 and 3 of the Directive were implemented in the intellectual property Acts mentioned, but not, generally, in the CCP.[119]

2   Article 11: Injunctions

a   *Introduction*

Article 11 of the Directive requires that an injunction can be issued against the infringer aimed at prohibiting the continuation of the infringement. Noncompliance with an injunction shall, where appropriate, be subject to a recurring penalty payment, with a view to ensuring compliance.

This provision is already present in the different Dutch intellectual property Acts, together with the articles on tort (Articles 6: 162 etc. CC) and Article 3: 296 CC. Article 3: 296 CC stipulates that the court, at the request of the person entitled, can order the party who is obliged to give something, to do something, or not to do something, to do so.

The penalty payment is provided for in the Articles 611a-i CCP.

---

118. Art. 10 of the Directive was implemented in the same way in the other intellectual property Acts.
119. Kamerstukken II, 2005-2006, 30 392, MvT, No. 3, p. 26.

b   *Implementation in Intellectual Property Acts*

The last sentence of Article 11 requires Member States to ensure that rightholders are in a position to apply for an injunction against intermediaries whose services are used by third parties to infringe an intellectual property right.

Only this part of Article 11 was implemented in the different intellectual property Acts. An example thereof is Article 26d of the Copyright Act. The injunction is solely aimed at prohibiting the continuation of the infringement. The court will have to weigh the interests of the intermediary and the rightholder. It has to take into account the contribution or the involvement of the intermediary with regard to the infringement and whether the intended purpose of the claim and the interests of the rightholder are more important than the disadvantage for the intermediary, or the harm it will cause to that person. The intermediary should also be able to fulfil the claim, without incurring disproportionate costs. If the claim can be served on the infringer himself without too many obstacles, the claim against the intermediary should be rejected. So, the claim against the intermediary must have an autonomous aim that cannot be achieved in any other way via the infringer himself.[120]

G   SECTION 6: DAMAGES AND LEGAL COSTS

1   **Article 13: Damages**

a   *Introduction*

Article 13 of the Directive is almost completely provided for in different Dutch laws. Article 6: 162 (Civil Code) CC is the general basis to claim damages and applies to the infringer who knowingly engaged in an infringing activity, or should reasonably have known that he was engaging in such activity. To claim damages under Article 6: 162 CC the defendant should be accountable for his actions. Under Article 6: in 96 paragraphs 1 and 2 CC financial losses may be claimed, as well as emotional damages pursuant to Article 6: 106 CC. Furthermore, intellectual property acts, like the Copyright Act, provide for special rules on damages.

Article 13 of the Directive provides for two methods in which the damages, to be paid by the infringer, can be determined by the court. Pursuant to Article 13 paragraph 1(a) damages are determined by taking into account all appropriate aspects, such as the negative economic consequences, including lost profits, which the injured party has suffered, any unfair profits made by the infringer and, in appropriate cases, elements other than economic factors, such as emotional damage. As already said, paragraph 1(a) does not need to be implemented, because the general article on damages, Article 6: 106 CC already provides for this kind of moral damages. In different Acts on intellectual property, damages for moral prejudice can also be taken into account.

---

120.   Kamerstukken II, 2005-2006, 30 392, MvT, No. 3, p. 26.

Article 13 paragraph 1(b) of the Directive sets the damages as a lump sum on the basis of elements such as at least the amount of royalties or fees which would have been due if the infringer had requested authorization to use the intellectual property right in question. The determination of damages, especially in intellectual property cases, is set out in Article 6: 95 etc. CC. The surrender of profits is regulated in several intellectual property Acts.

Articles 27 and 27a Copyright Act provide for damages as well as the surrender of profits. Nonetheless, Article 13 paragraph 1(b), providing competence to fix a lump sum, was implemented in different intellectual property acts.

Article 13 paragraph 2 of the Directive is an optional provision. This paragraph, which allows damages to be claimed from an infringer who knowingly engaged in infringing activities, or should reasonably have known that he was engaging in such activities, is not in conformity with Dutch law.[121] As mentioned, to claim damages under Article 6: 162 CC the defendant should be accountable for his actions. Therefore, this paragraph will not be implemented.

b   *Implementation in Intellectual Property Acts*

In Article 27 Copyright Act a new paragraph 2 has been inserted which explicitly states that, in appropriate cases, the court can set the damages by way of a lump sum. Furthermore, Article 13 paragraph 1(b) is implemented in the Neighbouring Rights Act under Article 16, in the Database Act under Article 5d, and in Article13a paragraph 5 of the Agricultural Quality Act.

2   Article 14: Legal Costs

a   *Introduction*

Article 14 of the Directive stipulates that reasonable and proportionate legal costs and other expenses incurred by the successful party shall, as a general rule, be borne by the unsuccessful party, unless equity does not allow this. Contrary to the provision of Article 14 the Explanatory Report mentions that the legal costs and other expenses incurred by the successful party shall be borne by the unsuccessful party. For that reason the government was of the opinion that Article 14 had to be implemented, which took place in Article 1019h CCP.[122] Furthermore, it is not clear why the Explanatory Report did not mention the restriction that the legal costs should be reasonable and proportionate, although in Article 1019h CCP the requirements 'reasonable' and 'proportionate' have been inserted. Legal practice, when confronted with the explanation in the Explanatory Report, started to claim in intellectual property cases all the legal and extrajudicial costs already from the

---

121.   This is a translation of the Dutch official text of the Directive. The official English text reads: 'did not knowingly, or with reasonable grounds knowingly, engage in infringing activity …'.
122.   Kamerstukken II, 2005-2006, 30 392, MvT, No. 3, p. 16.

date of implementation, as set by the Directive.[123] These claims were, in many cases, awarded by the courts.

This practice gave rise, during the legislative procedure, to questions in the Upper House. The Memorandum of Reply[124] emphasizes the importance of flexibility in awarding legal costs and other expenses in intellectual property cases.[125] Although this point of view is not unreasonable, it is not in conformity with the compensation of costs in civil procedures in general.

Legal literature has ventured the opinion that this practice is also contrary to the principle of legal certainty, because the full compensation of legal and extra-judicial costs is a too abrupt deviation from the compensation of costs by Dutch courts in general.[126]

Moreover, one can state that the Dutch government is not consistent in its point of view with regard to legal costs and other expenses. This might be illustrated on the basis of the following example. Directive 2000/35/EC[127] states in Article 3 paragraph 1(e):

> Unless the debtor is not responsible for the delay, the creditor shall be entitled to claim reasonable compensation from the debtor for all relevant recovery costs incurred through the latter's late payment. Such recovery costs shall respect the principles of transparency and proportionality as regards the debt in question. [...].

At that time, the Dutch government was of the opinion that this provision did not need to be implemented because Dutch law was in conformity with this paragraph of the Directive. There was quite some disagreement concerning the point of view taken by the Minister of Justice.[128]

The government does not explain why, a few years later, the same way of calculating the legal costs and other expenses by a European instrument is no longer in conformity with Dutch law.

b   *Article 1019h CCP*

Article 1019h CCP stipulates:

> If necessary and contrary to the provisions on costs [in civil procedure], as laid down in Articles 237-245 and Article 843a para. 1 CCP, the unsuccessful

123. See also Sections I and I.A.
124. Kamerstukken I, 2006-2007, 30 392, C.
125. Mention is made, referring to the proposal of the Directive, COM (2003) 46 def., of which costs can be claimed.
126. M. Driessen, De willekeur van de proceskostenveroordeling, *Bijblad Industriële Eigendom* (2007): 343-350.
127. Directive 2000/35/EC of 29 Jun. 2000 on combating late payments in commercial transactions: OJ 2000, L 200/35.
128. M. Freudenthal, Implementation of the Directive on Late Payments in the Netherlands, in *La Armonización del Derecho de Obligaciones en Europa*, eds F. Badosa Coll & E. Arroyo i Amayuelas (Valencia: Tirant Lo Blanch, 2006), 407-427.

party will, upon request, be ordered to pay the reasonable and proportionate legal and other expenses incurred by the successful party, unless equity does not allow this.

The government was of the opinion that Article 14 of the Directive obliges a broad compensation of costs. In the Netherlands the statutory rules on the compensation of court fees is laid down in Articles 237-245 CCP. Although Article 237 CCP determines that the party which is declared to be the unsuccessful party in the judgment should be ordered to pay the costs of the action, in legal practice the successful party will only receive part of the costs which he has incurred, especially where it concerns lawyers' fees. This is due to a special non-statutory recommendation called *liquidatietarief* (court-approved scale of costs) and which is normally followed by the courts.[129]

The court-approved scale of costs determines the fees of lawyers by using two parameters. The first parameter relates to the activities of the lawyer. Each of his activities is valued by a number of points. The second parameter relates to the subject of the claim. These points are expressed in monetary terms depending on the kind of claim or in the case of a monetary claim on the amount of the claim. For instance, for pleading the lawyer is given two points. If the money claim is, for instance is less than 10,000 Euros, a point is worth 384 Euros. Even if the lawyer claims a fee of 1500 Euros, the court will merely award 768 Euros.

The compensation of extrajudicial costs is regulated under Article 6: 96 paragraph 2 sub. b and c CC. The compensation of these costs is subject to even greater vagueness. By virtue of this provision extrajudicial costs may be claimed as far as they are reasonable. This provision is limited to the extent that these costs are not taken into account as court costs (Article 241 CCP). So, the statutory rule under Article 6: 96 paragraph 2 sub. c, CC distinguishes between extrajudicial costs and court fees. For legal practice this distinction is important because in principle the *liquidatietarief* does not apply to extrajudicial costs and as a consequence these costs should be fully compensated.[130] However, in legal practice there is a non-statutory recommendation which provides rules concerning the awarding of extrajudicial costs.[131]

This recommendation is generally applied by the courts. Although this recommendation was intended to harmonize the awarding of extrajudicial costs, in legal practice the result is the opposite of harmonization. Due to Article 242 CCP the judge can, if he is of the opinion that these costs are too high, mitigate the amount of the extrajudicial costs or even not award any extrajudicial costs at all. The discretionary competence of the judge to mitigate the amount of the

---

129. This *liquidatietarief* was approved by the Netherlands Bar Association and the Netherlands Association for the Judiciary.
130. Another problem is as long as this provision is used by the judiciary there are different opinions between the judiciary and legal practice concerning the activities that are to be included in court costs and which costs are included in extrajudicial costs.
131. This recommendation, entitled 'rapport Voor-werk II', has been approved by the Netherlands Association for the Judiciary.

extrajudicial costs may even set aside an agreement between the parties concerning extrajudicial costs.[132]

Although there is a great deal of opposition regarding the renumeration of lawyers' fees and extrajudicial costs, the government was convinced, up until the implementation of the Directive on enforcement of intellectual property rights, that no changes would have to be made.

According to Article 1019h CCP the regime of compensating costs in intellectual property cases will be different from the provisions in other civil cases. The court will have to check whether the costs are reasonable and fair. Reasonableness may be taken into account in the order to pay costs if the infringer has acted in a bona fide manner. In that case the order to pay costs can be based on the current rules for the renumeration of costs, as described before. On the other hand, for commercial infringements, according to the provision of Article 1019h CCP, all the legal costs and other expenses may be awarded.[133] It has been discussed by scholars whether this point of view is in accordance with Article 14 of the Directive, because the Directive is not explicitly limited to commercial infringements or piracy (see Article 2 paragraph 1 and recital 13) and if the Directive is limited to commercial infringements, it explicitly states this (see Articles 8 and 13).[134]

Under Article 1019h CCP the court can, at the request of the claimant, award the costs for lawyers, representatives, and experts, which could not be claimed under Article 6: 96, paragraph 2, sub. b or c CC. Furthermore, a claim under Article 6: 96 CC can only be instituted by the claimant, whereas under Article 1019h CCP every successful party can claim the more liberal compensation of costs.

i   Case Law
According to the case law, the courts are not consistent concerning the compensation of costs. The reason for this inconsistency is the double-check on the reasonableness and the proportionality of the costs on the one hand, and the fairness of the costs on the other. This leaves a lot of room for the courts to determine the costs, and as a consequence legal certainty is at stake. Recent case law has shown that, for successfully compensating costs, it is important that the parties have to provide for a clear insight into the costs requested. If the costs are not well-founded the court may award merely a part of the costs.

In a *kort geding* procedure, the District court in The Hague decided that the claimant probably would not have a solid case in the procedure on the merits. For

---

132. The Supreme Court already decided on 22 Jan. 1993, NJ 1993, 597 that such an agreement is valid. Nonetheless, the judiciary and the Supreme Court almost always decide otherwise: HR 11 Jul. 2003, NJ 2003, 566, where the party had to pay 15% of the debt as extrajudicial costs, which is considered to be a normal percentage, was set aside by the judge and the Supreme Court upheld the decision.
133. Kamerstukken II, 2005-2006, 30 392, MvT, No. 3, p. 26.
134. D.J.G. Visser & A. Tsoutsanis, De volledige proceskostenveroordeling in IE-zaken, *NJB* (2006): 1940-1946.

that reason, the court decided that the successful party mentioned in Article 14 not only refers to the claimant, but also to the defendant. After all, Article 14 mentions 'the successful party' and the costs borne by the 'unsuccessful party'. Therefore, the defendant will be compensated for costs.[135]

H   SECTION 7: PUBLICITY MEASURES

1   Article 15: Publication of Judicial Decisions

a   Introduction

Article 15 stipulates that in legal infringement procedures, the judicial authorities may order, at the request of the applicant and at the expense of the infringer, appropriate measures for the dissemination of the information. These measures are meant to deter future infringers and to contribute to the awareness of the public at large.

b   Implementation in Intellectual Property Acts

The publication of judicial decisions is already present in Civil procedural law. It is quite usual for the publication of the judgment to be ordered or an order is given to inform buyers by mail. The provision is implemented in several intellectual property Acts.

Article 28 Copyright Act will be supplemented with a new paragraph 10. Publication may take different forms, e.g., an advertisement in a newspaper, periodical or journal, or through a press release, or as already mentioned by mail to persons who have been, involved with the infringement in the past, such as distributors or the retailers of the infringing goods.

IV   ARTICLES OF THE DIRECTIVE WHICH HAVE NOT
           BEEN IMPLEMENTED

A   INTRODUCTION

Although the general opinion in the doctrine was that Dutch law was already fairly in conformity with this Directive, several changes have taken place. As we have seen before, Articles 1019-1019h CCP will have quite some impact not only on the enforcement of intellectual property rights, but also on Dutch civil procedural law in general. A few Articles of the Directive have not been implemented. They will be discussed shortly in this section. Before doing so, Article 1019i CCP, which is the last Article in the new title 15 of the CCP, will be discussed

---

135.   Voorzieningenrechter The Hague Court, 8 Aug. 2006, KG ZA 06-619, Visser/Heto.

1   **Article 1019i CCP: Article 50 paragraph 1 TRIPs**

Article 1019i CCP was not mentioned in the foregoing section because it is not a
new article. Article 1019i CCP replaces Article 260 CCP which is the implementation of Article 50 paragraph 1 TRIPs. The text of Article 1019i CCP is exactly
the same as Article 260 CCP. Until the implementation of the Directive, Article
260 CCP was one of the provisions concerning the *kort geding*. Although the text
of Article 1019i CCP is the same, by replacing Article 260 with Title 15, Book 3
CCP, the Article will not merely relate to the *kort geding* but to all intellectual
property rights procedures which are covered by Title 15. For trade names, it will
mean a change because they did not fall within the TRIPs Convention.

a   *Case Law*

A *kort geding* decision in an intellectual property case was strengthened with a
penalty payment. The defendant in the procedure invoked his right to declare that
the provisional measures, including the penalty payment, be revoked or otherwise
cease to have effect under Article 260 paragraph 1 CCP (replaced by Article 1019i
CCP). It is clear that the proceeding leading to a decision on the merits of the case
was not instituted within the time decided by the court. Although the defendant
was of the opinion that the penalty payment had ceased to have retroactive effect,
the court of appeal decided otherwise. Article 260 paragraph 1 and Article 1019i
CCP stipulate that provisional measures will cease to have effect at the moment
the defendant's declaration is submitted. This does mean that the declaration does
not have retroactive effect, and the forfeited penalty payments will also not cease
to have effect.[136]

In a case discussed already under subsection III.C.2.b.ii the court decided that
a seizure of evidence under Article 1019a CCP does have to be followed by a
procedure on the merits. A procedure, like the *kort geding* procedure, being a provisional measure itself, does not suffice.[137]

B   SECTION 1: ARTICLES 3 AND 4 DIRECTIVE, GENERAL
                  PROVISIONS

Article 3 paragraphs 1 and 2 obliges Member States to provide for measures, procedures, and remedies which are necessary to ensure the enforcement of intellectual property rights. Those measures, procedures and remedies have to be fair and
equitable and not unnecessarily complicated or costly. They should be effective,
proportionate and dissuasive. The parties cannot invoke the provision
themselves.

---

136. Hof Arnhem, 13 Feb. 2007, JBPr 2007/49, Test & Drive/Veka Best.
137. Voorzieningenrechter The Hague, 25 Jul. 2007, LJN: BB2652, Abbott/Teva. The court
      referred to the decision of the CJEC, 16 Jun. 1998, C-53/96, Hermès.

The optional Article 4 concerns the persons entitled to apply for the application of the measures, procedures and remedies. This Article has also not been implemented. As for the holders of intellectual property rights, according to Article 4 (a) it is out of the question that these persons are entitled to all procedures and measures to enforce their rights. The rightholder himself will have to decide against which person(s) he will take action and which procedural measures he wants to utilize. The rightholder may also confer on a professional defence body by proxy the right to act against infringements and to appear in the proceedings. Which persons amount to rightholders is regulated in the different intellectual property rights Acts. The same holds true for the licensee under Article 4 (b). It should be noted that, according to Dutch law, the licensee is not allowed to act independently against an infringement. This depends on the consent of the rightholder and the conditions of the licensee contract. The Directive does not oblige one to deviate from national law.

Furthermore, under Article 4 (c) and (d), officially recognized collective rights-management bodies and professional defence bodies who represent the holders of intellectual property rights may be entitled to take action against infringements. Dutch law, in Article 3: 305a CC, provides for a general provision on collective claims. This Article, in the opinion of the Dutch government, offers sufficient opportunities for collective claims.[138] Anyway, it is up to the rightholder to allow himself to be legally represented by these professional defence bodies.

C   ARTICLE 12: ALTERNATIVE MEASURES

The optional provision of Article 12 has not been implemented either. This provision permits pecuniary compensation to be ordered instead of the measures provided for in Articles 10 and 11, if the person acted unintentionally and without negligence, if the execution of the measures as mentioned in Articles 10 and 11 would cause disproportionate harm and if pecuniary compensation to the injured party appears reasonably satisfactory. Article 12 has not been implemented as it is not in conformity with Dutch law. There is no Dutch statutory rule which allows compensation to be ordered if a person is not responsible. In the literature another objection is made. Article 10 paragraph 3 of the Directive already provides for the principle of proportionality. To introduce a double proportionality check would be undesirable, especially in intellectual property cases. In legal practice, an injunction is almost always awarded to the rightholder so that he can prohibit the continuation of the infringement, even if the defendant is not responsible.[139]

---

138.   Kamerstukken II, 2005-2006, 30 392, MvT, No. 3, p. 11. Since 2005 Dutch procedural law contains the possibility of a 'class-action': Arts 1013-1018 CCP.
139.   C. Gielen, De richtlijn handhaving IE-rechten, *NTER* (2005): 6-11.

Chapter 4

Implementation of Directive 2004/48/EC in English Civil Procedure

I   IMPLEMENTATION

As noted in Chapter 2, the correct implementation of a directive comprises three closely related but nevertheless distinguishable issues: the first concerns the content of the measures which are adopted with a view to implementation; the second relates to the requirements regarding the nature of these measures; and the third relates to their effective application and enforcement in practice.

More generally, the Member States must decide which body is to be charged with the responsibility of applying a directive. Further and in particular, the Member States must act in conformity with the obligations laid down therein. In this respect, the requirements of clarity and precision of the implementing measures and legally binding nature are crucial for avoiding their misapplication: in short, the requirements imposed by the European Court of Justice (ECJ)[1] as to the content of the measures and their nature must guarantee the correct application of a directive. The very purpose of directives is their implementation in national law. As a rule, therefore, their provisions should apply within the national legal order in their converted form, i.e., as provisions of national law.

Apart from some rather isolated instances of harmonization of different procedural aspect such a Regulation 2913/92 European Economic Community (EEC), two kinds of situations occur in Community law: either no provisions on procedure and remedies are established or the Member States are obliged by some very generally worded provisions to provide for judicial protection in the area concerned. In principle, it would not seem to be important whether there are some very

---

1.   Cases such as: *Commission v. Germany*, Case No. C-131/88 (1991) ECR I 825, *Commission v. Germany* Case C-59/89 (1991) ECR I 2607, *Commission v. Italy*, Case No. C-306 /91 (1993) ECR I 2133.

general provisions or no provisions at all as the former are usually rather non-committal. In both situations it is left to the Member States to determine the competent courts and to lay down rules for the legal proceedings in which Community law is to be enforced.[2] Whenever a directive has not been correctly implemented or has not been implemented at all, an individual may find that although a provision exists which should be considered to be a part of the national legal order and which is intended to grant him rights or to allow him to benefit in other ways, the Member State's inadequate action or inaction appears to prevent him from exercising his rights or at least from enjoying full implementation of a directive. In such a situation the individual may have to resort to a national court with a view to compelling observance of a particular directive. As noted earlier in Chapter 2, in order to so do, the national courts may make recourse to three concepts which have been developed by the ECJ in the event of either an incorrect transposition or an absence of a transposition of a directive: that is, the doctrine of direct effect, the interpretation of national law in conformity with the directive and the principle of State liability for harm caused to individuals by breaches of Community law. More generally, it is to be noted that directives may be implemented either by specific new legislation or by current existing legislation which the national court has a duty to interpret in conformity with the obligations contained within a particular directive.

In England and Wales, patent and registered design litigation is conducted in accordance with the Civil Procedure Rules (CPR) except where CPR Part 63 or Practice Direction (PD) 63 provides otherwise in according with the Chancery Guide. The Patents Court is thus part of the Chancery Division of the High Court.[3] Section 97 of the Patents Act (1977) (the Act) provides for appeals to the Patents Court from many decisions of the comptroller under the Act or rules. Many other sections of the 1977 Act provide for proceedings, e.g., concerning alleged infringement of patents, to be brought in the court. With respect to England and Wales, the expression in the Act, 'the court', refers to the High Court where proceedings involve either the Patents Court or the Patents County Court (PCC).[4] Under section 61 of the Supreme Court Act (SCA) 1981 and Schedule 1 to that Act, all causes and matters in the High Court which concern patents trade marks, registered designs or copyright are assigned to the Chancery Division. Proceedings in the High Court under the Patents Act 1977, the Registered Designs Act 1949 and the Defence Contracts Act 1958 and all proceedings for the determination of a question or the making of a declaration relating to a patent under the inherent jurisdiction of the High Court shall be assigned to the Chancery Division and

---

2. See *Rewe*, Case No. 33/76 (1976) ECR 1989 and *Comet*, Case No. 45/76 (1976) ECR 2043.
3. The Constitutional Reform Act 1981 (c. 54) provides for the Lord Chief Justice to appoint judges and deputy judges in the High Court. Proceedings before the Patents Court are regulated by the CPR, particularly, Part 63 entitled 'Patents and other Intellectual Property Claims' CPR 63. This part was introduced into the CPR 1998 by the Civil Procedure (Amendment No. 2) Rules 2002 (SI 2002 No. 3219) which entered into force on 1 Apr. 2003. Part 63 together with the PD which supplements CPR 63.
4. As set up under ss 287-292 of the Copyright, Designs and Patents Act 1988.

taken by the Patents Court. The areas in which those differences occur include pleadings, case management, disclosure, trial and post trial proceedings. The PCC in London is an alternative venue to the Patents Court of the High Court for bringing legal cases involving certain matters concerning patents, registered designs and more recently trade marks including Community trade marks and designs where the courts of England and Wales are competent as well as other intellectual property (IP) cases where a normal county court may be competent such as for many copyright matters. Jurisdiction: no limit to the level of damages after which the case must be heard by a higher court – usually by a judge of the Patents Court. There is also no limitation on the jurisdiction of the PCC by virtue of the complexity of the law or facts. Cases are sent from the Patents Court quite frequently and on occasions cases are also sent to the Patent Court form the PCC as well. The judge of the PCC usually has specific and additional jurisdiction to sit in the Patents Court.

Implementation: primarily by means of IP (Enforcement etc.) Regulations (2006)[5] and the CPR in particular CPR 63 as well as the associated PD.

II   EXAMINATION OF THE IMPLEMENTATION
                OF EACH ARTICLE OF THE DIRECTIVE

Article 1
Subject Matter

The Directive was implemented by the IP (Enforcement, etc.) Regulations 2006 with supporting changes to the court rules.

Article 2
Scope

CPR 63 and PD applies to all IP rights with the exception of model rights and trade names which are not covered by either UK or Community Rights and therefore implements this article

Article 3
General Obligation: Costs

With respect to costs the General Obligation provides that 'Member States shall provide for measures, procedures and remedies necessary to ensure the enforcement of IP rights. Those measures, procedures and remedies shall not be unnecessarily complicated or costly ...'. The matter of costs will be dealt with under the heading of Article 14 in so far as it would appear that unlike the other elements of

---

5.   Intellectual Property (Enforcement etc.) Regulations 2006 (SI 2006/1028) <http://www.opsi. gov.uk/si/si2006/20061028.htm> and <http://www.statutelaw.gov.uk/>.

the General Obligation of Article 3, the CPR does not effectively implement this obligation.

Article 4
General Obligation: Rights of Standing for Four Categories of Persons

As noted earlier, the objective of this article is to identify categories of persons who are entitled to apply for the remedies which are provided in the context of the Directive. In the Consultation Paper, The UK Implementation of the Directive on the Enforcement of IP Rights (2004/48/EC), the Patent Office (DTI) observes that no changes in the CPR or otherwise are required in order to implement this obligation.[6] However, that conclusion would appear to depend upon the manner in which the scope of the substantive obligation is interpreted. As noted earlier, Article 4 of the Directive establishes that 'Member States shall recognize as persons entitled to seek application of the measures, procedures and remedies referred to in this chapter'. However, the Directive then provides what appears to constitute a limitation on the scope of the substantive obligation: that is, in relation to rights holders the standing is to be provided 'in accordance with the provisions of the applicable law'. Further, in relation to licensees, rights management groups and professional defence bodies, the obligation on the Member State appears, at least initially, to be only 'in so far as permitted by and in accordance with provisions of the applicable law'. Accordingly, as noted in Chapter 3, it is possible that there are two interpretations for notably for Article 4 (c) and (d).[7] The first interpretation might be termed restrictive in that, following it, neither of those sections imposes an obligation on Member States to introduce such representation into their national systems of procedures where the procedural mechanism for representation does not already exist. The second interpretation of Article 4 (c) and (d) which might be termed the wide interpretation is that it may be the case that neither of the two

---

6. Explanatory Note: Intellectual Property (Enforcement etc.) Regulations 2006/1028 Para. 7.3 '... Article 4 of the Enforcement Directive requires the Member States to provide the same remedies to, amongst others, exclusive licensees as they provide to right owners but only as far as national law permits. Thus, there is not a Community obligation to provide such rights to exclusive licensees and granting them a right of action goes beyond what is required by the directive'.
7. Category (b) is already provided for in English law. Rights holders and persons authorized to use those IP rights are already permitted to bring proceedings pursuant to statute. The Patent Office in 'Representation Actions for Enforcement of Intellectual Property Rights' (R A)(consultation closed on 18 Dec. 2006 and no recommendations yet produced) observed at para. 1 therein that while generic multiple provisions exist in the form of the Group Litigation Order (GLO – CPR 19. 10-15) (and the Representative Rule, (CPR 19.6) it was not an adequate solution for representative actions under Dir. 2004/48/EC even more so that the 'Directive did not require us to make specific provisions'. The RA also notes at para. 11 that although generic multiple party provisions exist they were not suitable for the enforcement of IP rights in that parties are required to share a similar interest (CPR 19.6 (1)) or common related issues (CPR 19.10) which prevents trade associations from enforcing proceedings on behalf of members by reason of absence of ownership of the IP rights. Therefore the RA suggests at para. 26-29 the introduction of a new representative action.

phrases cited in the two sections serves to restrict the scope of the substantive obligation on the part of a Member State to provide for the standing to the four categories for the following reasons:

> first, following the case notably of *Commission v. UK*,[8] effective implementation of the Directive, as required by Article 3 thereof as well as European Community (EC) Articles 249 (3) and 10, would seem to require that legal standing be provided for all four categories of persons enumerated within the Directive in order in order to ensure its effective implementation notably in relation to Article 3: that is, in order to ensure effective judicial protection for the four categories of beneficiaries of the obligation; in order to ensure a reduction of the disparities in enforcement capacity of the national procedural systems and in order to reduce costs in conformity once again with Article 3.

In the aforementioned case, the ECJ held that the UK had infringed its obligations under Directive 77/187/EC by failing to provide for designation of employee representatives as required by Article 6 of that directive. UK legislation did not contain such a mechanism for designation of employee representatives. Further, the UK argued that the words: 'as provided for by the law or practises of the Member States …' restricted the obligation on the part of Member States to provide such representation to those circumstances where such provisions already existed in the national legislation. Therefore, Directive 77/187/EC did not require that the UK introduce such representation. The ECJ, relying partially upon EC Article 5 (now EC Article 10) rejected this restrictive analysis of the scope of the obligation for two reasons: firstly, it would deprive the directive and particularly Article 6 of its 'full effect';[9] in short 'The intention of the Community legislature was not therefore to allow different national legal systems to accept a situation in which no employee representatives are designated since such designation is necessary to ensure compliance with the obligations laid down in Article 6 of the directive';[10] second, national legislation which 'makes it possible to impede protection unconditionally guaranteed to employees by a directive is contrary to Community law'.[11]

Further, the meaning of Article 4 of the Directive may be analyzed as follows: it is recalled that Recital 10 establishes that:

> The objective of the Directive is to approximate legislative systems so as to ensure a high, equivalent and homogenous level of protection in the internal market.

---

8. *Commission v. UK*, Case No. 382/92 (1994) ECR I 2435.
9. *Commission v. UK*, Case No. 382/92 (1982) ECR 2, ibid., at para. 17: 'The interpretation proposed by the UK would allow Member States to determine the cases in which employee representatives can be informed and consulted since they can be informed and consulted only in undertakings where national law provides for the designation of employee representatives. It would thus allow Member States to deprive Art. 6 of the directive of its full effect.'
10. *Commission v. UK*, Case No. 382/92 (1982) ECR 2435, ibid., at para. 18.
11. *Commission v. UK*, Case No. 382/92 ECR 2601, ibid., at para. 20 and for the full argument, see paras 8-31.

It is submitted that the objective of the Directive requires, therefore, an 'equivalent and homogenous level of protection in the internal market' for both rights holders and those who have, following Recital 18, a 'direct interest'. Therefore, it would appear that 'equivalent and homogenous protection' as provided for in Recital 10 and supplemented by Recitals 7, 8 and 9 would, therefore, necessitate that standing be provided for the four categories of persons as provided by Article 4 of the Directive. Such an implementation would ensure national compliance not only with the objective of the Directive as stated in Recital 10 but would also preclude the 'disparities between the systems of the Member States as regards the means of enforcing intellectual property rights' referred to in Recitals 7, 8 and 9 of the Directive. Accordingly, following this second interpretation of Article 4 (c) and (d) it is submitted that effective implementation requires that the purpose of the Directive as set forth in Recital 10 be achieved. Moreover, following *Commission v. The UK*,[12] the two phrases 'in accordance with the provisions of the applicable law' and 'in so far as permitted by and in accordance with the provisions of the applicable law' are to be construed as simply assigning the Member States, pursuant to EC 249(3) the role of ensuring such locus standi.[13]

Second, it is submitted that the source of procedural rights, namely, the granting of standing to act legally to the four categories of beneficiaries derives fundamentally from the clear wording of Article 4 of the Directive and also partially from the implementing measures: that is, the Directive identifies clearly the classes of beneficiaries of the right: namely, rights holders and those other parties who have a direct interest in the enforcement of IP rights. The category of those parties with a direct interest in enforcement is in turn divided into three sub-categories, namely, (b) other persons authorized to use the rights such as licensees, (c) IP collective rights management bodies which are regularly recognized as having a right to represent holders of IP rights and (d) professional defence bodies recognized as having a right to represent rights holders. It is submitted that the three subcategories are in turned defined by the Directive in so far as they are composed of individuals who have a direct interest in the enforcement of the IP rights. The nature

---

12. *Commission v. UK*, Case No. 382/92 (1982) ECR 2601, ibid., at para. 16: 'Contrary to the UK's contention, the wording of Art. 2 (c) of the directives does not cast any doubt on the interpretation of Art. 6. Art. 2 (c) is not simply a renvoi to the rules in force in the Member States on the designation of employee representatives. It leaves to Member States only the tasks of determining the arrangements for designating the employee representatives who must be informed and consulted under Article 6 (1) and (2)'.
13. S. Prechal, *Directives in EC Law* (Oxford: Oxford University Press, 2005), ibid., 198 'The words "as far as possible" merely refer to the nature of the judicial function as such and no longer to the methods of construction under national law' [and n. 86 at 198. D. Curtin … S. Prechal … and A. Tanney … also suggest that national rules of interpretation are no longer relevant. Wherever possible, should in his view be under stood as 'where there is no irreconcilable conflict as a matter of language'.] Similarly this approach seems to imply that the question whether the national courts is still within the boundaries of its judicial role or not would in the ultimate analysis be a matter of Community law as opposed to national (constitutional) laws.

of the right is defined as entitlement 'to seek application of the measures, proce-dures and remedies referred to in the chapter'[14] which can be said to constitute a procedural right as opposed to a substantive right.[15] Further following the case of Verholen,[16] it follows that the category of person who may rely upon the Directive includes those who have a direct interest in the application of the rules and not merely those who are directly protected by the rules at issues. In the instant case, it would seem that the three categories of persons to whom standing must be granted include not only those named within the Directive but also according to Recital 18, those who have a direct interest. Third, it may possibly be that the expressions 'in accordance with the provisions of the national law' and 'in so far as permitted by and in accordance with the provisions of the national law' operate in a manner which might be equivalent to granting discretion to the Member States to derogate from its contents: here the usual form of expression is: 'does not pre-vent the Member States from [applying different provisions]' or that the directive is 'without prejudice to the right of the Member States to …'. If this were the case which is not obvious, then the Member States in exercising their discretion would nevertheless be bound by the substantial content of the directive and in the instant case the substantive obligation in Article 4 to provide for locus standing for rights holders.

More particularly, the implementation of the Directive overall is subject, as noted earlier, to the principles of legal certainty, effectiveness and effective legal protection of rights. It is submitted that seeking to justify a refusal to implement the substantive legal obligation in Article 4 with respect to the legal standing for all four groups of rightsholders, and notably, 4 (c) and (d) on the basis of the expressions 'in so far as permitted by and in accordance with the provisions of national law' would, as noted earlier, be precluded by the terms of Article 4 of the Directive: that is, the substantive obligation of the Directive coupled with the prin-ciples of notably clarity, effectiveness and, in particular, the effective legal protec-tion of rights would require full implementation of the locus standi for the four categories of rights holders.

Thus far, bearing in mind that the Patent Office has undertaken a consultation upon the appropriateness of modifying the rules of procedure so as to ensure stand-ing for all four categories of persons enumerated in Article 4, it would seem that

---

14. As noted earlier, a separation is made between the creation of rights and direct effect. See S. Prechal, *Directives in EC Law* (Oxford: Oxford University Press, 2005), ibid., 283.
15. Other examples of directives which create procedural rights as opposed to substantive rights are.
16. *Verholen*, Joined Case Nos C-87/90 and C-88/90 (1991) ECR I 3757 The inferences to be drawn from this judgment are that Community law requirements may influence national stand-ing rules and that in the ultimate analysis, the persons concerned should be given under certain circumstances locus standi even in situations where they have no standing under national law if this is necessary to safeguard effective judicial protection. See also *Rewe,* Case No. 158/80 (1981) ECR 1805 and *MRAX*, Case No. C-459/99 (2002) ECR I 6591 at para. 101.

the UK has provided only partial implementation. In this regard the Memorandum[17] which accompanies Regulations 2006/1028 states with respect to Article 4 of the Directive:

> this article imposes no obligation on Members. Instead it requires Member States to ensure that where a person has a direct interest and legal standing under UK law they should have access to the measures, procedures and remedies provided for in the Directive.

(a) Category of rights holders: the category of rights holders is restricted to the following statutes:

- S 14 Trademarks Act (1994) (rights of proprietor)
- S 61 Patents Act (1977) (rights of proprietor)
- S 96 Copyright Designs and Patents Act (1998) (rights of copyright owner)
- S 229 Copyright Designs and Patents Act (1998) (rights of unregistered design owner)
- S 7 A Registered Design Act (1949) (rights of design owner)

It is submitted that these sections constitute an effective implementation of the Article 4 (a) of the Directive in the sense that they correspond to the criterion of clarity, they are legally binding and provide full effect and finally, they appear to constitute effective legal protection of the rights: that is the content of the implementing measures are clear and precise notably in so far as they are destined to protect procedural rights of the owners of IP rights. There is nothing ostensibly ambiguous about the wording of the implementing measures. However, the courts must apply these sections in a manner which ensures effective implementation of the Directive.

(b) Category of Licensees: the category of licensees provided that they can qualify as 'exclusive' are provided for by specific articles within the same statutes:

- S 31 Trademarks Act (1994) (rights of exclusive licensee)
- S 67 Patents Act (1977) (rights of exclusive licensee)
- S 191 L Copyright Designs and Patents Act (1998)
- S 234 Registered Designs Act (1949) (rights of exclusive licensee)

Paragraph 3 of Schedule I of Regulations 2006/1028 inserts section 24 F into the Registered Designs Act (1949) (rights of exclusive licensee)

Exclusive Licensee is defined in the Patents Act (1977) as follows: 'exclusive license' means a license from the proprietor of or applicant for a patent conferring on the licensee or on him and persons authorized by him to the exclusion of all other persons 'including the proprietor or applicant' any right in respect of the invention to which the patent or application relates and further, 'exclusive licensee'

---

17. Explanatory Memorandum to the Intellectual Property (Enforcement etc.) Regulations 2006 No. 1028.

and 'non-exclusive licence' shall be construed accordingly'.[18] Paragraph 2 of Schedule 1 of Regulations 2006/1028 inserts into the Registered Designs Act (1949) a definition of an 'exclusive licensee' which corresponds to the definition used in other IP legislation.

In so far as Article 4 (b) may be construed as limiting the category of licensee to an exclusive licensee it is submitted that the sections constitute an effective implementation for the above reasons. However, it is not clear, for reasons which will be developed concerning the manner of interpretation of Article 4 (c) and (d) that Article 4 (b) of the Directive can be restricted to the class of exclusive licensees: in short, it is not clear that Article 4 (b) precludes the possibility of a non-exclusive licensee. Therefore it would appear that the scope of the obligation on the part of the Member State may be such as to require provision for non-exclusive licensees which clearly are not dealt with by the implementing legislation.

(c) As noted earlier, the interpretation of Article 4 and in particular sections (c) and (d) can only be determined definitively by the ECJ. Therefore, it is also appropriate to consider the possibility that those sections do not impose any obligation on the Member States to introduce representative actions into their national procedure where such does not already exist. The only purpose of these articles under what might be termed a narrow interpretation would seem to be to encourage Member States whose systems of procedure do not contain such forms of representation to introduce such into their rules of procedure. If the ECJ were to adopt such an interpretation, then clearly, the duty to implement the Directive correctly and adequately would extend only to Article 4 (a) and (b) requiring thereby respect of the principles of clarity, effectiveness and effective legal protection. Under such an interpretation it is submitted that the implementation of Articles 4 (a) and (b) by the UK is adequate in that it conforms with such principles that the implementing measures are clear, precise and unambiguous and are appropriate for the creation of rights.

In the alternate it is also necessary as noted earlier to consider what might be termed the wider interpretation of Articles 4 (c) and (d) whereby these two sections impose an obligation on the Member States to ensure that representative actions exist within the national legislation for the two categories of rightsholder therein defined. Starting with section (c), the category of collective rights management bodies, this category of rightsholder may use CPR 19 either to bring or defend an action where all parties including the collective rights management body have the same rights. No provision is made within the CPR for an action to be brought or defended by a rights management body which does not have the same interest as the other members in the sense of being able to bring a substantive action in its own right. It is submitted that CPR 19 cannot implement Article 4 (c) by reason of the requirement that the representative have the same interest as the parties represented precluding thereby representation where no such similar interest exists.

---

18. Section 29(1) Trade Marks Act (1994) 'In this Act an "exclusive licence" means a licence (whether general or limited) authorising the licensee to the exclusion of all other persons including the person granting the licence to use a registered trade mark in the manner authorised by the licence.'

CPR 19 (6) (1) provides:

Where more than one person has the same interest in a claim

a) the claim may be begun; or
b) the court may order that the claim be continued
by or against one of the persons who have the same interest as representing
any other persons have that interest.

It is clear that a condition precedent for the court to exercise its discretion to make such an order is that the eventual representative 'has the same interest in a claim' as the parties represented. Accordingly, CPR 19 is unable to implement Article 4 (c) of the Directive whose scope is not restricted to parties who have the same interest as those of the representing party.

(d) the category of defence management bodies may use CPR 19 to either bring or defend actions where all, including the defence body, have the same interests. No provision is made for an action to be brought or defended by a defence body which does not have the same interest as the other members in the sense of being able to bring in its own right a substantive action for the reasons above. In short, by reason of the requirement of 'same interest' CPR 19 does not implement Article 4 (d) adequately the scope of which is not restricted to parties having the same interest.

As noted earlier, arguably the aforementioned Recitals of the Directive would seem to be such as to preclude assigning a limited scope to Article 4 (c) and (d): that is, the harmonization and the requirement of effective remedies required by Article 3 would preclude limiting representation to those instances where as in CPR 19 the representative and the parties represented must share the same interest. Moreover, this wide interpretation of the duty which is provided by the Directive in Article 4 (c) and (d) precludes the requirement of CPR 19 that the representative share the same interest. On the contrary, by reason of Article 3 of the Directive in conjunction with the aforementioned Recitals, the implementation of Article 4 (c) and (d) by the Member States must be ' effective'. Accordingly, following the *Commission v. UK*,[19] the expressions, as 'as provided by ...' cannot be construed in light of the Recitals and Article 3 of the Directive as constituting a derogation or an exception from the obligation to implement Article 4 (c) and (d). In short, the purpose of the Directive as provided in Recital 18 coupled with the duty to provide effective implementation as provided in Article 3 arguably require that the category of representative include a party who does not share the interests of those who are represented in contrast to CPR 19.

Following upon the wide interpretation of Article 4 (c) and (d) as opposed to the narrow interpretation thereof which does not impose any obligation on the Member States, one may make the following observations concerning the consequences of the non-implementation or incorrect implementation of those two sections: arguably, as noted earlier in Chapter 2, there are three methods for a

---

19. *Commission v. UK*, Case No. 382/92 (1994) ECR I 2435, op. cit.

party who benefits from the rights provided by a directive where they are notably sufficiently clearly defined therein as is arguably the case with the Directive 48/2004/EC in terms of the nature of the obligation and, in particular; the category of beneficiaries, to protect his rights in the event of either non-implementation or incorrect implementation thereof: these methods are namely, the concept of direct effect, the concept of interpretation in conformity and that of State liability for non-implementation or incorrect implementation of EC law. The concept of direct effect will not be utilized by reason of the degree of discretion which the Member States enjoy in terms of the implementation of notably the practical designation of the category of beneficiaries of rights:[20] that is the text of the Directive does not indicate how the representative of the class is to be chosen, for example, by the parties, by the court, or by the responsible minister on the basis of specific criterion as in the case of the Competition Appeal Tribunal (CAT).[21] Further the doctrine of direct effect does not apply in horizontal or party to party enforcement. Accordingly, it is necessary to consider the use of the doctrine of interpretation in conformity on the one hand and on the other, that of State liability. It is submitted that the essential limitation in the circumstances to the use of the doctrine of consistent interpretation is the fact that there is no legislation either pre-existing or adopted subsequently which can reasonably be interpreted in conformity with Article 4 (c) and (d) of the Directive: that is, the limitation on the group action arguably cannot be removed in the sense of permitting a representative body which does not in itself have a cause of action similar to the other members of the group action so as to permit the use thereof to implement Article 4 (c) and (d) of the Directive. Accordingly, it would appear that an attempt to remove the requirement imposed by CPR 19 that a representative have a cause of action similar to that of the members would impose an interpretation on that article which is fundamentally opposite to its natural and indeed purposive meaning, namely, to provide for collective actions where the representative has a similar cause of action to those represent. The contrary meaning produced

---

20. *Francovich*, Case Nos C-6/90 and C-9/90 (1991) ECR I 5357, op. cit., at para. 26.
21. Section 19 of the Enterprise Act (2002) inserted s. 47 B into Competition Act (1998) (CA) allowing thereby a body designated in an order made by the Secretary of State to bring a claim under s. 47 A of the CA on behalf of at least two individuals in respect of the supply of goods or services which such individuals receive or should receive otherwise in the course of business from someone who supplies those goods or services in the course of business. In order to be designated as a specified body to bring a claim on behalf of consumers an organization must meet the criterion published by the Secretary of State. Designations are made by means of a Statutory Instrument. See: Claims on Behalf of Consumers: Guidance for Prospective Specified Bodies, <www.berr. gov.uk.files/file11957.pdf> 550; Mulheron 'From Representative Rule to Class Actions: Steps Rather than Leaps', *CJQ* 24 (2005): 42. For pro-opt-out class actions see R. Mulheron, 'Justice Enhanced: Framing an opt out Class Action in England', *ML R* 70 (2007), op. cit.: who argues at 580 that 'England has two generic multi party actions but it requires a third ... the principle of "access to justice" being recognised both in case law (*Thai Trading Co. v. Taylor* (1998) QB 781 and by the Human Rights Act (1998) Art. 6.1 to be a human right the ongoing lack of such a regime [opt out representative actions] in England's civil procedure both discredits the legal system and frustrates those with grievances in their access to justice.'

by the removal of that requirement would arguably not be possible by reason of its violation of the principle of legal certainty:[22] that is, the limitation on the scope of the principle of consistent interpretation, namely, that the national court is under an obligation to proceed 'as far as possible' with consistent interpretation, would be exceeded in that an interpretation of CPR 19 which would result in an entirely different meaning would violate the principle of legal certainty. More particularly, it is submitted that the concept of legal certainty which forms part of the EU principles that govern the scope of the interpretation in conformity which a national court may make of the Directive implies that the application of the law to a specific situation must be predictable.[23] An additional argument may be that Article 4 (c) in itself does not provide a sufficiently detailed basis for an effective consistent interpretation: that is, the method of appointment or choice of the representative body is in no way provided by the current CPR 19. Accordingly, by reason of this insufficiency of certainty within the Directive itself it may be that a consistent interpretation would be impossible.[24] Therefore, it is necessary to consider the possibility of an action in damages against the State. As noted earlier, three requirements must be fulfilled in order that a damages action may be brought successfully against the State for either non-implementation or for incorrect implementation. The first of these conditions is that the relevant obligation must be sufficiently clear. It is submitted that the relevant obligation in terms of its nature and scope and in particular the category of the beneficiaries would seem indeed to be sufficiently clear.

---

22. Case No. C-60/02X (2004) ECR I 651 para. 59.
23. *Kolpinghuis*, Case No. 80/86 (1987) ECR 3969, confirmed in Case C-60/02 X (2004) ECR I-651, C. Plaza Martin 'Furthering the Effectiveness of EC Directives and the Judicial Protection of Individual Rights Thereunder', *ICLR* 26 (1994): 30-32, *Koppenburg*, Case No. 70/83 (1984) ECR 1075 at para. 11: 'Community legislation must be unequivocal and its application must be predictable for those who are subject to it'. H. Schermers & D. Waelbroeck, *Judicial Protection in the European Union* (The Hague: Kluwer, 2001), 64, and S. Prechal, *Directives in EC Law* (Oxford: OUP, 2005), op. cit., 206: 'On the other hand, the concept of legal certainty implies that the application of the law to a specific situation must be predictable. This implies that depending on the circumstances and, in particular, on its wording, a rule cannot be construed as bearing a meaning which would fly in the face of the meaning one may expect the rule to have'. *Faccini Dori*, Case No. C-91/92 (1991) ECR I-3325 para. 27, where the ECJ accepts that possibility that consistent interpretation is not always possible: 'If the result prescribed by the directive cannot be achieved by way of interpretation … Community law requires the Member States to make good the damages caused to individuals through failure to transpose the directive … .'
24. See Art. 33 (1) and (2) of the Rules of the CAT, SI 2003/1372, which implements s. 47 B of The Competition Act 1998 and see n. 20 *supra*. See also *The Consumers Association v. JJB Sports PLC*, Case No. 1078/7/0: Claim for damages under s. 47 B CA (1998) CAT; see also Office of Fair Trading 'Private actions in competition law: effective redress for consumers and business' Discussion Paper, Apr. 2007, and Consultation Responses 31 Aug. 2007 <www.oft.gov.uk/advice_and_resources/resource_base/consultation/private> considers the use of representative actions in private enforcement actions for competition law. See also 'Private Actions in Competition Law: Effective Redress for Consumer Affairs: Recommendations of the Office of Fair Trading, 26 Nov. 2007, in particular, Chs 5, 6, and 7 dealing with representative actions for consumers and small businesses.' <www.oft.gov.uk/news/press/2007/162-07>

Notwithstanding, it is also submitted that the method of the choice or the appointment of the representative of the class is unclear as noted previously: that is, it is not apparent whether the definition of the class of the beneficiaries may be affected by the method through which the representative is designated which is not defined by the Directive and which depends upon the measures adopted by the Member State to ensure implementation.[25] However, it is necessary to bear in mind that the degree of certainty required for implementation is arguably less than that required for direct effect.[26] Therefore, in the event that the rights were defined with sufficient clarity for the purposes of implementation in the sense that the absence of a method provided by the Directive to designate a class representative has no effect thereon, then the next step would be for the beneficiary to prove loss and damage resulting from what had been established and proved as an incorrect or the non-implementation of the Directive: that is if the rights are sufficiently clearly defined to establish an action in State liability it would be necessary to prove that the current national implementation constitutes an inadequate implementation of the Directive which thereby would constitute a breach by the Member State of its duty pursuant to EC Articles 249 (3) and 10. In the instant case, it is submitted, as noted previously herein, that a failure to provide standing for the persons in Article 4 (c) and (d) of the Directive may breach the principal of effective judicial protection[27] as developed in Johnston,[28] Heylens[29] which governs, as noted earlier in Chapter 2, the implementation of directives in general: in short, the principle of effective legal protection[30] would seem to require that all categories of rights holders provided by Article 4 (a)-(d) of the

---

25. S. Prechal, *Directives in EC Law* (Oxford: OUP, 2005), op. cit., 283.
26. S. Prechal, *Directives in EC Law* (Oxford: OUP, 2005), ibid., 128-129. Furthermore, as noted earlier, even, which is not submitted, Art. 4 did not create rights, albeit to be implemented through national legislation, the Member State would still be enjoined to ensure effective implementation. Further, in *Francovich*, Case No. 6/90 and 9/90 (1991) ECR I-5357, op. cit., the body charged with the duty to compensate not being defined by Directive 80/987, the application of the doctrine of direct effect was prevented. However the terms of the directive were sufficiently certain so as to provide for an action in State liability for damages.
27. S. Prechal, *Directives in EC Law* (Oxford: OUP, 2005), ibid., 143-144 observes that the principle of effective judicial protection is based on the rationale that in 'a Community based on the rule of law everyone must have the opportunity to assert his rights before the court and … the protection must be effective'. See also Unibet London, Case No. C-432/05 (unreported); Opinion of AG Sharpston at para. 38. '… the principle of effective legal protection reflects a general principle of law which underlines the constitution traditions common to the Member States. That principle, the right to a "fair trail" is embodied in Art. 6 (1) of the ECHR and is now recognised as a general principle of Community law by virtue of Art. 6 (2) EU'.
28. *Johnston v. Chief Constable of Ulster*, Case No. 222/84 (1986) ECR 1651, op. cit.
29. *Unectf v. Heylens*, Case No. 222/86 (1987) ECR 4097, op. cit.
30. S. Prechal, *Directives in EC Law* (Oxford: OUP 2005), op. cit., 142-145; M. Dougan, *National Remedies Before the Court of Justice*, (Oxford: Hart 2004) Ch. 1; *Unibet London*, Case No. C-432/05 (unreported) para. 42-43 and 73 and Opinion of AG Sharptson at para. 38: *Safalero*, Case No. C-13/01, (2003) ECR I 8679, paras 49-50 and Opinion of AG Stix-Hackl at paras 66-68. See also potentially, the effect of Art. 47 of the Charter of Fundamental Rights as implemented by Art. 6 of the Lisbon Treaty [rejected by Ireland on 13 June 2008] subject to Protocols mentioned in n. 7 of Ch. 2.

Directive be able to effectively exercise their procedural rights.[31] Arguably, this reasoning would also apply to Article 4 (b) in so far as non-exclusive licensees are not provided for. More generally, it would seem that effective legal protection would require that the holder of the IP rights be able to enforce them either directly in personam or indirectly by means of the additional parties enumerated in Article 4 of the Directive[32] which constitutes, it is submitted, the hard core obligation of this article. Accordingly, it would appear that failure to provide for all four categories of persons set out in Article 4 may constitute an infringement of the principle of effective judicial protection unless justifiable in terms of the European Court of Human Rights (ECtHR) case law[33] and also contravene EC Articles 249(3) and 10.[34] In this regard, the ECJ held in Verholen[35] not only that the category of persons who may enforce a directive include those who are not specifically named but also those who have a direct interest and that further, a failure to provide legal standing for both categories would breach the principle of effective judicial protection. However, it is not clear that Article 4 (a) (b) (c) and (d) of the Directive define sufficiently clearly the nature of the rights and the category of the beneficiary and that the Member State has breached its obligation pursuant to EC Articles 249(3) and 10 such that the first limb of an action for State liability can be established. With respect to breach, and on the condition that the interpretation of Article 4 (c) and (d), if necessary by means of a reference to the ECJ, is indeed held to provide for standing in the form of a representative action for those two categories of beneficiaries then following Dillenkopfer[36] non-implementation in due time would sound as a serious breach. However causation and loss must also be proved in order to establish a successful cause of

31. Recitals 2, 3 and 32. See also Art. 17.2 of the Charter of Fundamental Rights and Ch. 2, n. 7 therein concerning the Charter of Fundamental Rights and Freedoms and the Lisbon Treaty [rejected by Ireland on 13 June 2008] and notably the Protocols applicable to the UK and Poland. I am grateful to Prof. A Dashwood for personal communication of his paper 'The Charter of Fundamental Rights and its Protocol: Drawing the Teeth of the Paper Tiger' Feb. 2008.

32. S. Prechal, *Directives in EC Law* (Oxford: OUP, 2005), op. cit., 143 'Moreover, it is similarly important to note in this context that the principle does not apply solely where a person relies directly on provisions of a directive, but also where the national law provisions implementing the directive are invoked and applied. In other words, even if a directive which, in contrast to Directive 27/207 – does note contain a provision relating to judicial protection, is as such correctly implemented in national law, the Member States must ensure that the rights under the national implementing measures can be asserted by judicial process by the individuals concerned. The absence of such a possibility will amount to inadequate implementation'.

33. *Unibet*, Case No. C-432/05 (2007) ECR I 2271, op. cit., <www.curia.europa.eu> Opinion of AG Sharpston at para. 38 who cites notably: *Golder v. UK* (1979-80) 1 EHRR 524 at para. 36; *Klass v. Germany* (1994) 18 EHRR 305 at para. 49; *Ashingdane v. UK* (1985) 7 EHRR 528 at para. 55-57; *Lithgow v. UK* (1986) 8 EHRR 329. see also *Van der Weerd* unreported Case No. C-225/05 judgement 7 Jun. 2007, and generally A. Arnull "Unibet" (2007) CMLRev 6, 1763 who argues that van der Weerd follows Unibet.'

34. *Petersen v. Council & Commission*, Case No. 382/92 (1994) ECR I-2435 para. 24-27.

35. *Verholen*, Case No. C-87/90, C-88/90 and C-89/90 (1991) ECR I-3757.

36. *Dillenkofer*, Joined Cases No. C-178/94 (1996) ECR I 4845, op. cit.; C-179/94, C-188/94, C-189/94 and C-190/94 and *Brinkman*, Case No. C-319/96 (1998) ECT I 5255.

action. Certainly, causation is a matter of fact and must be assessed in the context along with loss of the actual case at hand. Conspicuously these elements of the cause of action are absent.

Finally, it is perhaps useful in this regard to contrast Article 4 (c) and (d) of the Directive with Articles 2 and 3 of Directive 98/27 EC which require Member States to provide for the granting of injunctions to a representative party known as 'qualified entity' 'which being a properly constituted according to the law of a Member State, has a legitimate interest in ensuring that the provisions referred … are complied with "against businesses which breach the directive"'.

Directive 98/27/ EC

Article 2
Actions for an Injunction

1. Member States shall designate the courts or administrative authorities competent to rule on proceedings commenced by qualified entities within the meaning of Article 3 seeking: (…)

Article 3
Entities Qualified to Bring an Action

For the purpose of this Directive a 'qualified entity' means any body or organization which, being properly constituted according to the law of a Member State, has a legitimate interest in ensuring that the provisions referred to in Article 1 are complied with, in particular:

(a) one or more independent public bodies specially responsible for protecting the interest referred to in Article 1 in Members in which such bodies exist and /or

(b) organizations whose purpose is to protect the interests referred to in Article 1 in accordance with the criterion laid down by their national law.

The UK has implemented Directive 98/27/ EC and in particular Articles 2-3 by means of Part 8 of the Enterprise Act (2002) which provides as follows notably with respect to 'qualified entity':

213 Enforcers
(2) A designated enforcer is any person or body (whether or not incorporated) which the Secretary of State
a) thinks has as one of its purposes the protection of the collective interests of consumers and
b) designates by order
(3) The Secretary of State may designate a public body only if he is satisfied that it is independent

(4) The Secretary of State may designate a person or body which is not a public body only if the person or body (as the case may be) satisfied such criteria as the Secretary of State specifies by order.[37]

Therefore, the overall conclusion would seem to be that, following at least what might be termed the wide as opposed to the narrow interpretation of Article 4 and notably of sections (c) and (d) therein the non-implementation of those sections by the UK contravenes EC Articles 249 (3) and 10. More particularly, it would appear that the wording of the Directive coupled with the relevant Recitals under at least the wide interpretation as opposed to the narrow interpretation establishes sufficiently clearly both the nature of the obligation and the category of beneficiary at least for the purposes of an action in damages against the State. However, as noted earlier, breach of the duty pursuant to EC Articles 249 (3) and 10 will not suffice to establish a cause of action until damage and causation have been proved. Finally, one might only reiterate that the definitive interpretation of Article 4 (c) and (d), as to whether it is narrow or wide, can only be rendered by the ECJ.

Directive 2004/48/EC

Article 5
Presumption of Ownership

Regulations 2006/1028, section 10 of Schedule 2 in conjunction with sections 104, 105 and 107 (6) of the Copyright, Designs and Patents Act (1988) appear to adequately implement this article: that is, the implementation is clear, legally binding, effective and ensures effective judicial protection.

One notes for example Regulations 2006/1028 which constitutes specifically adopted legislation:

1) In proceedings brought by virtue of this part, with respect to rights in a performance where copies of a recording of the performance is issued to the public bear a statement that a named person was the performer, the statement shall be admissible as evidence of the fact state and shall be presumed to be correct until the contrary is proved.

Similarly, section 104 (2) of the Copyright Designs and Patents Act (1988), which is pre-existing legislation:

Where a name purporting to be that of the author appeared in copies of the work as published or on the work when it was made the person whose name appeared shall be presumed until the contrary is proved

---

37. See Lord Chancellor's Department Consultation Paper: 'Representative Claims', Feb. 2001; also 'Representative Actions', DTI, 4 Oct. 2006, <www.berr.gov.uk/files31886.pdf> and 'Private Actions in Competition Law: Recommendations', OFT, 26 Nov. 2007 <www.oft.gov.uk/shared_oft/reports/comp_policy/oft916resp.pdf>.

a) to be the author of the work ... .

S 105 (1) In proceedings brought by virtue for this chapter with respect to a sound recording as issued to the public bear a label or other mark stating

a) that the named person was the owner of copyright at the date of issue ... the label or mark shall be admissible as evidence of the facts stated and shall be presumed to be correct until the contrary is proved

Article 6
Evidence

The purpose of this article is to ensure that a party who has advanced evidence in support of his claims may be able to obtain documentary evidence from the other party subject to protection of confidential information. The scope of the substantive obligation appears to involve the following:

> First, Article 6 (a) of the Directive indicates: '... the competent judicial authorities may order that such evidence be presented by the opposing party ...': it is submitted that the term evidence be presented refers to both disclosure and inspection of a specific document or documents. This is provided for by CPR 31.12. (2) and (3).

Article 6 (b) of the Directive uses the term 'communicated' rather than 'presented'. However, it would seem that the effect is the same as presented, that is, the scope of the obligation concerns both disclosure and inspection. Further, the term 'documents' rather than 'evidence' is used such that article (b) would appear to limit the scope of article (a): that is, the availability of specific disclosure is required only in relation to banking, financial and commercial documents only where the breach is of a commercial nature. Following Recital 14 of the Directive, this apparent limitation does not prevent protection on a wider scope which would ensure the availability of specific disclosure with respect to documentary evidence both on a commercial and non-commercial basis notably with respect to banking, financial and commercial documents subject to protection for commercial documents.

The White Book[38] notes: 'a litigant is not entitled to claim privilege for documents and information merely because they were supplied to him in confidence by a third party'. However, as Zuckerman observes:[39]

> Nevertheless, quite apart from its managerial discretion under these rules the court has a long-standing jurisdiction to limit disclosure in order to protect other interest. These may be interests recognised by statute, by the ECHR or by popular morality. ... as a matter of general principle the court may accord protection to the interest of privacy and confidentiality to the extent that it

---

38. Lord Justice Waller (ed.), *The White Book Service: Civil Procedure*, Vol. 1 (London: Sweet & Maxwell, 2007), para. 31.3 at 36.
39. A.A.S. Zuckerman, *Civil Procedure* (London: Lexis-Nexis, 2003), op. cit., 437.

can be done without compromising the administration of justice. The court may, hold proceedings behind closed doors in order to maintain the secrecy of sensitive commercial information. Similarly the court may have regard to the need to protect privacy and confidentiality when making inter partes orders for disclosure and inspection or when it is asked to order a non-party to disclose documents or other information.

It is clear that the implementation of this rule requires consideration of the element of costs as provided in Article 3 of the Directive: that is, it is noted that standard disclosure is normally dispensed with in the PCC specifically in order to reduce costs which will be dealt with in greater detail under Article 14. In particular, the use of judicial case management as provided by the CPR as the context in which CPR 35.12 operates can in itself serve to increase costs of discovery notably in terms of the compliance required by solicitors.[40] However, over all it would seem that this article is effectively implemented in terms of clarity, full effectiveness and effective legal protection provided that the national court in the context of implementation ensures interpretation in conformity of CPR 35 with Articles 3 and 14 of the Directive.

Article 7
Measures for Preserving Evidence

The power to grant interim orders so as to preserve evidence is arguably found in the both the inherent discretion of the court as well as is S37 of the SCA (1981) and section 38 of the County Courts Act (1988). Additional powers are conferred by section 33 of the SCA and section 7 of The Civil Procedure Act 1997.

The rules of the CPR 25 in turn provide for the implementation of the Article 7 in the following manner:

Article 7 (1)

CPR 25. 1 provides as follows:
(c) (i) for the detention, custody or preservation of relevant property;
(ii) for the inspection of relevant property;
(g) an order directing a party to provide information about the location of relevant property or assets or to provide information about relevant property or assets which are or may be the subject of an application for a freezing injunction
(h) an order (referred to as a 'search order' under section 7 of the Civil Procedure Act 1997 (order requiring a party to admit another party to premises for the purpose of preserving evidence etc.);[41]

---

40. J. Peysner & M. Seneviratne, *The Management of Civil Cases: The Courts and Post-Woolf Landscape*, DCA Research Series 9/05, Nov. 2005.
41. This section puts on a statutory basis the jurisdiction to make Anton Piller orders as developed in the case of *Anton Piller KG v. Manufacturing Processes* (1976 Ch. 55 (1976). The Civil

(j) an order under S 34 of the Supreme Court Act 1981 or section 53 of the County Courts Act 1984 (order in certain proceedings for disclosure of documents or inspection of property against a non-party)

It is clear that CPR 25 (1) makes a distinction between, on the one hand, injunctions which are provided for in section (a) and interim orders which are provided for in section (c). It is immediately apparent that this list consists broadly, albeit presented under the uniform denomination of 'Interim Remedies', of two different types of interim orders which have little in common apart from the fact that they are not meant to finally determine the issues in dispute. Zuckerman observes:[42]

> The second type consists of measures designed to facilitate access to information or regulate the litigation process in some way. These are very different measures. There is a profound difference between an order restraining a defendant from pulling down a building to which both he and the claimant assert a right of ownership and an order directing disclosure of documents or directing a person to allow inspection of property. The former involves pre-judgment interference with substantive rights albeit on a temporary basis. Since an interim order restraining conduct may affect the very rights in dispute the court must take great care to ensure that its interim decision does not harm the very rights that it may itself endorse after trial. However, where the order is only concerned with the procedure to be followed as where the court has to decide whether to order pre-trial disclosure or inspection, it has no effect on the disputed rights or their exercises though it may assist one or other of the parties to establish his rights. Indeed, since such orders are not temporary in nature, it is hardly justified to describe them as interim. An order requiring a defendant to allow inspection of property or to disclose certain documents requires a one-off act of compliance leaving no further decision to be make on the point in final judgment.

The CPR permits enforcement of Article 7 in the following manner:

> Before Commencement: CPR 25.2 (1) provides that an order for an interim remedy may be made at any time, including
> (a) before proceedings are started; and
> (b) after judgment has been given

Application without notice:

> CPR 25. 3 (1) provides: The Court may grant an interim remedy on an application made without notice if it appears to the court that there are good

---

Procedure Act 1997, s. 7 (8) confers the jurisdiction to make search order only on the High Court. Only a judge sitting in the PCC of a High Court judge sitting in the County Court may make a search order. However, a county court may vary a search order with the agreement of all parties.

42. A.A.S Zuckerman, *Civil Procedure* (London: Nexis Lexis, 2003), op. cit., 265.

reasons for not giving notice. Ex parte, that is, without notice proceedings, may be justified only on grounds of unavoidable necessity and, therefore, the applicant must persuade the court both of an imminent threat to his interest and of the necessity to forego notice to the respondents. Arguably there are two types of situations in which an application may be made ex parte: first in situation of urgency and second in situations demanding secrecy with Mareva injunctions being an example of the latter.[43]

DEFENCE RIGHTS: CPR 23.9 provides:
  (1) This rule applies where the court has disposed of an application which it permitted to be made without service of a copy of the application notice;
  (2) Where the court makes an order, whether granting or dismissing the application, a copy of the application notice and any evidence in support must, unless the court orders otherwise, be served with the order on any party or to any other person –
  (a) against whom the order was made; and
  (b) against whom the order was sought.

However it is to be noted that Article 7 (1) appears to remove the discretion of the courts which CPR 23.9 (2) provides: namely 'unless the court orders otherwise': that is, Article 7 (1) establishes a substantive obligation to provide notice: 'Where measures to preserve evidence are adopted without the other party having been heard, the parties affected shall be given notice without delay after the execution of the measures at the latest'. It is submitted therefore that were the court to exercise its discretion to order 'otherwise', it would breach Article 7 (1) of the Directive.
Application to set aside:

  CPR 23.10 (1): A person who was not served with a copy of the application notice before an order was made under 23.9 may apply to have the order set aside or varied.
  (2) an application under this rule must be made within 7 days after the date on which the order was served on the person making the application.

Article 7 (2)

Article 7 (2) will be dealt with in conjunction with Article 7 (4).

Article 7 (3)

Article 7 (3) of the Directive has been implemented by CPR 25 (2) (3) which provides that 'Where the Court grants an interim remedy before a claim has been commenced the Court should give directions requiring a claim to be commenced'.

---

43.   A.A.S. Zuckerman, *Civil Procedure* (London: Nexis-Lexis, 2003), ibid., 105 and 306.

However, it is submitted that the discretion of the Court to establish the period for the commencement of the substantive action will be subject both to the principle of full effectiveness and the principle of effective judicial protection notably as they may apply to ensuring the protection of rights of the defence.

This alteration was effected by SI 2005 No. 3515 (L32). The difficulty, however, is that arguably the words 'should give directions' do not implement the Article 7 (3) as clearly as possible: that is following the White Book:[44]

> In the penultimate draft of r. 25.2 (3), it was stated that 'the court must give' directions requiring a claim to be commenced and r. 25.2. (4) created obvious exceptions. However in the form in which it was enacted in 1998, the provision (perhaps surprisingly) was made permissive, stating that the court 'may give' directions ... . This remained the position until r. 25. 2. (3) was strengthened by the Civil Procedure (Amendment No. 4) Rule 2005 so as to state that the 'court should give' directions.

It is submitted that a clearer and more fully effective implementation of Article 7 would contain the words 'the court must give' which in turn would bring it into harmony with the wording of the PD for Interim Injunctions: (PD) Urgent Applications at point 4.4.:

> 1) in addition to the provisions set out at 4.3 above unless the court orders otherwise either the applicant must undertake to the court to issue a claim form immediately or the Court will give direction for the commencement of the claim.

It is submitted that unlike ' Court should give directions', the verbal expression 'the Court will give' is synonymous to 'the Court must give'; that is, 'should give' indicates an element of discretion. Further, it would have been appropriate for reasons of legal certainty to have indicated a period of time as in PD 4.4 (1) namely, 'immediately'.

Furthermore, it is to be noted that Article 7 appears to establish only one consequence or penalty attendant upon setting aside notably for 'any injuries caused by the measures'. This is in the form of compensation from the undertaking in damages. There remains, however, the situation in which an ex parte application is set aside by reason of lack of full and frank disclosure by the applicant. In this situation it would appear that the PD for CPR 32 which would be coupled with the applicant's duty for full disclosure[45] would still apply subject to the doctrine of

---

44. Lord Justice Waller (ed.), *The White Book Service*, Vol. 1 (London: Sweet & Maxwell, 2007), para. 25.2.6 at p. 618.
45. *Brink's-MAT Ltd v. Elcombe* [1988] 3 All E 188 established a wide scope for the duty of disclosure. 'the duty of disclosure ... applies not only to material facts know to the applicant but also to any additional facts which he would have know if he had made inquiries'. *Behbehani v. Salem* [1989] 2 All ER 143 at 157 per Nourse, J 'all proper inquiries must be made before the ex part application is launched their extent depending on all of the circumstances including the nature of the case which the applicants is making'.

effectiveness and judicial protection as noted above. This PD provides for a large number of possible penalties including civil imprisonment for contempt of court:

Penalty: CPR 32 PD

28 (1) Where a party alleges that a statement of truth or a disclosure statement is false the party shall refer that allegation to the court dealing with the claim in which the statement of truth or disclosure statement,

(2) the court may –

(a) exercise any of its powers under the rules;

(b) initiate steps to consider if there is a contempt of court and where there is, to punish it.

(The practice direction to RSC Order 52 (Schedule 1) and CCR Order 20 (Schedule 2) makes provision where committal to prison is a possibility if contempt is proved);

(c) direct the party making the allegation to refer the matter to the Attorney General with a request to him to consider whether he wishes to bring proceedings for contempt of court.

Penalty: CPR 32 PD

28 (1) Where a party alleges that a statement of truth or a disclosure statement is false the party shall refer that allegation to the court dealing with the claim in which the statement of truth or disclosure statement,

(2) the court may –

(a) exercise any of its powers under the rules

(b) initiate steps to consider if there is a contempt of court and where there is, to punish it.

(The practice direction to RSC Order 52 (Schedule 1) and CCR Order 20 (Schedule 2) makes provision where committal to prison is a possibility if contempt is proved)

(c) direct the party making the allegation to refer the matter to the Attorney General with a request to him to consider whether he wishes to bring proceedings for contempt of court.

Article 7 (2) and (4)

The courts enjoy inherent discretion to order a cross-undertaking in damages which apparently serves to fulfil adequately the obligation set forth in both sub-paragraphs (2) and (4). The County Court obtains this discretion from statute. The undertaking in damages is given to the court and not to the party against whom the interim order is made. The requirement of an undertaking in applications for interim injunctions, freezing orders, search others and other interim injunctive relieve is seal with in paragraph 5 of Practise Direction 25A:

Any order of an injunction, unless the court orders otherwise, must contain, (1) an undertaking by the applicant to the court to pay any damages which the respondent(s) (or any other party served with or notified of the order) sustain which the court considers the applicant should pay.

Given that the manner in which the discretion is to be exercise is not specified within the Directive, the CPR Overriding Objective will apply albeit subject to the principle of effectiveness and effective judicial protection of rights as well as the articles of the EC Treaty.

Article 7 (5)

Article 7 (5) provides that the identity of witnesses may require non-disclosure. This obligation is implemented effectively by CPR 39 (4) (2). The court may order that the identity of any party or witness not be disclosed if it considers non-disclosure necessary in order to protect the interests of that party or witness. It is clear that CPR 39 (4) (2) derogates from the general principle of publicity which is expressed in CPR 39 (2) (1) 'The general rule is that a hearing is to be in public'.

It is submitted that the court's discretion will be exercised following the same principles as in the previous section.

It would seem that over all the current existing rules of the CPR in conjunction with substantive law permits the fully effective implementation of this article coupled respecting thereby the principles of legal certainty and effective judicial protection coupled with the principle of interpretation in conformity.

Article 8
Right of Information

The substantive obligation here concerns the duty on the part of the Member States in the context of infringements on a commercial scale to ensure that in proceedings a national court be able to order that the infringer or third party provide the following: namely, 'information on the origin and distribution networks of the goods or services which infringe the IP rights'. CPR 31. 16 ensures pre-action disclosure of documents thereby exceeding the requirements of Article 8 of the Directive which provides for post-action disclosure. CPR 31.17 provides for disclosure of documents against a non-party upon the commencement of documents. CPR 31.18 in conjunction with section 34 (4) of the SCA (1981) and the County Courts Act (1984) ensure that rules 31.16 and 31.17 do not limit any other power which the court may have to order:

(a)   disclosure before proceedings have started; and
(b)   disclosure against a person who is not a party to proceedings

Accordingly, the court is able to invoke its powers to order, notably, a non-party to provide information both pre-action and post-action[46] commencement which

---

46.   Lord Justice Waller (ed.), *The White Book Service*, Vol. 1 (London: Sweet & Maxwell, 2007), op. cit., para. 31.18.3 at 804: Disclosure of the identities of infringers and other wrongdoers may also be obtained by an interlocutory order in proceedings for other relief in relation to the same subject matter (*RCA Corp. v. Reddingtons Rare Records* [1974] 1 WLR 639; See *Loose v.*

deals with such matters as the identity of a wrongdoer in particular circumstances: namely, where the innocent part has become involved in the commission of wrong.[47] This power is the modern form of the old Chancery procedure used in aid of common law actions know as the 'bill of discover'.[48] At the present day, such orders are largely directed not so much to disclosure of documents as to disclosure of the identity[49] of a particular person being either the person who has committed the wrong or the person into whose hands property subject of the action has passed. In this regard the classic modern case is that of Norwich Pharmacal[50] in which the House of Lords held that:

> if through no fault of his own a person gets mixed up in the tortious acts of others so as to facilitate their wrong doing he may incur no personal liability but he comes under a duty to assist the person who has been wronged by giving him full information and disclosing the identity of the wrongdoers.[51]

It would seem that the wrong doing which would justify the imposition of an obligation to provide such information may involve not only a tort but also a breach of a contract or some other form of civil wrong.[52] It is necessary, however, that the non-party come within the category of person who is said to have become 'mixed up in the tortious acts of other'. Article 8 of the Directive provides that oral information which deals with the identity of wrongdoers '... is to be furnished by individuals 'involved in the manufacture, production and distribution of the goods or the provision of services'. For this reason, it would seem that in so far as such persons who are involved correspond to those who can be described as 'being mixed up' whether voluntarily or not, they would come within the parameters of Norwich Pharmacal. The case of *CHC Software Care v. Hopkins & Wood*[53] would seem to indicate that the class of information is not limited to that of the identification of the wrong doers. Lord Woolf noted in *Ashworth Hospital Authority v. MGN Ltd*[54] that the availability of the remedy of the Norwich

---

Williamson [1978] 1 WLR 639 (disclosure of identity of parties removing shellfish from the claimant's sole and several fishery and sea ground). But disclosure of customer's names in a copyright infringement action will not be order because until those persons have notice of the claim they are not wrongdoers (*Roberts v. Jump Knitwear Ltd* [1981] FSR 527).

47.   Lord Justice Waller (ed.), *The White Book Service*, Vol. 1 (London: Sweet & Maxwell, 2007), ibid., at para. 31.18.1: 'this form of claim will be unnecessary where the Court's powers to order disclosure and production against a non-party during proceedings under s. 34 of the SCA 1981 can be invoked but will retain its usefulness where such powers cannot be invoked. Section 34 provides for pre-action disclosure against a potential defendant'.

48.   *Gait v. Osbaldeston* (1826) 1 Russ 158, *Mendizabal v. Machado* (1826) 2 Russ 540, P. Matthews and H.M. Malek QC, *Disclosure* (London: Sweet & Maxwell, 2001), 26.

49.   or address as in *The Coca – Cola Company v. British Telecommunications plc* [2999] FSR 518.

50.   *Norwich Pharmacal Co. v. Customs and Excise Commissioners* [1974] AC 133.

51.   *Norwich Pharmacal Co. v. Customs and Excise Commissioners* [1974] AC 133, ibid., at 175.

52.   *Ashworth Hospital Authority v. MGN Ltd* [2002] UKHL 29.

53.   *CHC Software Care v. Hopkins & Wood* [1993] FSR 241.

54.   *Ashworth Hospital Authority v. MGN Ltd* [2002] UKHL 20, op cit.

Pharmacal is discretionary in the sense that it will only be ordered if it is established as being necessary and proportionate in the circumstances. However, it is submitted that the judicial implementation of Article 8 of the Directive will involve consistent interpretation of CPR 31 and section 37 of the SCA (1981) as concerns the exercise of the court's discretion notably in relation to the principles of the doctrine of full effectiveness, effective judicial protections and the articles of the Treaty as well as principles of EU law. These principles would apply, in particular, in order to ensure that the category of information which the Norwich Pharmacal order may produce will cover that which is provided by the Article 8 of the Directive.

In this regard, Lord Woolf observed in Ashworth:

> New situations are inevitably going to arise where it will be appropriate for the jurisdiction to be exercises where it has not been exercises previously. The limits which applied to its use in its infancy should not be allowed to stultify its use now that it has become a valuable and mature remedy.[55]

It is to be noted that following Recital 14 of the Directive, the scope of the English protection provided in terms of the disclosure of information in relation to both parties and non-parties and pre-action and post-action commencement is greater than that required by Article 8 of the Directive: that is, it is not restricted to simply commercial situations and it also provides for pre-action disclosure. This higher standard of protection however, is to be implemented as noted earlier in the context of consistent interpretation taking into consideration not only the wording of Recital 14 but also that of the Directive generally in the context of conformity with the principles of clarity, full effectiveness, effective judicial protection and articles of the EC Treaty.[56] Overall, it is concluded that the implementation of Article 8 conforms with the principles of legal certainty, full effectiveness and effective legal protection.

Article 9
Provisional and Precautionary Measures

Article 9 1 (a)

This article requires that Member States ensure that judicial authorities be able to grant an interlocutory injunction on the application of the applicant against an infringer of IP rights which includes intermediaries in three contexts:

- First, to prevent an imminent infringement of an IP right.

---

55. *Ashworth Hospital Authority v. MGN Ltd* [2002] UKHL 20, ibid., at 57.
56. S. Prechal, *Directives in EC Law* (Oxford: OUP, 2005), op. cit., 44 'On the other hand, where the Community has opted for minimum harmonization, the Member States are still free to maintain or adopt more stringent standards. However, the latter must be compatible with other Community law in particular the Treaty. In other words, the member States are free to maintain or adopt national measures, with the directive as the floor and the Treaty as the ceiling.'

- Second, to prevent the continuation of the infringement of an IP right sub-ject to a recurrent penalty where appropriate.
- Third, to make the continuation of the infringement of an IP right subject to the 'lodging of guarantees intended to ensure the compensation of the right holder'.

A   INTERLOCUTORY INJUNCTIONS AGAINST INTERMEDIARIES

Pursuant to section 37 of the SCA (1981) and following section 38 of the County Courts Act,[57] the High Court and the County Court respectively are able to grant an injunction. CPR 25 (1) (a) in turn embodies this power within the CPR. Injunctions being effectively forms of relief may normally only be granted if the applicant has a substantive cause of action. Lord Diplock observed in The Siskina:[58]

> A right to obtain an [interim] injunction is not a cause of action. It cannot stand on its own. It is dependent upon there being a pre-existing cause of action against the defendant arising out of an invasion, actual or threatened by him, of a legal or equitable right of the [claimant] for the enforcement of which the defendant is amendable to the jurisdiction of the court. The right to obtain an [interim] injunction is merely ancillary and incidental to the pre-existing cause of action. Thus, an applicant cannot obtain an interim injunction to restrain conduct that is not unlawful even if the act might be characterised as unfair. Nor is an interim injunction obtained in aid of a cause of action that has not yet arisen.[59]

Accordingly, it is necessary to consider whether it is possible in English law for a substantive cause of action to exist with respect to intermediaries. In this regard, no particular legislation has been adopted to implement Article 9 (1) of the Directive in order to provide a substantive cause of action against an intermediary such that an injunction may be granted. This is unlike the situation which prevailed with Article 8 (3) of Directive 2001/29 EC which contains the same wording with respect to third parties as does Article 9 (1) of the Directive with respect to intermediaries:

> Pursuant to Article 8 (3), Member States shall ensure that rights holders are in a position to apply or an injunction against intermediaries whose services are used by a third party to infringe a copy right or related right.
> Article 9 (1) (a) establishes that Member States shall ensure that rights holders are in a position ... an interlocutory injunction may be issued against intermediaries whose services are used by a third party to infringe an

---

57. County Court Remedies Regulation 1991 S.I. 1991/1222.
58. *The Siskina* [1979] AC 210.
59. A.A.S. Zuckerman, *Civil Procedure* (London: Nexis Lexis 2003), op cit., 326, *Sucker v. Tyndal PL* [1992] 1 All ER 124.

intellectual property right.

Article 8 (3) of Directive 2001/29 EC was implemented by section 97 A of the Copyright and Related Rights Regulations 2003 which provides that the High Court shall have power to grant an injunction against a 'service provider' where that service provider has actual knowledge that another person who uses the services of the 'service provider' is breaching the copyright. In section 97 A 'service provider' is given the meaning which is provided by Article 2 of the Electronic Commerce (EC Directive) Regulations which is any person who provides a service to an information society. However, although no definition is given in the Directive concerning an 'intermediary' or a service provide it would seem that the meaning is wide: that is, intermediary or service provider is to apply to any person who provides a service which is used to infringe an IP or facilitates such an infringement. Accordingly, the definition of service provider would seem to be too narrow in order to implement the concept of intermediary as provided in the Directive. More particularly, no specific legislation has been adopted in order to implement the Directive. Accordingly, it would seem to be necessary to ascertain whether the substantive cause of action for infringement of IP rights notably as provided by the Copyright, Designs and Patents Act (1998),[60] the Patents Act (1977),[61] the Trade Marks Act (1994)[62] can serve to implement the concept of intermediary provided by Article 9 (1) of the Directive. This process will require the use of the doctrine of interpretation in conformity.

B   APPLICATION OF THE DOCTRINE OF INTERPRETATION
          IN CONFORMITY WITH SUBSTANTIVE LEGISLATION

In short, it is submitted that the national court will be obliged to interpret the aforementioned statues which provide for a substantive cause of action concerning a breach of IP rights in conformity with Article 9 (1) (a) of the Directive. It would seem that the instant case is an example of where the United Kingdom has not adopted any implementing legislation by reason of the fact that it feels that the already existing legislation either constitutes or may constitute, subsequent to judicial interpretation, adequate implementation of Article 9 (1) of the Directive. Accordingly, the application of the doctrine of interpretation in conformity is necessary in the instant case in order to ensure that the scope of the substantive causes of action within the three aforementioned statutes may be interpreted sufficiently widely so as to provide a cause of action against an intermediary thereby permitting the rights hold to obtain interlocutory relief: that is, the scope of the substantive cause of action must encompass not only what might be termed a primary infringer who infringes an IP right directly but also a secondary infringer

---

60. Sections 17, 18, 18A, 19, 20, 21, 22, 23, 24, 25, & 26 Copyright Designs and Patents Act (1988).
61. Section 60 (2) Patents Act (1977).
62. Section 10(5) Trade Marks Act 1994.

such as an intermediary as provided by Article 9 (1) (a) who infringes such right indirectly. In the instant case it is submitted that the application of the doctrine of interpretation in conformity may proceed in the following manner: the method of interpretation which the English Court will used to interpret the Copyright Designs and Patents Act (1998), the Patents Act (1977) and the Trade Marks Act (1994) so as to implement Art 9 (1) of the Directive will be that of Community law rather than English law. This teleological method will necessarily require consideration of the purpose of Article 9 (1) as established both in the text of the that article and as set forth in the Recital 23.[63] From this combination of sources it is clear that the purpose of Article 9 (1) is indeed to ensure that a rightholder is able to apply for an interlocutory injunction against an intermediary in order to enforce and protect his IP rights: that is, the English court must construe the aforementioned statutes in relation to the purpose set forth in the directive thereby giving a meaning to the concept notably of infringer and infringement which are the basis of the three statutes. In so doing, the court will ensure the fully effective implementation of the Article 9 (1) of the Directive. In this regard, it is recalled that following Marleasing[64] the duty of the national court is to provide an interpretation which ensures conformity 'as far as possible' with the Directive using once again the concept of teleological interpretation[65] both to pre-existing legislation as in the instant case, as well as specially adopted legislation. It is submitted that in the instant case, such an interpretation of the three English statutes in conformity with the text and purpose of the Directive is possible: the result of such a possible interpretation would be to extend the scope of the concept of infringer and infringement so that it includes not only direct infringers or infringements but also indirect infringers which would include normally intermediaries. It is submitted that such a wide interpretation firstly, conforms with the purpose of the Directive and secondly, it does so in a manner which results in neither an artificial or strained construction of the words used in the legislation to express the concepts of infringement and infringer. In this regard, the ECJ in Marleasing in fact proceeded in the opposite manner, namely, by reducing the scope of the national legislation in order to ensure conformity with the EC directive dealing with grounds of nullity for companies.

C   CONTEXT OF THE AVAILABILITY OF THE INTERLOCUTORY INJUNCTION

As noted earlier, Article 9 (1) of the Directive provides that the applicant may apply for an injunction both where there is an imminent infringement of his right

---

63. Recital 23, Directive 2004/48 EU: ' … rightholders should have the possibility of applying for an injunction against an intermediary whose services are used being use by a third party to infringe the rightholder's industrial property'.
64. *Marleasing*, Case No. C-106/89 (1990) ECR I-4135.
65. S. Prechal, *Directives in EC Law* (Oxford: OUP, 2005), op. cit., 198.

and or where an infringement has taken place both. It is submitted that CPR 25 ensures fully effective implementation of (1) in this regard. However, arguably, the purpose of Article 9 (1) (a) is to expand the protection available to the rights holder in the following two ways:

i) first, where an injunction is refused perhaps because damages are viewed as capable of compensating the eventual loss, continuation of the infringement is made 'subject to the lodging of guarantees'. Therefore, it would seem that this provision serves to protect the rights holder in the situation where an injunction, for example, has been refused because damages at trial were held to constitute sufficient compensation but where the court felt it necessary to provide specific protection for the period between the application for the injunction and the judgment on the substantial issue: that is, it serves to expand the power of the court to award damages in lieu of an injunction but in so doing potentially augments the protection available to the right of the applicant for the injunction by means of the imposition of the guarantees which seem to constitute a form of monetary compensation for loss suffered. It would seem that such guarantees may be viewed as the counterpart to the undertaking in damages which an English court normally requires from an applicant in order to obtain an injunction in order to protect the rights of the defendant: This would seem to presuppose that such guarantees could serve to compensate for loss during the period which would have been covered by the granting of an injunction but which cannot perhaps be covered by damages on the substantive cause of action. In this regard, it would appear that at a minimum the court in exercising its power pursuant to S 37 of the High Courts Act (1981) or the County Courts Act (1984), would be required by reason of the doctrine of interpretation of conformity to exercise their discretion in a manner which would permit effective implementation of Article 9 (1) (a). In reality, however, CPR Or 25 1 (p) was specifically adopted in order to ensure that the court has the jurisdiction to make such an order and provides as follows:

'(p) an order under Article 9 of Council Directive (EC) 2004/48 on the enforcement of intellectual property rights (order in intellectual property proceedings making the continuation of an alleged infringement subject to the lodging of guarantees)'.

In this regard, the White Book observes

'It is clear that the court has a discretion to award damages in lieu of an injunction but it will not normally exercise this discretion to sanction future infringements. It would seem that sub paragraph (p) was added to r. 25 1(l) for the purpose of making it clear that the court has jurisdiction to make an interim order permitting the continuation of alleged infringement subject to the lodging of guarantees'.

ii) second, by expanding the scope of the method of enforcement for non-compliance with the terms of the injunction so as to provide for the imposition, where appropriate, of a 'recurring penalty' for non-compliance one notes as follows: in English law, non-compliance with or breach of an injunction constitutes contempt of court which is punishable by imprisonment or sequestration. The contempt must be proved beyond reasonable doubt. Clearly the person against whom the order is made will be in contempt if he or she acts in breach of an injunction after having notice of it.[66] To establish contempt by a non-party it must be demonstratèd both that the non-party's acts defeated in whole or in part the court's purpose in granting the injunction and that the non-party appreciated that this would be the effect. It would seem, therefore, that the imposition of recurring penalties would constitute an alternative to the sanction of contempt of court and or sequestration thereby increasing the scope of the methods of enforcement. Accordingly, the methods of enforcement would range potentially from the imposition of recurring sanctions to civil contempt of court and sequestration. This range would seem to comply with the principle of proportionality which is set for in the Article 3 (2) of the Directive. It would appear, therefore, that the courts in applying this article may be required to exercise their discretion pursuant to S 31 of the SCA (1981) in a way which would permit fully effective implementation of Article 9 (1) (a) at least in those circumstances where, following the Directive, the court feels it 'appropriate'. This last mentioned aspect of Article 9 appears to require that the court should have the power to order security for damages against an alleged infringer whilst permitting the infringement to continue. It is clear that the court has a discretion to award damages in lieu of an injunction but it will not normally exercise this discretion to sanction future infringements. It would seem that sub-para (p) was added to rule 25 1 (1) for the purpose of making it clear that the court has jurisdiction to make an interim order permitting the continuation of alleged infringement subject to the lodging of guarantees. Article 9 expressly states that where an interim remedy is granted before proceedings have been commenced, the procedural law of Member States shall ensure that upon the request of the defendant such remedy shall be revoked or cease to have effect if the applicant does not institute within a reasonable period proceedings leading to a decision on the merits. With respect to Article 9 (1) (b) it would appear that CPR 25 (1) (1) (c) (i) would permit effective implementation thereof.

Article 9 (2)

With respect to Article 9 (2) it would appear that CPR 25 (1) (1) (g) would permit the seizure of assets by means of the Mareva injunctions thereby effectively and clearly implementing that article.

Article 9 (3)

More complicated is Article 9 (3) which harmonizes the ground on which an injunction is to be granted. This article requires that the national courts have the

---

66. S. Sime, *A Practical Approach to Civil Procedure*, 5th edn (Oxford: OUP, 2002), 376 (*Z Ltd v. A-Z and AA-LL* (1982) QP 558 per Eveleigh LJ) (*A-G v. Punch Ltd* (2001) 2 WLR 1713.

authority to require the applicant to provide any reasonably available evidence to satisfy themselves of two matters: first, that the applicant is the rights holder and second, that his rights have been infringed. It is submitted that the expression in Article 9 (3): ' ... to satisfy themselves to a sufficient degree of certainty that the ... applicant's right is being infringed or that such infringement is imminent' signifies that the merits of the substantive action for infringement of IP rights must be considered. It is submitted that the meaning of this phrase is clear and unambiguous: 'to satisfy themselves to a sufficient degree of certainty that the ... applicant's right is being infringed or that such infringement is imminent' signifies that consideration be given to the merits of the applicant's case for breach of the substantive cause of action. It is only having considered the likelihood of success of the claimant's case for breach of an IP right that the courts are able to 'satisfy themselves to a sufficient degree of certain that ... the applicant's right is being infringed.' It would appear, therefore, that effective implementation of this article would require that the courts use their discretion so as not apply the principles advanced in American Cyanamid[67] which generally preclude consideration of the merits of the case. In this regard, it is recalled that in American Cyanamid, the House of Lords established, certeris paribus, the following: firstly, that the applicant merely had to show that he had a serious issue to be tried concerning the substantive cause of action as opposed to a case on the merits. Lord Diplock described a serious issue to be tried in the following terms: 'that the claim is not frivolous or vexations: in other words that there is a serious question to be tried'. Secondly, the matter of the merits of the case was normally not to be considered. Indeed the very purpose of the American Cyanamid guidelines was to preclude the determination on affidavit evidence of the merits of the case concerning the substantive cause of action.

Lord Diplock observed:

> It is no part of the court's function at this stage of the litigation to try to resolve conflicts of evidence on affidavit as to fact on which the claims of either party may ultimately depend nor to decide difficult question of law which call for detailed argument and mature considerations. These are matters to be dealt with at the trial.

Zuckerman observes:

> This statement was latter interpreted to mean that beyond ensuring that the applicant had an arguable case, thee strength of the parties' claims and their respective chances of success on the merits had not role to play in the exercise of the jurisdiction.

However, it may be that the correct interpretation of American Cyanamid is rather as follows: in truth, the House of Lords simply expanded the scope of the discretion which national courts enjoy pursuant to CPR 25 in two situations: first, where

---

67. *American Cyanamid Co. v. Ethicon Ltd* [1975] AC 396 at p. 398, HL (E), A.A.S. Zuckerman, *Civil Procedure* (London: Nexis Lexis 2003), 325.

there is a strong case on the merits that a breach of the substantive cause of action is made out and second, in default of a strong case on the merits, where there is a serious issue to be tried coupled with considerations based upon the balance of convenience. In Factortame No. 2, Lord Goff although upholding American Cyanamid, regarded the primary purpose of the latter as being as follows: that is 'to remove a fetter which appears to have been imposed in certain previous cases viz. that a party seeking an interlocutory injunction had to establish a prima facie case for substantive relief'. Indeed, it is submitted that the line of cases which are said to constitute exceptions to American Cyanamid in that the merits of the case are considered, in reality constitute the primary basis for the granting of an injunction. Following Lord Goff, it would seem to be that the real effect of American Cyanamid is to permit the granting of injunctions in cases where there is no prima facie case for substantive relief. The cases in which the merits of the case are regularly considered are as follows: defamation;[68] cases where the facts were clear and there was no material dispute about them;[69] mandatory injunctions;[70] where the granting of the injunction is likely to dispose of the action and therefore tantamount to a final judgment.[71] It is submitted[72] that effective implementation of Article 9 (3) of the Directive will simply return the basis upon which courts exercise their discretion at least with IP to its underlying status: namely, that the court normally exercises its discretion by considering the merits of the case for substantive relief. Laddie J in Series 5 *Software v. Clarke* observed in this regard:

> In my view Lord Diplock did not intend by the last quoted passage to exclude consideration of the strength of the cases in most applications for

---

68. *Bonnard v. Perryman* [1891] 2 Ch 269, *Cambridge Nutrition v. BBC* [1990] 3 All ER 523 (CA).

69. *Smith v. Inner London Education Authority* [1978] 1 All ER 411, *Alfred Dunill Ltd v. Sunoptic SA* [1979] FSR 337, *David (Lawrence) Ltd v. Ashton* [1991] 1 All ER 385 at 393 (CA).

70. *Hounslow London Borough Council v. Twickenham* [1971] Ch 223, *Shepherd Homes v. Sandham* [1971] Ch 340, *Bryanston Finance Ltd v. de Vries* No. 2 [1976] Ch 63; see *Software Cellular Network Ltd v. T Mobile (UK) Ltd* (2007) EWHC 1790 (Ch) 17 Jul. 2007 the court, following the Court of Appeal in *Zockoll Group Ltd v. Mercury Communications Ltd* (1988) FSR 354 held: 'But finally even if the Court is unable to feel any high degree of assurance that the plaintiff will establish his right there still may be circumstances in which it is appropriate to grant a mandatory injunction at an interlocutory stage. Those circumstances will exist where the risk of injustice if this injunction is refused outweights the risk of injustice if it is granted'. See, A. Zuckerman, *Civil Procedure* (London: Lexis-Nexis, 2003), 302-303 concerning the reasons why there should be no conceptual distinction between mandatory and prohibitory injunctions.

71. *NWL Ltd v. Woods* [1979] 3 All ER 614, *Cayne v. Global Natural Resources plc* [1984] All ER 224 (CA), *Lansing Linde Ltd v. Kerr* [1991] 1 All ER 418.

72. A. Zuckerman, *Civil Procedure* (London: Lexis-Nexis, 2003), Series 5 *Software v. Clarke* (1996) 1 All ER 853, op. cit., 280. 'The existence of these exceptions undermines the justification for the American Cyanamid doctrine ... Admittedly deciding on the basis of affidavits may not be as good a method of determining issues as testing them by the normal processes but it must be better than maintaining total ignorance in all situations and not just where the exceptions apply.'

interlocutory relief. It appears to me that what is intended is that the court should not attempt to solve difficult issues of fact or law on an application for interlocutory relief. If, on the other hand, the court is able to come to a view as to the strength of the parties' cases on the credible evidence, then it can do so... If it is apparent from that material [the affidavits] that one party's case is much stronger than the other's then that is a matter the court should not ignore. To suggest otherwise would be to exclude from consideration an important actor and such exclusion would fly in the fact of the flexibility advocated earlier in American Cyanamid. As Lord Diplock pointed out in Hoffmann-LaRoche, one of the purpose of the cross-undertaking in damages is to safeguard the defendant if this preliminary view of the strength of the plaintiff's case proves to be wrong.

D   Consistent Interpretation: Judicial Implementation

As noted earlier, it would seem that the case of von Colson[73] established a duty on the part of the Member States and, in particular, on the part of the national courts, to interpret national law in conformity with EU law irrespective of whether a deficiency in the implementation has taken place or not. Accordingly, it is submitted that the national court would be obliged to implement Article 9 (3) of the Directive by interpreting the national law in conformity therewith. It is to be noted that national law for the purposes of the principle of consistent interpretation includes more than simply legislation: it comprises what might be termed unwritten principles of national law as well as judge made case law.[74] The national law in the present instance would include such case law as that based upon Series 5 *Software v. Clarke* in addition to those cases noted where the granting of the injunction is likely to have the following characteristics: first, disposing of the matter and therefore be tantamount to a final judgment; second, cases where the fact are clear; third, mandatory injunctions, and fourth, actions in defamation among others. In short, it is not sufficient that the Member State transpose the directive into national legislative measures: the obligation on the part of the Member State requires that the objective contained within the Directive notably as pertains to Article 9 (3) therefore be effectively achieved in terms of both law and the actual application of the transposing national measures to fact: in the present instance, case law provides the possibility for the use of the grounds which are based upon the merits of the case. Therefore, the judicial application of the consistent interpretation would now require that the court consider using such cases as the basis of granting an injunction in order to effectively implement Article 9 (3) of the Directive.

---

73. See also *Commission v. Germany*, Case No. C-361/88 (1991) ECR I-2567, op. cit., para. 24; *Marks & Spencer*, Case C-62/00 (2002) ECR I-6325, *Commission v. Belgium*, Case No. C-42/89 (1990) ECR I-2821, *Commission v. Gree*, Case No. C-103/00 (2002) ECR I-1147.
74. *Centrosteel*, Case No. 456/98 (2000) ECR I-6007.

Article 9 (4)

Article 9 (4) provides that the application for the injunction may take place without the defendant being heard, in particular, where delay may result in irreparable harm to the rightsholder. In such a case the party is to be informed without delay and is to be permitted to make an application for a review to take place within a reasonable time. CPR 25.3 (1) permits an application for an injunction to be made ex parte, that is without notice, where there appear to be good reasons which would seem to include irreparable harm. The PD (Interim Injunctions) section 5. 1 (2) provides that any order for an injunction, unless the court orders otherwise, must contain, if made without notice to any other party, an undertaking by the applicant to the court to serve on the respondent as soon as practical the application notice, the evidence in support and any order made. The PD paragraph 4. 3 (3) provides that 'except in cases where secrecy is essential, the applicant should take steps to notify the respondent informally of the application'. Further, section 5 (3) of the PD provides that any order for an injunction must contain if the application for the injunction is made without notice to any other party, a return date for a further hearing at which the other party can be present. CPR 23.9 (2) and (3) require that where an application for an injunction as been granted ex parte that a copy of the evidence and the order must be served on the defendant unless the court orders otherwise. In particular, CPR 23.9 (3) requires that 'the order must contain a statement of the right to make an application to set aside or vary the order under rule 23.10.' Finally, CPR 23.10 permits the defendant to make an application to have the injunction set aside or varied within seven days of service thereof on him.

It is submitted that the provisions of CPR 23 herein cited implement Article 9 (4) of the Directive clearly and effectively.

Article 9 (5)

Article 9 (5) seeks to uphold the protection of the rights of the defence by ensuring that where an injunction is granted pre-commencement the applicant must commence the substantive action within a reasonable period of time. CPR 25 r.2 provides that an order for an interim remedy may be made at any time including pre-action commencement. In particular, CPR 25 r 2 (3) provides: 'Where it grants an interim remedy before a claim has been commenced, the court should give directions requiring a claim to be commenced' The operative term here is 'the court should give directions'. However, this rule is to be read in conjunction with section 4.4 (1) of the PD for Part 25: 'in addition to the provisions set out at 4.3 above, unless the court orders otherwise, either the applicant must undertake to the court to issue a claim form immediately or the court will give directions for the commencement of the claim'. Accordingly, the combination of section 4. 4 (1) of the Practise Direction arguably ensures through the use of the words 'the court will give' that the substantive action must give directions for the commencement of the claim in the event that the claimant does not do so. Accordingly, it would seem that the conjunction of both the claimant and the court will preclude the absence of a fixing of the substantive cause of action. Therefore, it would appear that these rules of the CPR and the Practise Directive permit effective and clear implementation of Article 9 (5) of the Directive.

Article 9 (6)

Article 9 (6) requires that the granting of an injunction may be made subject to the lodging of security such that the party against whom the order is made may receive compensation in the event that the injunction is found to have been wrongly made. Section 5 (1) of the Practise Direction for Part 25 provides that any order for an injunction must, unless the court orders otherwise, contain an undertaking by the applicant to the court to pay damages which the defendant may sustain and which the court considers that the applicant should pay. It is to be noted that the undertaking in damages is given to the court and not to the party against whom the interim order is sought.[75] It is submitted that the Practise Direction ensures effective and clear implementation of Article 9 (6) of the Directive.

Article 9 (7)

Article 9 (7) requires that the court have authority to order payment of compensation in the event that these measures are revoked or lapse due to any act or omission of the applicant or here it is subsequent found that there has been no infringement of an IP right. It would seem that section 5 (1) of the Practise Direction for Part 25 would provide for the undertaking as provided in the previous section:

> 5.1 Any order for an injunction, unless the court orders otherwise, must contain
> (1) an undertaking by the applicant to the court to pay any damages which the respondent sustains which the court considers the applicant should pay.

It is noted that pursuant to paragraph 5.1 of the PD, the Court enjoys discretion as to whether or not to order that the applicant pay any damages suffered by the respondent. This discretion appears to be consistent with the wording of the Directive which requires that 'the judicial authorities shall have the authority to order the applicant'. This is as opposed to removing the discretion of the national courts by imposing an obligation that they requiring the applicant to provide an undertaking in all cases. Accordingly, it is submitted that the national court would thereby effectively and clearly implements Article 9 (7) of the Directive.

---

75.   The Court apparently has discretion to dispense with the undertaking in damages. Thus far this dispensation has been confined to situation where a public body seeks an interim injunction as a means of enforcing the law. See *Hoffmann-La Roche & Co. AG v. Secretary of State for Trade* [1975] AC 295. However a public body is not entitled to dispensation where it bring proceedings for enforcement of a property, contract or other private law right.

Article 10
Corrective Measures

Article 10 (1)

Article 10 (1) requires that Member States ensure that the courts be able to order appropriate measures in order to ensure that goods found to be infringing as well as materials and implements used in the manufacture or creation of the goods involved in the infringement where necessary. These measures are to include where necessary the ability to recall the goods from the channels of commerce or destroying the goods or related materials. The implementation consists, arguably, in the following: first the inherent discretion which the court enjoys; and second, specific substantive legislation: section 99, 100 and 114 of the Copyright, Designs and Patents Act (1988) in relation to a copy right: section 230 of the same act in relation to unregistered designs; in addition section 229 provides that any relief available with respect to injunctions, damages accounts or otherwise as is available for any other right. Further, sections 16 and 19 of the Trade Marks Act (1994) provide for the delivery up and destruction where appropriate of infringing goods. Section 61 (1) (b) of the Patents Act (1997) provides for the delivery up and the destruction of any patent material in relation to which the patent is infringed or compromised. Paragraph 3 of Schedule 1 to Regulations 2006/1028 inserts section 24 A into the Registered Designs Act 1949 which accordingly makes clear that relief by way of damages, injunctions, accounts etc. are available for the infringement of registered design rights. This paragraph also inserts section 24 C and 24 D into the Registered Designs Act 1949 which provide for delivery up and disposal of articles which infringe the registered design. Further, Paragraph 3 of Schedule 1 of Regulations 2006/1028 also inserts section 24 F into the act:

> 24 F Rights and Remedies of an Exclusive Licensee:
> '1) In relation to a registered design, an exclusive licensee has except against the registered proprietor, the same rights and remedies in respect of matters occurring after the grant of the licence as if the licence has been an assignment'

However, although section 24 F (1) of the Registered Designs Act (1949) provides standing for an exclusive licensee in conformity with Article 4 (b) of the Directive no provision is made by any of the substantive law measures cited in order to ensure implementation of Article 4 (b) (c) or (d) of the Directive. Beyond the question of standing provided in Article 4 (b), (c) and (d) of the Directive it is submitted that the substantive law measures cited above implement the remainder of the obligation within Article 11 of the Directive. Interpretation in conformity in the context of judicial implementation will require the court to exercise its discretion pursuant to section 37 of the SCA (1981) and similarly with respect to the aforementioned statutory based powers, However, it is submitted that the scope of interpretation in conformity in the context of judicial implementation is such that it will not permit the creation of the standing required by Article 4 (b) (c) and (d) so as those categories of rights holders to apply for interim relief either pursuant to CPR 25 or pursuant to the courts inherent discretion pursuant to section 37 of the SCA (1981).

Article 10 (2)

Article 10 (2) provides that the court shall be able to order that such measures be carried out at the expense of the infringer. It would appear that the court enjoys broad discretion both within its inherent jurisdiction and pursuant to CPR 44. This latter provides that the court may establish the conditions in which costs are payable. Normally, it would seem that the basic principle is that the party ordered to do something will also bear the costs of executing the order. It is submitted that the court would following the duty of interpretation in conformity be able to exercise its discretion to order the defendant to pay for the execution of an order made in the context of Article 10 (2) of the Directive.

Article 10 (3)

Article 10 (3) provides that the national court be able to take into consideration the principle of proportionality. The CPR provides in the Overriding Objective that the principle of proportionality can be taken into consideration.

Accordingly, it is submitted that the CPR Overriding Objective implements this article effectively and with legal clarity.

Article 11
Injunctions

Article 11 requires that Member States ensure that the national courts be able to provide a permanent injunction both against the direct infringer and against the intermediary whose services are being used by a third party to infringe an IP right. Section 37 (1) of the SCA (1981) provides that a court may grant an injunction which would include a final injunction and following section 37 (2) on such conditions as it thinks fit. This article requires only that the national courts posses the power to order such a measure. It does not apparently seek to harmonize, unlike with the interlocutory measure in Article 9 the conditions under which the final injunction is to be given. It seeks only to ensure that such a measure is available.

The White Book observes at paragraph 25.1.10:

> The Supreme Court Act (1981) S 37 states that the High Court may by order whether interlocutory or final, grant an injunction in all cases in which it appears to the court to be and convenient to do so (S 37 (1). Any such order may be made either unconditionally or on such terms and conditions as the court thinks just (s. 37 (2)).

The jurisdiction of the County Court is derived from section 38 of the County Courts Act 1984 and the County Courts Remedies Regulation 1991, S.I. 1991/1222.

A final injunction is usually granted to an IP right holder who proves at trial that his rights have been infringed by the defendant as in *Chiron v. Organon* (No. 10).[76] As a general rule a defendant who interferes with a proprietary right will be injuncted. The principles were most recently stated in: *Navitaire Inc. v. Easyjet Airline Co.* (No. 2):[77]

> 1. An injunction would generally be granted where the invasion of a property right was demonstrated and where repetition was threatened, but not where the effect of the injunction was oppressive. The court might in its discretion award damages instead. *Jaggard v. Sawyer* [1995] 1 W.L.R. 269; [1995] 2 All E.R. 189 at 208 (CA per Millett L.J.) followed.
> 2. The grant or refusal of a final injunction was not merely a matter of convenience.
> 3. The discretion to award damages was not exercised merely because the defendant was willing to pay. If the effect of the grant of an injunction were not oppressive, the defendant could not buy his way out of it even if the price, objectively ascertained, would be modest. By 'oppressive' in this context was meant that the effect of the grant of the injunction would be grossly disproportionate to the right protected.[78]

With respect therefore to Article 11 of the Directive and final injunctions, consistent interpretation of section 37 of the SCA (1981) in the context of judicial implementation would require the discretion of the court be exercised in a manner which would ensure implementation which would conform with the principles of clarity, effectiveness and effective judicial protection. In this context principles developed notably in Chiron and in Noita would be applied. It is to be noted that the doctrine of consistent interpretation would be unable to assist with the non-implementation of Article 4 (c) and (d) and the partial implementation of Article 4 (b) as it pertains to application for a final injunction pursuant to Article 11.

Article 12
Alternative Measures

Article 12 provides that Member States may ensure that the national courts be able to grant compensation – damages in lieu of injunction where the infringer acted unintentionally and the imposition of an injunction would be disproportionate. Pursuant to section 50 of the SCA (1981) and section 38 of the County Courts Act (1984) the Court may award damages as opposed to an injunction. Accordingly, the

---

76. *Chrion v. Organon (No. 10)* [1995] FSR 325.
77. *Navitaire Inc. v. Easyjet Airline Co. (No. 2)* [2006] RPC 4: I am grateful to the chambers of 11 South Square, Gray's Inn, London for an electronic copy of this judgment.
78. *Shelfer v. City of London Electric Lighting Co.* [1895] 1 Ch 287 at 315-316, 322-323, 64 L.J.Ch. 216 at 225, 229 (CA per Lindley, A.L. Smith L.JJ.) applied. *Banks v. CBS Songs Ltd* (No. 2) [1996] E.M.L.R. 452 (Jacob J.) and *Ludlow Music Inc. v. Williams* [2002] F.S.R. 57 (Pumfrey J.) distinguished.

principle of consistent interpretation would require in the context of judicial implementation that the court exercise its discretion pursuant to the aforementioned statutes in conformity with the provisions set forth in Article 12 of the Directive.

Article 13
Damages

Article 13 requires that Member States ensure that the national courts be able to award damages to the rightsholder which will compensate for the loss caused by the infringement.

The first section concerns infringements carried out with knowledge on the part of the infringer:

(1) Member States shall ensure that the competent judicial authorities, on the application of an injured party, order the infringer who knowingly or with reasonable grounds to know, engaged in an infringing activity, to pay the rightsholder damages appropriate to the actual prejudice suffered by him/her as a result of the infringement

In such circumstances the national court is obliged to take into account the following factors:

When the judicial authorities set the damages:
a) they shall take into account all appropriate aspects, such as the negative economic consequences, including loss of profits, which the injured party has suffered, any unfair profits made by the infringer and in appropriate cases, elements other than economic factors such as the moral prejudice caused to the right holder by the infringement

E   IMPLEMENTATION

Article 13 (1) (a)

Paragraph 3 of the Intellectual Property (Enforcement, etc.) Regulations 2006/1028 implements Article 13 (1) in conjunction with paragraphs 1-5 of Schedule 11 thereof which are set forth in footnote 79 below. Indeed, Paragraph 3 of the Regulations implement Article 13 (1) (a) of the Directive by almost verbatim transposition thereof as can be observed through the comparison of the texts herein presented at footnote 80 herein.[79]

---

79. In this regard the Explanatory Memorandum to the Intellectual Property (Enforcement etc.) Regulations 2006/1028 states in this regard: 'Art. 13 (1) sets out a range of factors which must be taken into account in awarding damages. It includes a number of terms the meaning of which is unclear: for example "actual prejudice", "moral prejudice". It does not seem appropriate to attempt to translate these terms into those of national law and accordingly to ensure that

Paragraph 3 of the Regulations provides as follows:

Assessment of Damages:

(1) Where in an action for infringement of an intellectual property right the defendant knew or had reasonable grounds to know that he engaged in infringing activity, the damages awarded to the claimant shall be appropriate to the actual prejudice he suffered as a result of the infringement:

(2) When awarding such damages –

   a) all appropriate aspects shall be taken into account, including in particular –

      i) the negative economic consequences, including any lost profits which the claimant has suffered and any unfair profits made by the defendant, and

      ii) elements other than economic factors including the moral prejudice caused to the claimant by the infringement; or

   b) where appropriate they may be awarded on the basis of the royalties or fees which would have been due had the defendant obtained a licence.

3) The regulation does not affect the operation of any enactment or rule of law relating to remedies for the infringement of intellectual property rights except to the extent that it is inconsistent with the provision of this regulation.[80]

---

our approach is in compliance with Art. 13(1), the copy out approach has been adopted. However it is necessary to avoid the implication that Art. 13(1) provides a complete code which displaced the national law of damages (in particular any suggestion that it introduces punitive damages). Accordingly, Reg. 3(3) makes it clear that the existing rules of national law are preserved except to the extent that there is an actual inconsistency.'

80. Schedule 2 Amendments to other primary legislation: Amendments of the Patents Act 1977 supplements para. 3 of the Regulation in terms of implementation of Art. 13 (1) of the Directive.

'1. The Patents Act 1977 shall be amended as follows.
2. In s. 62 (restrictions on recovery of damages for infringement) in subs. (3) for the words from 'no damages' at the end of the subsection there shall be substituted:
'the court or the comptroller shall, when awarding damages or making an order for an account of profits in proceedings for an infringement of the patent committed before the decision to allow the amendment take into account the following:
(a) whether at the date of the infringement the defendant or defender knew, or had reasonable grounds to know that he was infringing the patent;
(b) whether the specification of the patent was famed in good faith and with reasonable skill and knowledge;
(c) whether the proceedings are brought in good faith'.
3. In s. 63 (relief for infringement of partially valid patent) in subs. (2) for the words from ' not grant relief' to the end of the subsection there shall be substituted:
'when awarding damages, costs or expenses or making an order for an account of profits, take into account the following:
(a) whether at the date of the infringement the defendant or defender knows, or had reasonable grounds to know, that he was infringing the patent;

F   IMPLEMENTATION

Article 13 (1) (b)

The Directive also provides an alternative which the national courts may use in place of the calculations provided in the previous section and which constitutes a form of lump sum damages:

> b) as an alternative to (a), they may, in appropriate cases, set the damages as a lump sum on the basis of elements such as at least the amount of royalties or fees which would have been due if the infringer had requested permission to use the intellectual property right in question.

It is clear that by reason of the term 'may'. Article 13 (1) (b) does not place an obligation on the national courts to use this method of assessment of damages.

Article 13(2)

Article 13 (2) provides as follows:

> 2. Where the infringer did not knowingly, or with reasonable grounds know, engage in infringing activity, Member States may lay down that the judicial authorities may order the recovery of profits or the payment of damages which may be pre-established.

Article 13 (2) of the Directive is not specifically implemented. Arguably, this article contains no obligation which enjoins the national courts to pre-establish the amount of either profits to be recovered or damages to paid. Indeed the position at law in England would seem to prevent the awarding of damages against an innocent infringer. Cornish observes:

> Thus, in the Acts relating to patents, designs and copyright it is explicitly provided that no damages are payable for a period in which the infringer did not know and had not reasonable grounds for supposing that the right existed:

(b) whether the specification of the patent was framed in good faith and with reasonable skill and knowledge;

(c) whether the proceedings are brought in good faith.

And any relief granted shall be subject to the discretion of the court or the comptroller as to costs or expenses and as to the date from which damages or an account should be reckoned'.

4. In s. 68 (effect of non-registration on infringement proceedings):

(a) the words from 'the court or comptroller shall' to 'occurring' shall be omitted; and

(b) before the word 'unless' there shall be inserted 'in proceedings for such an infringement, the court or comptroller shall not award him costs or expenses'.

5. (1) In s. 130 (interpretation) in subs. (1), in the definition of 'formal requirement' for 's. 17' there shall be substituted 's. 15A'.

(2) Subpara. (1) does not apply to an application for a patent to which Art. 20, 21 or 22 of the Regulatory Reform (Patents) Order 2004 applies'.

(PA 1977 s 62 (1), RD 1949 s 9(1), CDPA 1988 ss 97 (1), 233 (also affecting secondary infringement). RPC 279) though a discretionary remedy such as an account might be refused.[81]

In terms of implementation of Article 13 (1) by means of the non specifically adopted substantive law, arguably the position in English law is that damages are intended to compensate the victim of a wrong and damages and therefore are to be appropriate to the actual prejudice suffered. They are designed to make good, so far as possible, the pecuniary or non-pecuniary loss suffered by the victim by putting him or her into as good a position as if no wrong had occurred. IP torts are civil wrongs, which are either statutory torts as with infringement of a patent or common law torts such as passing off. The owner of IP rights is able to claim financial compensation from an infringer either as compensation for the owner's loss or by the infringer accounting for his profit following in conformity with Article 13 (1) (a).[82] The equitable remedy of an account of profits is very well-established, and it is laid down in statute that an account of profits may be ordered for infringement of a patent,[83] infringement of copyright,[84] infringement of design right,[85] and infringement of performer's property rights. 'Aggravated damages' may be awarded as compensation for a claimant's mental distress, which can be equated to moral prejudice that may be caused to a right holder by an infringement. It is not clear exactly however as to the scope or meaning of the term 'moral prejudice'.[86] 'Additional damages' are provided for infringement of copyright, design right or performer's property rights under the Copyright, Designs and Patents Act 1988. To award such damages the court considers all the circumstances and in particular the flagrancy of the infringement and any benefit accruing to the defendant by reason of it.[87] It is to be noted the Recital 27 establishes that the Member States are not required to introduce exemplary damages albeit

---

81. W. Cornish & D. Llewelyn, *Intellectual Property, Patents, Copyright, Trademarks and Allied Rights*, 5th edn (London: Sweet & Maxwell, 2003), 78.
82. W. Cornish & D. Llewelyn, *Intellectual Property: Patents, Copyright, Trade Marks and Allied Rights*, 5th edn (London: Sweet & Maxwell, 2003), ibid., 74-78, H.D. Mc Gregor QC, *McGregor on Damages* (London: Sweet & Maxwell, 2005) and 2nd supplement to the 17th edition (2005), D. Bainbridge, *Intellectual Property*, 5th edn (London: Longman, 2002), 417-419.
83. Section 61(1)(d) Patents Act 1977.
84. Section 96(2) Copyright, Designs and Patents Act 1988.
85. Section 229(2) Copyright, Designs and Patents Act 1988.
86. A. Kur, 'The Enforcement Directive – Rough Start, Happy Landing', *ICC* 35, no. 7 (2004): 821 at 828, op. cit.
87. W. Cornish & D. Llewelyn, *Intellectual Property: Patents, Copyright, Trade Marks and Allied Rights*, 5th edn (London: Sweet & Maxwell, 2003), op cit., see generally Ch. 2, Remedies in Civil Actions. For exemplary damages see *Rookes v. Barnard* (1964) AC 1129 per Lord Devlin, at 1225-1226, and *Kuddus v. Chief Constable of Leciestershire Constabulary*, <www.publications.parliament.uk>, and The Law Commission, Report on Aggravated, Exemplary and Trestitutionary Damages (1998) Law Com. No. 247, and The Department of Constitutional Affairs, Consultation Paper: The Law on Damages: 4 May 2007, <www.dca.gov.uk/consult/damages/dp090>, in particular, Ch. 7.

they are available in English law.[88] Accordingly, it would appear that Article 13 is adequately implemented in terms of substantive law by reason of the clarity of the measures.

It is necessary, however, to consider the availability of damages in relation to representative actions as provided by Article 9 (1) of the Directive as discussed under that section. As noted in the discussion in relation to Article 4, there are two hypothesis: first, that notably Article 4 (c) and (d) do not impose any obligation on Member States to introduce representative actions into their national procedure where such do not already exist. Following this hypothesis, the requirements for damages pursuant to Article 13 will arguably require no modifications of the English system of damages. However, following the second hypothesis, namely, that Article 4 (c) and (d) do impose upon Member States the obligation to introduce representative actions where such do not already exist in the national systems, the following observations may be made: Andrews argues[89] that the inability of English courts 'to award damages at large or globally without reference to the particular loss suffered by members of the relevant class ... is the nub of the matter and the reason that English representative actions remains a procedural backwater rather than a flourishing style of multi-party litigation'. Nevertheless, it is necessary to bear in mind the existence of a representative action for consumers pursuant to section 47 B of the Competition Act (1998).[90] It is true that this provision is limited in scope and nature allowing bodies specified by the Secretary of State to bring follow-on actions on behalf of consumers before the CAT. Further, this form of representative action appears to avoid the difficulties raised by Andrews for the following reasons: in a representative action, a body representing the interests of those harmed by an unlawful practice (the representative body) brings an action on behalf of those who have suffered loss which can be totalled up.

---

88.   See n. 86 *infra* in particular *Rookes v. Barnard* (1964) AC 1129 per Lord Devlin at 1125-1226 ibid.

89.   N. Andrews, 'Multi-party Proceedings in England: Representative and Group Actions' *Duke J of Comp. & Int'l L* 11 (2001): 249 at 250 'A representative cannot use representative proceeding to make a claim if he does not have a cause of action in his own right. *Chocosuisse: Union des Fabricants Suisses de Chocolat v. Cadbury Ltd*, The Times 15 Mar. 1999, 'Trade Association Cannot Sue Over Passing-Off'. The Court of Appeal held that the association lacked capacity to sue on behalf of affected Swiss traders because it own interest had not been damaged by the wrong.

90.   See *The Consumers Association v. JJB Sports PLC*, Case No. 1078/7/0: Claim for damages under s. 47 B CA (1998) CAT; see also Office of Fair Trading 'Private actions in competition law: effective redress for consumers and business' Discussion Paper, Apr. 2007, and Consultation Responses 31 Aug. 2007 <www.oft.gov.uk/advice_and_resources/resource_base/consultation/private> considers the use of representative actions in private enforcement actions for competition law.

G   MEASURES RESULTING FROM A DECISION ON THE MERITS
OF THE CASE

It is convenient to group under this heading the measures which are provided by Articles 10, 11 and 13 of the Directive in so far as they result from the finding of a merits on the substantive cause of action for a breach of IP rights.

It is recalled that Article 10 provides: '… that appropriate measures be taken with regard to goods that they have found to be infringing an IP right … ': clearly an infringement of the substantive rights must have been made.

Article 11 declares: '… that where a judicial decision is taken finding an infringement of an IP right …'

Article 13 establishes: ' … Member States shall ensure that the competent judicial authorities … shall order the infringer who knowingly, or with reasonable grounds to know, engaged in an infringing activity …' clearly presupposes an infringement finding. More particularly, it is submitted that in order to ensure that the procedural rights which are involved in the aforementioned articles may be effectively implemented pursuant to Article 3 (1) and (2) of the Directive it is necessary that the court ensure that it be able to evaluate expert evidence adequately: that is, the finding of infringement is dependent upon the judge's ability to evaluate the expert evidence, particularly in the sense of understanding the scientific terminology involved with IP. This is notably so in cases where the trial judge does not possess a scientific background which would facilitate comprehending and evaluating the expert evidence which may be presented before the court. Accordingly, it is submitted that following in particular Recitals 3 and 17 coupled with Article 3 of the Directive, it is necessary in such cases for the court to consider using its discretion in order to appoint an assessor pursuant to CPR 35. 15.[91] It is to be noted, however, that it may be necessary to make a reference to the ECJ pursuant to Article 234 in order to confirm the exact scope of the substantive rights contained within Articles 10, 11 and 13 of the Directive in order to ensure that their scope indeed requires what is setforth herein as the effective form of their implementation.

H   EVALUATION OF EXPERT EVIDENCE

1   **High Court, Chancery Division, CPR and Assessors**

CPR 35.15 provides as follows:

> (1) This rule applies when the court appoints one or more persons (an assessor) under S 70 of the Supreme Court Act (1981) or S 63 of the County Courts Act (1984)

---

91. Sir L. Blom-Cooper (ed.), *Experts in the Civil Courts*, *Expert Witness Institute* (Oxford: OUP, 2006) Ch. 8, 113-117.

(2) The assessor shall assist the court in dealing with a matter in which the assessor has skill and experience

(3) An assessor shall take such part in the proceedings as the court may direct and in particular may –
   a) direct the assessor to prepare a report for the court on any issue in the proceedings
   b) direct the assessor to attend the whole or any part of the trial to advise the court on any such matter

(4) If the assessor prepares a report for the court before the trial has begun –
   a) the court will send a copy to each of the parties; and
   b) the parties may use it at the trial

(5) The remuneration to be paid to the assessor for his services shall be determined by the court and shall form part of the costs of the proceedings....

The Practise Direction for CPR 35.15 provides:

7.1 An assessor may be appointed to assist the court under rule 35.15. Not less than 21 days before making such an appointment the court will notify each party in writing of the name of the proposed assessor of the matter in respect of which the assistance of the assessor will be sought and of the qualification to the assessor to give that assistance.

7.2 Where any person has been proposed for appointment as an assessor objection to him, either personally or in respect of his qualification may be taken by any party.

7.3 Any such objection must be make in writing and filed with the court within 7 days of receipt of the notification referred to in paragraph 6.1 and will be taken into account by the court in deciding whether or not to make the appointment.

7.4 Copies of any report prepared by the assessor will be sent to each of the parties but the assessor will not give oral evidence or be open to cross-examination or questioning.

Lord Woolf sets forth the purpose and in particular the costs advantages of the assessor in the Interim Report[92] at paragraph 24:

In complex litigation, it could often be of considerable assistance to the judge if he was provided with an assessor. This only happens with any degree of regularity in the Admiralty Court and the practise should be extended. Expense will be involved in employing the expert but this is likely to be justified by substantial savings in the length of the hearing. In particular, it should be possible for the assessor to preside over meetings of the parties' experts and assist them to reach agreement.

---

92. Lord Woolf, *Interim Report on Access of Civil Justice*, Jul. (1995) <www.gov.uk/civil/report.htm>

In his Final Report Lord Woolf[93] sets forth at paragraphs 58-60 his definitive view on the role of the assessor:

> 58 In the Interim Report, I recommended that the courts should make wider use of the powers to appoint expert assessors to assist the judge in complex litigation and in appropriate cases to preside over meetings between the parties' experts and help them reach an agreement.
>
> 59 There has been some resistance to these proposals largely on the ground that an assessor would usurp the role of the judge. I do not agree that this would necessarily be the case: where there are complex technical issues the assessors function would be to 'educate' the judge to enable him to reach a properly informed decision. In the most complex cases, this function could be performed by two assessors, one instructed by each party.
>
> 60 Clearly the use of an independent assessor in addition to the parties' experts and the judge will not be cost effective except in the heaviest cases.

The nature of the intervention of the assessor, however, is restricted to giving advice to the judge as part of the court concerning technical information but not evidence. Accordingly, the assessor may not be cross-examined as no evidence is presented and the assessor intervenes as part of the court in order to assist the judge in his judicial functions. Blom-Cooper[94] however, argues that this system of providing advice to a judge which is not subject to cross-examination is likely to contravene Article 6.1 European Convention on Human Rights (ECHR). He writes:

> The assessor system being advice by an expert not under oath given to the court on matters not disclosable for cross examination by either party would be regarded today as being incompatible under S 3(1) of the Human Rights Act. 1988 as a violation of Art. 6.1 ECHR.

Nevertheless, it is submitted that this analysis may possibly not apply in the following situations: first, where the assessor provides information which the court uses in order to take judicial notice of non controversial matters:[95] second, in those circumstances where the rights of the defence do not require cross-examination,

---

93. Lord Woolf, *Final Report on Access to Civil Justice*, Jul. (1996) <www.dca.gov.uk/civil/report. htm>
94. L. Blom-Cooper QC, 'Experts and Assessors', *CJQ* 21 (2002): 345, op. cit., at 348, See also A. Edis QC, 'Privilege and Immunity: Problems of Expert Evidence' *CJQ* 26 (2007): 40, D.M. Dwyer, 'The Causes and Manifestations of Bias in Civil Expert Evidence', *CJQ* 26 (2007): 425, Protocol for Experts to Give Evidence in Civil Claims, Civil Justice Council, Jun. 2005, <www.justice.gov.uk>
95. A.A.S. Zuckerman, *Civil Procedure* (London: Lexis-Nexis, 2003), op. cit., 640 'Assessors fulfil a different role from that of expert witnesses. Assessors sit with the judge and assist the court in its deliberations both during the presentation of evidence and argument and after they have been concluded. Since an assessor assists the court in its judicial role, an assessor cannot be cross-examined.'

the proposition being that defence rights do not require in all situations the right to cross-examination in order to be upheld notably when then are accompanied by an effective system of appeal.

2   Assessors CPR 35.15 and Practice Direction Paragraph 7

Etymologically, assessor signifies a person who is authorized to sit with others in order to assist directly in the taking of decisions. In practice, the role of the assessor may vary widely. Indeed, for some, such as Viscount Simon LC,[96] an assessor may intervene exclusively on matters which require an explanation of the meaning of technical terms. Moreover, an assessor, being unsworn may not give evidence. Others, such as Viscount Dunedin,[97] believe that an assessor may provide a source of facts beyond simply the meaning of words. For Zuckerman, the assessor in providing either the information concerning the meaning of words or more generally, facts, assists the judge in his judicial capacity.[98] Therefore, the assessor cannot be cross-examined. Dwyer[99] observes that:

> it is settled law that an assessor acting in a normal civil capacity or under a particularly statutory form of proceedings is not an evidentiary source and almost certain constitutes part of the tribunal as scientific adviser under S 70 (3) of the Supreme Court Act (1981) and CPR 35.15.

3   Method of Intervention of the Assessor

One method of analysing the function of the assessor is to relate it to the process of judicial notice. Indeed, Lord Denning[100] observed that a judge in using the advice of the assessor 'equips himself in order to take judicial notice'. In terms of a definition judicial notice may be defined as a compendious method of proof. Further, the facts which may be noticed judicially vary between those of which the veracity is indisputable to those which require some type of proof. Restricting judicial notice to the category of indisputable facts entails a procedural advantage:

---

96. *Richardson v. Redpath Brown & Co. Ltd* [1944] AC 67, speech of Viscount Simon LC at 70.
97. *SS Australia v. SS Nautilus (Cargo Owners) The Australia* [1927] AC 145 at 150.
98. A.A.S. Zuckerman, *Civil Procedure* (London: Lexis-Nexis, 2003), op. cit., 640.
99. D. Dwyer, 'The Future of Assessors under the CPR', *CJQ* 25 (2006): 219 at 230 refers to *The White Book Service* (London: Sweet & Maxwell, 2006) at 962: 'The assessor assists the judge in discharging his judicial role. His function is to educate the judge and to enable him to reach a properly informed decision', contrary to Sir Louis Blom-Cooper QC who observes at p. 350 'There has been significant uncertainty as to the status of the advice given to judges by assessors.'
100. *Baldwin & Francis v. Patents Appeal Tribunal* [1959] AC 663 at 691 where Lord Denning explains that the purpose of the appointment of assessors is '... the court is equipping itself for its task by taking judicial notice of all such things as it ought to know in order to do its work properly'.

it explains both why an assessor cannot be cross examined and why such absence of cross-examination cannot violate the rights of the defence:[101] namely, that the veracity of the facts noticed judicially is indisputable. If, on the other hand, the concept of judicial notice is expanded so as to include not only indisputable but also disputable matters then the rights of the defence may be ensured in two ways: firstly, by means of appeal and secondly, by the right of the parties to respond in some way before judgment to the information given to the judge by the assessor through judicial notice.[102] With regard to the type of facts which may be judicially noticed the distinction is sometimes made between adjudicative facts which are not disputable and legislative facts which are disputable. Indeed, Davis[103] includes both types of facts, legislative and adjudicative, within the concept of judicial notice. Accordingly, it will be argued here that a judge when sitting with the assessor takes judicial notice by means of the information which the assessor provides him of facts some of which are indisputable and others which are disputable.

In order to ensure that the functions of the assessor correspond to the notion of the judge taking judicial notice, it may be that the doctrine of efficacy and non-discrimination will require certain changes to the structure of CPR 35. 15. One may consider the following.

First, it is submitted that CPR 35. 15 (3) and (4) may be ultra vires of the enabling statutes.
The editor of the White Book observes:

'CPR 35 (15) (3) provides that an assessor may take part 'in the proceedings as the Court may direct.' This seems wider than the former provisions and without the statutory provision. S 70 (1) of the 1981 Act says that the Court 'may hear and dispose' of the case 'with their assistance' and S 63 (1) of the 1984 Acts states that the assessor 'may sit with the judge'.[104]

---

101. A.A.S. Zuckerman, *Principles of Criminal Evidence* (Oxford: OUP, 1989), op. cit., 98: 'Where there can be no reasonable dispute between parties it is wasteful to insist on a full trial of fact. The doctrine of judicial notice relieves the parties of the burden of proving facts which are not reasonably disputable and thereby solves the problems when an indisputable fact is taken for granted it clearly cannot be said that one of the parties has been deprived of the opportunity to present his case.'
102. K.C. Davis, 'Judicial Notice', *Columbia Law Review* 55 (1955): 945 at 978.
103. K.C. Davis, 'Judicial Notice', *Columbia Law Review*, 55(1955): 945, ibid., 976.
104. SCA (1981) s. 70 provides: '(1) In any cause or matter before the High Court the court may, if it thinks it expedient to do so, call in the aid of one or more assess specially qualified and hear and dispose of the cause or matter wholly or partially with their assistance.
      (2) The remuneration, if any, to be paid to an assessor for his services under subs. (1) in connection with any proceedings shall be determined by the court and shall form part of the costs of the proceedings.
      (3) Rules of Court shall make provision for the appointment of scientific advisors to assist the Patents Court in proceedings under the Patents Act 1949 and Patents Act 1977 and for regulating the functions of such advisors.
      (4) The remuneration of any such adviser shall be determined by the Lord Chancellor with the concurrence of the Minister for the Civil Service and shall be defrayed out of the money provided by Parliament.'

In short, a court may only direct assessors to '… take part in the proceedings' as in conformity with the Supreme Court Act (1981) (SCA) and the County Court Act (1984) (CCA). More particularly, it would seem that CPR 35.15 (3) and (4) permit the assessor to provide what could be construed as evidence in so far as the report can be relied upon by the parties. Accordingly, this possibility arguably exceeds the scope of both the SCA (1981) and the CCA (1984) but also tends to obliterate the distinctions as to the appropriate function of a court expert: that is an expert appointed ex officio by the court in contrast to the current single expert provided by CPR 35. This would approximate the former court expert under the Rules of the Supreme Court (RSC) 40 rule 1.[105]

It would seem, therefore, that the elimination of CPR 35.15 (3) and (4) may be required by application of the doctrine of consistent interpretation notably with respect to Article 3 of the Directive coupled with compliance with EU principles such as, that of legal clarity, full effect[106] and effective judicial protection of rights so as to ensure that the operation of the assessor comes squarely within the ambit of SCA (1981) and CCA (1984). Following this analysis, the restriction of CPR 35.15 to the parameters of the enabling statutes ensures, thereby, that the rôle of the assessor is in turn limited to one of assisting the judge to take judicial notice of the meaning of technical words. It is submitted that this restriction of the role of the assessor ensures, thereby, the incorporation of its functions into those of the tribunal. It would seem, therefore, that the assessor operating in this manner may contribute to ensuring that Articles 3, 10, 11 and 13 of the Directive are enforced and implemented in a manner which also complies with the aforementioned EU principles such as effective judicial protection, full effect and legal clarity. Similarly, in order to ensure more fully the reduction in the scope of the assessor which would result from the removal of CPR 35.15 (3) and (4), arguably, the doctrine of consistent interpretation may require an amendment of Practice Direction (PD) 7. 4:[107]

---

105. L. Blom-Cooper, 'Experts and Assessors: Past Present and Future' *CJQ* (2002) 341, at 347 notes that RSC Or 40 r. 1 which is now replaced by CPR 35 provided:

'1. In any cause or matter which is to be tried without a jury and in which any question for an expert witness arises, the Court may at any time; on the application of any party, appoint an independent expert of if more than once question arises, two or more such experts, to enquire and report on any question of fact or opinion involving questions of law or of construction. An expert appointed under this paragraph is referred to as a court expert.

2. Any court expert in a cause or matter shall, if possible be a person agreed between the parties and failing agreement, shall be nominated by the court.

3. The question to be submitted to the court expert and the restrictions (if any) given to him shall, failing agreement between the parties, be settled by the court.

4. In this rule 'expert' in relation to any question arising in a cause or matter means any person who has such knowledge or experience of or in connection with the question that his opinion on it would be admissible in evidence.

RSC 40 r 1 (2) is the germ of the idea for the single joint expert provision in CPR 35.7 and one wonders why the court appointed expert provision was dropped.'

106. *Commission v. Germany*, Case No. 29/84 (1985) ECR 1661 para. 18, *Commission v. UK*, Case No. 340/96 (1999) ECR I-2023.

107. L. Blom-Cooper, 'Experts and Assessors: Past Present and Future', *CJQ* (2002) 341, op cit., at p. 352 (n. 11 *supra*) argues that the 'advice' which the assessor may provide to the judge

specifically, the words 'copies of any report prepared by the assessor will be sent to each of the parties would be removed in order to more effectively prevent the production of evidence by an assessor. In the event that the judge were to feel that his judgment is likely to be influenced by the advice of the assessor with respect to the meaning of particular words then it may be appropriate that he indicate to the parties the nature of this advice before judgment.[108] This will more easily enable the parties to exercise their rights of defence in the following manner: firstly, they are indirectly able to respond to the assessor's advice by commenting thereupon to the judge before judgment despite the exclusion of oral cross-examination of the assessor by section 7.4 of the PD: and secondly, the parties are able to use this information given by the judge in order to assist in forming eventual grounds of appeal from the judgment.[109] Accordingly, the rights of the defence would appear to be adequately

pursuant to CPR 35.15 in fact is evidence: 'Under r 35.15 the "advice" will qualify as evidence (35.15 (4)(b) and Practice Direction 7.4 and to the extent that a pre-trail report from the assessor is directed by the court, the parties will have sight and the facility to make use of its contents.'

108. *Richardson v. Redpath* [1944] AC 62 at 71, Viscount Simon, 'It would seem desirable in cases where the assessor's advice, within its proper limits, is likely to affect the judge's conclusion for the latter to inform the parties before him of the advice which he has received from the assessor.'

109. L. Blom-Cooper QC, 'Experts and Assessors, Past Present and Future', *CJQ* 21 (2002): 350 and n. 11 *supra*: 'The assessor system being advice by an expert no under oath given to the court on matters not discloseable for cross examination by either party before judgment and qualifying as evidence would be regarded today as being incompatible under s. 3 (1) of the Human Rights Act 1998 as a violation of Art. 6 (1) of the European Convention of Human Rights' and similarly in L. Blom-Cooper QC (ed.), *Experts in the Civil Courts, Expert Witness Institute* (Oxford: OUP, 2006), 117 Clearly, this view is based upon an interpretation of ECHR Art. 6 (1) as providing a right to direct oral cross examination as the only method of ensuring the rights of the parties to respond to the case being made against as provided by *van Orshoven v. Belgium* (1997) (26) EHRR 55. However, it is not absolutely clear that Art. 6 (1), and such cases such van Orshoven require that that the right to respond is coterminous with the right to direct oral examination as opposed to the right to respond indirectly coupled with written notice of the information which in turn forms the basis for an eventual appeal. D. Dwyer, 'The Future of Assessors under the CPR', *CJQ* 25 (2006): at 219 argues at 225 that 'Four distinct functions can be identified for assessors within the current scope of CPR 35.15: tribunal member, court expert, court officer and scientific adviser … . The assessor as scientific adviser would seek to clarify technical points of evidence for the judge and might suggest to the judge possible areas for further questioning in relation to a CPR r 35.2 expert's opinion. This appears to be the type of assessor Mackay J. had in mind in *XYZ v. Schering Health Care* [2002] EWCA 1420 (QB) at 148-149, when he considered expert evidence involving algebra.' It would seem the Dwyer feels that the function of scientific adviser may not require cross-examination: she notes at 229 'The final point in applying Art. – (1) to the use of assessors is that one must have regard to the extent to which a particular practice might affect the substantive fairness of the process taken as a whole rather than in isolation. Thus the use of assessors to give opinions on the acceptability of the conduct of the parties might reasonably be considered to have a significant effect on the trial and so procedure surrounding such a use should be subject to Art. 6 (1) scrutiny. On the other hand, the use of assessors to advise the judge in general terms or to suggest further lines of question might be see has having significantly less impact on the case as a whole. See generally D. Dwyer, 'Changing Approaches to Expert Evidence in England and Italy', *Intl. Commentary on Evidence* (2003): <www.law.qub.ac.uk/ice/papers/expert2pdf>

protected by a combination of the aforementioned two provisions: namely, the possibility for the parties to respond directly although not through oral cross examination of the assessor to the information contained in his written report prior to the entry of judgment: and additionally, the opportunity of using the judge's written comments to assist in making an appeal against the judgment where he relied upon the information provided by the assessor in making his judgment. This does not prevent a reference on the matter of the use of the assessor in relation to the rights of the defence pursuant to EC 234 to the ECJ in so far as these proposed amendments apply in relation to the enforcement of the Directive.

Finally, it may be that the use of an assessor is proportionately cheaper and quicker than would be the case if an additional expert were appointed. This reflects what appears to be the historic advantages of the use of the assessor and of judicial notice.[110] As noted, however, the doctrine of consistent interpretation may also apply in order to ensure that the assessor does not give expert evidence and thereby retains the function of part of the court which does not give evidence and is not subject to cross-examination. Accordingly, it is submitted that the doctrine may apply so as to eliminate, thereby, the use of CPR 35.15 (3) and (4) in conjunction with Article 7.4 of the Practise Direction.[111]

I   PROBLEMS WITH LEGAL PROFESSIONAL PRIVILEGE, EXPERT WITNESS IMMUNITY, RIGHTS OF THE DEFENCE AND THE EVALUATION OF EXPERT EVIDENCE BY A JUDGE

As noted earlier, in order to ensure compliance with Article 3 (1) and (2) of the Directive implementation of Articles 10, 11 and 13 in so far as they involve taking measures which result from a decision on the merits of the case, may require the use of an assessor in certain circumstances in order to assist a judge to understand expert evidence. However, it may be that the ability of the judge to assess evidence, and notably with the assistance of an assessor, may be undermined along with possibly the rights of the defence, by a combination of a legal profession privilege and the immunity of expert witnesses in contravention of Article 3 (1) and (2) of the Directive. The eventual solution to this problem would be through the doctrine of consistent interpretation preceded by a possible reference to the ECJ pursuant to EC Article 234 in order to ascertain the precise scope of the substantive obligation contained within Articles 10, 11 and 13 in conjunction with Article 3 (1) and (2) of the Directive.

---

110. K.C. Davis, 'Judicial Notice', *Columbia Law Review* 55 (1955): 945, op. cit., at 983 and J. Dickey, 'Assessors', *MLR* (1970): 494, op. cit., at 501.
111. Sir Louis Blom-Cooper QC, 'Experts and Assessors', *CJQ* 21 (2002): 345, op. cit., at 354 notes: 'Why can the court not use the assessor system under part 35.15 as a court appointed expert? With Case Management in force the appointment of an assessor under CPR 35.15 can be made before trial. Is it not time for the courts to use the new modified assessor system at least where the expert issue is complex?' This view appears to be shared by J.A. Jolowicz QC, 'A Note on Experts' *CJQ* (2004): 408, op. cit., at 410.

1   **Disclosure of Expert Reports**

The CPR sought to improve various difficulties which Lord Woolf identified in both his Interim[112] and Final[113] Reports. With respect to partiality of expert evidence presented in an adversarial fashion Lord Woolf noted at paragraph 5 of his Interim Report:

> Most of the problems with expert evidence arise because the expert is initially recruited as part of the team which investigates and advances a party's contentions and then has to change roles and seek to provide the independent expert evidence which the court is entitled to expect. As Lord Wilberforce, in the Ikarian Reefer (1993 2 Lloyd's reports 68) stated: 'It is necessary that expert evidence presented to the court should be and should be seen to be the independent product of the expert uninfluenced as to the form or content by the exigencies of litigation'.

Indeed in his Final Report Lord Woolf noted at paragraph 31 that he had been obliged to restrict the scope of his original recommendation as regards the information to be disclosed by the expert in his expert report:

> One of the recommendations in my interim Report was that once an expert had been instructed to prepare a report for the use of a court, any communication between the expert and the client and his advisers should no longer be the subject of legal privilege. My intention was to prevent the suppression of relevant opinion or factual material which did not support the case put forward by the party instructing the expert. There is, I believe, no disagreement with that intention but it has been put to me very strongly that waiver of legal privilege is not the way to achieve it.

In reality these difficulties were of two orders;[114] first, that the adversarial use of experts tended to provide partisan expert opinion favourable to the instructing and paying party rather than presenting an objective opinion with which the court could evaluate the matters in dispute; and second, that the costs involved in the pre-CPR adversarial experts were high and apparently not subject to effective control.[115] While the second problem may have been in some measure controlled by the measures introduced by the CPR whereby the extent of the use of expert

---

112. Lord Woolf, Interim Report, Access to Justice (1995), Department of Constitutional Affairs (Expert Evidence), op cit., <www.dca.gov.uk/civil/interim/woolf.htm>

113. Lord Woolf, Final Report, Access to Justice (1996), Department of Constitutional Affairs (Expert Evidence), <www.dca.gov.uk/civil/final/index/htm> also House of Commons, Constitutional Affairs Committee: First Report: (Small Claims Track) Session 2005-06, op cit., <www.publications.parliament.uk>

114. A. Zuckerman, 'Editor's Note: Disclosure of Expert Reports', *CJQ* 24 (2005): 293, D. Davies, 'Current Issues: Expert Evidence: Court Appointed Experts', *CJQ* 23 (2004): 367; A. Edis QC, 'Privilege and Immunity: Problems of Expert Evidence', *CJQ* 26 (2007): 40, D. Dwyer, 'The Effective Management of Bias in Civil Expert Evidence', *CJQ* 26 (2007): 57.

115. A. Edis QC Privilege and Immunity: Problems of Expert Evidence', *CJQ* 26 (2007): 40 observes at 42:

evidence and its form are controlled by the judge, arguably the partisan nature of evidence presented in an adversarial manner remains. In this regard, Sir Anthony Clarke MR[116] observed as follows:

> Does that problem exist today? I think the answer must, at any rate to some extent, be yes, because it seems to be to be inevitable. It is inevitable because it is human nature. I am open to persuasion that I am wrong about this but it does seem to me that there is at least a serious risk that a person who is asked to express an opinion by a party or prospective party to litigation, however honest and however hard he or she tries to be entirely objective will or may trim his or her opinion to meet the interests of the client, or at any rate in the grey areas which experience suggests exist in almost every case. Chapter 11 in this book [Experts in Civil Courts] provides a cautionary note to those who think that the new regime for expert evidence will automatically instil an attitude of independence and impartiality on the part of experts.

In order to achieve control over notably the partisan element of expert evidence presented in an adversarial manner.
CPR 35.10 (3) was adopted. This rule provides:

> (3) The expert's report must state the substance of all material instructions, whether written or oral, on the basis of which the report was written.

Of significance is the fact that the Court of Appeal in Jackson[117] interpreted the expression 'all material instructions' narrowly simultaneously retaining a wide scope for Legal Professional Privilege (LPP). Longmore LJ of the Court observed:

> Paragraph 13: There can be no doubt that if an expert makes a report for the purpose of a party's legal adviser being able to give legal advice to their client or for the discussion in a of a party's legal advisers such a report is the subject matter of litigation privilege at the time it is made. It has come into existence for the purpose of litigation. It is common for drafts of expert reports to be circulated among the party's advisers before a final report is prepared for exchange with the other side. Such initial reports are privileged.

Further, CPR 35.10 (4) provides:

> The instructions referred to in paragraph (3) shall not be privileged against disclosure but the court will not, in relation to those instructions:
> a) order disclosure of any specific document; or
> b) permit questioning in court, other than by a party who instructed the expert,

---

Expert evidence is a major source of difficulty in dealing justly with cases. It is expensive and causes delay in the proceedings while it is obtained and disclosed. These problems are probably inevitable and the new power to control the admissibility of expert evidence and to impose conditions on its being adduced is probably as much as can be done to address them.

116. Sir A. Clarke MP, 'Foreword', in *Experts in the Civil Courts*, ed. Sir L. Blom-Cooper (Oxford: OUP, 2006) at p. V.
117. *Jackson v. Marley Davenport Ltd* (2004) EXCA Div. 1225.

unless it is satisfied that there are reasonable grounds to consider that statement of instructions given under paragraph (3) to be inaccurate or incomplete.

Longmore LJ then went on to interpret CPR 35.10(4) in the following manner:

> Paragraph 14: I cannot believe that the CPR were intended to override that privilege. CPR 35.5 provides that expert evidence is to be given in a report unless the court directs otherwise. CPR 35.10 then changed the previous law by providing in subrule (3) that the expert's report must state the substance of all material (whether written or oral) on the basis of which the report was written. By sub-rule (4) it is moreover expressly provided that these instructions shall not be privileged. But the reference in Rule 35.10 to the 'expert's report' is and must be a reference to the expert's intended evidence, not to earlier privileged drafts of what may or may not in the due course become the expert's evidence.

Therefore following Longmore LJ, communications between an expert and his instructing solicitors were protected form disclosure by LPP.

The essential difficulty however with the narrow interpretation of 'all material instructions' coupled by a what might be termed a wide interpretation LPP as performed by Longmore LJ is as follows: the various exchanges between the expert and notably the party and his legal counsel arguably forms overall the evidence which is placed before the judge and eventually the assessor as well as to the opposite side. It is clear that there are two imperatives which must be balanced here: on the one hand LPP exists in order to ensure that a party be able to feel free to discuss his case with the expert, correct inaccuracies, change or modified theories in order to prepare his case as effectively as possible; on the other hand however, there arguably must be some proportionality in the protection granted by means of the LPP so an to ensure that the court is able to effectively evaluate if necessary with an assessor the expert opinion which is provided and that similarly the opponent be able to ensure his rights of the defence. In short, it is submitted that it is necessary for the court to be able to evaluate the expert evidence in light of the entirety of the instructions given to the expert as well as the communications which have taken place in the course of the preparation of the report which is presented to the judge as expert evidence. That is, it is not only the initial instructions which have helped the expert's opinion but also the comments which the party and his legal adviser's make on the expert's various drafts prior to the drafting of the final evidence. In short an appreciation of all of this material is required in order for the court to evaluate the evidence and for the opposite side to exercise his rights of defence. Accordingly, the narrow interpretation of the Court of Appeal in Jackson and in particular the opinion of Longmore LJ also does not enhance the ability of the CPR 35.10 (3) and (4) to reduce the potential partiality and partisanship of expert evidence arguably in violation of Article 3 (1) and (2) of the Directive: that is, it is submitted that the restrictive interpretation lof CPR 35.10 (3) so as to preclude all of the communications which served to form the expert evidence may contravene the principle of effective judicial protection as in Steffensen[118] in which the ECJ established that evidential rules must comply with the requirements arising from fundamental rights such as Article 6 (1) of the ECHR: in short, it is submitted that the restricting the access of the court and the opposing party to all of the relevant communications involved in the formation of the expert evidence in favour of a wide LPP to protect one of the parties is a disproportionate: that is, the extent of the protection granted by the wide scope of LPP in Jackson is not justifiable in that its consequence is an excessive restriction of the ability of both the court and the opposing party to evaluate the quality of the expert evidence particularly with respect to partiality of the expert.

However, even if the interpretation of CPR 35.10 (3) by the Court of Appeal in Jackson were found not to contravene Article 3 (1) and (2) of the Directive and in particular the principle of effective judicial protection, it is submitted that an eventual contravention may result in the following conditions: that is, where the current interpretation of CPR 35.10 (3) is considered in conjunction with the other element which characterizes expert evidence albeit not formally part of the CPR: namely, the immunity of experts. Practically speaking the immunity results in the absence of any formal method for enforcement of the duty of impartiality which the CPR seeks to enforce, that is, by reason of expert immunity. The objective of the immunity is apparently to ensure that expert witnesses should not be deterred from assisting the court by fear of possible consequences if any party suffers damages by reason of their opinions. The immunity was developed relatively recently in the case of *X (Minors) v. Befordshire*[119] per Lord Browne-Wilkinson approving a decision of Drake J in Evans[120] However, following Edis[121] would seem that this justification is extremely tenuous in light of the abandonment of the main principle, namely, that social workers in child protection cases cannot be sued because there is no duty of care. These essential difficulty arises from the fact that although the court can make an appropriate costs orders[122] or a reference can be made to the expert's professional body[123] the immunity prevents an action either in negligence or breach of contract against an expert. It is submitted that the expert immunity when coupled with the restrictive interpretation of CPR 35.10 (3) produces a system in which of expert evidence which disproportionately undermines the ability of the court as well as the opposing party in terms of his rights of defence to deal among other things with partiality and partisan evidence. Accordingly, this combination of expert immunity and the restrictive interpretation of CPR 35.10 (3) may be said to contravene Article 3 (a) and (b) of the Directive and in particular the principle of effective judicial protection and proportionality. Notwithstanding

---

118. *Steffensen*, Case No. C-276/01 (2003) ECR I-3735 in particular at para. 80, see *Evans*, Case No. C-63/01 (2003) ECR I-14447 for an aspect of fair hearing.
119. *X (Minors) v. Bedfordshire CC* (1995) 2 AC 633 at 754-755 per Lord Browne-Wilkinson.
120. *D v. East Berkshire Community Health NHS Trust* (2005) 2 AC 373.
121. A. Edis QC, 'Privilege and Immunity: Problems of Expert Evidence', *CJQ* 40 (2007), op cit., 50.
122. *Philipps v. Symes* (2005) 1 WLR 2043: a cost order against a non-party under s. 51 of the SCA (1981).
123. *GMC v. Professor Sir Roy Meadow* (2006) EWCA Civ. 1390.

this analysis, it would seem that it would be necessary to ensure that a reference were made on this point to the ECJ pursuant to EC Article 234 in order to ensure the scope of the application of Article 3 (a) and (b) in the context of Articles 10, 11 and 13 as affected by CPR 35.10(3).

Pursuing therefore the analysis of non conformity, in order to ensure adequate implementation of Articles 3 (a) and (b) and 10, 11 and 13, and notably the principle of effective judicial protection, it is submitted, that following the doctrine of interpretation in conformity, it will be necessary for the English court to interpret CPR 35.10 (3) and in particular the expression 'all material instructions' widely so as to include eventually all communications oral and written between the expert, the client and the legal adviser which have lead to and influenced the expert evidence submitted: that is, at least to the degree necessary to ensure that the court if necessary accompanied by the assessor and the opposing party are able to evaluate the accuracy of the evidence so as to comply with Article 3 (a) and (b) and in particular the principles of effective judicial protection and proportionality.[124] Once again it is stressed that a definitive interpretation of the scope of the substantive and ancillary obligations contained within the aforementioned articles would be required by means of a reference to the ECJ pursuant to EC Article 234.

Article 14
Legal costs

For reasons of convenience it has been decided to deal in this section with both the subject of costs as provided both by Article 14 and by the General Obligation which is established under Article 3. As noted earlier, Article 3 (1) requires that 'The measures, procedures and remedies provided shall not be ... costly' and 3 (2) that such measures, procedures and remedies 'shall also be ... proportionate ...' With respect to Article 14, the substantive obligation consists in ensuring that in using the indemnity rule Member States ensure that 'reasonable and proportionate legal costs ...' incurred by the winning party be borne by the losing party. In short, it is submitted that overall the CPR generally does not in its current form ensure that costs are reasonable and proportionate in conformity with Article 14 nor following Article 3(1) that the '... measures, procedures and remedies shall not be

---

124. Quaere to what extent solution to the problem of impartiality of experts remains that which was proposed initially by Lord Woolf in his Interim Report at paras 20-23, namely a court appointed expert, however, with its use being extended to multi-track commercial litigation. Sir A. Clarke MR observes in his Foreword to *Experts in Civil Courts*, ed. Sir L Blom-Cooper QC (Oxford: OUP, 2006), at p. viii. 'The second point is that I sometimes wonder whether the adversarial process is a sensible way of putting expert evidence before the court.' A. Jolowicz 'A Note on Experts', *CJQ* 23 (2004): 408 at 409 speaking of a court appointed expert observes: 'On the other hand it is suggested that the present English rules on expert evidence which attempt to get away from the adversary system without offending to much the die hard supporters of our traditional system cannot be expected to survive for ever. When the time comes for an experiment with a new system, the solution is to hand.'

(unnecessarily)[125] costly' and 3 (2) 'shall be ... proportionate'. This is notably the case in relation to enforcement of IP rights by both the Patents Court and the Patents Country Court (PCC).

J   NATURE OF THE OBLIGATION

As noted in the previous chapter, arguably a substantive obligation exists which requires the following: first, pursuant to Article 3 of the Directive, that Member States implement a system of procedure which 'shall not be ... costly' and 'shall be ... proportionate'; and second, following Article 14, that where the indemnity rule applies, then not only must the measures not be 'costly' but also, in the particular circumstances of the case ' reasonable and proportionate'. In order to be able to evaluate more clearly the type of implementing measure which may be appropriate it is necessary to ascertain whether or not the provisions dealing with costs in Articles 3 and 14 can be said to constitute rights. In this regard, it is important to ascertain whether the nature of the right is clear and whether it benefits a specific category of beneficiary. Arguably, the category of right, namely, access to a system of judicial measures and procedures which are not costly, is generally clear in the sense that it is intended to establish a right or benefit for litigants in legal proceedings which involve IP rights as opposed to simply regulate administrative interests. Further, one may add that the category of the beneficiary which benefits directly therefrom is in fact two fold: first, it is the rightsholder at least with respect to Article 3 and second, with respect to Article 14 it is arguably the defendant in IP litigation. However, the actual form of the right to what might be termed 'non costly procedure' is not determined by the Directive but rather by the implementing national legislation.[126] As noted earlier, where a directive, as in the instant case, provides for rights, those provisions must be enacted with clarity and precision so that the beneficiary may understand without difficulty the exact nature of his rights and the possibility of their enforcement before a national court. However, even were it the case that Articles 3 and 14 did not provide for rights, nevertheless, their implementation would still be subject to the principles of clarity and legal certainty in order to prevent misapplication by the national courts in addition to the doctrine of full effect albeit the degree of clarity required may be

---

125. Arguably the word 'unnecessarily' in Art. 3 (1) is restricted to 'complicated' and does not apply to 'costly'.

126. S. Prechal, *Directives in EC Law*, 2nd edn (Oxford: OUP, 2005), op. cit., 96: 'As regards the content of the relationship, in some cases the obligations and rights may be laid down in the provision of the directive very precisely and in concrete terms. In other cases, the content and scope must subsequently be defined with more precision by national or Community measures. However, even in the latter cases it should be possible to establish whether a directive or particular provisions aim to confer rights or imposed obligations on individuals or whether they are intended to regulate for instance the relations between administrative bodies. The answer to the question will only be facilitated by precision and consequently more concrete working.'

somewhat less than were rights involved. Most significantly, perhaps, is the fact that the implementation of Articles 3 and 14, notably in so far as they do provide for rights, is subject to the principle of effective judicial protection. This is particularly so in the sense that the principle of effective judicial protection when related notably to Article 6.1 of the ECHR requires access to justice in terms of costs as provided in Airey.[127] As noted earlier, the principle of effective legal protection was introduced into EU law notably by the case of Johnston[128] following on from von Colson.[129] Accordingly, the national legislation which seeks to implement Articles 3 and 14 must be not only clear and binding, it must also conform with the principle of effective judicial protection in terms of access to justice with respect to costs.

K   EFFECTIVE IMPLEMENTATION OF THE DIRECTIVE

1   **Background: High Costs of Intellectual
                   Property Litigation**

Before examining the specific implementation of Articles 3 and 14 of the Directive it is useful to consider the general background of costs as they apply to litigation involving IP rights in particular and litigation in general before the English courts: the purpose would be to ensure a clearer understanding first, of why the CPR implements inadequately, notably for economic reasons, the Directive and second, of the form which adequate implementation might take in terms of substantive content particularly in light of economic analysis. It is clear, however, that any such economic content must ensure that the implementation of the Directive complies with the aforementioned principles of legal clarity, full effectiveness and above all, effective legal protection.

With respect to IP litigation in England and Wales, Judge Fysch of the PCCs[130] observes first that IP litigation is expensive and second identifies the facts which contribute thereto:

---

127. *Airey v. Ireland*, application 6289/73 [1979] ECHHR (32) 305, *Johnston*, Case No. 222/84 [1986] ECR 1651, *von Colson*, Case No. 14/83 [1984] ECR 1891.
128. *Johnston*, Case No. 222/84 (1986) ECR 1651, op. cit.
129. *Von Colson*, Case No. 14/83 (1984) ECR 1891, op. cit.
130. Michael Fysch QC SC Judge, PCC 11 Feb. 2003 IP Centre, St Peter's College, Oxford: Concerning the PCC in terms of costs effectiveness see: University of Melbourne: Intellectual Property Research Institute of Australia (IPRIA) Sep. 2002 para. 5. 'The creation of the Patents County Court was supported by industry but there are now differing views as to its success (Lord Chancellor's Dept: Access to Justice: Final Report 1995 Ch. 19 (15) The fact that the procedure of the court means that a matter can be brought to trial without there necessarily first being discovery has been regarded as a major costs advantage (although this front loading of costs means that it is more expensive to initiate proceeding in the Patent County Court than in the High Court). On the other hand the expense involved in providing detailed pleadings at an early stage in the proceedings may mean that costs are initially greater in the

6.0 Costs: It is notorious that IP litigation and patent litigation in particular has become prohibitively expensive. This is to some extent an inherent problem because:

i)   The nature of patent law, its complexities and in the common law system its reliance on binding authority of higher courts. Litigants in person find research in the substantial corpus of UK, European and often Commonwealth authorities particularly difficult.

ii) Procedural complications:

   a) first, because of the impact of the Common Law system (disclosure, interrogation) in the field of IP law. This can lead to mamouth exercises in disclosure which in my experience are to the benefit principally of solicitors and supplier of photocopy paper.

   b) second, and potentially worse, particularly in pharmaceutical cases the frequent use of experiments to prove fact. These often take place overseas and involve substantial delays.

   c) third, the need to cross-examine (usually) all witnesses whether of fact or experts.

iii) The trial of damages issues (enquiry as to damages –account of profits, interest on accrued damages) after the adjudication of validity. This usually involved the use of particularly costly services of litigation accountants.

Judge Fysh advocates observes further:

> These matters inevitably pose a real challenge to the requirements of fair and effective administration of justice in a court which after all was set up to cater for the small and medium enterprise companies and not to be forgotten litigant in person. The new 'Streamlined Procedure' has been available to litigants in English patent proceeding since 1 April 2003. The normal procedures for UK patent litigation provide for an extremely thorough examination of the issues with requirements for disclosure of documents, reliance on experiments provided they are repeated and witnessed by all sides meticulously prepared experts and a strong oral tradition including sometimes lengthy cross-examination. The new Streamlined Procedure will dispense with disclosure of documents and experiments and restrict cross-examination with a trial taking no longer than one day usually with 6 months. The Streamlined Procedure can be varied in accordance with circumstances of the case in question. Both the High Court and the Patents County Court can make use of the procedure.

Patents County Court than in the High Court (see A. Webb, 'Patent Litigation in the UK', *EIPR* 6 (1991): 203 at 207').

However, the Gower Report on IP[131] would seem to indicate that neither the streamlined system of litigation nor indeed the existence of the PCC has contributed significantly to the reduction of costs in patent litigation:

> 6.30 Following the Woolf reforms to the Civil Law system in 1999 all courts in England and Wales now work on the same procedure. The reform led to the three tracks of legislation: small clams fast and multi track claims. Cases are allocated largely according to the amount in dispute. Anything over £15,000 which includes nearly all IP case is heard on the multi track. Accordingly, many of the benefits of the fast tract system such as capped costs, limited trail length and limited disclosure do not apply to IP cases. This means that PCC is almost as expensive and complex as High Court litigation. High costs at the PCC and the High Court act as a barrier to all potential litigants and the SMEs in particular.
>
> 6.31 Litigation of patents is extremely expensive in England and Wales with costs of comparable cases in English Oxford patent courts up to four times greater than in Germany. … Professional fees in England & Wales are generally higher and the patent proceedings more complex. This leads to lengthier cases and higher costs. This can make it more difficult for SME's to enforce (or depend) any infringement claim. Chapter 6 will consider how the current England and Wales court structure can be improved to reduce costs.
>
> Alongside reforming the courts in England and Wales the number of cases reaching litigation should be reduced by alternative methods of dispute resolution.

One notes, in passing, that the observations of the Gower Report concerning the high costs of patent litigation in England as opposed to other EU Member States are corroborated by a judgment of the French Cour de Cassation in *Gustave Pordea v. The Times Newspapers.*[132] In this case the French claimant brought defamation proceedings against the defendant newspaper in the English High Court. He was asked to provide security for costs and failed to do so. As a result, his action was dismissed. The defendant then obtained an order for costs from the High Court which it sought to enforce in France. The Cour de Cassation found that it would be contrary to public policy to enforce such an order because the costs were set at a disproportionately high level.[133] The high costs of litigation had presented an obstacle to the original claimant's access to justice contrary to ECHR Article 6 (1).

---

131. Gowers Review of Intellectual Property Dec. 2006 H.M Treasury <www.hm-treasury.gov. uk/medi/583/91/pbr06_gowers_report_755.pdf>
132. (2000 IL Pr 763 Cases (F) Cour de Cassation, France).
133. Arguably preserved by: Art. 26 Regulation 864/2007 (Rome II) of the European Parliament and Council of 11 Jun. 2007 on the law applicable to non-contractual obligations (OJ 2007, L 199/40) 'The application of a provision of the law of any country specified by this regulation may be refused only if such application is manifestly incompatible with the public order of the forum.'

2   Nature of the Costs Difficulties Generally in English Litigation

Arguably, the market for legal services in England possesses a specific character-istic which distinguishes it from that of other EU countries, namely, high legal costs.[134] It is, accordingly, useful to consider the phenomenon of high legal costs as analyzed in various studies, firstly in England, and secondly, by the European Commission in order to better define the problem, its origin and eventual method of cure so as to ensure compliance with the Directive.

With respect to studies undertaken in England, one notes, firstly, that Lord Woolf in his Interim Report on Access to Justice (1995)[135] defined the nature of the problem concerning high legal costs in England as attributable in particular to the failure of market forces to regulate legal fees. His lordship observed as follows in Chapter 25 of his report:

> Point 5: There is a misconceived view that the entire problem is due to the scale of the lawyer's costs. This is not so. It is however, the case that market forces which in other contexts have acted as a restrain on prices operate rather weekly in relation to the supply of professional legal services. Factors associated with legal charging are to be found in this field: notably the restrictions on access to the market and the regulating controls necessary to maintain proper professional standards and the integrity of the legal system.

His lordship then goes on to consider the influence of the method of calculation of the legal fees in the context of a market where the normal competitive forces do not function:

> Point 8: In Chapter 3, I refer to the common practice of lawyers charging their clients by the hours (or by the day in the case of barristers). I believe that this has an inflationary effect on costs. Regular litigators appreciating this, are moving towards costs agree in advanced for a range of legal services … . In addition to requiring information to be given as to fees, the professional bodies should encourage lawyers to enter into fixed fee agreements where practical.

---

134. Ashurst Report (Waelbroeck, Salter & Even-Shoshan), *Study on the Conditions of Claims for Damages: Comparative Report*, prepared for the European Commission, Aug. 2004, states at 96: ' … in all countries it appears that on the basis of a EUR 1 million claims where the level of damages is relatively easy to establish costs would run into tens of thousands of euros. In the UK and Ireland, this figure is higher going well above GBP 100,000'. It is submitted that these figures demonstrate that origin of the high costs in English is not attributable to the influence of lawyers established in other EU member states including Ireland. It is exclusively English in origin; see also OFT 'Private actions in competition law: effective redress for consumers and business' Discussion Paper, Apr. 2007, at para. 3.4 'potential exposure to liti-gation costs may act as a major disincentive to the bringing of well-founded competition law actions …' and para. 5.
135. Lord Woolf, *Interim Report Access to Justice* (1995), op. cit., <www.dca.gov. uk/civil/interim/chap25.htm>

Zuckerman asserts in the same manner as Lord Woolf, that high legal costs in England are attributable to two factors: first, what might be termed as will be seen later in this analysis, supplier induced demand, and second, the manner of calculating the costs and control: namely, ex post as opposed to ex ante cost calculation and control:

> The failure of the present system to curb costs is due to two factors: first, costs are determined by reference to what is considered by the profession to be reasonably necessary work and by the prevailing standards of fees and overheads. In other words, the judicial pitching of costs follows the forensic practise and expectations and not the other way around. Second, taxation is conducted retrospective so that it reflects the way in which the parties chose to conduct the case. In other words, retrospective taxation does not influence the steps taken in the litigation.[136]

Lord Hoffmann, in turn, identifies the problem of high legal costs as one which is attributable to the absence of any objectively established global method for calculating the amount of the costs which extends beyond the immediate case at hand. In order to achieve some objective method of costing his lordship adverts to the need for legislative intervention:

> the criterion prescribed by the CPR for determining whether costs are reasonably framed operate entirely by reference to the facts of the particular case. Once one invokes a global approach designed to produce a reasonable overall return for solicitors, one moves away from the judicial function of the costs judge and into the territory of legislative and administrative decisions.[137]

The solution to this problem according to Lord Hoffmann is as follows:

> A legislative decision to fix costs at levels calculated to provide adequate access to justice in the most economical way seems to me to be a more rational approach than to leave the matter to an individual costs judge. If it is considered the most appropriate way to secure value for money when the expenditure is borne by the public as a whole (e.g., fixing of graduated fees for criminal legal aid) it should be no less appropriate when the expenditure is born by a section of the public, namely, the motorists. Not only would this be likely to keep the actual costs within the reasonable levels but it would also greatly reduce the costs of disputes over costs.[138]

---

136. A.A.S. Zuckerman, 'Devices for controlling the Cost of Litigation through Taxation', paper presented to the Woolf Inquiry Team by A.A.S. Zuckerman, JILT (1996) (1)<ww2.warwick.ac.uk/fac/soc/law/elj/jilt/1996_1/woolf/costs>.
137. *Callery v. Gray* [2002] UKHL 28, judgment date 27 Jun. 2002, Lord Hoffmann, point 34 <www.publications.parliament.uk>
138. *Callery v. Gray* [2002] UKHL 28, judgment date 27 Jun. 2002; Lord Hoffmann point 34 ibid.

3   Aggravation of the Problem of High Costs by the CPR

This situation of high legal costs has been further aggravated by at least three factors which concern specifically the operation of the CPR: the first problem concerns the use of the conditional fee coupled with the shifting of an uplift of up to
100% by the indemnity rule;[139] the second, arises from the use of judicial case
management;[140] and the third is attributable to the also very limited use of the
concept of cost capping notably in the context of the allocation questionnaires.

*a   Conditional Fees, Success Fees and the Operation of the
          Indemnity Rules*

In order to analyze the operation of conditional fee arrangements (CFA), and success fees it necessary to consider briefly their legislative basis. The system of
conditional fee agreements was originally introduced in England under section 58
of the Courts and Legal Services Act (1990). At that time, the legislation did not
provide for the recovery of the uplift or success fee as it was called in section 58
(2) (b) from the losing party. However, section 58 A of the 1990 Act which was
introduced by section 27 (1) of the Access to Justice Act (AJA) (1999) modified
that: section 58 A (6) provides that a costs order made in any proceedings may,
subject in the case of court proceedings to rules of court, include provision requiring payment of any fees payable under a conditional fee agreement which provides
for a success fee. Conditional fee arrangements cannot be the subject of an
enforceable conditional fee agreement in criminal proceedings or family proceedings as per section 58 (1) and (2). Subject to those exceptions the system is available to litigants, pursuant to section 58 A (6), in 'any proceedings'. In contrast to
the position in Scotland,[141] litigation may be conducted in such cases in England
on the basis that if the client is successful the losing party will be obliged to pay
the success fee by reason of the operation of the indemnity rule. In this regard CPR
rule 44. 3 A provides for the inclusion of a funding arrangement and a success fee
within the assessment of costs. The basis of the assessment is set out in rule CPR
44.4, paragraph (2). This rule provides that, where the amount of costs is to be
assessed on the standard basis, the court will only allow costs which are proportionate to the matters in issue. Further, any doubt which it may have as to whether
costs were reasonable incurred or reasonable and proportionate in amount is to be
resolved in favour of the paying party. CPR 43. 2 (1) defines the expression 'costs'

---

139. A.A.S. Zuckerman, 'Editor's Note', *CJQ* 24 (2005): 1 at 3: 'What was not predictable at the
      time of the Woolf Report was that the structure of the CFA legislation would combine with
      the existing inflationary factors to inflame the situation even further'; A.A.S. Zuckerman,
      'Editor's Note', *CJQ* 26 (2007): 271 generally; K. Ashley & C. Glasser 'The Legality of
      Conditional Fee Uplifts', *CJQ* 24 (2005): 83-103.
140. For non-English lawyers a concise account of conditional fees and up lifts see generally the
      opinion of Lord Hoffmann in *Callery v. Gray* [2002] UKHL 28, judgment date 27 Jun. 2002
      op. cit.
141. *Campbell v. MGN* (2005) UKHL 61 at para. 43, speech of Lord Hope.

so as to include any additional liability by way of a percentage increase incurred under Conditional Fee Agreement (CFA). These definitions are reflected in section 9.1 of the Practise Direction which provides that under an order for payment of costs the costs payable will include an additional liability incurred under a funding arrangement which include a Conditional Fee Agreement. However, it is then necessary to consider the effect of section 11.5 of the Practise Direction. This section provides that, in deciding whether the costs claimed are reasonable and (on a standard basis) proportionate the court will consider the amount of any additional liability separately from the base costs. Section 11. 9 establishes that a percentage increase will not be reduced simply on the ground that, when added to the base costs, the total appears disproportionate. Following Lord Hoffmann in *Campbell v. MGN* at paragraph 11, it is clear that section 11.5 when read in conjunction with section 11.9 provides that the test of proportionality and reasonableness is applied only to the basic costs. It is not applied to the total sum for which the losing party may be liable after the addition of the success fee. This is explicitly recognized in the PD. Section 11.5 states: 'In deciding whether the costs are reasonable and (on a standard basis assessment) proportionate, the court will consider the amount of any additional liability separately from the base costs. The consequence is spelled out in section 11.9' A percentage increase will not be reduced simply on the ground that, when added to the base costs which are reasonable and (where relevant) proportionate, the total appears disproportionate'.[142]

Accordingly, the result would seem to be that the situation with respect to Conditional Fee Agreements and success fees (uplifts) is as follows:

– First, section 11.9 of the PD for CPR 44 apparently violates both Articles 3 (2) and 14 of the Directive with respect to proportionality in the strictly literal sense of its meaning: that is, there is no requirement that the percentage increase of the success fee be proportionate to the base costs in a particular case of litigation;

– Second, following *Campbell v. MGN*, the conditional fee system coupled with the uplift and the indemnity rule may well appear to constitute overall a system which is proportionate to the objective of increasing access to justice. However, in reality, following notably Lord Hoffmann, it would seem that this system of funding which is appears to be proportionate to the objective of increasing access to justice nevertheless produces a level of costs which is disproportionate in relation to that very objective.[143] It is submitted that this disproportionate level of costs is caused by the factors noted earlier, namely, hourly based charging of legal costs and lack of objective cost assessment

---

142. It would appear the Lord Hope interprets the section as still permitting the application of the criterion of proportionality overall.
143. *Campbell v. MGN* (2005) UKHL 61 op. cit., speech of Lord Hoffmann at para. 18 'This is not however a problem which arises in the present case. There has, as I have said, been no assessment in which the level of the success fees might be contested. The challenge is to the allowance of any success fee at all.'

criterion.[144] Lord Hoffmann specifically notes that the system of fee capping ex poste ante while desirable is inadequate to deal with such costs. Similarly ex post control in the form of costs judge assessments is insufficient in so far as they are not based upon market based indicators.[145]Accordingly, these factors prevent the system of conditional fees and success fees coupled with the indemnity rule from constituting a proportionate method of increasing access to justice by producing excessive levels of costs and for this reason violate both Articles 3 (2) and 14 of the Directive as well as the principle of effective judicial protection of rights and Articles 6.1 ECHR following Airey. On the contrary, the high level of costs thereby generated may decrease access to justice notably by undermining the ability of a defendant or in some cases a claimant from asserting their legal rights for fear of being confronted, if unsuccessful, with legal costs which include a success fee of up to a 100%. Following Ashby and Glaser,[146] the only apparent exception is the field of personal injuries where the amount of the fees has been negotiated by the insurance industry and lawyers. Arguably, in such circumstances where the fees are thereby controlled, the conditional fee coupled with a success fee does not constitute a disproportionate level of costs in relation to the objective pursued of increasing access to justice. This is in contrast to other areas of law which do not involve personal injuries where no such agreements exist and therefore, where, according to Ashby and Glaser the success fee not only does not represent the cost of actual legal work but constitutes a form of legal penalty for losing to a party with a conditional fee agreement in place: the authors observe:

In King, Brooke L.J. accepted that the effect of the Conditional Fee Agreement (CFA) uplift is to impose costs at a level that would not ordinarily be regarded as proportionate or reasonable. Nor does the argument that CFAs improve access to justice in these cases have any particular legitimacy because there is nothing to stop the rich litigant entering into a CFA in an action against an opponent of limited means.[147]

Therefore, the fundamental problem with the system of conditional fees coupled with the success fee of up to 100% and the indemnity rule which shifts the entire amount to the losing party is that, in practice, the level of costs produced may contravene the EC principle of effective judicial protection as well as ECHR

---

144. *Willis v. Nicolson* [2007] EWCA Civ. 199 Buxton, LJ, 'One element in the present high cost of litigation is undoubtedly the expectation as to the annual income of the professionals who conduct it. The costs system as it is at present operates cannot do anything about that because it assesses the proper charge for work on the basis of the market rates charged by professions rather than attempting the no doubt difficult task of placing an objective value on the work.'
145. Points 34 of Lord Hoffmann's judgment in which he indicates that cost capping will not suffice to control costs: and that costs judges are handicapped by lack of objective costings.
146. K. Ashby & C. Glasser, 'The Legality of Conditional Fee Uplifts', *CJQ* 24 (2005): 130. Also, *Airey v. Ireland* (1997) 2 EHHR 305 op. cit.
147. K. Ashby & C. Glasser 'The Legality of Conditional Fee Uplifts', *CJQ* 24 (2005): 134, ibid.

Article 6.1:[148] in short the disproportionately high amount of costs notably calculated on hourly fees may well serve to dissuade a party from exercising his rights before a court and thereby, perversely, restrict access to justice in a way which has no justification.[149] With respect to the principle of effective judicial protection the problem is arguably that the disproportionate level of costs engendered by the conditional fee system coupled with a success fee of 100% which itself is exempted from the principle of proportionality and in turn is shifted to the losing party does not appear to be justifiable: that is, whilst the system itself may be proportionate to the objective of increasing access to justice, the method of calculation of costs to which it is connected constitutes the fundamental problem of disproportion for which there appears to be no justification in the following sense: namely, there would appear to be alternative methods for calculating costs, in particular fixed costs, which, notably when coupled with budget capping, can produce a proportionate result; and second, it is submitted that this is a fortiori the case in so far as, following cases such as *Campbell v. MGN*, the disproportionate level of the costs produced by the system, may, perversely, have the effect of decreasing access to justice thereby impairing the existence of the right without justification.

b   *Judicial Case Management*

The study by Peysner[150] and Seneviratne corroborates what has been anticipated for some time:[151] namely that the use of judicial case management has lead to an increase of costs by reason of increased involvement of lawyers for compliance: this augmented forensic activity has lead to an increase of costs which are calculated on an hourly basis. In short, the indirect method of controlling costs through the judicial case management coupled with an attempt at simplifying the rules of civil procedure has not succeeded in reducing overall legal costs. Accordingly, the reform of the CPR has not lead to a reduction of costs but rather in some cases an increase in costs.

---

148. K. Ashby & C. Glasser, 'The Legality of Conditional Fee Uplifts', *CJQ* 24 (2005), ibid., 130, see also S. Prechal, *Directives in EC Law*, 2nd edn (Oxford: OUP, 2005) at 108 'Although for the purposes of the principles of effective judicial protection the Court may refer to the principles enshrined in Art. 6 and Art. 13 of the ECHR the scope of the protection requires is much broader than (civil) rights'.
149. *UNIBET*, Case No. 432/05 (2007) ECR I 2271 23 Mar. 2007, op cit. AG Sharpston observes at para. 38 possible limitations to judicial access under Art. 6.1 ECHR '… limitations to such access are compatible with Art. 6 (1) only where they do not impair the essence of that right, where they preserve a legitimate aim and where a reasonable relationship of proportionality exists between the means employed and the aim sought to be achieved'.
150. J. Peysner, & M. Seneviratne, 'The Management of Civil Cases: the Courts and the Post – Woolf Landscape' (Dec. 2005), op cit., <www.dca.gov.uk/research/2005/9_2005.htm>
151. J. Peysner, & M. Seneviratne, 'The Management of Civil Cases: DCA Research Series 9/05', Nov. 2005, op cit., <www.dca.gov.uk/research/2005/9_2005.htm>; RAND, Institute for Civil Justice, 'Just, Speedy and Inexpensive: An Evaluation of Judicial Case Management under the Civil Justice Reform Act' (1996) <www.rand.org/pubs/monograph_report/MR800>

c   *Costs Estimates: Cost Capping*

CPR 26 requires parties to complete an allocation question. One of the pieces of information that must be provided in this document and similarly in the later pre-trial checklist is the party's estimates of costs incurred to date and of likely future costs to the date and of likely costs to the end of the proceedings (CPR PD 6). In principle CPR 26 through the mechanism of the cost estimates as contained within the allocation questionnaire can serve in conjunction with the concept of cost capping to limit costs on an ex ante basis providing thereby foreseeable costs and legal certainty. However, by reason of its judgment in *Leigh v. Michelin Tyre PLC*,[152] the Court of Appeal reduced the effectiveness of this provision: that is, the court held that a low costs estimate in the allocation questionnaire would not serve to prevent a litigant from claiming much higher costs than those provided at the allocation stage. In short, it would appear that a costs estimate as provided in the questionnaire is relevant only in so far as a litigant who presents a much higher costs bill must justify them. Accordingly, the cost estimates as applied by the courts under CPR 26 do not seriously impede a party from recovering much higher costs if they can be justified by the traditional standards of reasonableness. Whilst reducing, however, the effectiveness of cost estimates, the Court of Appeal never-theless, expressed the view in *Leigh v. Michel Tyre PLC* that what might be termed costs capping orders provided a better means of achieving this goal. A costs cap-ping order determines in advance or ex ante the maximum amount that a party would be allowed to recover by way of costs should that party be successful.[153] However, the scope of the jurisdiction to make cost capping orders and thereby the benefits which they could offer for cost control has been reduced by the courts. According to Gage LJ in *Smart v. East Cheshire NHS* Trust the function of the jurisdiction is to place a prospective limit on recoverable costs when:

> there is a real and substantial risk that without such an order costs will be disproportionately or unreasonably incurred and that this risk may not be managed by convention case management and a detailed assessment of cost after a trial.[154]

That is, with the exception of public law and group litigation, the jurisdiction is exercisable only where there is a real risk that the costs incurred by a litigant may be disproportionate. What might be termed the narrow interpretation of the scope of costs capping orders has arguably substantially diminished their effectiveness for reducing the costs of the parties within a particular trial. This was recognized

---

152. (2003) EWCA CIV 1766; (2004) 2 All ER 175.
153. A. Zuckerman 'Cost Capping Orders: The Failure of the Third Measure for Controlling Litigation Costs': Editor's Note *CJQ* 26 (2007): 271, op. cit., feels that 'The jurisdiction to make [cost] orders effectively introduces into English law a form of fixed cost litigation similar to the cost recovery systems followed in some European countries.'
154. (2003) EWHC 2806.

in Henry[155] which illustrates this point. However, Zuckerman questions whether this judgment which restricts the availability of cost capping is well founded:

> The limitation of the costs capping jurisdiction to case where there is a risk of costs getting out of control is puzzling. For as already noted no matter how much a successful party has spent the court cannot order the unsuccessful party to pay more than reasonable and proportionate costs. Hence by definition there is no room for abuse in the sense of being able to recover more than reasonable and proportionate costs (ignoring for the present discussion the effect that the success fee can have where the successful party has been represented on a conditional fee basis). The upshot is that having failed to control costs by means of court management directions which the Woolf reforms sought to achieve, having failed to control costs by holding parties to their estimates, the Court of Appeal has now abandoned a third measure for achieving costs control by reducing the practical usefulness of the jurisdiction of making cost capping orders to a vanishing point in ordinary civil litigation.

For the instant purposes it is of significance to note that the restriction on the availability of costs orders following the criterion established by Gage LJ was applied in the context of IP litigation by Mann J. in Knight[156] wherein the learned judge held:

> I consider Gage J's indication that costs capping should be done if the normal post trial costs assessment would or might not achieve justice to be important and a guideline that is applicable to me in this case.

d   *Economic Definition of the Problem of High Costs
              in English Litigation*

In order to assist in producing possible solutions for the problem of the CPR non-compliance with Articles 3 and 14 both in relation to the conditional fees but also to the system of judicial case management it would seem appropriate to consider certain economic aspects thereof. As such, it is submitted that the nature of the problem of costs in the English system of litigation, in particular, as described by Lord Woolf and Zuckerman may be defined generally in the following manner:

> First, from an economic point of view the problem of high legal costs arises from the inability of market forces to function within the field of legal services by reason among other things of lack of client information: this may be termed asymmetry of information.[157] This asymmetry of information leads to what

---

155. *Henry v. BBV* (2005) EWHC 2503 (2006) 1 ALL ER 154.
156. *Knight v. Beyond Properties PTY Ltd* (2007) FSR 7.
157. *Cipolla v. Fazari*, Case No. C-94/04 and *Macriono and Capodarte v. Meloni*, Case C-202/04, joined cases, judgment in date of 5 Dec. 06 at para. 68 (2006) ECR I 11421 <www.curia.europa.eu>

might be termed as the problems of moral hazard[158] and producer induced consumption notably in the markets of private clients and small businessmen: that is, it is these two groups of consumers of legal services who lack the knowledge which is necessary in order to assess the quality of the legal services and thereby make comparisons notably as to legal cost. Van den Berghe[159] describes succinctly the nature of the general market for legal services and the problems therein for consumers which is that to which the observations of Lord Woolf, Lord Hoffmann and Zuckerman refer:

The definition of professional service demonstrates some characteristics of the market in which such services are offered and acquired. It involves specialised skills and it is safe to say that the information of the consumer concerning the particular service will be at best sketchy. There exists an imbalance in information between the provider of the service who may asses the quality of his serve and the consumer who has no information about the quality of the service he is about to acquire and only in the case of experienced goods can access information of the service he purchased. This is a far cry from the ideal of perfect information necessary for perfect competition

Van den Berghe, in turn, defines the two specific problems which can result from this information asymmetry and which arguably characterise accurately the market for legal services in England, namely, adverse selection and moral hazard. Arguably it is the problem of moral hazard or that of supplier induced demand which describes most accurately the aforementioned observations of Lord Woolf and Zuckerman:

Adverse Selection:

Economic theory has shown that this information asymmetry between the provider and the consumer may culminate in a so called market for lemons. Since the consumer cannot judge the quality of the service he will acquire he will not be willing to pay a high price for quality. As a result providers of high quality (with higher prices) are driven out of the market which results in a market with sub optimal quality services. This process is known as adverse selection. Another problem resulting from the information asymmetry is moral hazard.

Moral Hazard: supplier induced demand:

The moral hazard concept signifies that there is a discrepancy between the goods of the agent and the objective of the principal. The provider of the service (agent) is supposed to act in the best interest of his customer (principal). However, since the principal cannot express the price quality relationship he desires the agent has every incentive to oversupply quality in order to charge high prices even if his client would be better served with a lawyer quality at a

---

158. R. van der Bergh & Y. Motagnie, Theory and Evidence in the Regulation of the Latin Notary Profession, ECRI Report 0604, Jun. 2006; <www. mediaseor.neon.estrate.nl/publications/theory-and-evidence-regulation-latin-profes.pdf>

159. R. van den Bergh & Y. Montagnie, Theory and Evidence in the Regulation of the Latin Notary Profession, ECRI Report 0604, Jun. 2006, ibid.; <www.mediaseor.neon.estrate.nl/publications/theory-and-evidence-regulation-latin-profes.pdf>, ibid., at 7-8.

more reasonable price. The same goes for supplying services the client does not need (supplier induced demand).

Significantly, this lack of consumer information or asymmetry of information leads as noted to certain problems which may not only justify if not indeed require regulation which is the very point advanced in particular by Lord Hoffmann as noted previously. The Copenhagen Economics[160] report concludes that the market failures attributable to the information asymmetry which characterises the provision of legal services generally requires regulation:

> The usual starting point for an economist is that a free market without regulation gives the best legal solution with optimal allocation of resources and the correct combination of price and quality. However, there are two important exceptions – asymmetric information and externalities – which means that a totally free market for legal services will not function optimally. These exceptions are relevant to the legal profession and in turn make it advantageous to have a certain degree of regulation.

Second, the problem of the moral hazard or the producer lead consumption is exacerbated by the manner in which lawyers calculate their costs namely on an hourly rather than primarily on by means of an aggregated sum which is calculated in relation to the overall value of the matter concerned in the litigation. This is in essence the very point which was made by Lord Woolf. Interestingly, the Copenhagen Economics prepared for the Danish Bar and Law Society report observes in this regard:

> Fees only calculated from hours used could give some lawyers a vested interest in using more hours on a case than necessary. There is a risk that fees only calculated from hours used lead to complaints regarding the amount of hours used by lawyers.[161]

---

160. Copenhagen Economics, The Legal Profession: Competition and Liberalisation: Jan. 2006 at p. 8 <www.copenhageneconomics.com/publications/The_legal_profession.pdf>
161. Copenhagen Economics, The Legal Profession: Competition and Liberalisation: Jan. 2006, ibid., at p. 13: … (A.M. Polinsky & D. L. Rubinfeld (2001) 'Aligning the Interest of Lawyers and Clients', The Berkley Law and Economics Working Papers, Col. 2001, Issue 2, Fall2001<www. copenhageneconomics.com/publications/The_legal_profession.pdf>, R. van den Bergh & Y. Motagnie, Theory and Evidence in the Regulation of the Latin Notary Profession, ECRI Report 0604, ibid., at p. 7-10. This report is referred to also in the CCBE Economic Submission to the Commission Profess Report on Competition in Professional Services (2006) 1: <www. ccbe.org/doc/En/ccbe_economic_submission_310306_en.pdf>. See also, *Jemma Trust & Co. Ltd v. P. D'Arcy et al.* [2003] EWCA Civ. 1476, Case 2002 2588 72, Mance LJ at para. 37: '… In some circumstances, the certainty of a charge based purely on a percentage of value could well have advantages for clients. Some legal system (e.g., the German, absent written agreement to the contrary BRAGO 26 Jul. 1957) fix lawyers fees ion the basis of the value of the subject matter even in contentious cases; One feature of hourly charging for which even the most skilled costs judge may, I imagine, fit it difficult to allow, is the propensity to reward plodding work or and this is I suspect, as if not more relevant its propensity to encourage and reward excessive diligence whether by an individual or in the form of excessive deployment of man or woman power.

e   *European Commission and Legal Costs:*
                      Professional Services

Turning now to the next stage of the analysis, one notes generally that the intervention of the Commission in terms of procedural costs is arguably explicable in the following manner: specifically, the cost of legal proceedings in so far as they affect enforcement of EC law by national courts has become a concern for the Commission.[162] Accordingly, the Commission undertook in particular studies on competition in the field of professional services in 2003[163] and 2004.[164] In its Follow Up Paper of 2005[165] the Commission defines the problems including costs with respect to liberal professions, including law as being attributable to excessive regulation prevents the operation of market forces: that is a lack of competition. Notwithstanding this apparently anti-regulatory observation, the Commission, nevertheless, does conclude that in two markets, namely, those of private clients and small businesses, the failure of market forces is attributable not to excessive regulation but rather to information asymmetry. In short, not all problems can be resolved by reduction of regulation. On the contrary, in certain instances, regulation is required in order to compensate for the lack of market forces. The Commission observes under the heading of 'public interest' as follows:

I can therefore wee why it might be appropriate for solicitors to be able to charge on a pure percentage of value basis even without agreement'.

162. EC Regulation 1/2003 Art. 6: 'National courts shall have the power to apply Arts 81 and 82 of the Treaty' which therefore permits the national domestic courts to grant exemptions pursuant to EC Art. 81 (3).

163. Institut für Höhre Studien, Economic Impact of Regulation in the field of Liberal Profession in different Member State for the European Commission DG Competition: Wien, Jan. 2003. It is necessary to consider the critique of this report made in particular by RBB Economics Economic Impact of Regulation in Liberal Professions, A critique of the IHS report. 9 Sep. 2003.

164. EC Commission Report on Competition in Professional Services (COM (2004) 83) 9 Feb. 2004. A. Riley & J. Peysner, 'Damages in EC Anti-Trust Actions: Who pays the Piper', *ELRev* 31 (2006): Oct 748, approach the problem of costs in EC competition litigation and their effect upon access to justice and effective enforcement in light of the Commission Green Paper: Damages Actions for Breach of the EC Anti-Trust Rules COM (2005) 672, 19 Dec. 2005, and Commission Staff Working Paper, SEC (2005) 1732 from the perspective of funding: apparently feeling that national procedural problems such as damages – notably interest – following Case C-271/91, *Marshall v. Southampton* (No. 2), as well as discovery can be solved by the application of Community law to national procedure, the authors propose, having eliminated the use of capped contingency fees, a Contingency Legal Aid Fund (CLAF) which would be established throughout the EU.

165. EC Commission Follow up Report on Competition in Professional Services, COM (2005) 405 Final SEC (2005) 1064:
Point 6 'The Commission focussed upon 6 professions including lawyers' and a point 7 'In many instances, tradition restrictive rules in these areas are serving to restrict competition. Such regulation may eliminate or limit competition between service providers and thereby reduce the incentives between service providers and thus reduce the incentives for professionals to work cost efficiently, lower price increase, quality or to offer other market services', See also: European Parliament Resolution of 12 Oct. 2006, (2006/2137 (INI)) which supports the Commissions Follow up Report.

Better defining of the public interest:

Point 10 There are reasons why some carefully targeted regulation of professional services may be necessary:

Firstly, because there is an asymmetry of information between customers and service providers of professional services in that they require practitioners to display a high level of technical knowledge. Consumers may not have this knowledge and therefore find it difficult to judge the quality of services.

Secondly, the concept of externalities whereby the provision of a service may have an impact on third parties as well as the purchaser of the service.

Thirdly, certain professional services are deemed to produce 'goods' that are of value for society in general. For example, the correct administration of justice. It is possible that without regulation there might be an inadequate or under supply of these services.

In its Staff Working Document[166] the Commission makes the following observation apparently in relation to the information provided in the previous analyzes:

KEY FINDING OF ANALYSIS

21 A further differentiation of the markets of professional services would allow a better identification of the public interest involved and of the degree of regulation indispensable to protect this. This can be arrived at by assisting what is needed for the different types of customers or users. The above analysis shows that one off users – generally individual customers and households may have a greater need of some carefully targeted protection (e.g., price regulation may be needed) for the lower paid to ensure proper access to legal advice and representation in certain areas of law. On the other hand the main users of business services – business and public sector – may have no or little need given that they are better equipped to chose providers that best suit their needs. The position of small business is not entirely clear and further economic analysis is needed to arrive at a conclusion on the facts.

Therefore, and arguably despite its emphasis upon introduction of market forces facilitated through regulation,[167] the Commission nevertheless concludes by

---

166. Competition in Professional Services, Commission Staff Working Document COM (2005) 405 Final.

167. See for a criticism of the HIS Report for the Commission that of RBB Economics, Economic Impact of Regulation in Liberal Professions: A Critique of the HIS Report: 9 Sep. 2003: <www.ccbe.org/doc/En/rbb_ihs_critique_en.pdf> at para. 2.2.2 of its report the following with respect to the HIS Report: 'The theoretical overview seems to have a bias towards contra-regulation theories as the authors do not even consider the possibility that there could be too little regulation. Where there are benefits and costs of regulation it is clearly possible that in effort to curtail costs, government have reduced the level of regulation below the optima level ... . In general the theoretical discussion does not provide any framework for the empirical analysis. It therefore gives no clear guidance as to the relationship which should be investigated and how the results arising from the relationship should be interpreted. In par-

recognizing the following with respect to the market for legal services:[168] first, that the market for professional services in particular legal services involves information asymmetry and second, that accordingly, some regulation of costs may be necessary; and third, that the regulation should be directed to two groups of consumers in particular, namely, individual users and small business.[169]

Therefore, it is submitted that the Commission's conclusion in this regard coincides with the observations made by Lord Woolf, Lord Hoffmann and Professor Zuckerman cited earlier; namely, that free market forces in themselves are insufficient in order to reduce legal costs in England[170] Clearly, the Commission's acceptance of some market regulation in what is generally a deregulatory, market forces based analysis of costs is confined to two specific consumer groups for legal services, namely, private clients and small businesses. Overall, therefore, the conclusion must be that correct implementation of the Directive and in particular those articles which deal with costs will take place in a context where costs are excessive in English civil procedure.

f   *Methods of Correct Implementation of Articles 3 and 14'*
            of the Directive

Having thus considered the general background of costs and litigation involving IP rights before the English courts it is appropriate now to turn to the implementation of Articles 3 and 14 of the Directive. As noted earlier, the implementation of Articles 3 and 14 are apparently inadequate in two respects: first, with respect to the operation of the conditional fees and the indemnity rule and second, with regard to party to party costs and eventually solicitor's own costs although this latter will not be considered. Accordingly, it is appropriate to consider the concepts of interpretation in conformity and Member State liability developed by the ECJ which exist for remedying either non-implementation or in adequate imple-

---

ticular, the authors do not specify how it may be possible to decide whether there is too much or too little regulation within the profession.'

168. Competition in Professional Services, Commission Staff Working Document COM (2005) 405 Final.

169. See A. Ogus, 'Some Reflections on the Woolf Interim Report', *Journal of Current Legal Issues*, <www.ncl.ac.uk/-nlaw;www./1996/issue1/>; B. Main & A. Peacock, 'What price Civil Justice' (1998) Hume Institute <www.econ.ed.ac.uk /papers/confmp3.pdf>, at 6 'There are two types of purchases of civil legal services. The first is the one time buyer whom the costs of obtain and evaluating information on the range and quality of legal services can be high. Purchases are therefore typically make on faith and for this type of buyer legal service is a credence good where it can be argued that some kind of third party regulation is beneficial. The second type is a professional or repeat buyer who may be a business enterprise. Here there is ample opportunity to gain information on the nature of supplies and to make informed purchases based upon experience. To these buyers legal services are an experienced good where the normal stricture of caveat emptor leads to an efficient outcome.'

170. The Commission specifically identifies England the EU Member State – along possibly with IRELAND where the legal costs are the highest throughout the EU. See also, C. Hodges 'Europeanisation of Civil Justice: Trends & Issues', *CJQ* (2007): 96 at 120.

mentation of directives. As observed earlier, the third possible remedial method, namely, direct effect will not be considered by reason of the fact that the nature of the rights involved under Articles 3 and 14 of the Directive appear to be insufficiently clear in that they require among other things implementation by the Member States in order to be fully realized. Moreover, the scope of direct effect is restricted in that it is of no avail for enforcement of rights, horizontally, between individuals.

g   *Interpretation in Conformity: Implementation*
                of the Directive: Conditional Fees

It is submitted that CPR may be used in modified form to implement the Directive. However, as noted earlier, arguably, the concept of interpretation in conformity under von Colson[171] extends to the process of implementation itself. It is not simply a corrective procedure although in the instant case, it would seem that both applications of the principle are necessary. Accordingly, the national court, and in particular, the Patents Court, will be obliged to implement the Directive and notably Articles 3 and 14 by construing the relevant legislation in conformity therewith subject to the principles which govern implementation such as clarity, legal certainty, full effectiveness and, in particular, effective judicial protection of rights. In short, the pre-existing national legislation and specifically sections of the CPR and the AJA constitute an inadequate implementation of the obligations contained within Articles 3 and 14 of the Directive as well contravening the principle of effective judicial protection. In this regard, it would seem that remedial interpretation in conformity as well as possibly the use thereof in the context of judicial implementation would be utilized in the following manner as regards pre-existing legislation, and in particular, the CPR in relation to Article 14 of the Directive:

first, one notes that section 51 (1) SCA (1981)[172] empowers the court to decide three issues two of which are particularly relevant to the shifting of costs in relation to conditional fees and up lifts: that is, the court may exercise its discretion to decide:

    i)   whether costs are payable by one of the parties;
    ii) the amount of those costs.

This power would be exercised in conjunction with:

---

171. *Von Colson*, Case No. 14/83 (1984) ECR 1891, op. cit., S. Prechal, *Directives in EC Law*, 2nd edn (Oxford: OUP, 2005), op. cit., 187-193.
172. Section 51(1) SCA 1981: the court has discretion as to:
    (1) whether costs are payable by one party to the other;
    (2) the amount of those costs; and
    (3) when they are to be paid.
    In the Civil Division of the Court of Appeal, the High Court and the County Courts, the CPR identifies as a general rule that: *the unsuccessful party will be ordered to pay the costs of the successful party; but the court may make a different order* (Rule 44.3(2)).

S 27 A(6) of the Access to Justice Act which empowers the court to decide the following issue:
A costs order made in any proceedings may, subject in the case of court proceedings to rules of court include provisions requiring the payment of any fees payable under a conditional fee agreement which provides for a success fee.

In short, it is submitted that the expression '… may … include' simply empowers[173] the court to exercise its discretion so as to include a success fee within the fees payable by a losing party in the context of a conditional fee agreement. It does not enjoin the court to include such fees as a matter of obligation: that is, the court enjoys the discretion not to include such fees and therefore not to shift them to the losing party. It is submitted that the principle of interpretation in conformity may require the court to consider exercising its discretion in the aforementioned manner: specifically, so as not to include the success fee which is included in a conditional fee agreement and not to shift it to the losing party. Arguably, it is in this way that the court appears to be able to implement Articles 3 (a) and (b) and 14 of the Directive, that is, in conformity with the wording not 'costly' and 'proportionate' which constitute part of the substantive obligation in those two articles. In so doing, the court would specifically not apply either section 9. 1 or section 11. 9 of the PD for CPR 44: that is, the court would exercise its discretion pursuant to section 51 of the SCA (1981) and section 27 A (6) of the AJA (1999) so as not to shift the costs involving the success fee thereby avoiding the consequences of section 9.1 and the inclusion of the success fee which according to section 11.9 need not comply with the principle of proportionality.[174] In short, it is submitted that in order to correctly implement Articles 3 and 14 of the Directive, the principle of consistent interpretation in light of von Colson and, notably, Marleasing[175] the national court called upon to interpret national law is required to do so, as far as possible, in light of the wording and purpose of the Directive. In short, in the present case, it would be necessary for the national court to exercise its discretion pursuant to section 51 of the SCA (1981) so as not to include the costs of the success fee notably in those cases where a limit thereto has not been fixed as in the personal injuries: specifically, the court in exercising its power pursuant to section 51 would thereby override section 9.1 of the PD for CPR 44[176] except in cases such as personal injuries.

---

173. It is submitted that following Marleasing, Case No. C-106/89 (1990) ECR I-4135 op. cit., it may be that the rules of interpretation to be used are not the national rules but rather what might be termed EU rules: see generally, A. Tanney '*Comment on Webb v. EMO Air Cargo (UK) Ltd*' (1992) CMLR 1021, op. cit., S. Prechal, *Directive in EC Law*, 2nd edn (Oxford: OUP, 2005), op. cit., 197-199.
174. Civil Justice Council, Improved Access to Justice: Funding Option and Proportionate Costs, Jun. 2007, <www.civiljusticecouncil.gov.uk> 46 in particular para. 101. 'A good example is the CFA regime as it operated prior to the introduction of recoverability in Apr. 2000. Originally under the 1990 Courts and Legal Services Act, the uplift on the success and any premium incurred were taken from client damages… . There is no evidence of client dissatisfaction with this regime … .'
175. Marleasing, Case No. C-106/89 (1990) ECR I-4135 , op. cit.
176. S. Prechal, *Directives in EC Law*, 2nd edn (Oxford: OUP, 2005), op. cit., 196-198.

This is the preferred solution in terms of compliance notably with both the text of Articles 3 and 14 of the Directive and notably the principle of effective judicial protection: that is effectively, the winning party would bear the burden of the success fee[177] which would restore the position provided by the Courts and Legal Services Act (1990). With respect to the operation of the principle of remedial consistent interpretation, following cases such as Case X[178] arguably the principles which govern the application and in particular the scope thereof are EU principles. In short, the result of the operation arguably consists in the substitution of the already existing general powers of the national court which enable it to exercise its discretion with respect to the calculation of amount of costs and designation of the paying party thereof for the particular powers which are provided in the CPR and notably in the PD. The purpose of this substitution is to ensure the following: first, that Articles 3 and 14 of the Directive are implemented effectively and that second, the implementation conforms with the principle of effective judicial protection as it pertains to costs. Accordingly, it would appear that this substitution of the general power for the particular power in order to ensure effective implementation of Articles 3 and 14 of the Directive and in order to ensure compliance with the principle of effective judicial protection does not exceed the limits on the scope of the concept of interpretation in conformity: that is, one might say that following Marleasing, the principle of legal certainty and its component of contra legem have not be breached. Contra legem here is interpreted as proscribing the attribution to a national provision of a meaning which deviates from the literal reading of the national provisions concerned.[179] Nor arguably has there been any alteration with respect to the judicial capacity of the national court which already enjoy the existing power under section 51 (1) of the SCA of 1981.[180]

An alternate manner of dealing with this inadequate implementation of Articles 3 and 14 of the Directive would be to ensure that by means of remedial consistent interpretation, following the arguments just advanced in the previous paragraphs, the scope of section 9.1 of the PD be restricted.[181] Therefore, this section would be applied only in those circumstances such as personal injuries where the percentage of the success fee is determined ex ante by a fixed tariff. Beyond that, the national court would exercise its discretion pursuant to section 51 of the SCA (1981). Otherwise, the costs engendered by the uncontrolled success fee notably where the legal costs are based upon hourly calculations which cannot be

---

177. K. Ashby & C. Glasser 'The Legality of Conditional Fee Uplifts', *CJQ* 26 (2005): 135, op. cit., and A.A.S. Zuckerman, 'Editor's Note', *CJQ* 24 (2005): 1, op. cit., at 15 proposes that CFA legislation be modified so as to empower courts to 'dispense with payment of a even a reasonable success fee when to do so would cause injustice it might be possible to resolve the incompatibility [with Art. 6.1 ECHR] issue'.

178. Case No. C-373/90 X (1992) ECR I-131 and *Kolpinghuis*, Case No. 80/86 (1987) ECR 3969, op. cit.

179. Y. Galmot & J.-C. Bonichot, 'La Cour des Justice des Communautées Européennes et la Transposition des Directives en Droit National', *RDDA* (1998) 1, op. cit.

180. S. Prechal, *Directives in EC Law*, 2nd edn (Oxford: OUP, 2005), 201-203, op. cit.

181. S. Prechal, *Directives in EC Law*, 2nd edn, (Oxford: OUP, 2005), 210, op. cit.

objectively assessed and where information asymmetry prevails as with small companies and private clients would not only constitute a disproportionate method of funding in contravention to Articles 3 and 14 of the Directive: significantly, it would also violate the principle of effective judicial protection of the parties, and notably violate Article 6 ECHR specifically as in *Airey v. Ireland.* It is to be noted that in Airey the ECtHR decided that the costs of legal proceedings could in certain circumstances contravene Article 6.1 by preventing access to a court and thereby to a fair trial. It is submitted that there is no justification in the instant case within the CPR for using conditional fees with success fees when the consequence is that that one of the parties, namely, the party likely to lose, may be effectively discouraged from defending his rights before the court by fear of paying double the normal amount in costs of his opponent who uses the conditional fee with a 100% success fee. This is particularly the case where private individuals and or small companies are involved in the defence of IP rights under the Directive. As observed, there is no justification for this restriction of the principle of effective legal protection and the violation of the principle of proportionality contained in Articles 3 and 14 of the Directive given that a different system for the calculation of legal costs, for example, a system of fixed legal costs, could be used. Such a system would produce not only lower costs but would have the advantage of producing an objective method for assessment of costs and, over all, would assist in ensuring that conditional fees and success fees comply with both the principle of proportionality and that of effective judicial protection. Regretfully, although the CPR constitutes an attempt to simplify the previous RSC thereby corresponding to an example noted by the ECtHR in Airey, namely, the possibility of simplifying rules in order to ensure compliance with ECHR Article 6.1, nevertheless one notes as follows: namely that the CPR at least in relation to conditional fee agreements and success fees has created the following problem: that is, a system whereby the success fee of up to 100% based upon costs which are calculated on an hourly basis and not subject to the control of market forces are shifted to the loser who is a private party or a small business in IP litigation has the result of being disproportionate to the aim of increasing access to justice: more specifically, the operation of the conditional fee agreement coupled with the success fee of up to 100% which is shifted by means of the indemnity rule impairs the very right of effective judicial protection. This system of financing discourages the eventual and or actual losing party from exercising his right of access to the court simply by reason of the magnitude of the costs which could be awarded against him in the event of losing. In short, what is required, as noted earlier, at a minimum is that the conditional fee system and success fee be based upon an objective method of legal costing, for example, fixed legal costs, which will serve to control legal costs by among other things taking into account of the information asymmetry which prevails in the market of legal services for small companies and private individuals.[182] Further and in the alternative, it is submitted that section 11.9 of the Practise

---

182. A.A.S. Zuckerman, see notes 153 and 177 *infra.*

Direction might be interpreted in conformity with the Directive and notably with the principle of effective judicial protection in the following manner: that is, following the ratio of Marleasing, the phrase 'A percentage increase will not be reduced simply on the ground that when added to the base costs which are reasonable the total appears disproportionate' ought to be interpreted as applying strictly to a situation where the ground is 'disproportionate'. Section 11.9 should not apply to a situation where there are multiple grounds. Accordingly, such a strict interpretation limited to reduction simply on grounds of disproportion would not prevent a reduction on multiple grounds such as disproportion coupled with a violation of the principle of effective judicial protection and eventually contravention of ECHR Article 6.1 or indeed simply on the ground of violation of the principle of effective judicial protection: that is, correct implementation of Articles 3 and 14 of the Directive will require that section 11. 9 of the PD be interpreted in such a manner that it does not prevent a reduction of the percentage increase of the success fee where such an increase could result in a violation of effective judicial protection in the sense of depriving notably the losing party of the possibility of access to judicial protection. Therefore, it is in this manner that the obligations contained within the text of Articles 3 and 14 of the Directive would be respected and further, the implementation thereof would conform with the principle of effective legal protection. Nevertheless, as noted previously, the preferred method is for the court, following what might be termed a remedial form of consistent interpretation with the Directive, to exercise its discretion pursuant to SCA (1981) so as not to include the success fees within the costs which will be shifted to the losing party by means of the indemnity rule. It is submitted that this method ensures most adequately the implementation of Articles 3 and 14 of the Directive notably with respect to the principle of effective judicial protection notably in a context where legal fees cannot be objectively assessed and controlled.

h   Costs Estimates: Fee Capping

The jurisdiction for fee capping is to be found in section 51 of the SCA (1981) and arguably subsection (2) therefore which provides that the Court has discretion as to the amount of costs in conjunction with CPR 3(2) (m) which provides as follows:

> Except where these Rules provide otherwise, the Court may (m) take any other step or make any other order for the purpose of managing the case and furthering the overriding objective.

It is submitted that judicial interpretation in conformity of the relevant pre-existing legislation herein cited with the Directive would lead to the following implementation: that is, interpretation in conformity with both Articles 14 and 3 of the Directive and in particular with the principle of effective judicial protection as reflected in ECHR Article 6 would ensure that the court exercises its discretion pursuant to section 51 of the SCA (1981) and CPR 3 (2) (m) to establish a fee cap in a manner which is not restricted by the principle or test established by Gage J in *Smart v. East Cheshire NHS Trust*: that is there will be no requirement that the jurisdiction is exercisable only where there is a real risk that the costs incurred by a litigant may get out of hand. Arguably, the intervention of the principle of effective judicial protection which notably the judicial implementation process involving consistent interpretation must respect would require the restriction of the application of the test created by Gage J such that it would not apply with respect to the enforcement of the Directive. The purpose of such a restriction would be to ensure effective access to the courts in terms of costs and thereby adequate implementation of Articles 3 and 14 of the Directive in so far as they refer to costs. Accordingly, the system of cost capping would then supplement the system of conditional fees wherein the winner would pay the uplift and overall contribute to ensuring that the latter operates in a proportionate manner in relation to costs in order to ensure access to justice notably for the losing party. Further, it would seem that this analysis and notably the principle of effective judicial protection would apply with regards to the use of the court's discretion in relation to CPR 26 as it concerns the application of the details provided in the allocation questionnaire: that is, the court would exercise its discretion in such a manner as to ensure that the budget estimates provided in the allocation questionnaire pursuant to CPR 26 were respected by the parties in the sense of not permitting deviation therefrom without good reason. The national court would thereby render more effective the control of costs through cost capping.

i   Proportionality

CPR 44. 4 (2) provides:

> Where the amount of costs is to be assessed on the standard basis, the court will
> a) only allow costs which are proportionate to the matters in issue; and
> b) resolve any doubt which it may have as to whether costs were reasonably incurred or reasonable and proportionate in amount in favour of the paying party.

It is submitted that consistent interpretation of this rule with notably Article 3 (2) of the Directive which, as recalled, imposes a substantive obligation on Member States to ensure that 'Those measure, procedure and remedies shall be ... proportionate ...' will also require that CPR 44. 4. (2) be effectively applied. This however is in the sense that overall the method used for funding litigation is proportionate to the end which is pursued, namely, the increase of access to justice.[183] It

---

183.   See for example, *Suid – Hollandse*, Case No. C-174/05 (2006) ECR I-2443 at para. 28, and *Alrosa*, Case No. T-170/06, unreported judgment in date of 11 Jul. 2007 at para. 98 for a definition of proportionality; G. De Burca observes 'Proportionality in EC Law', *Yearbook of European Law* 13 (1993): 105 at 146 concerning ECJ case law on proportionality: '... there appear to be three stages in the proportionality enquiry: ... first whether the measure was an appropriate and effective way of achieving this legitimate aim; second whether the measure was a necessary way of achieving its aim in that there was no less restrictive alternative and thirdly, whether even if the first two stages are satisfied the adverse effect on the interest

would appear that effective application of CPR 44. 4. (2) in turn will require that cost capping and cost estimates provided at the allocation stage be effectively implemented by the Patent Court, as the national court, in order to ensure compliance with the wording of Article 3 (2) of the Directive as it pertains to proportionality. The judicial implementation of this article through consistent interpretation will also require that the principle of effective judicial protection be respected as noted earlier in order to ensure access to justice in terms of costs. As noted previously, in order for Article 3 (2) to be effectively implemented as it relates to proportionality, it will be necessary for the system of conditional fees and the success fees to be based upon a system of costs, arguably, fixed costs which can then ensure notably with respect to private parties and small businesses involved in IP litigation that the costs are objectively controlled. It is only in this manner that the conditional fees and the uplifts can in some measure function in a manner which is proportionate to the objective pursued, namely, the increase of the access to justice and notably if the success fee is not shifted to the losing party.

j   *Obligation that Procedure not be Unnecessarily Costly*

However, consistent interpretation of section 51 (1) of the SCA (1981) in conjunction with section 27 (a) (6) (AJA) (1999) is unable to ensure adequate implementation notably of the obligation 'shall not be unnecessarily costly' contained in Article 3 of the Directive as noted above: that is, clearly, the non inclusion of the success fees does not in itself determine substantively the aggregate level of costs which as noted, earlier, at least for individual litigants and small businesses are not subject to market forces, that is, neither information asymmetry nor objective control through the intervention of costs judges either through budgeting, cost capping or through ex post factum assessment. The essential problem remains, as noted above, that the costs generated by the structural economic factors, such as information asymmetry and moral hazard, produce amounts which cannot be objectively assessed and which are disproportionate to the values at stake in the litigation. Overall, consistent interpretation of the aforementioned statutes can only partially ensure that costs are proportionate. As observed earlier, consistent interpretation cannot suffice unless the basic pre-existing or specifically adopted legislation exists: as Prechal observes: the basics for a consistent interpretation must exist in terms of the national legislation.[184] In the instant case, no fixed cost legislation exists beyond that in Road Traffic accidents.

k   *Legislative Modification of the CPR*

By reason of this analysis, it may be useful to consider possible amendments to the CPR which could assist in the implementation of Articles 3 and 14 of the

---

or right affected was disproportionate or excessive when weighed against the aim of the measure'.

184. S. Prechal, *Directives in EC Law*, 2nd edn (Oxford: OUP, 2005), op. cit., 163.

Directive from the point of view of not only of full effectiveness[185] but also legal certainty, clarity and perhaps above all, conformity with the principle of effective legal protection as provided in such cases as Unibet and Airey. First, legislative intervention in the form of a system of fixed costs or mandatory maximum fees. Van den Berghe[186] notes:

> In some professions the fees to be paid by the consumer of professional services are regulated to a certain extent. Such regulation can impose hourly rates, specific fees for certain services or fees calculated as a percentage of the value of the transactions. Fee regulations can take several forms. The most restrictive form of regulation is the imposition of mandatory fixed fees which leaves no freedom whatsoever to regulate fees between professionals and their clients. Mandatory maximum fees or minimum fees are less restrictive since they allow the professional to charge lower or higher fees.

Therefore, fixed costs represent what might be termed the potentially most restrictive method of controlling costs as opposed to mandatory maximum and or minimum fees. It would seem that the advantage of the fixed costs would be the following; in Airey,[187] the ECtHR held that it was the responsibility of the State to ensure effective access to the legal system. Fulfilment of this obligation might in certain circumstances involve provision of legal aid. In other circumstances, the obligation may involve the simplification of the rules of civil procedure. As noted earlier, the CPR represents the effect of the attempt to simplify the rules of civil procedure in England and Wales.[188] For this reason it would seem that the only method procedurally which remains available to control costs given that the mechanisms of budgeting and cost capping in themselves have been observed notably by Lord Hoffmann to be insufficient is through some form of fixed costs

---

185. *Commission v. Germany*, Case No. 29/84 (1985) ECR 1661 para. 18, *Commission v. UK*, Case No. 340/96 (1999) ECR I-2023.
186. R. van den Bergh & Y. Montagnie, Theory and Evidence on the Regulation of the Latin Notary Profession, ECRI Report 0604 Jun. 2006 at p. 7-8.
187. *Airey v. Ireland* application 6289/73 (1979) ECHRR (32) 305, op. cit., see also potentially, Art. 47 (right to an effective remedy) of the Charter of Fundamental Rights as implemented by Art. 6 of the Lisbon Treaty [rejected by Ireland on 13 June 2008] subject to the Protocol for Poland and the UK.
188. It is submitted that the case of UNIBET, albeit applying to a situation where the rules of national procedure were not subject to a directive as in the instant case nevertheless produces an interpretation of the concept of effective judicial protection which may be of use or at least warrants consideration where procedure is subject to a directive and the implementation thereof is subject to the principle, as in the instant case, the principle of effective judicial protection: arguably, the ECJ held in *UNIBET*, Case No. C-432/05 (2007) ECR I 2271, op. cit., para. 55-58 that it is necessary to consider in deciding whether the principle is infringed whether, although a specific procedure does not exist whether other procedures available which albeit 'indirect' are effective and equivalent may be used. In the instant case, before deciding on the introduction of fixed costs in order to ensure compliance with effective judicial protection it is arguably necessary to consider whether other procedural changes – perhaps less drastic – have first of all been attempted – as is the case with the CPR – but have proved to be ineffectual directly or indirectly in controlling the costs in English civil procedure.

or fixed maximum costs[189] which arguably will comply effectively with the principle of judicial protection of rights notably as illustrated in Airey. It is perhaps this principle of effective judicial protection expressed in Airey and in Unibet which may most significantly justify if not require some form of fixed maximum costs given that the other methods of controlling costs such as the reform of the CPR and case management have signally failed. Accordingly, some more direct method of controlling the costs would seem to be required in order to specifically ensure that the implementation of the Directive with respect to costs as provided by Articles 3 and 14 is not only clear; fully effective but most significantly ensures effective judicial protection of the rights of litigants, and notably defendants, in terms of costs. Interestingly, Peysner and Seneviratne conclude their report on the judicial case management by raising as a possible solution for the increase in costs the possibility of using fixed costs:

Towards the end of the research period, the promotion of fixed costs by the Civil Justice Council was on the mind of the interviewees. The merits of fixed costs in principle divided interviewees with judges taking the view on the Fast Track it would be the most effective way of dealing with disproportionate costs.[190]

Second, it would seem that the introduction of the fixed costs with respect to party to party costs would correspond precisely to the objectives of legal certainty and predictability which are part of the Overriding Objective of the CPR,[191] notably, saving expense and ensuring speedy disposition. This is recognized as a possibility in turn by the LECG – Office of Fair Trading report[192] in March 2001:[193]

---

189.   Bearing in mind that litigation involving intellectual property is different from that of personal injuries, one notes nevertheless that system of fixed legal costs is not unknown to the CPR. Indeed the CPR provides for such with respect to Road Traffic injuries in the context of the Fast Track procedure. Furthermore, the Civil Justice Council in Recommendation 3 of its report, Access to Justice, August 2005, <www.civiljusticecouncil.gov.uk> proposes that the fixed cost system under CPR 45 Part II be expanded from Road Traffic Injuries to include personal injuries within the Fast Track whose limit would be extended to £ (GBP) 50,000 and optionally up to £ (GBP) 50,000.

190.   J. Peysner & M. Senviratne, The Management of Civil Cases, DCA Research Series 9/05, at p. 69: '… Practitioners feel that issues of proportionality should be addressed by encouraging sensible charging by opponent and in any event fixed costs did not fit well with the rigorous requirement to comply fully with a set of complex rules.' The report continues at p. 71: '… The failure of estimate as a cost control measure was noted but in the absence of prospective cost control (fixed costs, …) … it is hard to see how estimate on their own could constitute an effective restriction on costs. … Rules alone cannot achieve proportionality, economy, predictability and certainty of costs. Policy solutions are required.'

191.   CPR 1.1 (2) (b) saving expense:
       (d) ensuring that it is dealt with expeditiously and fairly.

192.   LECG in 'Competition in the Professions: A Report prepared by the Director General of Fair Trading: OFT 2001 OFT 328, Mar. 2001. at 225.

193.   It is useful to note with respect to legal certainty that the ECJ held in Case 348/85 *Denmark v. Commission* (1987) ECR 5225 at para. 19: 'Furthermore, as the Court has decided on numerous occasions, community legislation must be certain and its application must be foreseeable by those subject to it. That requirement of legal certainty must be observed all the more strictly in the case of rules liable to entail financial consequences in order that those concerned may know precisely the extent of the obligations which they impose on them'.

An alternative form of charging has emerged for some contentious work for example, Fast Track (claims valued up to £10,000). In these cases lawyers' costs are fixed in accordance with one of the aims of the Woolf reforms. By making fees more transparent before a service is purchases, this type of charging may increase competition, help bring down costs and provide more certainty for clients.

Necessarily, such a system would permit implementation of the Directive which would comply with the principle of legal clarity and certainty in addition to the obligation of proportionality contained both in Articles 3 and 14 of the Directive: for this reason, the fixed costs or fixed maximum costs would be related to the amounts in dispute. Moreover, if the fixed costs or fixed maximum costs were established by the Civil Justice Council, notably, the eventual Costs Council and or the LSB[194] ensures compliance with what might be said to be a restrictive interpretation of the Member State's duty pursuant to EC Articles 10: that is, for example, in the field of EC competition law, a Member State following Advocate General Poiares Maduro[195] and the ECJ in Cipolla,[196] complies with its duty pursuant to EC Article 10 to avoid breaching EC Articles 81 and 82 by the adoption of anti-competitive measures provided that it supervises, as the State, the adoption and implementation of the measures so that they retain a legislative character.[197] In short, it is submitted that Civil Procedure Act (1997) imparts such a state legislative character to the amended CPR 45, specifically by means of and by reason of state supervision of the amending process. This would avoid the problem raised by notably Lord Hoffmann with respect to the use of costs judges of calculating objectively the amounts of legal costs: that is a lack of objective criterion. Moreover, following the comments of the Commission in conjunction van der Berghe and Copenhagen Economics, it would seem appropriate to limit the scope

---

194. Legal Services Bill 2006-2007.
195. *Cipolla*, Joined Cases No. C-94/04 and C-202/04, (2006) ECR I 1141, para. 31: 'While it is true that Art. 86 (now Art. 82) is directed at undertakings, nevertheless it is also true that the Treaty imposes a duty on a Member State not to adopt or maintain any national measures which would deprive that provision of its effectiveness. However the Court subsequently gave a restrictive interpretation of the requirements under Art. 10 and Art. 81 EC. According to case law these articles are regarded as having been infringed only in two cases ... second, where the State divests its own rules of the character of legislation by delegating to private economic operators responsibility for taking decisions affecting the economic sphere see generally: M. Illmer, 'Lawyers' Fee and Access to Justice: Cipolla & Macrino, *CJQ* 26 (2007): 301.
196. *Cipolla*, Joined Cases No. C-94/04 and C-202/04, (2006) ECR I 1141, ibid., In this case the ECJ held that the Italian law which established a system maximum and minimum costs for both party to party and solicitors own client costs did not contravene EC Art. 81. However, the ECJ held that although fixed minimum costs may violate EC Art. 49, it would fall to the Italian court to establish whether such a restriction, if proportionate, could be justified on the basis of proper administration of justice, consumer protection.
197. It is of interest to note that the ECJ does not link compliance with Art. 10 EC and discretion (which the English court is able to exercise under the current CPR 45 in order to increase fees) as did the Advocate General in para. 46 of his opinion.

of the application of such a system to individuals or small companies. Arguably, with respect to IP litigation it would be necessary to include all categories of rights holders as provided in Article 4 of the Directive. Finally, in order to ensure compliance with EC Articles 49 and 81 it may be necessary following such cases as Cipolla,[198] to ensure that the fixed costs contain a fixed maximum but no minimum and second that the system apply to lawyers within England and Wales but not those from other EU countries.

Overall it is submitted that some type of modification of the CPR is required along the lines as described above in order to ensure adequate implementation of Articles 3 and 14 of the Directive notably with respect to the principles of legal certainty, effectiveness and in particular effective judicial protection.

4   Action for Damages against the State

Arguably, the remedy of damages against the State would only be available in the event that the doctrine of interpretation in conformity proved to be ineffective in both the interpretative and remedial sense.[199] It would appear, on the contrary, that interpretation in conformity may render the implementation of Articles 3 and 14 of the Directive effective to the extent the national legislation exist. To the extent, however, that consistent interpretation, notably, both through judicial implementation and in remedial application do not suffice to ensure effective enforcement of the aforementioned Articles 3 and 14, it would be appropriate to consider the possibility of an action in damages. Moreover it is not clear that the concept of State liability would indeed apply in particular with respect to Article 3 and possibly Article 14. Indeed, it is submitted that in the instant case, the wording of the Directive does not define the category of the right sufficiently clearly: that is, although the wording does provide for a right for beneficiaries that procedure 'shall not be unnecessarily costly' the Member State enjoys considerable discretion in the manner and form in which the right is to be implemented. For this reason, it is concluded that the Directive does not define sufficiently clearly the category of the right so as to permit an action for damages against the State. In this regard Prechal[200] observes:

> Obviously, a right laid down in the directive in a rudimentary form will make it impossible to determine the loss and damage incurred by the individual. A directive must therefore provide sufficient guidance in this respect.

---

198.   *Cipolla*, Joined Cases No. C-94/04 and C-202/04, (2006) ECR I 1141 <www.curia.europa. eu>, op. cit., para. 54.
199.   S. Prechal, *Directives in EC Law*, 2nd edn (Oxford: Oxford University Press, 2005), op cit., 301, see *Miret*, Case No. C-334/92 (1993) ECR I-6911, *Faccini Dori*, Case No. C-91/92 (1994) ECR I-3325, *Carbonair*, Case No. C-131/97 (1999) ECR I-1103, and *Dorsch*, Case No. C-54/96 (1997) ECR I-4961 would seem to indicate that it is only if direct effect or consistent interpretation are impossible that State liability may be considered.
200.   S. Prechal, *Directives in EC Law*, 2nd edn (Oxford: OUP, 2005), ibid., 283.

This is, arguably, in contrast to the clarity with which the nature of the obligation and in particular the category of beneficiaries are defined in Article 4 of the Directive as previously analyzed. Secondly, even if the rights were sufficiently clear, the two other components of State liability must be established: namely, that the breach is sufficiently serious and that loss has thereby been caused. With respect to the matter of whether the breach is sufficiently serious, there is a range of factors which the court may take into consideration: among others are the clarity and precision of the rule breached, whether the infringement and the damage caused was intentional or involuntary and whether any error of law was excusable or inexcusable. Following therefore British Telecom[201] it may be that the rights described in Articles 3 and 14 of the Directive lack sufficient precision. Therefore, although the existing national legislation does not adequately implement these articles, nevertheless, because of the lack of their clarity, it might be said their use and the interpretation of the Directive by the UK are not manifestly contrary to the wording thereof. Following such cases as Brinkmann,[202] it is submitted that the meaning of the words clarity and precision with regards to State liability is different from that which is utilized in the context of direct effect. Rather clarity and precision in the context of State liability signifies that there is really no dispute as to the meaning of the text. In short, if the ECJ were to decide that Articles 3 and 14 do not possess the requisite degree of clarity then the breach by the Member State of its duty to correctly implement the directive may be excusable in the sense of not constituting a breach which is serious and manifest. One might also add that the broader the discretion which the Member State enjoys in terms of appreciation the more difficult it may be to establish a breach which is sufficiently serious to engage liability. Following Haim II,[203] the discretion at issue and above all its scope are to be determined by EC law principles and not national principles. Finally, causation can only be assessed in light of the actual facts of the case albeit it would appear that it is for the ECJ to decide on the nature thereof given that causation forms one of the components of the conditions for liability of a Member State.[204]

Article 15
Publication of Judicial Measures

Article 15 requires that the Member States ensure that the national courts may order, at the request of the applicant, the infringer to ensure the dissemination of the decision if necessary through publication thereof at his own expense. Recital 27 indicates that the purpose of this article is to increase the effectiveness of the deterrent factor of the enforcement decision. In so far as such an order may constitute a mandatory injunction then the Court would enjoy the power to so order

---

201. *British Telecom*, Case No. C-392/93 (1996) ECR I-1631, para. 43-44.
202. *Brinkmann*, Case No. C-319/93 (1996) ECR I-5255, op cit. para. 30-32, *Lindöpark*, Case No. C-150/99 (2001) ECR I-493 para. 39-41.
203. *Haim II*, Case No. C-424/97 (2000) ECR I-5123 at para. 40.
204. *Brasserie du Pêcheur*, Joined Cases No. C-46/93 and C-48/93 (1996) ECR I-1029.

pursuant to section 39 of the SCA (1981) and section 38 of the County Courts Act (1984). Effective implementation of this article is ensured by section 29.2 of the PD for CPR 63 which provides as follows:

> Section 29.2 Where the court finds that an intellectual property right has been infringed, the court may, at the request of the applicant, order appropriate measures for the dissemination and publication of the judgment to be taken at the defendant's expense.

Arguably, the exercise of the court's discretion exercised pursuant to section 29.2 in order to achieve such an objective would seem to constitute something akin to an order ad personam to a party within the court's jurisdiction as a result of the proceedings where as noted the objective is to ensure the effectiveness of the enforcement of the judgment as opposed to seeking to protect the rights of the applicant. As such the situation might possibly be viewed as being analagous to a so-called Mareva injunction which is rather more an order ad personam than an injunction which directly affects procedural or substantive rights. Therefore, a different and less demanding standard would be utilized to obtain an order under section 29.2 than would be the case were a form of a mandatory injunction used as the basis of the order to publish the judgment.[205]

Article 16
Sanctions by the Member States

Article 16 provides that the measures provided for within the Directive do not preclude the adoption and application of other appropriate measures such criminal sanctions by the Member States.[206]

Article 17
Codes of Conduct

Article 17 provides that Member States shall first, encourage trade and professional association to develop codes of conduct at the Community level which contribute to the enforcement of IP rights; and second that the Member States shall encourage the submission of draft codes thereof to the Commission. In this regard one observes first, that the time for compliance with such ancillary obligations is not stated and second, the obligation to encourage the communication of such draft codes to the Commission constitutes only a measure destined to inform the

---

205. A. Zuckerman, *Civil Litigation* (Oxford: Lexis-Nexis, 2003), op.cit., 303-305.
206. A guide to the criminal sanctions available can be found at <http://www.patent.gov.uk/crime/crime-whatis/crime-whatis-offenceguide.htm>
    The Annual Enforcement Report (<http://www.patent.gov.uk/enforcereport2005.pdf>) presents details of UK enforcement in the field of counterfeiting and piracy.

Commission. It is submitted that non-compliance in particular with the second obligation has no legal consequences.[207]

Article 18
Assessment

Article18 requires Member States to submit copies of their implementation of the Directive three years subsequent to the implementation date. According to the text of this article, the relevant period of time, namely, three years, has not yet elapsed.

Article 19
Exchange of Information and Correspondents

The Patent Office (Mr Jeff Watson[208]) has been nominated as the contact point for implementation of this Directive.

Article 20
Implementation

It is submitted that the SI 2006 No. 1028 and in particular the Explanatory Memorandum, The IP (Enforcement) Regulation (2006) comply with the first limb of this article.

Article 21
Entry into Force

The date by which the implementation is to have taken place is 28 April 2006. Accordingly, not only inadequate implementation but non-implementation of the Directive will result by reason of the implementation date having passed.[209]

---

207. In contrast see *Security*, Case No. C-194/94 (1996) ECR I-2201 where the ECJ found that a failure to observe the notification obligation constituted a substantial procedural defect which rendered the national technical regulation In question inapplicable and therefore unenforceable against individuals.
208. Patent Office: my thanks to Mr Watson for having so kindly and frequently replied to my questions concerning the implementation of the Directive in England. All errors and omissions in this regard are that of the author of this chapter.
209. *Dillenkofer*, Case No. C-178/94 jointed cases (1996) ECR I-4845 para. 28, failure to implement a directive in time constitutes per se a sufficiently serious breach for the purposes of State liability. See n. 35, op. cit.

Implementation of Directive 2004/48/ EC into German Civil Procedure

I   RECEPTION OF THE DIRECTIVE IN GERMANY

Directive 2004/48/EC was received rather sceptically in the German academic world. While there were mixed opinions as to whether the Directive was necessary in the first place,[1] it was criticized that the preparatory work for the Directive was sketchy and imprecise.[2] There was also a general belief that the speed of the legislative process was too rapid, and that the quality of various provisions might have been improved in a longer consultation process.[3] Some authors expressed doubt whether Article 95 EC provided the European Communities with a

---

1. The Directive was welcomed by H. Harte-Bavendamm H., 'Der Richtlinienvorschlag zur Durchsetzung der Rechte des geistigen Eigentums', in *Festschrift für Winfried Tilmann*, eds E. Keller, C. Plassmann & A. v. Falck (Köln: Heymanns, 2003), p. 798; R. Knaak, 'Die EG-Richtlinie zur Durchsetzung der Rechte des geistigen Eigentums und ihr Umsetzungsbedarf im deutschen Recht', [2004] GRUR Int, 746; and viewed more critically by J. Drexl, R. Hilty & A. Kur, 'Vorschlag für eine Richtlinie über die Maßnahmen und Verfahren zum Schutz der Rechte am geistigen Eigentum – eine erste Würdigung' [2003] GRUR Int, 606; H-P. Meyer and O. Linnenborn, 'Kein sicherer Hafen: Bekämpfung der Produktpiraterie in der Europäischen Union' [2003] K&R, 321; A. Peukert and A. Kur, 'Stellungnahme des Max-Planck-Instituts für Geistiges Eigentum, Wettbewerbs- und Steuerrecht zur Umsetzung der Richtlinie 2004/48/EG zur Durchsetzung der Rechte des geistigen Eigentums in deutsches Recht' [2006] GRUR Int, 293.
2. A. Metzger & W. Wurmnest, 'Auf dem Weg zu einem Europäischen Sanktionenrecht des geistigen Eigentums?' [2003] ZUM, 928; T. Hoeren, 'High-noon im europäischen Immaterialgüterrecht' [2003] MMR, 300.
3. D. Frey and M. Rudolph, 'EU-Richtlinie zur Durchsetzung der Rechte des geistigen Eigentums' [2004] ZUM, 522; D. Seichter, 'Die Umsetzung der Richtlinie zur Durchsetzung der Rechte des geistigen Eigentums [2006] WRP, 392; J. Jaeschke, 'Produktpiraten sollen Schiffbruch erleiden' [2004] JurPC, Web-Dok. 258/2004 n. 3.

competence to act,[4] and whether it was expedient to propose identical enforcement measures for all types of intellectual property (IP) rights and to cover both commercial and private actions.[5] Finally, it was felt that the provisions of the Directive were ambiguous, imprecise and inconsistent and were therefore inadequate to achieve the Directive's aim to harmonize the sanctions for IP infringements in the laws of the Member States[6] – in particular as many of the differences might be attributed to differences in the Member States regarding enforcement efforts, rules of evidence, evaluation of evidence and the infringer's opportunities to delay proceedings.[7]

II   STEPS TAKEN TOWARDS IMPLEMENTATION OF
            THE DIRECTIVE INTO GERMAN LAW

A   THE FAILURE TO IMPLEMENT DIRECTIVE 2004/48/EC WITHIN
            TIME

Whilst the Directive was met with a lukewarm reception in the German academic world, the political world approached implementation at a snail's pace. The Federal Ministry of Justice submitted a draft in the form of a *Gesetz zur Verbesserung der Durchsetzung von Rechten des Geistigen Eigentums* (Act to Improve Enforcement of IP Rights) on 3 January 2006, i.e., not even four months before the Member States were enjoined to bring into force the provisions necessary to comply with the Directive (29 April 2006, cf. Article 20 of the Directive). It was not until 24 January 2007 that the Federal Cabinet adopted the only slightly revised Draft Act as a Government Bill.[8] The Bill was referred to the Committee on Legal Affairs, to the Committee on Economics and Technology, to the Committee on Food, Agriculture and Consumer Protection and finally to the Committee on Education, Research and Technology Assessment. It was deliberated by the Bundesrat (German Federal Council) on 9 March 2007 and went through a first reading in the Bundestag (German Federal Parliament) on 26 April 2007. None of these bodies doubted the necessity of introducing changes to the existing IP legislation.

---

4. A. Metzger & W. Wurmnest, 'Auf dem Weg zu einem Europäischen Sanktionenrecht des geistigen Eigentums?' [2003] ZUM, 925.
5. D. Frey and M. Rudolph, 'EU-Richtlinie zur Durchsetzung der Rechte des geistigen Eigentums' [2004] ZUM, 522 et seq.
6. D. Frey and M. Rudolph, 'EU-Richtlinie zur Durchsetzung der Rechte des geistigen Eigentums' [2004] ZUM, 529; D. Seichter, 'Die Umsetzung der Richtlinie zur Durchsetzung der Rechte des geistigen Eigentums' [2006] WRP, 392.
7. D. Frey and M. Rudolph, 'EU-Richtlinie zur Durchsetzung der Rechte des geistigen Eigentums' [2004] ZUM, 529; J. Drexl, R. Hilty and A. Kur, 'Vorschlag für eine Richtlinie über die Maßnahmen und Verfahren zum Schutz der Rechte am geistigen Eigentum – eine erste Würdigung' [2003] GRUR Int, 606; H-P. Meyer and O. Linnenborn 'Kein sicherer Hafen: Bekämpfung der Produktpiraterie in der Europäischen Union', [2003] K&R, 321.
8. Gesetzesentwurf der Bundesregierung, 'Entwurf eines Gesetzes zur Verbesserung der Durchsetzung von Rechten des Geistigen Eigentums', BT-Drucks. 16/5048, 20 Apr. 2007.

In the meantime, the European Commission decided to pursue infringement procedures against the German state for failure to transpose the Directive into national law. On 12 October 2006, the Commission decided to formally ask Germany to implement the Directive. On 23 August 2007, the Commission brought an action against the Federal Republic of Germany seeking a declaration of the European Court of Justice (ECJ) that Germany had failed to fulfil its obligations under Directive 2004/48/EC.[9]

At the time of writing it was unclear when and how the Directive would be implemented. Naturally, this uncertainty constitutes a challenge for any author commenting on the implementation. The following analysis pursues a dual strategy: In a first step, the existing German law is examined as to the extent of which it already complies with the requirements set forth by the Directive, thereby taking into account the duty of consistent interpretation. In a second step, the reform provisions as suggested by the Government Draft are explained and their suitability to transpose the Directive is discussed. The *Gesetz zur Verbesserung der Durchsetzung der Rechte des Geistigen Eigentums* (Act to Improve the Enforcement of IP Rights) was adopted on 7 July 2008,10 after the manuscript for this book was submitted. The Act follows the proposals of the Government Bill as discussed herein. The description of the status of law previous to the implementation remains valid for any breaches of intellectual property rights before the Act's entry into force on 1 September 2008.[10]

B   THE GOVERNMENT BILL TO IMPROVE ENFORCEMENT OF
           INTELLECTUAL PROPERTY RIGHTS

Even though recital 17 of the Directive proclaims that '[t]he measures, procedures and remedies provided for in this Directive should be determined in each case in such a manner as to take due account of the specific characteristics of that case, including the specific features of each IP right', the Directive follows a general approach by providing for identical sanctions for infringements of all IP rights. The German Government Bill does not follow this horizontal approach, nor are the proposed provisions primarily viewed as a matter of civil procedure. Instead, the Bill basically pursues a dual strategy: Where the provisions of the Directive reflect procedures generally available to all rights holders under the German Code of Civil Procedure (Zivilprozessordnung – ZPO) or the German Civil Code (Bürgerliches Gesetzbuch – BGB), as is, i.e., the case for interlocutory injunctions and precautionary seizure (Article 9 of the Directive), injunctions (Article 11 thereof) and legal costs (Article 14 thereof), the general provisions of the ZPO/BGB are declared to be adequate and sufficient. Where this is not the case, it is primarily suggested to introduce substantive rights

---

9. *EC Commission v. Germany*, Case No. C-395/07, OJ No. C 247, 20 Oct. 2007, p. 19.
10. BGBl. I 2008, p. 1191.

which are to be inserted in each of the various IP statutes, using almost identical wording.

The Bill therefore does not envisage any changes to the ZPO, but seeks to institute more or less corresponding changes to

- the Patent Act (Patentgesetz – PatG);
- the Industrial Designs Act (Gebrauchsmustergesetz – GebrMG);
- the Trademark Act (Markengesetz – MarkenG);
- the Copyright Act (Urheberrechtsgesetz – UrhG);
- the Designs Act (Geschmackmustergesetz – GeschmMG);
- the Plant Variety Protection Act (Sortenschutzgesetz – SortschG);
- the Topographies of Semiconductor Products Act (Halbleiterschutzgesetz – HalblSchG).

C   THE DUTY OF CONSISTENT INTERPRETATION

Until the Government Bill is enacted, the German law must be viewed in the light of Directive 2004/48/EC. Following Article 249(3) EC, a directive is binding upon each Member State as to the result to be achieved, but leaves to the national authorities the choice of form and methods. While this excludes a direct effect of directives in principle, the ECJ has consistently ruled that directives are capable of being directly effective if particular criteria have been met:[11]

(a) The time limit given for the implementation of the directive has expired.
(b) The provision must be sufficiently clear and precisely stated.
(c) It must be unconditional or non-dependent.
(d) The provision must confer a specific right for the citizen to base his or her claim on.

However, the Court was equally consistent in pointing out that 'a directive cannot of itself impose obligations on an individual and cannot therefore be relied upon as such against an individual'.[12] It follows that a direct effect is possible only in vertical (party to state) relations as opposed to horizontal (party to party) relations. The matter is less clear for directives with a dual character such as Directive 2004/48/EC, which imposes obligations upon the Member States and benefits private parties by stipulating the introduction of procedural rights, while at same time factually encumbering the opponents of the beneficiaries in IP proceedings.[13]

Clearly, the Directive does not of itself impose obligations on an individual. Nonetheless, it is proposed that the cumbersome effect of the procedural rules on individuals is to be equated with the direct imposition of obligations by a directive.

---

11. *Ratti,* Case No. 148/78, [1979] ECR 1629.
12. *Marshall v. Southhampton,* Case No. 152/84, [1986] ECR 723, para. 48; *Paola Faccini Dori v. Recreb Srl,* Case No. C-91/92, [1994] ECR I-3325, para. 20 et seq.
13. For an overview of the discussion refer to J. Eisenkolb, 'Die Enforcement-Richtlinie und ihre Wirkung' [2007] GRUR, 388 et seq.

It needs to be recalled that the ECJ's case law regarding the direct effect of Community law is primarily based upon the idea of 'venire contra factum proprium', respectively the principle of estoppel, seeking to prevent a Member State from 'taking advantage of its own failure to comply with community law'.[14] Where the directive does not have an adverse effect upon a Member State, but upon another private party, this principle does not come into play. There is also a difference with respect to the principle of legal certainty: Whereas a Member State in breach of its obligation to transpose community law should be aware of the content of an European Union (EU) directive, a private party adversely affected by the provisions of a directive is allowed to live in legal ignorance until the directive is implemented into national law.

Quite apart from these principal considerations, it has been convincingly argued that the most prominent articles of the Directive lack the characteristics of sufficient precision, requiring the exercise of too much discretion on the part of the German legislator.[15] Despite the fact that Germany failed to implement the Directive within the time period stipulated in Article 20 thereof, the provisions of the Directive consequently do not possess a direct effect upon the parties to an IP dispute.[16]

This being said, the Directive nonetheless already influences IP disputes heard before the German courts. The ECJ is adamant that,

> the Member States' obligation arising from a directive to achieve the result envisaged by the directive and their duty under [Article 10] of the Treaty to take all appropriate measures, whether general or particular, is binding on all the authorities of Member States, including, for matters within their jurisdiction, the courts… [W]hen applying national law, whether adopted before or after the directive, the national court that has to interpret that law must do so, as far as possible, in the light of the wording and the purpose of the directive so as to achieve the result it has in view and thereby comply with the third paragraph of [Article 249] of the Treaty. [17]

With respect to criminal proceedings, the Court further expounded that

> The obligation on the national court to refer to the content of the directive when interpreting the relevant rules of its national law is limited by the general principles of law which form part of Community law and in particular the principles of legal certainty and non-retroactivity.[18]

---

14. *Paola Faccini Dori v. Recreb Srl*, Case No. C-91/92, [1994] ECR I-3325, para. 22 et seq.
15. *Supra*, Ch. 2, I.E.6; J. Eisenkolb, 'Die Enforcement-Richtlinie und ihre Wirkung' [2007] GRUR, 390 et seq.; F. Koch, , Die Enforcement-Richtlinie: Vereinheitlichung der Durchsetzung der Rechte des geistigen Eigentums in der EU [2006] ITRB, 42.
16. J. Eisenkolb, 'Die Enforcement-Richtlinie und ihre Wirkung' [2007] GRUR, 390 et seq.; A. Auer-Reinsdorff, 'Der Besichtigungsanspruch bei Rechtsverletzungen an Computerprogrammen' [2006] ITRB, 85.
17. *Paola Faccini Dori v. Recreb Srl*, Case No. C-91/92, [1994] ECR I-3325, para. 26 with further references.
18. *Kolpinghuis Nijmegen BV*, Case No. 80/86, [1987] ECR, 3969, para. 13.

The consequences of this latter case law for a directive pertaining to civil law or civil procedure are not quite clear. It would seem that the courts of the Member States enjoy rather more freedoms in interpreting provisions of civil procedure according to the respective Member State's legal methodology than with respect to criminal law, where the principle of *nulla poena sine lege* is enshrined both in Article 7(2) of the European Human Rights Convention and Article 49(1) of the Charter of Fundamental Rights of the EU. Consequently, it is proposed that if a Member State's methodology allows for an interpretation in the light of the Directive, that interpretation should be preferred under all circumstances. Accordingly, the German Federal Court of Justice has upon several occasions reversed its previous case law in the light of community law.[19]

In view of Germany's failure to transpose Directive 2004/48/EC in time, it is of particular interest and will be addressed repeatedly in the following, whether an interpretation consistent with the Directive may be achieved with the help of an analogy. Under German doctrine, the application of an analogy requires the following

(a) The factual situation is not covered by a statutory rule.
(b) This legal gap was unintended for by the legislature (i.e., the legislature failed to notice that the situation required statutory regulation).
(c) There are common factual and legal characteristics between this factual situation and another situation covered by statutory rule which justify a transfer of the legal rule from the latter to the former.

In trying to achieve an interpretation of domestic law which is consistent with community law, an analogy based upon the said criteria might oftentimes fail because the German Parliament initially did not intend to provide statutory rules for a specific situation (i.e., because it felt that only the holders of copyright should benefit from a presumption of ownership, whereas the holders of rights related to copyright were not in need of an equivalent protection, see in contrast Article 5 of the Directive). Thus, in theory, the legal requirements for an analogy are not met.

Nonetheless, it would seem that the legislature's failure to implement the provisions of a directive in time decidedly changes matters and justifies the application of an analogy in such instances. Arguably, there exists a presumable intention of bodies of the Member States to comply with their obligation under Article 10 EC to take all measures, whether general or particular, to ensure compliance with the obligations arising out of the Treaty. Thus, once the deadline for the implementation of a directive has transpired, the legal gap that might have initially been intentional has become objectionable and undesired in the the legislature's view. It follows that an analogy is appropriate if the factual situation is not covered by German statutory rule, but should be covered according to the directive that has not yet been transposed.

---

19. I.e., BGH [1998] GRUR, 824 (826) – *Testpreis-Angebot*; BGH, [2006] GRUR, 962 (966) – *Restschadstoffentfernung*.

III   ENFORCEMENT OF IP RIGHTS IN GERMANY *DE LEGE LATA* AND *DE LEGE FERENDA*

A   ENTITLEMENT TO APPLY FOR THE MEASURES, PROCEDURES AND REMEDIES OF THE DIRECTIVE

Article 4 enjoins the Member States to allow specific persons or groups to request application of the measures, procedures and remedies provided by the Directive. As has already been noted[20], Article 4 (a) differs from Article 4 (b) to (d) in that an application right is granted to the holder of IP rights 'in accordance with the provisions of the applicable law', whereas the application rights of other persons authorized to use those rights as well as the application rights of collective rights-management bodies and professional defence bodies are subject to the additional limitation that the applicable law so permits.

The interpretation given to this distinction by the Explanatory Report of the Government Draft is the following: While Article 4 (a) is seen as compulsory, the application rights of the groups named in Article 4 (b) to (d) are regarded as options granted to the Member States.[21] There is some doubt regarding this reading of Article 4 since the wording of the Directive consistently distinguishes between obligatory and discretionary provisions: while the former are characterized by the words 'The Member States shall [...]', the latter are typified by the phrase 'The Member States may [...]' (i.e., Article 7 (5), Article 12, Article 15 sent. 2, Article 16). Article 4 is devised as an obligatory provision. Possibly, this may simply be attributed to the history of the provision, as the Commission's first proposal sought to oblige the Member States to provide *locus standi* for all the persons and organizations named in Article 4.

A different interpretation might be that the wording 'where the applicable law so permits' refers to questions of substance. It needs to be recalled that the content of the Directive is mainly procedural in nature, and that the jurisdiction of one Member State as assigned by the Brussels I Regulation[22] may coincide with the application of the substantive law of a different Member State, as determined by Article 8 of the Rome II Regulation.[23] Article 4 could therefore oblige the Member States to provide legal standing for the persons named therein, if and insofar as the applicable substantive law allows them to seek redress. I.e., if a professional defence body seeks an injunction against an alleged infringer in Member State A,

---

20.   *Supra*, Ch. 3, Art. 4.
21.   Begründung RegE, BT-Drucks. 16/5048, p. 26.
22.   Council Regulation (EC) No 44/2001 of 22 Dec. 2000 on jurisdiction and the recognition and enforcement of judgments in civil and commercial matters, OJ L 12, 16 Jan. 2001, p. 1-23. Cf. also Art. 90 et seq. Council Regulation (EC) No 40/94 of 20 Dec. 1993 on the Community trade mark, OJ L 11, 14.1.1994, p. 1-36; Art. 79 et seq. Council Regulation (EC) No 6/2002 of 12 Dec. 2001 on Community designs, OJ No. L 3, 5 Jan. 2002, pp. 1-24
23.   Regulation (EC) No 864/2007 of the European Parliament and of the Council of 11 Jul. 2007 on the law applicable to non-contractual obligations (Rome II), OJ No. L 199, 31 Jul. 2007, pp. 40-49.

and the applicable substantive law of the Member State B gives the professional body the entitlement to such an injunction, Member State A is obliged to grant the professional body *locus standi*.

Irrespective of the interpretation of Article 4 of the Directive, it is argued that there is no necessity to transpose the said provisions into German law. The general principle of *Prozessführungsbefugnis* in German civil procedure implies that any person who asserts a right of its own before a court possesses legal standing, irrespective of whether the asserted right is based upon German substantive law or the law of a different country.[24]

B   PRESUMPTION OF AUTHOR- OR OWNERSHIP

§ 10 (1) UrhG (German Copyright Act) contains a presumption of authorship, respectively ownership, as required by Article 5 (a) of the Directive.[25] § 69a (4) UrhG extends this presumption to computer programs, since Article 1 (1) Dir 91/250/EC requires Member States to protect computer programs by copyright as literary works under the Berne Convention.[26] Furthermore, the editor of scholarly editions of works previously unprotected by copyright as well as the creators of photos that do not constitute artistic works equally enjoy a corresponding presumption under §§ 70(1) and 72(1) UrhG. In contrast, other holders of rights related to copyright currently do not benefit from such a presumption. The Government Bill sets out to fill this gap and to achieve a faithful transposition of Article 5 of the Directive with the proposed §§ 71(1), 74(3), 85(4), 87(4), 87b(2), 94(4) UrhG, relating to the publishers of works published for the first time after the expiry of copyright, performers, producers of phonograms, broadcasters, producers of databases and producers of films. However, the draft overlooks companies that arrange for the presentation of a performer and who attain a related right of their own under § 81 UrhG.[27]

Until the transposition of Dir 20044/48/EC by the German Parliament, the question arises whether the goal of Article 5 may be attained by means of a consistent interpretation, namely by an analogy to § 10(1) UrhG for the holders

---

24.   Regarding the application of licensees cf. L. Pahlow, 'Anspruchskonkurrenzen bei Verletzung lizenzierter Schutzrechte unter Berücksichtigung der Richtlinie 2004/48/EG' [2007] GRUR, 1001 et seq.

25.   Begründung RegE, BT-Drucks. 16/5048, p. 26; M. Grünberger, 'Die Urhebervermutung und die Inhabervermutung für die Leistungsschutzberechtigten' [2006] GRUR, 900. There is some debate whether the requirement of § 10 UrhG that the work has appeared is in line with the Directive, cf. Grünberger, ibid at 897 (for) and G. Spindler and M-P. Weber, 'Die Umsetzung der Enforcement-Richtlinie nach dem Regierungsentwurf für ein Gesetz zur Verbesserung der Durchsetzung von Rechten des geistigen Eigentums' [2007] ZUM, 258 (against).

26.   Council Directive 91/250/EEC of 14 May 1991 on the legal protection of computer programs, OJ No. L 122, 17 May 1991, pp. 42-46.

27.   M. Grünberger, 'Die Urhebervermutung und die Inhabervermutung für die Leistungsschutzberechtigten' [2006] GRUR, 902.

of the related rights enumerated above. In the year 2002, the Federal Court of Justice in the decision *P-Vermerk* rejected the idea of an analogous application of § 10(1) UrhG to the producers of phonograms[28] (the decision applies *mutatis mutandis* to the producers of films and to broadcasters[29]). It would seem that this case law needs to be reconsidered in the light of Germany's obligation to adhere to community law. The Federal Court of Justice had based its rejection of an analogy upon two arguments: (a) it was doubtful whether an unintentional legal gap existed and (b) it held that the evidentiary position of the author of a literary or artistic work was decidedly more difficult than the evidentiary position of a producer of phonograms, since the author is oftentimes on his/her own during the process of creation whereas the organization and the technical process of recording can usually be documented and supported by witnesses.[30]

In the current situation, with the Directive requiring a presumption of ownership for the holders of related rights and in view of the failure of the German legislature to transpose the Directive within the time limit set by Article 20(1) thereof, these arguments lack persuasion. Article 10 EC obliges the courts of the Member States to take appropriate measures to bring national law into line with community law requirements.[31] Thus, it should be reconsidered whether an analogy is possible in the circumstances. Arguably, once the deadline for transposition of the Directive transpired, the legal gap, which the Federal Court of Justice had declared to be missing in the decision *P-Vermerk* was retroactively created. In a similar vain, the argument that an analogy is inadequate due to the favourable evidentiary position of the holders of related rights is no longer persuasive: As Article 5(2) bestows on the holders of related rights the same presumption as on the authors of literary and artistic works, community law obviously considers them to be equally worthy of protection.[32]

---

28. BGH [2003] GRUR, 228 – *P-Vermerk*; concurring LG Mannheim, [2007] MMR, 335. See also M. Grünberger, 'Die Urhebervermutung und die Inhabervermutung für die Leistungsschutzberechtigten' [2006] GRUR, 902, who remarks that the decision *P-Vermerk* remains relevant with respect to the finding that a 'P'-mark does not constitute a sufficient appearance on the work 'in the usual manner', opposing view held by G. Spindler and M-P. Weber, 'Die Umsetzung der Enforcement-Richtlinie nach dem Regierungsentwurf für ein Gesetz zur Verbesserung der Durchsetzung von Rechten des geistigen Eigentums' [2007] ZUM, 257.
29. D. Thum in A-A. Wandtke and W. Bullinger (eds), *Urheberrecht* (2nd edn, München, C.H. Beck, 2006), § 10 n. 49.
30. BGH [2003]GRUR, 228 (230 et seq.).
31. *v Colson und Kamann v. Land Nordrhein-Westphalen*, Case No. 14/83 [1984] ECR 1891; *Inter-Environnement Wallonie v. Région wallonne*, Case No. C-129/96 [1998] ECR I-7411.
32. Opposing view held by M. Grünberger, 'Die Urhebervermutung und die Inhabervermutung für die Leistungsschutzberechtigten' [2006] GRUR, 903, who argues that an analogy is solely adequate for performers, not for other holders of related rights. However, his main argument that § 10(1) UrhG has a strong association to the author's right of personality fails to consider that the purpose of the provision is of an evidentiary nature only.

C   EVIDENCE

1   The Obligations Imposed by Article 6 of the Directive

Member States are enjoined by Article 6 of the Directive to provide for rules
which allow the competent courts upon application of one party to order the production of evidence which lies within the control of the opposing party. The
implementation of this provision into German law constitutes a particular challenge for three reasons. First, German civil procedural law is historically adverse
to any type of disclosure and orders for the production of evidence. The procedural
principle of party presentation (*Beibringungsgrundsatz*), which implies that a
court may base its decision solely on information which has been introduced into
the proceedings by the parties, is often interpreted to contain the maxim that no
one is held to contribute to the production of evidence against his or her own
cause.[33] Thus, access to evidence in the sphere of the opposing party may only be
achieved by means of substantive provisions. Second, while Article 6 seems to
prescribe a procedural measure, German law traditionally allows for the production
of evidence in the sphere of the opposing party by virtue of substantive provisions.
Third, due to the historical lack of procedural provisions for disclosure, there are
no specific rules allowing for the protection of confidential information. In the
following, the German procedural principle 'Verbot des Ausforschungsbeweises'
is explained, followed by an examination of avenues contained in the current
German procedural and substantive law to order a party to present evidence. In a
final step, the measures stipulated by the Government Bill will be illustrated.

*a   The Prohibition of 'Exploratory Evidence' in German Civil
            Procedure*

Disclosure or access to evidence in the sphere of the opposing party may contravene a principle of German civil procedural law termed the 'Verbot des
Ausforschungsbeweises', i.e., the prohibition of exploratory evidence.[34] The
underlying idea is that, following the procedural principle of party presentation
(*Beibringungsgrundsatz*), each party has to plead and prove the facts which it is
relying on for its legal submissions. The term exploratory evidence is used to
describe a motion for the taking of evidence where there is no intention of proving
facts already pleaded by the respective party, but rather an unfocused attempt to

---

33. BGH [1990] NJW, 3151; A. Baumbach, W. Lauterbach, J. Albers, P. Hartmann,
     Zivilprozessordnung (66th edn, C.H. Beck, München, 2008), § 284 ZPO n. 29; critical
     A. Stadler, who argues this sentence should be put on mothballs in *Kommentar zur
     Zivilprozessordnung mit Gerichtsverfassungsgesetz*, H-J. Musielak (ed.) (5th edn, München,
     Franz Vahlen, 2007), § 142 ZPO n. 4.
34. BGH, [1998] NJW, 2100 (2101); BGH [1996] NJW, 3150.

spy out new facts or reveal as of yet unknown sources of information which would in turn enable the party to plead new facts.[35]

The concept of exploratory evidence seems much stricter than what might be deemed a 'fishing expedition' in Common Law terminology. At the same time, a clear-cut definition of the concept does not exist. The Federal Court of Justice tends to apply relatively lenient standards if the party bearing the onus of submission and proof is legitimately in the dark regarding factual matters resting within the sphere of the opposing party.[36] In such an instance, that party might submit assumptions and offer corresponding proof if there is ample ground for the correctness of the submissions and the party is not acting at random.[37] This would seem to correspond to the requirements of Article 6 that the applicant present reasonably available evidence sufficient to support its claims and in substantiating those claims specify evidence in the control of the opposing party. Thus, the prohibition of exploratory evidence does not per se constitute an insurmountable obstacle to the transposition of Article 6 of the Directive into German law.

b   *Substantive Rights to the Production of Evidence*

As has already been noted, disclosure of evidence under German law is traditionally achieved by virtue of substantive provisions. Following §§ 422, 371(2) of the Code of Civil Procedure (ZPO)

> The opponent is obliged to present the document [or item] if the demonstrator may require delivery or presentation of the document [or item] according to the provisions of civil law.

A substantive right to the presentation of documents and items may result from §§ 809, 810 of the German Civil Code (BGB).[38]

> § 809 BGB: Inspection of an item
> Any person who possesses a claim in respect of an item against its possessor or wishes to obtain certainty as to whether he has such a claim may, if inspection of the item is of interest to him for this reason, demand that the possessor present the item to him for inspection or permit inspection.
> § 810 BGB: Right to inspect documents

---

35. *Greger*, Zivilprozessordnung, Zöller (ed) (25th edn, Otto Schmidt, Köln, 2005), vor § 284 para. 5 et seq. with further references.

36. Cf. the case law cited by U. Foerste in *Kommentar zur Zivilprozessordnung*, H.-J. Musielak (ed.) (4th edn, Franz Vahlen, München, 2007), § 284 ZPO n. 17 and L. Rosenberg, K. H. Schwab and P. Gottwald, *Zivilprozessrecht* (16th ed, C.H. Beck, München 2004), § 115 para. 15 et seq.

37. BGH [2001] NJW, 2327 (2328); BGH [1996] NJW, 3147 (3150); BGH [1987] NJW-RR, 335.

38. The following translation is courtesy of the Langenscheid Translation Service (with some modifications by the author) and is available at <http://www.gesetze-im-internet.de/englisch_bgb/index.html>.

Any person who has a legal interest in inspecting a document in the possession of another person may demand from its possessor permission to inspect it if the document was drawn up in his interest or if the document serves to record a legal relationship existing between himself and another or if the document contains negotiations on a legal transaction that were engaged in between him and another person or between one of the two of them and a joint intermediary.

§ 811 BGB: Place of presentation, risk and costs

(1) Presentation must, in the cases of sections 809 and 810, be made at the place where the item to be presented is located. Each party may demand to have it presented at another place if there is a compelling reason for doing so.

(2) Risk and costs must be borne by the person demanding presentation. The possessor may refuse presentation until the other party advances the costs and provides security for the risk.

§ 810 BGB relates to documents and provides that a right to the presentation of documents exists in cases where the document was (a) created in the interest of the party seeking its disclosure, (b) professes a legal relationship between this party and another party or (c) contains negotiations regarding such a legal relationship. Consequently, § 810 BGB is of little help in IP infringement litigation.

§ 809 BGB is rather more interesting. On its face, the provision seems of promising value to any holder of an IP right who wishes to ascertain whether another person is infringing his or her rights. However, § 809 has been rendered virtually useless for IP disputes by a 1985 decision of the German Federal Court of Justice (BGH) and only as recently as 2002 has the rule slowly begun to change its part from sleeping beauty to effective measure.

In the 1985 decision *Druckbalken*,[39] the BGH reasoned that § 809 BGB could not be used to circumvent the procedural prohibition of exploratory evidence. In particular with respect to supposed patent infringements, the court warned of the risk that § 809 BGB might be used as an instrument to spy out the trade secrets of competitors in the industry. According to the decision, a right to inspect an allegedly patent-infringing item solely existed if there was a 'substantial degree of probability' that the patent was being breached. To make matters worse for IP rights holders, the court also interpreted the term 'inspection of the item' as embracing solely the viewing of that item and ruled that any interferences with the substance, i.e., the installation or removal of specific parts or the putting to operation of a machine were not covered by § 809 BGB.

The decision *Druckbalken* was widely criticized by academics,[40] but it was not until the year 2002 when a different senate of the BGH in its decision *Faxkarte* distinguished copyright from patents, pointed to the need to interpret § 809 BGB in the light of the Agreement on Trade-Related Aspects of Intellectual Property

---

39.   BGH [1985] GRUR, 512 et seq. – *Druckbalken*,.
40.   For references see BGH [2002] NJW-RR, 1617 (1620) – *Faxkarte*.

Rights (TRIPs), and established different criteria for the inspection of items alleg-edly infringing copyright.[41] Finally, in the decision *Restschadstoffentfernung*, which was handed down in the year 2006, the Xth senate (which possesses the competence for patent claims) agreed that § 809 BGB had to be interpreted in the light of TRIPs as well as Article 6 of Directive 2004/48/EC with respect to all Intellectual Property, including patents.[42]

Due to the fact that these developments are of a relatively recent nature, there is little case law to guide us regarding the prerequisites of a substantive right to the presentation of documents under § 809 BGB.[43] There is clarity regarding two points: First of all, the right to inspection under § 809 BGB might encompass interferences with the substance of the inspected item,[44] which constitutes a departure from the 1985 decision *Druckbalken*. It is furthermore clear that the right of inspection will be granted on the basis of a balance of the conflicting interests of the parties involved. On the one hand, the rights holder is to be pro-vided with an instrument to prove the infringement in cases in which proof might otherwise be very difficult to bring forward; on the other hand, the inspection cannot be granted in each and every case in which a rights holder alleges that his or her rights are being infringed, since there is a considerable risk that the claim might be used to – voluntarily or involuntarily – obtain superior knowledge about competitors and their products.[45] There is a variety of criteria to be considered when trying to achieve this balance of interest, such as the probability of an IP infringement, the protection of the opponent's confidential information, both the intensity of the infringement and the intensity of the disturbance of the opponent's rights and the possibility of proving the infringement by other reasonable and proportional means.[46]

It would seem that these criteria to a wide extent mirror the benchmark of Article 6 of the Directive, namely that the applicant has presented reasonably available evidence and that the confidential information of the opponent be pro-tected. In the indefinite number of cases in which the applicant has presented reasonable evidence *and* the secrecy interests of the opponent are affected, the courts of the Member States will have to balance the interests of the parties. The criteria set forth by the BGH in the decision *Faxkarte* and *Restschadstoffentfernung* aim at such a balance of interest, while taking into account the principle of pro-portionality as laid down in Article 3(2) of the Directive. However, it needs to be emphasized that § 809 BGB only allows for an inspection of goods known to be in the possession of the opposing party. The rule does not allow for an inspection

---

41. BGH, [2002] NJW-RR, 1617 (1619) – *Faxkarte*.
42. BGH [2006] GRUR, 962 (966) – *Restschadstoffentfernung*.
43. For an overview of the case law up to the year 2005 cf. T. Kühnen, 'Die Besichtigung im Patentrecht', [2005] GRUR, 185-196.
44. BGH [2002] NJW-RR, 1617 (1620) – *Faxkarte*.
45. BGH [2002] NJW-RR, 1617 (1620) – *Faxkarte*.
46. BGH [2002] NJW-RR, 1617 (1620) – *Faxkarte*; BGH, GRUR 2006, 962 (966 et seq.) – *Restschadstoffentfernung*.

of the other party's premises in order to 'spy out' whether particular items are in his or her possession.[47]

The fact that § 811(2) BGB requires the applicant to bear the cost of the inspection and to provide security for the risk involved seems unproblematic. Article 3(1) of the Directive stipulates that the measures provided for by the Member States shall not be unnecessarily costly, implying that the measures do not need to be provided to rights holders at no cost.[48] Consequently, it is proposed that § 809 in its current interpretation by the German courts sufficiently implements Article 6 of the Directive with respect to the inspection of items.

As has been noted above, however, the sister provision relating to documents, § 810 BGB will be of little help to rights holders. Insofar as Article 6 requires the Member States to enable the competent judicial authorities to order that documents be presented by the opposing party (be it general documents under paragraph 1 or banking, financial or commercial documents under paragraph 2), the substantive law is insufficient to meet the obligations imposed on Germany under Article 20 of the Directive.

c   *Presentation of Evidence Following §§ 142, 144 Code of Civil Procedure (ZPO)*

Both § 142 and § 144 of the Code of Civil Procedure (ZPO) contain modifications of the principle of party presentation insofar as they allow the court to take evidence upon its own initiative without a corresponding request made by one of the parties. The scope of these provisions was substantially enlarged in the course of the comprehensive ZPO-reform implemented on 1 January 2002. Whereas under the former provisions a court was only able to order a party to present documents in its possession if the party itself had referred to them, it is now possible to order a party to produce material that the opponent is relying upon. However, a 2004 report evaluating the ZPO-reform has shown that while judges tend to hold a favourable view of their amplified powers under §§ 142, 144 ZPO, they are more than reluctant to exercise their discretion and issue orders under these provisions.[49] Possibly, the appeal of the said rules will grow over time.

§ 142 ZPO[50]

(1) The court may order a party or a third person to present certificates or other documents in their possession, in case one of the parties has referred to them. The court may set a time limit for the production and

---

47. BGH [2004] GRUR, 420 (421) – *Kontrollbesuch*.
48. Should the inspection show that the opponent did infringe the applicant's intellectual property, the cost for the inspection will form part of the prejudice suffered by the injured party as a result of the infringement, Art. 13(1) of the Directive.
49. C. Hommerich, H. Prütting et. al., *Rechtstatsächliche Untersuchung zu den Auswirkungen der Reform des Zivilprozessrechts auf die gerichtliche Praxis – Evaluation ZPO-Reform*, <http://www.bmj.bund.de/media/archive/1216.pdf>, p. 4.
50. All translations, unless otherwise indicated, are by the author.

may order the documents to remain in the court office for a stipulated period of time.

(2) Third parties are not obliged to present documents if such production cannot reasonably be expected of them or in case they are entitled to refuse testimony under §§ 383 to 385. §§ 386 to 390 apply accordingly.

§ 144 ZPO

(1) The court may order the taking of evidence by inspection or the examination by an expert. For this purpose, it may order a party or a third person to produce a specific item and set a corresponding time limit. The court may also order a party to tolerate a measure taken under sentence 1, unless a residence is involved.

(2) Third parties are not obliged to present an item or tolerate said measures if this cannot reasonably be expected of them or in case they are entitled to refuse testimony under §§ 383 to 385. §§ 386 to 390 apply accordingly.

Apart from the courts' reluctance to make use of their powers under §§ 142, 144 ZPO, it is questionable whether these provisions are sufficient to implement Article 6 of the Directive into German law: Firstly, the wording of §§ 142, 144 ZPO leaves it to the discretion of the individual court whether to make an order for the presentation of evidence; secondly, the sanctions in case of non-compliance with the order are rather weak, and finally, courts will rarely be able to order the presentation of banking, financial and commercial documents under § 142 ZPO.

i   Discretion of the Courts

Article 6 of the Directive requires that the courts of the Member States be empowered to order a party to present evidence in its control upon the application of the opposing party, provided that the applicant has presented reasonably available evidence sufficient to support its claims and has specified evidence which lies in the control of the opposing party, subject to the protection of confidential information. It has been argued that §§ 142, 144 ZPO are inadequate to transpose Article 6 of the Directive as they provide the court with discretion whether to make or abstain from an order.[51] However, it would seem that the wording of Article 6 allows for provisions granting discretion to the courts of the Member States ('the competent judicial authorities may order'), in particular since the criteria for the making of such an order, namely the presentation of reasonably available evidence and the protection of confidential information are quite indeterminate, leaving to the courts a wide room for interpretation.

§§ 142, 144 ZPO are broader than Article 6 of the Directive in various aspects: The court may order the presentation of evidence following its own discretion, without party application, under sole the qualification that, in the case of documents, one of the parties has referred to the evidence. Furthermore, the order

---

51. Begründung RegE, BT-Drucks. 16/5048, p. 26.

may not only be directed against the opponent, but also against third parties. In the light of Article 2(1) of the Directive, which allows for more stringent national legislation, the fact that §§ 142, 144 ZPO name fewer prerequisites for an order than Article 6 is of no importance. It would seem that the additional requirements of Article 6, namely that the applicant has presented reasonably available evidence and the protection of confidential information, are safeguards for the proportionality of the measures as required by Article 3(2). The German rules are flexible enough to accommodate the obligation of proportionality, in particular since the German constitution (the Basic Law) compels the German courts to consider the principle of proportionality in any legal dispute.[52] In exercising its discretion, the court may take various factors into account, i.e., the intensity of the infringement, whether other means of proof are reasonably available and the protection of legitimate interests of the opposing party.

ii   Sanctions for Non-compliance

The Achilles' heel of §§ 142, 144 ZPO are the weak sanctions available in case the opposing party refuses the production of a document or an inspection by the court or an expert. The only disadvantage for the non-compliant party is that the court may take the refusal to produce the evidence into account when it forms its opinion as to whether the facts submitted by the parties are true (§§ 286, 371(3), § 422 ZPO analogical).[53] The ZPO does not provide an avenue of enforcing the court's order. Seeing that Article 3(2) of the Directive requires that the measures provided for the enforcement of IP rights are effective and dissuasive, such a procedural effect is certainly insufficient.[54]

iii   Communication of Banking, Financial or Commercial
              Documents

Finally, rights holders will find it difficult to base a request for the communication of banking, financial or commercial documents on § 142 ZPO, as the provision requires that one of the parties has referred to the documents. There is little case law to clarify what the verb 'referred to' signifies in this context, but certainly the sole allegation that such documents usually exist is insufficient[55] and the courts are held to prevent a spying in the opponent's sphere.[56] For this reason, German courts are likely to be hesitant in ordering the communication of such information on the basis of § 142 ZPO.

---

52. BVerfG (German Constitutional Court), MMR 2006, 375 (377).
53. *Greger*, Zivilprozessordnung, Zöller (ed) (25th edn, Otto Schmidt, Köln, 2005), vor § 142 para. 4; L. Rosenberg, K. H. Schwab and P. Gottwald, *Zivilprozessrecht* (16th ed, C.H. Beck, München 2004), § 118 para. 45; Baumbach A., W. Lauterbach, J. Albers, P. Hartmann, Zivilprozessordnung (C.H. Beck, 64th edn, München, 2006), § 142 ZPO n. 27.
54. Begründung RegE, BT-Drucks. 16/5048, p. 26.
55. A. Stadler in *Kommentar zur Zivilprozessordnung*, H.-J. Musielak (ed.) (4th edn, Franz Vahlen, München, 2007), §§ 142 ZPO n. 4.
56. T. Lüpke and R. Müller, ' "Pre-Trial Discover of Documents" und § 142 ZPO – ein trojanisches Pferd im neuen Zivilprozessrecht? ' [2002] NZI, 589.

d   *The Protection of Confidential Information*

Irrespective of whether the presentation of documents and/or the inspection of goods is based upon procedural or substantive rules, the courts are bound to balance the interests of the parties and to provide for the protection of sensitive data of the alleged infringer. The options for the protection of confidential information developed by the German courts or suggested by academics include the so-called 'Wirtschaftsprüfervorbehalt' and 'in camera' proceedings.

Insofar as the documents to be presented or items to be inspected pertain to sensitive data, the courts have developed the so-called 'Wirtschaftsprüfervorbehalt'. Originally developed with respect to substantive rights of information, the presentation or inspection is made subject to the proviso that the documents be handed over to a neutral certified accountant named by the plaintiff and paid for by the defendant. The Federal Court of Justice has only recently accepted that this reservation may also be made when the presentation or inspection is based upon the procedural measures of §§ 142, 144 ZPO.[57] However, engaging a certified accountant is only an option if the questions to be answered are of a simple nature (i.e., whether a specific undertaking appears in a list of clients). More complicated matters, such as the calculation of damages on the basis of the profit reaped by the infringer, include a legal assessment which is part of the role of the court and of the court only.[58] The same is true when experts are commissioned in IP disputes, i.e., to aid the court in making its legal assessment on whether a particular machinery makes use of the claimant's patent. Thus, the presentation to or inspection by a neutral third party sworn to secrecy will only rarely suffice to protect the alleged infringer's interest.

The obvious alternative are 'in camera' proceedings, which have little tradition in German law[59] and are not provided for in the Code of Civil Procedure. § 172 n. 2 GVG allows for the exclusion of the public from the hearing or a part thereof if an important business, trade or tax secret or a secret pertaining to an invention is being discussed. However, § 357(1) ZPO stipulates that the parties to a dispute are entitled to witness the taking of evidence, an important element of the right to be heard under Article 103(1) GG (the German Basic Law) and ultimately the right to a fair trial. Nonetheless, a party seeking to establish an infringement of IP rights will oftentimes voluntarily agree to a restriction of its right under § 357(1) ZPO, as it has nothing to lose: whilst its ability to challenge material presented to the court will be restricted, at least the material will be accessible to the court in the

---

57. BGH [2006] GRUR, 962 (967) – *Restschadstoffentfernung*.
58. BVerfG [2006] MMR, 375 (378); BGH [2006] GRUR, 962 (967) – *Restschadstoffentfernung*.
59. Cf. BVerfG [2006] MMR, 375 et seq., in which the Constitutional Court indicated for the first time that in camera proceedings may be compatible with Art. 103(1) of the Basic Law.

first place.[60] The choice between the right to a fair hearing and the effectiveness of justice would seem to be a simple one to make.[61]

Yet another matter is the revelation of such material to the claimant's attorney, since attorneys are obliged to inform their clients immediately under § 11 of the Federal Attorneys' Professional Code of Conduct (*Berufsordnung der Rechtsanwälte in der Bundesrepublik Deutschland – BRAO*) and the German law does not contain provisions debarring attorneys from disclosing information to their clients.[62] Again, however, it would be for the claimant to decide whether to agree to the attorney being sworn to secrecy or to forego the benefits of access to material in the opponent's sphere.[63] Finally, as the court (or the court in subsequent infringement proceedings) reviews the materials presented or inspected, it should have the option of lifting restrictions on the access to such material if it turns out that the information revealed is not particularly confidential, or if the balance of interest tips towards the claimant.[64]

e   *Summary of the Status Quo Regarding Access to Evidence*

De lege lata, the German rules requiring the alleged infringer to produce evidence at the request of the rights owner inadequately transpose Directive 2004/48/EC. Such an application may be based on procedural rules (§§ 142, 144 ZPO) which make the presentation of documents or items subject to the court's discretion, are little-used and provide weak sanctions in cases of non-compliance. Further, they are not suitable to procure bank, financial and/or commercial documents. As an alternative, since the Federal Court of Justice has effectively reversed the decision *Druckbalken*, § 809 BGB provides a substantive right to the presentation and inspection of an item in IP cases. In contrast, there is no substantive right to the

---

60.   J. Bornkamm, 'Der Schutz vertraulicher Informationen im Gesetz zur Durchsetzung von Rechten des geistigen Eigentums – In-camera-Verfahren im Zivilprozess?' in *Festschrift für Eike Ullmann*, H-J. Ahrens, J. Bornkamm and H-P. Kunz-Hallstein (eds) (Saarbrücken, juris, 2006), p. 903 et seq.

61.   P. Schlosser, 'Wirtschaftsprüfervorbehalt und prozessuales Vertraulichkeitsinteresse der nicht primär beweisbelasteten Prozeßpartei' in *Festschrift für Bernhard Großfeld*, U. Hübner and W. Ebke (eds) (Recht und Wirtschaft, Heidelberg, 1999), p. 1005 et seq.; L. Rosenberg, K. H. Schwab and P. Gottwald, *Zivilprozessrecht* (16th ed, C.H. Beck, München 2004), § 115 para. 45; G. Spindler and M-P Weber, 'Der Geheimnisschutz nach Art. 7 der Enforcement-Richtlinie' [2006] MMR 713 with a discussion of the constitutional relevance.

62.   P. Schlosser, 'Wirtschaftsprüfervorbehalt und prozessuales Vertraulichkeitsinteresse der nicht primär beweisbelasteten Prozeßpartei' in *Festschrift für Bernhard Großfeld*, U. Hübner and W. Ebke (eds) (Recht und Wirtschaft, Heidelberg, 1999), p. 1010.

63.   T. Kühnen, 'Die Besichtigung im Patentrecht' [2005] GRUR, 191; J. Bornkamm, 'Der Schutz vertraulicher Informationen im Gesetz zur Durchsetzung von Rechten des geistigen Eigentums – In-camera-Verfahren im Zivilprozess?' in *Festschrift für Eike Ullmann*, H-J. Ahrens, J. Bornkamm and H-P. Kunz-Hallstein (eds) (Saarbrücken, juris, 2006), p. 911.

64.   J. Bornkamm, 'Der Schutz vertraulicher Informationen im Gesetz zur Durchsetzung von Rechten des geistigen Eigentums – In-camera-Verfahren im Zivilprozess?' in *Festschrift für Eike Ullmann*, H-J. Ahrens, J. Bornkamm and H-P. Kunz-Hallstein (eds) (Saarbrücken, juris, 2006), p. 910 et seq.

presentation or inspection of documents which would be of help in IP infringement proceedings. Finally, there are no universally accepted instruments and standards allowing for the protection of confidential information in case of an order to procure such documents or items. Consequently, there is a clear need for a comprehensive implementation of Article 6 of the Directive.

f   *The Presentation of Evidence Following the Government Bill*

In view of the shortcomings of §§ 142, 144 ZPO and in the light of the currently changing, but not yet settled case law regarding § 809 BGB, the Government Bill proposes to introduce new provisions explicitly implementing Article 6 of the Directive. Even though the Explanatory Report acknowledges that Article 6 is of a procedural nature, the solution is seen in providing additional substantive rights of presentation and inspection. The report maintains that this transposition is more agreeable with the German system of evidence in place and does not necessitate the introduction of completely new procedural instruments.[65] § 140c PatG, § 24c GebrMG, §§ 19a, 128, 135 MarkenG, § 46a GeschmMG, § 101a UrhG, § 37c Sortenschutzgesetz, § 9(2) HalblSchG as proposed by the Government Bill read:

Right of Presentation and Inspection

(1) In cases of sufficient probability that a person [infringes an intellectual property right], the [rights owner] may require that person to present a document or to allow for the inspection of an item within that person's control, if such action is necessary to prove [the rights owner's] claims. If the circumstances show sufficient probability that the infringement was committed on a commercial scale, the right to the presentation of documents is extended to the communication of banking, financial or commercial documents. Should the alleged infringer submit that the information is of a confidential nature, the court provides for the appropriate measures of protection required in the particular instance.

(2) The right under subsection 1 is excluded if the presentation or inspection is disproportionate in the particular instance.

(3) The court may issue a provisional measure under §§ 935 to 945 of the Code of Civil Procedure (ZPO) in which the defendant is ordered to present documents or to allow for the inspection of an item. The court provides for appropriate measures to ensure the protection of confidential information, in particular if the provisional measure is ordered without a hearing of the defendant.

(4) § 811 of the Civil Code (BGB) as well as [§ 140b(8) PatG] find corresponding application.

(5) The applicant is required to compensate the alleged infringer for losses sustained if it is subsequently shown that an infringement or an impending infringement did not exist.

---

65. Begründung RegE, BT-Drucks. 16/5048, p. 27.

It is true that Article 249(3) EC declares that Directives are binding only regarding the result to be achieved, whereas the choice of form and methods is left to the Member States. Nonetheless, Article 6 of the Directive is a procedural instrument and it seems more appropriate to transpose it as such.[66] The fact that the Government Bill creates substantive rights irrespective of whether infringement proceedings have already been instituted creates a number of problems:

First, the presentation of reasonably available evidence (which is the main requirement under Article 6 of the Directive) is not a suitable criterion unless infringement proceedings have commenced. Instead, the proposed German provisions require that there is a sufficient likelihood of an infringement,[67] and the Explanatory Report advises that the principles set forth by the Federal Court of Justice in the decision *Faxkarte* (with respect to § 809 BGB) shall act as a guidance in the interpretation of the new right of presentation and inspection.[68]

Second, in the infringement proceedings envisaged by Article 6 of the Directive, the court will as a matter of course solely order the production of such evidence which is necessary to determine the validity of the claim. In contrast, the proposed right of presentation and inspection might be used as an instrument to spy out information without the true intention of raising an infringement claim.[69] Thus, the right is made subject to the requirement that the presentation or inspection is necessary to substantiate an infringement claim (which is possibly raised in another action). The procedural solution of Article 6 is rather more elegant and expedient because the court in the infringement proceedings will be in the best position to decide whether a presentation or an inspection is crucial.[70]

Third, the right of presentation and inspection is explicitly made subject to the principle of proportionality, whereas Article 6 simply provides for the discretion of the competent court.

Finally, the inspection of goods and the presentation of documents as envisaged by the proposed provisions may be narrower than the term 'evidence' as used in the Directive. This is a particular concern regarding the preservation of evidence with respect to processing patents.[71]

---

66. M-R. McGuire, 'Beweismittelvorlage und Auskunftsanspruch nach der Richtlinie 2004/48/EG zur Durchsetzung der Rechte des Geistigen Eigentums' [2005], 21, argues that Member States are bound to transpose Art. 6 as a procedural instrument.
67. The criterion of 'hinreichende Wahrscheinlichkeit' is criticized by Deutsche Vereinigung für gewerblichen Rechtsschutz und Urheberrecht (GRUR), 'Gemeinsame Stellungnahme der Ausschüsse für Patent- und Gebrauchsmusterrecht, Geschmacksmusterrecht und Urheberrecht zum Referentenentwurf für ein, Gesetz zur Verbesserung der Durchsetzung von Rechten des geistigen Eigentums' [2006] GRUR 394 at 4.2.
68. Begründung RegE, BT-Drucks. 16/5048, p. 40.
69. Begründung RegE, BT-Drucks. 16/5048, p. 40.
70. M-R. McGuire, 'Die richtlinienkonforme Auslegung des § 142 ZPO: Anmerkung zu BGH 1.8.2006 – X ZR 114/03 – Restschadstoffverwertung' [2007] GPR 36 et seq.
71. Deutsche Vereinigung für gewerblichen Rechtsschutz und Urheberrecht (GRUR), 'Gemeinsame Stellungnahme der Ausschüsse für Patent- und Gebrauchsmusterrecht, Geschmacksmusterrecht und Urheberrecht zum Referentenentwurf für ein, Gesetz zur Verbesserung der Durchsetzung von Rechten des geistigen Eigentums' [2006] GRUR 394 at 4.3; G. Spindler and M-P. Weber,

In conclusion, the path chosen by the Government Bill seems unnecessarily intricate, and it is unclear whether the criteria selected for the new § 140c PatG, § 24c GebrMG, §§ 19a, 128, 135 MarkenG, § 46a GeschmMG, § 101a UrhG, § 37c Sortenschutzgesetz and § 9(2) HalblSchG truly mirror the requirements of Article 6 in all instances.[72] The Explanatory Report correctly argues that the German system currently does not entail the enforcement of procedural measures against one of the parties. However, as §§ 142(2), 144(2), 390 ZPO show, enforcing procedural measures is not completely foreign to the German system of civil procedure and further development in this direction would be the preferable path for the implementation of Article 6.[73]

A further point of critique[74] concerns the fact that the Bill leaves the particulars of the protection of sensitive information to the courts without proposing a solution to the problems identified above (III.C.1.d). The Explanatory Report solely refers to the option of disclosing information to a third party under the pledge of secrecy as well as §§ 172, 174(3) GVG and § 353d no. 2 StGB.[75]

2   Measures for the Preservation of Evidence

a   Preservation of Evidence de lege lata

Article 7 of the Directive complements Article 6 by providing for measures for the preservation of evidence even before the commencement of proceedings on the

---

'Die Umsetzung der Enforcement-Richtlinie nach dem Regierungsentwurf für ein Gesetz zur Verbesserung der Durchsetzung von Rechten des geistigen Eigentums' [2007] ZUM, 264.

72. M-R. McGuire, 'Die richtlinienkonforme Auslegung des § 142 ZPO: Anmerkung zu BGH 1.8.2006 – X ZR 114/03 – Restschadstoffverwertung' [2007] GPR 37; W. Tilmann, 'Beweissicherung nach Art. 7 der Richtlinie zur Durchsetzung der Rechte des geistigen Eigentums' [2005] GRUR, 739, i.e., argues that 'reasonably available evidence' corresponds to a 'sufficient suspicion' rather than a 'sufficient probability'.

73. M-R. McGuire, 'Beweismittelvorlage und Auskunftsanspruch nach der Richtlinie 2004/48/EG zur Durchsetzung der Rechte des Geistigen Eigentums' [2005] GRUR, 17; of a different opinion W. Tilmann, 'Beweissicherung nach Art. 7 der Richtlinie zur Durchsetzung der Rechte des geistigen Eigentums' [2005] GRUR, 738.

74. Very explicit A. Peukert and A. Kur, 'Stellungnahme des Max-Planck-Instituts für Geistiges Eigentum, Wettbewerbs- und Steuerrecht zur Umsetzung der Richtlinie 2004/48/EG zur Durchsetzung der Rechte des geistigen Eigentums in deutsches Recht' [2006] GRUR Int, 302; see further J. Bornkamm, 'Der Schutz vertraulicher Informationen im Gesetz zur Durchsetzung von Rechten des geistigen Eigentums – In-camera-Verfahren im Zivilprozess?' in *Festschrift für Eike Ullmann*, H-J. Ahrens, J. Bornkamm and H-P. Kunz-Hallstein (eds) (Saarbrücken, juris, 2006), p. 912; G. Spindler and M-P. Weber, 'Die Umsetzung der Enforcement-Richtlinie nach dem Regierungsentwurf für ein Gesetz zur Verbesserung der Durchsetzung von Rechten des geistigen Eigentums' [2007] ZUM, 263; C. Frank and N. Wiegand, 'Der Besichtigungsanspruch im Urheberrecht de lege ferenda', [2007] CR, 486 et seq.; G. Spindler and M-P. Weber, 'Der Geheimnisschutz nach Art. 7 der Enforcement-Richtlinie' [2006] MMR 713.

75. Criminal sanctions for a breach of the secrecy obligation; cf. Begründung RegE, BT-Drucks. 16/5048, p. 41.

merits of the case, including a detailed description and the physical seizure of infringing goods, materials and implements used in the production and distribution of such goods and documents relating thereto.

The admissibility of the German 'Selbständiges Beweisverfahren' (independent proceedings for the taking of evidence) is governed by § 485 et seq. ZPO.

§ 485 ZPO

(1) During or before the commencement of proceedings on the merits of the case, the court may, on application by a party, order the taking of evidence by inspection, the hearing of witnesses or the examination by an expert if the opponent consents or if there is a risk of the means of evidence being destroyed or its use being impeded.

(2) Before the commencement of proceedings on the merits of the case, a party may apply for a written report of an expert examination if the party demonstrates a legal interest in the determination of
1. the condition of a person or the condition or value of an item
2. the cause of the damage to a person or to an item or the non-conformity of an item
3. the expenditure for the elimination of the damage to a person or an item or the non-conformity of an item.

A legal interest exists if the determination is suitable to prevent a legal dispute.

The provisions on independent evidence proceedings (§§ 485 et seq. ZPO) are of themselves insufficient to transpose Article 7 of the Directive, since they do not address access to the means of evidence or the taking of samples or the physical seizure of the infringing goods. §§ 142, 144 ZPO (which have been described above, III.C.1.c.) are only available in proceedings on the merits of the case. As noted above (III.C.1.b), access to material in the sphere of an alleged infringer of IP rights on the basis of § 809 BGB has only recently been granted by the German Federal Court of Justice. Thus, there is no established case law regarding the matters covered by Article 7 of the Directive. However, the practice of the Landgericht Düsseldorf ('Düsseldorf Practice') has obtained some publicity, and is mostly considered an expedient development,[76] even if its legitimacy under the current procedural rules is sometimes questioned.[77]

The 'Düsseldorf Practice' consists in a combination of an independent evidence proceeding and an interlocutory injunction ordering the opposing party to allow for the inspection.[78]

---

76. W. Tilmann, 'Beweissicherung nach Art. 7 der Richtlinie zur Durchsetzung der Rechte des geistigen Eigentums' [2005] 738; H-J. Ahrens, 'Gesetzgebungsvorschlag zur Beweisermittlung bei Verletzung von Rechten des geistigen Eigentums' [2005] GRUR 838.
77. H-J. Ahrens, 'Gesetzgebungsvorschlag zur Beweisermittlung bei Verletzung von Rechten des geistigen Eigentums' [2005] GRUR 838.
78. A detailed description is provided by T. Kühnen, 'Die Besichtigung im Patentrecht' [2005] GRUR, 185-196.

(a) The independent evidence proceeding is suited to procure a detailed description[79] in the meaning of Article 7(1) of the Directive, since the prerequisites of § 485(1) of § 485(2) no. 1 will generally be met in cases of alleged IP infringements.[80] If there is a risk that evidence will be destroyed, the application to commission an expert may be granted without a hearing of the defendant.[81]

(b) Should the item to be inspected not be publicly accessible, the order for an independent evidence proceeding is combined with a provisional measure ordering the alleged infringer to tolerate the inspection or to present evidence. The order may be based upon §§ 935 et seq. ZPO (subject to the requirement of exigency),[82] since the rights owner has a substantive right to the inspection of the item in cases of sufficient probability of an infringement (§ 809 BGB, supra III.C.1.b). To account for the protection of confidential information and avoid the rejection of the request for an interlocutory injunction, it is expedient for the applicant to limit (in a subsidiary motion) the application to an inspection or examination of the item in his absence, but in the presence of an attorney on his behalf who is sworn to secrecy. In cases of an expert examination, the parties (respectively their attorneys) will be heard by the court before the expert's report is transmitted to the applicant's attorney and to the opposing party. Depending on whether the proceedings or the report have revealed confidential information, the report will also be delivered to the applicant (possibly blackened in parts), and the attorney's secrecy obligation will be (partly) lifted. In those instances in which blackening the sensitive information would render the report incomprehensible, it is upon the court to

---

79. Obviously, the right to inspect the item entails the right to produce a description; an expert examination will anyhow result in a written report, cf. G. Spindler and M-P. Weber, 'Die Umsetzung der Enforcement-Richtlinie nach dem Regierungsentwurf für ein Gesetz zur Verbesserung der Durchsetzung von Rechten des geistigen Eigentums' [2007] ZUM, 264.

80. Opposing view held by H-J. Ahrens, 'Gesetzgebungsvorschlag zur Beweisermittlung bei Verletzung von Rechten des geistigen Eigentums' [2005] GRUR 838, who argues that the prerequisites of § 485(1) ZPO will oftentimes not be met. § 485(2) ZPO solely allows for the commissioning of an expert report, not for evidence by inspection (be it through an expert or otherwise). The question is whether Art. 7 of the Directive obliges to provide for preservation of evidence when the evidence is at no risk of being destroyed. The requirement of a 'demonstrable risk that evidence may be destroyed', which was contained in the Commission's first proposal, was later deleted at the suggestion of the European Parliament. However, Art. 7(1) sent. 3 indicates that the courts of the Member States are intended to have discretion whether to issue an order for the preservation of evidence, and that they are solely held to issue such an order in exigent cases (in particular, as an order may be considered unproportional if there is no particular need for a preservation of evidence). Arguably, therefore, § 485(1) ZPO sufficiently covers the situations described by Art. 7.

81. T. Kühnen, 'Die Besichtigung im Patentrecht' [2005] GRUR, 189.

82. If the alleged infringer refuses to tolerate inspection, he/she may be ordered to payment of a fine or imprisonment (§ 890 ZPO) or the applicant may request the support of a bailiff (§ 892 ZPO), who in turn may request the support of the police (§ 758(3) ZPO). Searches of private or business premises require a search warrant issued by a judge, § 758a ZPO.

decide whether an IP infringement exists and to correspondingly either accept the revelation of business secrets or to deny the transmission of the report to the applicant.[83]

Despite the inventiveness of the 'Düsseldorf Practice', the German civil procedure *de lege lata* does not completely conform with the requirements of the Directive. Article 7(1) mentions the taking of samples as one of the options, something which is currently not provided for by German law.[84] Further, as there is currently no right to the presentation of documents, their production cannot be required as part of a provisional measure.

With respect to Article 7(2) and (4), it is to be noted that the German law currently only provides for a right to compensation and for the lodging of a guarantee to ensure such compensation if the independent evidence proceedings are accompanied by provisional measures, §§ 936, 921, 945 ZPO. Also, a damages claim under § 945 ZPO requires that the provisional order was initially unjustified or later revoked. Since a provisional measure ordering the presentation of items on the basis of § 809 BGB solely presupposes sufficient probability of an infringement, a damages claim under § 945 ZPO will not arise if an infringement was sufficiently probable, but not existent; the rule must be therefore be extended to accommodate Article 7(7).

Finally, the order for a preservation of evidence does not lapse automatically; instead, the defendant has to request the court to set a period of time within which the applicant is to institute proceedings on the merits of the case, §§ 494a, 936, 926(2) ZPO. Arguably, this divergence is covered by Article 2(1) of the Directive (see infra III.E.3 for a discussion of the topic).

b   *The Changes Envisaged by the Government Bill*

The Government Bill seeks to transpose Article 7 of the Directive by stipulating that the courts may issue an interlocutory injunction ordering the alleged infringer to fulfil the applicant's substantive right to the presentation of documents and the inspection of items (*supra* III.C.1.f), subsection 3 of § 140c PatG, § 24c GebrMG, §§ 19a, 128, 135 MarkenG, § 46a GeschmMG, § 101a UrhG, § 37c Sortenschutzgesetz, § 9(2) HalblSchG respectively. Further, subsection 5 of the said provisions allows for compensation of the losses sustained by the alleged infringer if there was no (impending) infringement. The fact that

---

83. As already mentioned, this paragraph described the 'Düsseldorf Practice'; other courts handle the communication of the expert report to the parties differently, cf. the analysis and opinion given by C. Frank and N. Wiegand, 'Der Besichtigungsanspruch im Urheberrecht de lege ferenda' [2007] CR, 483.

84. W. Tilmann, 'Beweissicherung nach europäischem und deutschem Recht' in *Festschrift für Eike Ullmann*, H-J. Ahrens, J. Bornkamm and H-P. Kunz-Hallstein (eds) (Saarbrücken, juris, 2006), p. 1017; G. Spindler and M-P. Weber, 'Die Umsetzung der Enforcement-Richtlinie nach dem Regierungsentwurf für ein Gesetz zur Verbesserung der Durchsetzung von Rechten des geistigen Eigentums' [2007] ZUM, 264 et seq.

interlocutory injunctions under § 935 ZPO require exigency of the matter argu-ably does not create a divergence compared with the Directive: Article 7(1) sent. 3 thereof indicates that the courts of the Member States are intended to have discretion whether to issue an order for the preservation of evidence, and that they are solely held to issue such an order in exigent cases. Moreover, an order for the preservation of evidence would seem disproportionate if there is no conceivable risk that the evidence might be destroyed or the access to it impeded.[85]

The extremely slim transposition of Article 7 suggested by the Government Bill is cause for considerable debate: Some argue that the requirement of exi-gency must be deleted in the light of the Directive,[86] that a search warrant should be issued on a regular basis[87] and that the applicant be barred from using the information received if the court subsequently decides that there was no right of presentation or inspection or if the order is revoked.[88] Others criticize that the approach of § 144c(3) PatG-E et al. goes far beyond the requirements of the Directive,[89] as the suggested provisions do not solely preserve the evidence for an eventual proceeding on the merits of the case.[90] Instead, the right of presenta-tion and inspection alleged by the rights owner will be fulfilled before the pro-ceedings on the merits of the case have commenced. Since it is impossible to turn back the clock and make the presentation or inspection undone at a later point in time, the Government Bill's proposition is a departure from the princi-ple that provisional proceedings may not forestall the decision on the merits of the case.

---

85. Begründung RegE, BT-Drucks. 16/5048, p. 28; opposing opinion voiced by W. Tilmann, 'Beweissicherung nach Art. 7 der Richtlinie zur Durchsetzung der Rechte des geistigen Eigentums' [2005] GRUR, 738.
86. W. Tilmann, 'Beweissicherung nach Art. 7 der Richtlinie zur Durchsetzung der Rechte des geistigen Eigentums' [2005] 738; C. Frank and N. Wiegand, 'Der Besichtigungsanspruch im Urheberrecht de lege ferenda' [2007] Computer und Recht, 487.
87. H-J. Ahrens, 'Gesetzgebungsvorschlag zur Beweisermittlung bei Verletzung von Rechten des geistigen Eigentums' [2005] GRUR 839.
88. W. Tilmann, 'Beweissicherung nach Art. 7 der Richtlinie zur Durchsetzung der Rechte des geistigen Eigentums' [2005] 739; C. Frank and N. Wiegand, 'Der Besichtigungsanspruch im Urheberrecht de lege ferenda' [2007] CR, 486 et seq.
89. G. Spindler and M-P. Weber, 'Die Umsetzung der Enforcement-Richtlinie nach dem Regierungsentwurf für ein Gesetz zur Verbesserung der Durchsetzung von Rechten des gei-stigen Eigentums' [2007] ZUM, 265 claim that Art. 7(1) provides for the seizure of the infringing goods irrespective of the preservation of evidence, but overlook that sent. 2 solely specifies sent. 1 in giving examples and that sent. 1 refers to 'measures to preserve relevant evidence'.
90. A. Peukert and A. Kur, 'Stellungnahme des Max-Planck-Instituts für Geistiges Eigentum, Wettbewerbs- und Steuerrecht zur Umsetzung der Richtlinie 2004/48/EG zur Durchsetzung der Rechte des geistigen Eigentums in deutsches Recht' [2006] GRUR Int, 301 et seq.

D   RIGHT OF INFORMATION

1   Requiring Information from the Infringer

A right of information was codified in every German IP statute by means of the
1990 Brand Piracy Act (Produktpirateriegesetz[91]), cf. § 140b PatG, § 24b GebrMG,
§ 101a UrhG, § 19 MarkenG, § 46 GeschmMG, § 37b Sortenschutzgesetz, § 9(2)
HlSchG. Only geographic indications are currently not covered. The wording of
the said provisions is almost identical to § 101a UrhG.

> § 101a UrhG
>
> (1) Any person who, by producing or distributing reproductions, infringes
>   copyright or another right protected under this statute in the course of
>   trade may be called upon by the injured party to provide information
>   regarding the origin and distribution chain of these reproductions without
>   measurable delay, unless this is disproportionate in the particular case.
> (2) The information referred to in subsection 1 comprises the name and
>   address of the producer, of the supplier and of other previous holders of
>   the reproductions, of any commercial customer or client as well as the
>   quantity of the reproductions produced, delivered, received or ordered.
> (3) In instances of obvious infringement, an order that information be provided
>   may be issued as a provisional measure following the provisions of the
>   Code of Civil Procedure.
> (4) The use of such information in criminal or misdemeanour proceedings
>   against the person obliged to provide the information or a relative in
>   the meaning of § 52(1) of the Code of Criminal Procedure for an action
>   committed before the information was given is subject to the consent of
>   this person.
> (5) Further rights of information remain unaffected.

§ 101a UrhG and the corresponding provisions in the other IP statutes to a wide
extent already transpose Article 8 of the Directive, insofar as the Directive requires
that the infringer is obliged to disclose particular information.[92] This is hardly
surprising, since Article 8 was inspired by the German statutes,[93] which are more
beneficial to the rights owners than the Directive, because they do not require the
initiation of infringement proceedings. However, the said rights of information
currently do not extend to the price obtained for the goods or services in question.
Since Germany insofar failed to align the provisions with the Directive within the

---

91. 'Gesetz zur Stärkung des Schutzes des geistigen Eigentums zur Bekämpfung der Produktpiraterie'
     of 7 Mar. 1990, BGBl. I S. 422.
92. The IP statutes do not refer to 'goods and services which infringe an intellectual property
     right', but to 'products', 'items', 'reproductions' or 'material'. There is no difference in sub-
     stance compared to the Directive, cf. Begründung RegE, BT-Drucks. 16/5048, p. 29.
93. European Commission, *Proposal for a Directive of the European Parliament and of the
     Council on measures and procedures to ensure the enforcement of intellectual property rights*,
     COM (2003) 46 final, p. 23.

deadline stipulated by Article 20 thereof, there is a necessity to apply an analogy extending the right of information to such prices.

The situation is different with respect to requests of information directed against third parties. The rights of information as currently codified are directed against the 'infringer', i.e., a person who culpably commits an infringement or someone aiding and abetting the principal infringer. There is disagreement whether a request for information under § 140b PatG, § 24b GebrMG, § 101a UrhG, § 19 MarkenG, § 46 GeschmMG, § 37b Sortenschutzgesetz, § 9(2) HlSchG may be directed at parties acting without fault. It is settled case law that an injunction prohiting the continuation of an infringement of IP rights may also be directed against persons who interfere with IP rights irrespective of fault, the so-called 'Störerhaftung', i.e., 'interferer's liability'. The Federal Court of Justice considers any person an 'interferer' who

(a) contributes to the bringing-about or perpetuation of an illicit disturbance, i.e., by supporting the actions of the principal infringer without aiding or abetting, if

(b) this person possesses a legitimate option to stop the infringing actions[94] and

(c) was under a reasonable expectation to examine whether it was contributing to illicit actions.[95]

It is debated whether such an 'interferer' is to be regarded as an 'infringer' in the context of the right of information under the above-mentioned provisions and whether the interferer is therefore under an obligation to provide the rights owner with information.[96]

Irrespective of this matter, even if a right of information was derived by the 'interferer's liability', the existing provisions would be insufficient to correctly transpose the Directive, since Article 8(1) thereof requires the group of persons named in Article 8(1)(a)-(d) to answer to the claimant regardless of whether the requirements of due diligence and a legal option to stop the infringement according to the German 'interer's liability' have been met.

2   Proposition of the Government Bill

The Government Bill basically maintains the existing rules of information in the various IP acts, safe for some rephrasing. Furthermore, the particulars of the information to be given are amplified to include information regarding the prices of the

---

94. BGH [1955] GRUR, 97 et seq.
95. BGH [2001] GRUR, 1038 (1039) – *ambiente*; BGH, GRUR 1999, 418 – *Möbelklassiker*.
96. BGH [2004] MMR, 668 (672) – *Internetversteigerung* and OLG Frankfurt [2005] MMR, 241 (242 et seq.) do not consider the interferer to be an infringer under § 19 MarkenG, 191aUrhG; opposing view held by OLG München [2006] MMR, 739 (742). See further the references given by G. Spindler, and J. Dorschel, 'Vereinbarkeit der geplanten Auskunftsansprüche gegen Internet-Provider mit EU-Recht' [2006] CR 341, n. 4.

goods and services concerned and the names and addresses of service users. The provisions are then supplemented by a right of information directed towards third parties in each respective subsection 2, which closely follows Article 8 of the Directive. § 140b PatG, § 24b GebrMG, §§ 19, 128, 135 MarkenG, § 46 GeschmMG, § 37b Sortenschutzgesetz, § 9 HalblSchG are drafted as follows (there is a slight difference with respect to § 101 UrhG):

(1) Any person who [infringes intellectual property] may be called upon by the injured party to provide information regarding the origin and distribution chain [of the infringing goods] without measurable delay.

(2) In cases of obvious infringements or if [the rights owner] has brought an action against the infringer, the information may also be sought from any person who
   1. was found in possession of the infringing goods,
   2. was found to be using the infringing services,
   3. was found to be providing services used in infringing activities or
   4. was indicated by the person referred to in no. 1, 2 or 3 as being involved in the production, manufacture or distribution of the goods or the provision of the services on a commercial scale. The right under subsection 1 remains unaffected. A right of information does not exist if the said person was entitled to refuse testimony in legal proceedings against the infringer under §§ 383 to 385 ZPO. In case of an action brought to enforce the right under subsection 1, the court may stay the proceedings against the infringer until the dispute regarding the right of information has been settled. The person obliged to provide the information may request compensation of his/her expenses.

(3) The person obliged to provide information is to give particulars regarding
   1. the names and addresses of the producers, manufacturers, suppliers and other previous holders of the [goods or services] or the users of the services as well as the intended wholesalers and retailers, and
   2. the quantities manufactured, delivered, received or ordered, as well as the price obtained for the goods or services in question.

(4) The right of information under subsections 1 and 2 is precluded if the claim is disproportionate in the particular instance.

(5) The injured party is entitled to compensation for the loss sustained as a consequence of intentionally or grossly negligent incorrect or incomplete information.

(6) A person who has provided correct information without being obliged to do so under subsection 1 or 2 is only liable to third parties if he/she knew that he/she was not obliged to supply the information.

(7) In instances of obvious infringement, an order that the information be provided may be issued as a provisional measure under §§ 935 to 945 ZPO.

(8) The use of such information in criminal or misdemeanour proceedings against the person obliged to provide the information or a relative in the meaning of

§ 52(1) of the Code of Criminal Procedure for an action committed before the information was given is subject to the consent of this person.

(9) If the information can only be supplied using communications traffic data (§ 3 n. 30 of the Telecommunications Act), the injured party must previously request a court order regarding the admissibility of the use of this data.

a   *Information to be Provided by the Infringer*

Subsection 1 of the draft provisions recounted above mirrors the existing legislation and reinforces the infringer's obligation to provide the injured party with information. The Explanatory Report argues that 'interferers' (Störer) in the meaning described above are 'infringers' for the purpose of subsection 1. It is, however, unclear whether future case law will concur with this assessment. In particular, it needs to be noted that the concept of 'interferer's liability' has been shaped and transformed by case law over time and this process may not be completed yet. So far, the Federal Court of Justice has declined to consider parties it has regarded as 'interferers', i.e., Internet Service Providers (ISPs), as infringers in the context of the existing rights of information introduced by the 1990 Brand Piracy Act.[97] Moreover, parties which under German doctrine would be the typical example for an 'interferer', i.e., parties who were providing services used in infringing activities on a commercial scale, are quite obviously not considered 'infringers' in the wording of Directive 2004/48/EC (cf. Article 8 (1) (c) thereof). To promote harmonization, it seems advisable to interpret the German statutes in line with the Directive in this context.

b   *Information to be Provided by Persons other than the Infringer*

The respective subsection 2 of the draft provisions transposes the stipulation of the Directive that a rights owner may also require information to be provided by any non-infringer who acted on a commercial scale in one of the situations described in Article 8(1)(a) to (d). On its face, the Government Bill is more advantageous to rights holders than the Directive, which solely calls for the information to be given in the context of judicial proceedings. Following the Government Bill, the rights holder may also require information in cases of obvious infringements and by way of an interlocutory injunction.[98] The reason for this difference is the

---

97. BGH [2004] MMR, 668 (672) – *Internetversteigerung* and OLG Frankfurt [2005] MMR, 241 (242 et seq.) do not consider the interferer to be an infringer under § 19 MarkenG, 191aUrhG; opposing view held by OLG München [2006] MMR, 739 (742). See further the references given by G. Spindler, and J. Dorschel, 'Vereinbarkeit der geplanten Auskunftsansprüche gegen Internet-Provider mit EU-Recht' [2006] CR 341, n. 4.

98. Criticism regarding this excessive implementation is voiced by A. Peukert and A. Kur, 'Stellungnahme des Max-Planck-Instituts für Geistiges Eigentum, Wettbewerbs- und Steuerrecht zur Umsetzung der Richtlinie 2004/48/EG zur Durchsetzung der Rechte des geistigen Eigentums in deutsches Recht' [2006] GRUR Int, 297 et seq.

following: German rules of civil procedure do not allow for actions against unknown defendants.[99] Quite obviously, if the rights owner is unaware of the infringer's identity, he or she is unable to institute the infringement proceedings which would activate the right of information under Article 8 of the Directive in the first place.

There is currently a considerable debate amongst German jurists regarding the information obligations of ISPs. Rights owners, by approaching ISPs, try to unveil the identity of users of file sharing programs or members of electronic trading platforms who are allegedly infringing copyright or trademarks. The ISP is requested to reveal the alleged infringer's identity on the basis of an IP address or a user name. Article 8(1) of the Directive arguably may serve as a legal basis to oblige the ISP to provide the requested information, even though this is not as evident as generally presumed: Article 8(2)(a), in describing the content of the information to be given, solely refers to 'the names and addresses of the producers, manufacturers, distributors, suppliers and other previous holders of the goods or services, as well as the intended wholesalers and retailers'. Thus, Article 8 refers to the personal data of the various links on a distribution chain, not to the data of persons using services for infringing activities. Nonetheless, if one looks at the context of the provision, there is a strong argument that Article 8(2)(a) needs to be construed extensively since there would otherwise hardly be a point to Article 8(1)(b) and (c). It would seem that when Article 8(1)(c) was inserted at the suggestion of the European Parliament, there was simply a shortfall to adjust Article 8(2)(a) so that it would include an obligation to reveal the names and addresses of persons using the commercial services. The German draft seeks to fill this gap by including an obligation to disclose information regarding the 'users of the services'.

Even so, it should be noted that Article 8(3)(e) stipulates that 'paragraphs 1 and 2 shall apply without prejudice to other statutory provisions which govern [...] the processing of personal data.' It goes without saying that an obligation to reveal the names and addresses of ISP customers will generally conflict with data protection rules, in particular Directives 95/46/EC[100] and 2002/58/EC.[101] In its decision *Promusicae*, the ECJ declined to explain how to reconcile to the conflict between the fundamental rights protected by Directive 2004/48/EC and the Data Protection Directives, that is the Court declined to give a preference to the right of

---

99. Begründung RegE, BT-Drucks. 16/5048, p. 38 et seq. Apparently, it was emphasised during the negotiations in the Council that the Directive does not entail an obligation to introduce such actions, ibid at 39.

100. Directive 95/46/EC of the European Parliament and of the Council of 24 Oct. 1995 on the protection of individuals with regard to the processing of personal data and on the free movement of such data, OJ No. L 281, 23 Nov. 1995, pp. 31-50.

101. Directive 2002/58/EC of the European Parliament and of the Council of 12 Jul. 2002 concerning the processing of personal data and the protection of privacy in the electronic communications sector (Directive on privacy and electronic communications), OJ No. L 201, 31 Jul. 2002, pp. 37-47.

property over the right of privacy or vice versa.[102] Instead, the Court declared that it was for the Member States to achieve a fair balance between the right to property and the privacy rights of the users.

c   *Balancing the Right of Property with the Right of Privacy*

Before the ECJ handed down the decision *Promusicae*, the German Government, in line with most academics, presumed that Article 8 entailed a strict obligation for the Member States to provide for rules obliging ISPs to reveal the identity of their users in instances of alleged infringements. Thus, the Bill's Explanatory Report does not expound on a balancing of the right of property with the right of privacy. Instead, the report discusses on how to reconcile the right of information with the right of secrecy of telecommunications as constitutionally protected by Article 10 GG (the Basic Law).[103] The Government Bill proposes that, insofar as the performance of the information obligation entails the processing of communications traffic data, the communication of the identity of the alleged infringer be made subject to a judicial decree (subsection 8 of the draft provisions).[104] This proposition is highly disputed, most prominently by the Bundesrat (German Federal Council),[105] since it is obviously time-consuming and costly (the rules on costs included in the Bill suggests a court fee of 200,-EUR)[106] and will burden the courts with additional work. It will be interesting to see whether and how the ECJ's ruling in *Promusicae* will have an impact on the rules eventually adopted. In any case, the data protection provision contained in § 14 TMG (Tele Media Act) will also have to be aligned with the eventual transposition of Article 8.[107] Currently, § 14 TMG allows for the communication of personal data in the interest of the enforcement of IP rights only upon an order made by the competent authorities. The provision therefore does not allow for the communication of the identity of users in the 'obvious' infringement situations envisaged by subsection 2 of the draft provisions recounted above, in which a rights owner might ask an ISP to provide information without a court order.

---

102. *Promusicae v. Telefónica de Espana*, Case No. C-275/06, 29 Jan. 2008, n. 59, <curia.eu.int>.
103. For a discussion of whether the revelation of the identity of a user on the basis of the IP address affects the secrecy of telecommunications cf. G. Spindler, and J. Dorschel, 'Vereinbarkeit der geplanten Auskunftsansprüche gegen Internet-Provider mit EU-Recht' [2006] CR 342 et seq. with further references.
104. Begründung RegE, BT-Drucks. 16/5048, p. 39 et seq.; Gegenäußerung der Bundesregierung, BT-Drucks. 16/5048, p. 63; further F. Raabe, 'Der Auskunftsanspruch nach dem Referentenentwurf zur Verbesserung der Durchsetzung von Rechten des geistigen Eigentums' [2006] ZUM, 439 et seq.
105. Stellungnahme des Bundesrates, BT-Drucks. 16/5048, p. 55 et seq.
106. §§ 128c, 130(2),(5) KostO-E.
107. G. Spindler, and J. Dorschel, 'Vereinbarkeit der geplanten Auskunftsansprüche gegen Internet-Provider mit EU-Recht' [2006] CR 343 et seq.; D. Seichter, 'Die Umsetzung der Richtlinie zur Durchsetzung der Rechte des geistigen Eigentums' [2006] WRP, 398.

d   *Supplementary Rules*

The right of information as laid down by the draft § 140b(1) and (2) PatG and the corresponding draft provisions in other IP statutes is supplemented by rules which are not required by the Directive: Subsection 2, sent. 3 stipulates that third parties are to be compensated for their expenses (note that the right to compensation presupposes that the right of information cannot be based upon subsection 1, i.e., that the third party is neither an aider nor an abettor).[108] Further, in an attempt to set an incentive for a correct and comprehensive answer[109] subsection 5 grants the rights owner an entitlement to damages in cases of incorrect information. Finally, there is restriction of liability of the informant if he/she erroneously believed to be obliged to give the information away (subsection 6).

E   PROVISIONAL AND PRECAUTIONARY MEASURES

The provisional and precautionary measures envisaged by Article 9 of the Directive are to a large extent already in place as part of the general provisions of German civil procedure, §§ 935 et seq. ZPO. The Explanatory Report to the Government Bill solely proposes to implement Article 9(2) sent. 2, i.e., the order of communication or access to bank, financial and commercial documents in the case of an infringement committed on a commercial scale.

1   Interlocutory Injunctions and Provisional Sequestration

Article 9(1)(a) of the Directive requires Member States to enable rights holders to apply for interlocutory injunctions preventing an imminent infringement or prohibiting the continuation of an alleged infringement of IP. Such injunctions are covered by § 940 ZPO.

> § 940 ZPO
> Interlocutory injunctions are furthermore admissible for the purpose of regulating an interim state regarding a legal relationship in dispute, in particular regarding continuous legal relationships, in case this seems necessary for the avoidance of considerable detriment, for the prevention of imminent force or for other reasons.

Leaving aside the dogmatic brush which covers interlocutory injunctions prohibiting actions following §§ 935 et seq. ZPO, what is required is that the applicant demonstrate a substantive right requiring the opposing party to refrain from or to cease the infringement ('Verfügungsanspruch') and a reason for the interlocutory

---

108.   Begründung RegE, BT-Drucks. 16/5048, p. 39.
109.   Begründung RegE, BT-Drucks. 16/5048, p. 39.

injunction ('Verfügungsgrund'), i.e., the exigency of the injunction.[110] For the substantive right to request the prohibition of the continuation of an infringement, refer to the discussion of Article 11 of the Directive (infra, III.G.). The breach of an injunction under § 940 ZPO is sanctioned with penalty payments of up to EUR 250.000 and imprisonment, § 890 ZPO.

§ 938(2) ZPO provides for the sequestration of goods and effectively transposes Article 9(2)(b) of the Directive.

2   Precautionary Seizure

The precautionary seizure of the property of the alleged infringer as required by Article 9(3) of the Directive is addressed by the 'Arrest' following § 916 et seq. ZPO, according to which an order for the seizure of property is possible in order to ensure the enforceability of a monetary claim or a claim which may give way to a monetary claim.

> § 917(1) ZPO
> The seizure of property may be ordered if there is a concern that the enforcement of the decision will be frustrated or considerably impeded without the order.

The obvious difference between § 917(1) ZPO and Article 9(2) of the Directive is that the former requires that the recovery of the monetary claim be considerably impeded whereas the latter regards it sufficient that there is a likely endangerment of the recovery of the damages claim. According to the German Federal Court of Justice, § 917(1) ZPO does not allow for a seizure in situations in which the alleged infringer's financial standing is generally poor, as a footrace between the various creditors with the help of the courts is to be avoided.[111] Rather, what is required is evidence that the infringer is taking specific measures to impede the creditors' access to the property.[112] However, a poor financial standing of the infringer is certainly a circumstance likely to endanger the recovery of a damages claim (as Article 9(2) of the Directive stipulates). The Explanatory Report of the Government Bill tries to alleviate concerns that the wording of § 917(1) ZPO might be too narrow and thus inadequate to transpose Article 9(2) by arguing that the intended purpose of the Directive cannot consist in favouring the holders of IP over other creditors.[113] And indeed it would seem that such a preferential treatment of IP owners is incompatible with Article 20 of the EU Charter of Fundamental Rights.[114] Since the powers of the Community do not include the

---

110. Refer to recital 22 of the Directive which considers interlocutory injunctions as 'particularly justified where any delay would cause irreparable harm to the holder of an intellectual property right.'
111. BGHZ 131, 95 (105 et seq.) with further references.
112. Ibid.
113. Begründung RegE, BT-Drucks. 16/5048, p. 31.
114. Art. 6(1) of the Treaty on European Union as established by the Treaty of Lisbon is to read 'The Union recognises the rights, freedoms and principles set out in the Charter of

prescription of common standards for the seizure of property within the Member States, setting such standards via the back door of an IP enforcement measure should be equally impossible. Quite apart from these considerations, § 921 ZPO allows the court to order the precautionary seizure without demonstration of a considerable impediment to the recovery of the damages subject to the lodging of an adequate security (as allowed by Article 9(6) of the Directive). Thus, the German procedural provisions are *de lege lata* in line with the Directive.

However, there is currently no German provision which corresponds to Article 9(2) sent. 2 of the Directive.

3   Procedural Requirements under Article 9(3) to (7)

Article 9(3) to (7) specify the circumstances of a measure under Article 9(1) and (2). According to §§ 920(2), 936 ZPO, the applicant is to make credible both the substantive right entitling him or her to request the prohibition of an action on the part of the respondent and the exigency of the injunction. Following § 294 ZPO, any means of evidence may be used for this purpose, as long as it is immediately available. This reflects the authority of the courts under Article 9(3) of the Directive to satisfy themselves as to the alleged infringement.

Following §§ 922(1), 937(2) ZPO, the provisional measures of 'Arrest' and 'Einstweilige Verfügung' may be ordered without the defendant being heard in appropriate cases (as required by Article 9(4)). 'Appropriate cases' for interlocutory injunctions are defined by § 937(2) ZPO as (a) cases in which the application is denied and (b) urgent cases, i.e., situations in which a balancing of the interests of the parties shows that even a hearing at short notice will not suffice to satisfy the interests of the applicant. Again, this reflects the balance of interests expressed in Article 9(4) ('in particular where any delay would cause irreparable harm to the right holder'). With respect to orders of precautionary seizure, the hearing of the defendant lies in the discretion of the court, which will reach its decision by weighing the defendant's right to be heard with the applicant's interest in an immediate order without advance warning to the defendant.[115] If interlocutory injunctions or orders for provisional sequestration or precautionary seizure are made without a hearing of the opposing party, the decision needs to be served to that party by the applicant, §§ 922(2), 936 ZPO, thereby informing the defendant as required by Article 9(4) sent 2 of the Directive. However, there is a slight divergence in that § 929(3) stipulates that service of the order must be made within one week after the execution of the measure at the latest, whereas the Directive requires that information be given thereafter without delay. The orders are subject to a review upon the request of the defendant ('Widerspruch', §§ 924, 936 ZPO).

Fundamental Rights of the European Union of 7 Dec. 2000, as adapted at Strasbourg, on 12 Dec. 2007, which shall have the same legal value as the Treaties.'

115. M. Huber in *Kommentar zur Zivilprozessordnung*, H.-J. Musielak (ed.) (4th edn, Franz Vahlen, München, 2007), § 921 ZPO n. 2.

Furthermore, §§ 926, 936 ZPO provide for a revocation of the order if the applicant fails to institute proceedings on the merits of the case. Contrary to Article 9(5) of the Directive, in German procedure it is up to the defendant to request the court to set a period of time within which the applicant is to institute proceedings on the merits of the case. Obviously, Article 2(1) of the Directive allows the Member States to introduce or maintain more favourable means for rights holders.[116] On the other hand, Article 9(5) prescribes that, in the absence of a determination of the competent judicial authority, the statutory period granted to the applicant for the institution of legal proceedings may not exceed 20 working or 31 calendar days. Arguably, since Article 9(5) does not stipulate the point in time at which this period begins to run, there is room for the Member States to make the necessity of instituting legal proceedings subject to the defendant's request (cf. Article 50(6) TRIPs).[117]

It has already been noted that §§ 921, 936 BGB allow for the competent court to make its order subject to the lodging of a security by the applicant, in line with Article 9(6). Finally, the applicant is liable for damages under § 945 ZPO if it turns out that the interlocutory injunction or the precautionary seizure was unjustified *ab initio* or if the order is subsequently revoked, thereby effectively implementing Article 9(7).

4   Proposition of the Government Bill

As the general provisions of German civil procedure already comply with the stipulations of Article 9 of the Directive, the Government Bill solely proposes to transpose Article 9(2) sent. 2. It is envisaged to create a substantive right to the communication of bank, financial or commercial documents, and such communication may be ordered as part of an interim injunction. The draft versions of § 140d PatG, § 24d GebrMG, §§ 19b, 128, 135 MarkenG, § 101b UrhG, § 46b GeschmMG, § 37d SortenschutzG, § 9 HalbleiterschutzG read

(1) In case of a culpable infringement committed on a commercial scale, the injured party may require the infringer to present bank, financial or commercial documents or appropriate access thereto, if the documents are in the control of the infringer and are necessary for the enforcement of the damages claim, in case the performance of the damages claim is uncertain without the production or the access. Insofar as the infringer submits that

---

116. Begründung RegE, BT-Drucks. 16/5048, p. 31, 28.
117. W. Tilmann, 'Beweissicherung nach Art. 7 der Richtlinie zur Durchsetzung der Rechte des geistigen Eigentums' [2005] GRUR, 739 argues that the divergence is legitimate following ECJ's ruling in the case *Route 66*, Case no. C-89/99, [2001] ECR I-5951 n. 70. However, the ECJ explicitly refers to the 'absence of a Community rule on the point'. Thus, there is no guarantee that the court's interpretation would remain consistent after the creation of Art. 9(5) of the Directive. See further the analysis provided by N. v.Hartz, 'Beweissicherungsmöglichkeiten im Urheberrecht nach der Enforcement-Richtlinie im deutschen Recht' [2005] ZUM, 382 et seq.

the information is of a confidential nature, the court takes the appropriate measures to provide for the protection required in the particular instance.

(2) The right under subsection 1 is precluded if the presentation or inspection is disproportionate in the particular instance.

(3) The court may issue a provisional measure under §§ 935 to 945 of the Code of Civil Procedure (ZPO) in which the defendant is ordered to procure the documents referred to in subsection 1 if the damages claim is obviously legitimate. The court provides for appropriate measures to ensure the protection of confidential information, in particular if the provisional measure is ordered without a hearing of the defendant.

(4) § 811 of the Civil Code (BGB) as well as [§ 140b(8) PatG] find corresponding application.

Again, the Government Bill chooses to implement the production of documents as a substantive provision. Unfortunately, the recommended provision neither makes sense, nor does it meet the requirements of the Directive. The access to bank, financial or commercial documents under Article 9(2) sent. 2 of the Directive serves to enable the precautionary seizure of the alleged infringer's property ('to that end').[118] Thus, what is needed is obviously a quick access to financial information, i.e., a provisional measure. A proceeding on the merits of the substantive right of information as stipulated by the draft § 140d PatG and its sister provisions is already covered by Article 6(2) of the Directive and the draft § 140c(1) sent. 2 PatG and the respective provisions of other IP statutes as envisaged by the Government Bill.

The suggested provisions furthermore fail to transpose Article 9(2) correctly, as they stipulate requirements over and above the Directive:

(a) the documents must be necessary for the enforcement of the damages claim,

(b) the performance of the damages claim must be uncertain without the production of the financial documents,

(c) for the court to order an interim measure, the damages claim must be obviously legitimate.

None of these criteria find an express or implicit counterpart in Article 9(2) sent. 2.

F   CORRECTIVE MEASURES

Article 10 of the Directive enjoins Member States to provide for three corrective measures to be available at the request of the injured party, namely recall and

---

118. A. Peukert and A. Kur, 'Stellungnahme des Max-Planck-Instituts für Geistiges Eigentum, Wettbewerbs- und Steuerrecht zur Umsetzung der Richtlinie 2004/48/EG zur Durchsetzung der Rechte des geistigen Eigentums in deutsches Recht' [2006] GRUR Int, 302.

removal from the channels of commerce as well as the destruction of infringing items and the materials and implements used to create such goods.

1   Recall and Removal from the Channels of Commerce

The German IP laws do not explicitly provide for a right to the recall and/or removal of goods from the channels of commerce. There is some debate whether such a right may result from an analogous application of § 1004 German Civil Code (which deals with interferences with property). Following the long-established case law regarding a general analogy to § 1004 BGB,[119] the owner of an absolute right may require from any person who interferes with this absolute right a removal of the disturbance, irrespective of fault on the part of the interferer.[120] Recalling or removing goods from the channels of commerce would certainly remove the disturbance which the circulation of infringing goods causes to IP rights.[121] However, there is little case law regarding the matter;[122] it almost seems as if there was little interest in such an instrument on the part of rights holders.[123] Furthermore, based upon the analogy to § 1004 BGB, the rights holder can only generally request removal of the disturbance; there is no right to request a specific action, unless only this particular action will suitably remove the disturbance. It is therefore to be applauded that the Government Bill seeks to introduce provisions which clearly transpose Article 10(1)(a) and (b) of the Directive. In the meantime, the courts will have to consider granting an order for the recall or removal from the channels of commerce on the basis of an analogy to § 1004 BGB.

Naturally, the principle *impossibilium nulla est obligatio* applies to any such order. In the legislative process, the European Parliament had suggested an amendment to the Commission's proposal of the Directive stipulating that the recall of goods could only be enforced against third parties operating in the course of trade and only exceptionally if the goods had been purchased in good faith.[124]

---

119. Refer to the case law listed by J. Fritzsche in *Beck'scher Online-Kommentar BGB*, G. Bamberger and H. Roth (7th edn, München, C.H. Beck, 1.9.2007), § 1004 BGB n. 3.
120. For the interfers' liability cf. *supra* III.D.1.
121. K-H. Fezer, *Markenrecht* (3rd edn, München, C.H. Beck, 2001), § 18 MarkenG n. 46; G. Spindler and M-P. Weber, 'Die Umsetzung der Enforcement-Richtlinie nach dem Regierungsentwurf für ein Gesetz zur Verbesserung der Durchsetzung von Rechten des geistigen Eigentums' [2007] ZUM, 258.
122. Declining the the requested order for a recall under an analogous application of § 1004 BGB: LG Stuttgart [1994] CR, 162 (163 et seq.); OLG Hamburg [2000] NJWE-WettbR, 15 (16) – *Spice Girls*.
123. The Explanatory Report of the Government Bill proclaims the practical use of the right of recall/removal as 'questionable', Begründung RegE, BT-Drucks. 16/5048, p. 38; concurring D. Seichter 'Die Umsetzung der Richtlinie zur Durchsetzung der Rechte des geistigen Eigentums, [2006] WRP, 399.
124. European Parliament, Report on the proposal for a directive of the European Parliament and of the Council on measures and procedures to ensure the enforcement of intellectual property rights, Rapporteur J. Fourtou, A5-0468/2003, Amendment 34, p. 25.

Under German law, once a transfer of title has occurred, the recall or removal cannot be enforced against third parties at all;[125] the order might thus only require the infringer to inform his/her clients of the situation and to try to reacquire the goods.

2 Destruction of Infringing Items, Materials and Implements

The German IP statutes *de lege lata* provide for the destruction of goods which have been found to infringe IP (§§ 140a PatG, 24a GebrMG, 18 MarkenG, 9 HalbleiterschutzG, §§ 98, 99 UrhG, 43 GechMG, 37a SortenschG; there is no provision regarding geographic indications). The wording of these provisions more or less mirrors the wording of § 18 MarkenG:

§ 18 MarkenG

(1) The owner of a trademark or a business denomination may [in cases of infringement] request that the infringing items in the property or possession of the infringer be destroyed, unless the infringing condition of the items may be corrected in a different way and the destruction is disproportionate for the infringer or the proprietor of the item.
(2) Subsection 1 finds corresponding application to devices in the property of the infringer which exclusively or almost exclusively have been used or are intented for the illegal marking.
(3) Further rights to remediate action remain unaffected.

The said provisions differ in some respects from the corrective measure of destruction under the Directive: Firstly, the destruction is also an option if the intended illegitimate use of the implements can be proven, thus entailing for more favourable sanctions from the perspective of the rights owners than the Directive. On the other hand, where the Directive maintains that implements have been principally used in the production of the infringing goods, the German provisions state that an almost exclusive use is required. Since there is a material difference between 'almost exclusively' and 'principally', the statutes need to be revised. In the meantime however, the vague term 'almost exclusively' should be interpreted widely by the courts to allow for an interpretation as consistent as possible with the Directive.[126] Third, the German statutes do not address materials used in the creation of the infringing goods. The practical impact of this omission seems negligible, as materials principally used in the creation of infringing goods will

---

125. G. Spindler and M-P. Weber, 'Die Umsetzung der Enforcement-Richtlinie nach dem Regierungsentwurf für ein Gesetz zur Verbesserung der Durchsetzung von Rechten des geistigen Eigentums' [2007] ZUM, 259.
126. M. Bohne in A-A. Wandtke and W. Bullinger (eds), *Urheberrecht* (2nd edn, München, C.H. Beck, 2006), § 99 UrhG n. 6. See also K-H. Fezer, *Markenrecht* (3rd edn, München, C.H. Beck, 2001), § 18 MarkenG n. 18, who argues that the criterion of almost exclusive use is to be interpreteted in the light of Art. 46 TRIPs, i.e., as 'predominant' use.

generally be expended or transfigured in the process. Fourth, while the German provisions do not explicitly address the matter of costs, it is clear that the expenses are to be borne by the infringer since it is his or her obligation to arrange for the destruction.[127]

Finally, destruction under German law presupposes that the items to be destroyed are in the possession or form part of the property of the infringer. Both the German Federal Council[128] and academics[129] voiced fconcerns that the current provisions might fail to correctly implement Article 10(1)(c) for this reason. The Directive is silent as regards the ownership of the goods to be destroyed. Solely Article 10(3) – which addresses the interests of third parties – might give an indication that the Directive requires the destruction of items which is the property of third parties. However, it would seem that the origin of Article 10(3) can be traced to the European Parliament's suggestion of an amendment reading 'The recall of goods may only be enforced against third parties operating in the course of trade'.[130] There is nothing in the Directive or the legislative history to suggest that the silence of the Directive in this matter implies that the property of third parties need be destroyed; to the contrary: where the Directive provides for orders against third parties, it always stipulates so explicitly (cf. Article 8, 9, 11 of the Directive).[131]

3   Changes Proposed by the Government Bill

The Government Bill seeks to introduce changes to § 18 MarkenG and its sister provisions to bring them in line with the Directive by

(a) stipulating that materials and implements principally used in the creation or manufacture of the goods may be destroyed
(b) introducing a right to recall and removal from the channels of commerce and
(c) rephrasing the principle of proportionality in a separate subsection without a change in substance.[132]

---

127. Begründung RegE, BT-Drucks. 16/5048, p. 32.
128. Stellungnahme des Bundesrats, BT-Drucks. 16/5048, p. 54
129. T. Dreier, 'Ausgleich, Abschreckung und andere Rechtsfolgen von Urheberrechtsverletzungen: Erste Gedanken zur EU-Richtlinie über die Maßnahmen und Verfahren zum Schutze der Recht an geistigem Eigentum', [2004] GRUR Int., 712.
130. European Parliament, Report on the proposal for a directive of the European Parliament and of the Council on measures and procedures to ensure the enforcement of intellectual property rights, Rapporteur J. Fourtou, A5-0468/2003, Amendment 34, p. 25.
131. Begründung RegE, BT-Drucks. 16/5048, p. 31 et seq., further Gegenäußerung der Bundesregierung, BT-Drucks. 16/5048, p. 62, which addresses constitutional concerns (guarantee of the right of property); concurring G. Spindler and M-P. Weber, 'Die Umsetzung der Enforcement-Richtlinie nach dem Regierungsentwurf für ein Gesetz zur Verbesserung der Durchsetzung von Rechten des geistigen Eigentums' [2007] ZUM, 260.
132. Begründung RegE, BT-Drucks. 16/5048, p. 32.

§§ 128, 135 MarkenG now provide for corresponding rules for geographic indications.

It is doubtful whether the explicit introduction of the right to recall and removal from the channels of commerce will effect considerable change. If the infringing goods are still within the control of the infringer, an injunction prohibiting the circulation of the goods or an order for destruction is sufficient to achieve the desired result. If however the title has already passed, the recall and/or removal is unenforceable[133] and the infringer can solely be ordered to attempt to reacquire the goods.[134]

G   PROHIBITION OF THE INFRINGEMENT

The German IP statutes grant each IP owner the right to request from the infringer the cessation of the infringement. § 139 PatG, § 24 GebrMG, §§ 14, 128, 135 MarkenG, § 97 UrhG, § 42 GeschmMG, § 37 SortenschG, § 9(1) HalbISchG therefore effectively transpose Article 11 of the Directive. Compliance with a court order prohibiting the continuation of the infringement is achieved by virtue of § 890 ZPO, which enables the court to order, at the request of the injured party, penalty payments and imprisonment for each act of non-compliance.

Article 11 sent. 3 of the Directive further requires that the courts of the Member States be able to provide for an injunction against intermediaries whose services are used by a third party to infringe an IP right. German case law accomplishes such orders against intermediaries with the help of the concept of 'Störerhaftung' or interferer's liability. As has already been explained (supra III.D.1), the injunction prohibiting the continuation of an infringement may under German law be directed against anyone who unintentionally contributes to the illicit disturbance, i.e., by providing services which are used by the principal infringer, subject to the requirement that there is a legitimate option to stop the infringing actions and the person is under a reasonable expectation to examine whether it was contributing to illicit actions. There is no explicit counterpart to these two qualifications contained in the Directive, but they are obvious specifications of the principle of proportionality as laid down by Article 3(2) of the Directive.

---

133. Deutsche Vereinigung für gewerblichen Rechtsschutz und Urheberrecht (GRUR), 'Gemeinsame Stellungnahme der Ausschüsse für Patent- und Gebrauchsmusterrecht, Geschmacksmusterrecht und Urheberrecht zum Referentenentwurf für ein,, Gesetz zur Verbesserung der Durchsetzung von Rechten des geistigen Eigentums' [2006] GRUR, 393; Spindler and M-P. Weber, 'Die Umsetzung der Enforcement-Richtlinie nach dem Regierungsentwurf für ein Gesetz zur Verbesserung der Durchsetzung von Rechten des geistigen Eigentums' [2007] ZUM, 259.

134. Concurring G. Spindler and M-P. Weber, 'Die Umsetzung der Enforcement-Richtlinie nach dem Regierungsentwurf für ein Gesetz zur Verbesserung der Durchsetzung von Rechten des geistigen Eigentums' [2007] ZUM, 259; A. Peukert and A. Kur, 'Stellungnahme des Max-Planck-Instituts für Geistiges Eigentum, Wettbewerbs- und Steuerrecht zur Umsetzung der Richtlinie 2004/48/EG zur Durchsetzung der Rechte des geistigen Eigentums in deutsches Recht' [2006] GRUR Int, 295 et seq.

H   COMPENSATION INSTEAD OF RECALL, REMOVAL,
                             DESTRUCTION OR PROHIBITIVE INJUNCTIONS

Article 12 of the Directive contains an opening clause for the Member States under which the infringer may apply to the competent judicial authorities to pay pecuniary compensation instead of being subject to the corrective measures under Article 10 or an injunction under Article 11 of the Directive. This option is subject to the following requirements: (a) the addressee of the measure has acted without fault, (b) disproportionate harm would be caused by the corrective measure and (c) the pecuniary compensation appears reasonably satisfactory. Article 12 of the Directive is reminiscent of § 101 UrhG, § 45 GeschmMG.

> § 101 (1) UrhG
> If, in case of an infringement of one of the rights protected by this statute, the rights owner may claim removal or prohibit the continuation of the disturbance (§ 97) or may claim destruction or surrender of the copies (§ 98) or the implements (§ 99) from a person who has neither acted intentionally nor negligently, this party may avert the claims by way of pecuniary compensation if execution of the measures in question would cause him/her disproportionate harm and if pecuniary compensation to the injured party appears reasonable. The compensation due consists in the amount which would have been considered adequate as royalties or fees had there been a contractual agreement regarding the use. Once payment of the compensation has been effected, the injured party is presumed to consent to use on a common scale.

§ 45 GeschmMG possesses almost identical wording; however the German law does not provide for pecuniary compensation other than in cases of infringement of copyright and designs. Article 12 leaves it to the discretion of the Member States whether to allow for pecuniary compensation in appropriate cases, and the German Government Bill professes no intention of introducing corresponding provisions for industrial property.[135] In practice this will not make much of a difference, since the criteria for pecuniary compensation are so strict that they are very rarely met even in copyright and design cases,[136] and examples of the applicability in industrial property cases (which require action in the course of trade) are even harder to imagine.

§§ 101 UrhG, 45 GeschmMG follow a slightly different concept than Article 12 of the Directive: Whereas the Directive requires an application of the infringer to the court, the German provisions give the infringer a right to avert the injured

---

135. Begründung RegE, BT-Drucks. 16/5048, p. 32; critical A. Peukert and A. Kur, 'Stellungnahme des Max-Planck-Instituts für Geistiges Eigentum, Wettbewerbs- und Steuerrecht zur Umsetzung der Richtlinie 2004/48/EG zur Durchsetzung der Rechte des geistigen Eigentums in deutsches Recht' [2006] GRUR Int, 296.

136. S. Lütje in K. Nicolini and H. Ahlberg (eds), *Möhring/Nicolini, Urheberrechtsgesetz* (2nd edn, München, Franz Vahlen, 2000), § 101 UrhG n. 1; M. Bohne in Wandtke A-A. and W. Bullinger (eds), *Urheberrecht* (2nd edn, München, C.H. Beck, 2006), § 101 UrhG n. 1.

party's claims. Whereas the angle of the Directive is more procedural, German law again views the alternative measure as a matter of substantive law. It is upon the infringer to prove that the prerequisites of §§ 101 UrhG, 45 GeschmMG have been met.[137] A number of criteria may be used to determine whether pecuniary compensation appears reasonably satisfactory: i.e., the intensity of the infringement, whether licenses are usually granted regarding the material in question,[138] the prejudice to moral rights of the author,[139] the amount of the eventual compensation[140] as well as the infringer's ability to actually pay the compensation.[141]

I   DAMAGES

Article 13 of the Directive enjoins Member States to provide for a right of compensation in case of intentional or negligent IP infringements and provides for two options to be given to the courts to set the damages: either by taking into account 'all appropriate aspects', some of which are cited by Article 13(1)(a); or by fixing a lump sum on the basis of at least the amount of adequate royalties or fees. Naturally, the German IP statutes already provide for a claim for damages (§ 139 PatG, § 24 GebrMG, §§ 14, 128, 135 MarkenG, § 97 UrhG, § 42 GeschmMG, § 37 SortenschG, § 9(1) HalblSchG). The amount of damages is in principle calculated on the basis of the actual loss sustained (§§ 249 et seq. BGB); however, due to the specific difficulties of determining damages in IP cases, settled case law in IP cases stipulates that the injured party may choose between three methods of calculation:[142]

- the actual loss sustained, including loss of profits (this is the standard method of calculation for any civil law compensation claim following §§ 249, 252 of the Civil Code);
- foregone adequate royalties or fees;
- the profits of the infringer.

---

137. M. Bohne in A-A. Wandtke and W. Bullinger (eds), *Urheberrecht* (2nd edn, München, C.H. Beck, 2006), § 101 UrhG n. 2.
138. S. Lütje in K. Nicolini and H. Ahlberg (eds), *Möhring/Nicolini, Urheberrechtsgesetz* (2nd edn, München, Franz Vahlen, 2000), § 101 UrhG n. 14; M. Bohne in A-A. Wandtke and W. Bullinger (eds), *Urheberrecht* (2nd edn, München, C.H. Beck, 2006), § 101 UrhG n. 7.
139. M. Bohne in A-A. Wandtke and W. Bullinger (eds), *Urheberrecht* (2nd edn, München, C.H. Beck, 2006), § 101 UrhG n. 7.
140. M. Bohne in A-A. Wandtke and W. Bullinger (eds), *Urheberrecht* (2nd edn, München, C.H. Beck, 2006), § 101 UrhG n. 7.
141. S. Lütje in K. Nicolini and H. Ahlberg (eds), *Möhring/Nicolini, Urheberrechtsgesetz* (2nd edn, München, Franz Vahlen, 2000), § 101 UrhG n. 10.
142. BGH [1972] GRUR, 189 (190) – *Wandsteckdose II*; BGH [2001] GRUR, 329 (330 et seq.) – *Gemeinkostenanteil*. The choice between the three calculation methods is left to the injured party until the claim is fulfilled or until the final court decision, BGH [1993] GRUR, 55 (57) – *Tchibo/Rolex II*.

The Federal Court of Justice allows for the setting of damages double the amount of adequate fees solely with respect to the particularities of performance rights organizations.[143] On the other hand, § 139(2) PatG, § 24(2) GebrMG, § 42(2) GeschmMG, § 37 SortenschG, § 9(1) HalblSchG stipulate that the competent courts may, in cases of slight negligence provide for a compensation which ranges between the loss sustained and the profits reaped by the infringer. Finally, compensation of immaterial losses can only be claimed for infringements of copyright following § 97(2) UrhG, unless the breach of IP simultaneously infringes other rights, i.e., personality rights.[144]

Consequently, the German courts already take into account all the criteria named by the Directive, i.e., negative economic consequences for the injured party, unfair profits of the infringer, moral prejudice and adequate royalties or fees. The fact that the injured party may choose amongst the different options of fixing the damages amount is a deviation from the Directive which is covered by Article 2(1) thereof. Arguably however, the preferential treatment of slightly negligent infringements following § 139(2) PatG and its sister provisions contravenes the Directive, as Article 13 does not explicitly refer to the standard of culpability as a factor to be taken into account when setting the damages.[145] On the other hand, Article 13(a) calls for consideration of 'all appropriate aspects' and the criteria named are only examples. In any case, the German provisions furnish the courts with discretion whether to reduce the damages in cases of slight negligence, and until the scheduled Bill is enacted, the courts are held to make use of their discretion by considering Article 13(1) of the Directive.

The Government Bill intends to codify the existing case law by introducing the following sentence in § 139 PatG, § 24 GebrMG, §§ 14, 128, 135 MarkenG, § 97 UrhG, § 42 GeschmMG, § 37 SortenschG, § 9(1) HalblSchG:

> When setting the damages, the profits reaped by the infringer as a consequence of the infringement may also be considered. The damages claim may furthermore be calculated on the basis of the amount which the infringer would have had to pay as adequate remuneration, had the authorisation [to use the intellectual property right] been requested.

The draft provisions do not refer to the court's authority to consider the loss sustained by the injured party because this option is self-evident on the basis of §§ 249, 252 BGB. The Government Bill stands in contrast to the Directive in that it allows the courts to consider the moral prejudice suffered only if the claimant is an author, an editor of scholarly editions of works previously unprotected by

---

143.   BGH [1973] GRUR, 379 (380) – *Doppelte Tarifgebühr*, which argues that both an actual loss as well as the infringer's profit will be difficult to demonstrate with respect to music played in restaurants and other venues; on the other hand, setting the damage on the basis of a singular fee would not act as a deterrence, because it would put the infringer in no worse a position than someone who complied with the Copyright Act.
144.   Cf. BGH [2000] NJW, 2195 et seq. – *Marlene Dietrich*.
145.   Begründung RegE, BT-Drucks. 16/5048, p. 33.

copyright. a creator of photos which do not constitute artistic works or a perform-
ing artist (§ 97(1) UrhG-E). It would seem that this divergence can be justified, as
it is hard to imagine immaterial losses with respect to other IP rights.[146] The
Explanatory Report states that the Federal Court of Justice's case law with respect
to performance rights organizations should be left untouched,[147] but declines to
allow for a calculation of damages on the basis of multiple royalties in all other
instances. This refusal is subject to some criticism, notably by the Bundesrat
(German Federal Council) which suggested a rebuttable presumption that the
infringer's profit amounts to twice the standard royalty fees.[148] Nonetheless, the
government is adamant (and rightly so) that granting damages in the amount of
multiple fees would constitute a form of punitive damages which are incompatible
with the principles of German civil law.[149] Furthermore, the Government Bill
seeks to eliminate the preferential treatment for slight negligence. Finally, the
provisions clarify that other claims, i.e., on the basis of unjustified enrichment,
remain unaffected.

J   LEGAL COSTS

Article 14 enjoins Member States to ensure that reasonable and proportionate legal
costs and other expenses incurred by the successful party generally be borne by
the unsuccessful party. The German government correctly advanced the opinion
that the indemnity principle as set forth by the rules on costs in the Code of Civil
Procedure (ZPO) fully conforms with the requirements as set forth by the
Directive.[150]

Under § 91 ZPO the losing party in principle bears the cost of the proceedings, i.e., court and out-of-court fees. In cases of partial success, § 92 ZPO
provides that the costs be allocated proportionally. §§ 95 and 96 ZPO spell out
situations in which equity does not allow for the costs to be borne by the unsuccessful party (as Article 12 of the Directive puts it): If the successful party has
failed to attend a hearing or to meet a deadline or has by default caused an additional hearing to be fixed or a deadline to be prolonged, it needs to bear the corresponding costs (§ 95 ZPO). The same is true for 'a means of attack or defence
which proved to be unsuccessful', i.e., for any factual submission, contest or

---

146. Begründung RegE, BT-Drucks. 16/5048, p. 33; concurring A. Peukert and A. Kur,
     'Stellungnahme des Max-Planck-Instituts für Geistiges Eigentum, Wettbewerbs- und
     Steuerrecht zur Umsetzung der Richtlinie 2004/48/EG zur Durchsetzung der Rechte des gei-
     stigen Eigentums in deutsches Recht' [2006] GRUR Int, 293.
147. Begründung RegE, BT-Drucks. 16/5048, p. 37.
148. Stellungnahme des Bundesrates, BT-Drucks. 16/5048, p. 54; concurring D. Frey and M.
     Rudolph, 'EU-Richtlinie zur Durchsetzung der Rechte des geistigen Eigentums' [2004]
     ZUM, 528.
149. BGH [1992] NJW, 3096 (3103).
150. Begründung RegE, BT-Drucks. 16/5048, p. 33.

means of proof which caused additional costs and did not contribute to the party's eventual success in the proceedings (§ 96 ZPO).

The matter of reasonability and proportionality of legal costs is addressed by the Code on Court Fees (Gerichtskostengesetz – GKG) and the Attorney Fee Scheme (*Rechtsanwaltsvergütungsgesetz – RVG*). Both court and statutory attorney fees are generally defined in a digressive relation to the sum in dispute, while the procedural measures taken are also accounted for. The reimbursement of the opposing party's attorney fees is limited to the statutory rate stipulated by §§ 13 et seq. RVG and to the representation of one attorney only, § 91(2) ZPO. While client and attorney may agree on higher fees under § 4 RVG, such fees are not recoverable from the opposing party. Contingency and quota litis fees are considered inadmissible following § 49b(1), (2) of the Federal Attorney Regulation (*Bundesrechtsanwaltsordnung – BRAO*).[151]

K   PUBLICATION OF JUDICIAL DECISIONS

Following Article 15 of the Directive, Member States shall ensure that the injured party may apply for an order allowing the dissemination of the judicial decision at the expense of the infringer, i.e., by displaying or publishing it. Under German law, this is currently only possible with respect to copyright and designs, § 103 UrhG, § 47 GeschmMG.[152]

Publication of the Judgement

(1) If a claim has been raised on the basis of this statute, the court may grant the successful party the authority to communicate the decision at the expense of the opposing party, in case the former party demonstrates a legitimate interest. The decision may only be publicized after the final judgement, unless the court determines otherwise.

(2) Modalities and scope of the publication are determined in the decision. The authority to communicate the decision lapses unless the decision has been disseminated within 6 months after the final judgment.

These provisions mirror Article 15 of the Directive in that they grant the court discretion to order the publication of the decision at the expense of the infringer. Where the Directive uses the wording 'appropriate measures', the German law leaves modalities and scope of the publication to the court. However, under § 103 UrhG, § 47 GeschmMG the order is subject to the demonstration of a legitimate interest of the injured party, a criterion which is not contained in Article 15. Nonetheless, as the Explanatory Report of the Government Bill correctly points out, Article 15 of the Directive envisages that the national authorities be furnished

---

151. But see the decision of the Supreme Court regarding 'exceptional cases', BVerfGE 117, 163 et seq.
152. The wording of § 47 GeschmMG is identical.

with discretion as to whether to grant the order for the dissemination of the decision and that this discretion will have to be used in view of the principle of proportionality as set forth by Article 3(2) of the Directive.[153] § 103 UrhG, § 47 GeschmMG simply spell out that when deciding upon the applicant's request, the court will have to weigh the respective interests of the parties and thus respect the principle of proportionality.

What seems more of a concern is that according to the German provisions, the authority to make the decision public at the expense of the infringer lapses within six months, whereas the Directive does not contain such a time limit. The ECJ has been critical of time limits imposed by national legislation in other circumstances, notably in the case *Heininger*, in which the ECJ held that the prescription of a period of one year after the conclusion of contract for the exercise of the right of cancellation provided by Council Directive 85/577 (Doorstep Selling) breached the Member States' obligation to implement the provisions of that directive.[154] Clearly, *Heininger* can be distinguished from the obligations discussed at hand in that the Doorstep Selling Directive unconditionally grants consumers a right of withdrawal and clearly defines the time frame within which this right may be exercised, whereas Article 15 leaves the order on publication to the discretion of the competent judicial authorities and states nothing regarding the time frame. Again, it is suggested that the principle of proportionality allows for the limit prescribed by the German statutes, since the legitimate interest of the injured party to make the decision public will wane over time, and the risk that the publication is used for the sole purpose of harming the reputation or the purse of the opponent may increase correspondingly.

In any case, § 103 UrhG, § 47 GeschmMG are of little practical relevance since nothing generally prevents the injured party from taking the quicker and thus more effective path of communicating the decision on its own.[155] The main purpose of the provisions lies in burdening the infringer with the cost of the publication.

The other German IP statutes do not contain corresponding provisions. Due to the failure of the German legislator to transpose Directive 2004/48/EC within the time limit stipulated therein, the German courts are currently under an obligation pursuant to Article 10 EC to apply § 103 UrhG, § 47 GeschmMG by analogy to other IP infringements.

The Government Bill proposes to enact corresponding provisions for all other IP rights, § 140e PatG, § 24e GebrMG, §§ 19c, 128, 135 MarkenG, § 37e SortenschG, § 9 HalbleiterschG. However, the courts will only be entitled to order the immediate enforceability of the publication order of judgments that were not handed down by the final instance regarding infringements of copyright.[156] With respect to all other IP rights, the rights holder is bound to wait for the publication

---

153. Begründung RegE, BT-Drucks. 16/5048, p. 42.
154. *Heininger v. Bayerische Hypo- und Vereinsbank AG*, Case No. C-481/99 [2001] ECR I-9945, n. 44 et seq.; see also *Cofidis SA v. Fredout*, Case No. C-473/00 [2002] ECR I-10875.
155. M. Bohne in A-A. Wandtke and W. Bullinger (eds), *Urheberrecht* (2nd edn, München, C.H. Beck, 2006), § 103 UrhG n. 2.
156. The Explanatory Report of the Government Bill argues that there may be an exceptional overweighing interest of the author to have a decision communicated before final judgement,

until the final judgment in the interest of the opponent's reputation.[157] Furthermore, according to the proposition of the Government Bill, the authority to communicate the decision will in the future lapse within three months.

IV   ADDENDUM: REPORT OF THE COMMITTEE ON LEGAL AFFAIRS AND DELIBERATIONS OF THE BUNDESTAG

After the Committee on Legal Affairs rendered its report and recommendation on 8 April 2008, the Bundestag (German Federal Parliament) deliberated and adopted the Bill in a second and third reading on 11 April 2008. As a next step, the Bundesrat (German Federal Council) will consider the Bill. If the Federal Council voices its objection, the matter will be passed on to the Vermittlungsausschuss (Mediation Committee) and a further delay will ensue.

The deliberations of both the Committee on Legal Affairs and the Bundestag revolved around two issues: First, the right of information under Article 8 of the Directive and second, on a cap on recoverable attorney fees for cease and desist letters.

A   RIGHT OF INFORMATION

In its comment on the Government Bill, the Bundesrat had voiced three concerns regarding the transposition of Article 8 of the Directive (§ 140b PatG, § 24b GebrMG, §§ 19, 128, 135 MarkenG, § 46 GeschmMG, § 37b Sortenschutzgesetz, § 9 HalblSchG, § 101 UrhG as proposed by the Government Bill).

(1) The inconsistent use of the terms 'im geschäftlichen Verkehr' (in the course of trade) and 'in gewerblichem Ausmaß' (on a commercial scale).
(2) The proposed introduction of a court order when the information sought involves the processing of communications traffic data.
(3) The absence of a provision in the data protection acts authorizing the transmission of personal data.

1   **'In the Course of Trade' v. 'on a Commercial Scale'**

§ 101 UrhG as proposed by the Government Bill allows the holders of copyright to seek information from any infringer or, subject to qualifications, from third parties, if the infringer had acted 'im geschäftlichen Verkehr' (in the course of trade). Generally, however, the Government Bill followed the wording of the Directive and used the term 'in gewerblichem Ausmaß' (on a commercial scale).

---

cf. Begründung RegE, BT-Drucks. 16/5048, pp. 49 et seq. which refers to OLG Celle, GRUR-RR 2001, 126.
157. Begründung RegE, BT-Drucks. 16/5048, p. 42.

The Bundesrat commented that it would be desirable to use one of the two terms consistently throughout the Bill.

The Committee on Legal Affairs in its report proposed to use the term 'in gewerblichem Ausmaß' consistently, coupled with a clarification that the commercial scale could result both from the quantity and the gravity of the infringements. There were some deliberations on the appropriateness of this term in the Bundestag. In particular the Greens and the Liberal Democrats criticized that the concept of a 'commercial scale' was too vague and ambiguous, albeit drawing contrarious consequences: Whereas the Liberal Democrats proposed that the requirement of an infringement on a commercial scale be omitted, the Greens moved that the right of information be excluded if the infringer had acted in good faith (either regarding the commercial scale or regarding the entitlement to use the IP).[158] Neither of those motions received acceptance in the Bundestag. Thus, § 101(1) UrhG now reads:

> Any person who infringes copyright or any other right protected by [the Copyright Act] on a commercial scale may be called upon by the injured party to provide information regarding the origin and distribution chain [of the infringing goods] without measurable delay. The commercial scale may result both from the quantity of the infringements as well as the gravity of the infringement.

2   The Requirement of a Judicial Decree

For cases in which the information sought can only be disclosed if communications traffic data have previously been processed, the Government Bill stipulated that the injured party must first request a court order regarding the admissibility of the use of such data. This pertains in particular to requests that ISPs reveal the identity of their customers by means of an IP address which has been logged by the rights owner (i.e., the rights owner requests that the identity of an ISP customer be revealed whose computer was allocated a dynamic IP address which, at a particular point in time, was logged contacting a peer-to-peer-network). Currently, the most promising – if cumbersome – path for rights owners seeking to reveal the identity of internet users is to file a criminal complaint, upon which the access provider will reveal the identity of its customer (who, it should be born in mind, is not necessarily the infringer) during the preliminary criminal proceedings. The rights owner may then request access to the criminal files and is thus enabled to initiate infringement proceedings against the person named therein.

The Bundesrat agreed with the government's assessment that the current process is both unnecessarily time-consuming and intricate. However, the court order envisaged by the Government Bill was equally inadequate in view of the Bundesrat. The Bundesrat argued that such a court order is foreign to the existing rules of German civil procedure, puts an additional strain on the courts and burdens rights

---

158.   Beschlussempfehlung und Bericht des Rechtsausschusses, BT-Drucks. 16/8783, p. 58.

owners with considerable costs. The explanation provided by the Government Bill that the intent of introducing a judicial decree was to disencumber ISPs and telecom companies from assessing whether an infringement existed was dismissed by the Bundesrat with the argument that third parties (= access providers) are only obliged to reveal information in cases of obvious infringements. The Bundesrat's considerations were somewhat contradictory here: On the one hand, the Bundesrat argued that due to the high amount of information proceedings to be expected, the courts would be overburdened with work and the court fee of EUR 200 per request might render the request of no avail from an economic perspective. On the other hand, examining the information requests was supposedly not cumbersome for the third parties at whom the request was directed. What the Federal Council failed to acknowledge is that in the absence of a court order, it will be the ISPs who have to ascertain whether an 'obvious' infringement exists in each particular instance and who will be burdened with additional work. Since a third party disclosing information is entitled to compensation for this work according to the provisions proposed by the Government Bill, it is doubtful whether a EUR 200 court fee might not prove to be more advantageous to the rights holder (at least under the presumption that the ISPs actually scrutinize the existence of an infringement).

There was further disagreement on whether the revelation of the identity of a registered user on the basis of his or her communications traffic data clashes with the right of secrecy of telecommunications as constitutionally protected by Article 10 GG (the Basic Law). The Government Bill operated under the assumption that such a disclosure prejudices the secrecy of telecommunications, since the ISP will, in resorting to its charts, have to deduce the identity of its customer from the dynamic IP address used at a particular point in time.[159] The Bundesrat on the other hand argued that rights owners solely request the disclosure of the name and address of the ISP's contractual partner, data which by itself has no relevance to telecommunications.

By the time the Committee on Legal Affairs discussed the matter, the ECJ had handed down its decision *Promusicae*, in which it declared that it was for the Member States to find an equitable balance between the right of information under Article 8 of the Directive and the right to privacy as protected by data protection rules.[160] As a result, the parliamentary parties of the Greens and the Left proposed changes to the draft provisions on the right of information: While the Greens (focusing on ISPs as possible informants) proposed that the information to be provided should not include the disclosure of the identity of service users,[161] the Left suggested that the requirement of a court order be extended to all instances, irrespective of whether communications traffic data had to be processed in order to fulfil the information request.[162] The Christian Democrats and the Social Democrats

---

159. Most academics seem to agree with this assessment, cf. the references provided by G. Spindler, and J. Dorschel, 'Vereinbarkeit der geplanten Auskunftsansprüche gegen Internet-Provider mit EU-Recht' [2006] CR 342 et seq.
160. *Promusicae v. Telefónica de Espana*, Case No. C-275/06, 29 Jan. 2008, n. 59, <curia.eu.int>.
161. Beschlussempfehlung und Bericht des Rechtsausschusses, BT-Drucks. 16/8783, p. 57 et seq.
162. Beschlussempfehlung und Bericht des Rechtsausschusses, BT-Drucks. 16/8783, p. 61.

declared that the draft provisions of the Government Bill were expedient of their own right, and that the ECJ's decision *Promusicae* had clarified that the Member States were free to introduce such rules.[163] Accordingly, the Bundestag enacted the provisions regarding the right of information as proposed by the Government Bill.

Nonetheless, there seems to exist a consensus between the parliamentary parties to look further into the possibility of establishing a centre which acts as a clearing house and employs black box procedures,[164] such as the French example of the 'Accord Olivenne'.[165]

3   Provisions Authorizing the Data Transmission

Finally, the Federal Council had suggested to supplement the draft provisions on the right of information with a subsection each that authorized the transmission of personal data, in order to prevent the person required to disclose the information from having to breach data protection rules in the process. Currently, § 28(3) no. 1 BDSG (Federal Data Protection Act) allows for the transmission of personal data insofar as the transmission is necessary to protect the legitimate interests of third parties. However, § 14 TMG (Tele Media Act) contains specific and more restrictive legislation which precludes the recourse to § 28(3) BDSG[166] insofar as personal data of users of information services are concerned. Currently, § 14 TMG allows for the communication of personal data in the interest of the enforcement of IP rights only upon an order made by the 'competent authorities'. Following the scheme developed by the Government Bill, § 14 TMG thus allows service providers to fulfil information requests which involve the processing of communications traffic data, since the draft requires the rights owner to obtain a court order in those instances. In contrast, if the information request does not necessitate the processing of communications traffic data,[167] § 14 TMG does not authorize the ISP to transmit the data (failing an order made by competent authorities).

The Bundesrat had suggested to supplement the provisions on the right of information by subsections allowing for the transmission of personal data collected for the purpose of the conclusion and performance of the service contract (i.e., the user's name and address). For reasons undisclosed, the Committee on Legal Affairs as well as the Bundestag unfortunately failed to follow this suggestion. Thus, information services providers disclosing data on the basis of the German implementation of Article 8 of the Directive may under specific circumstances breach the data protection provision of § 14 TMG and possibly make themselves liable for damages as a consequence. In view of the legislature's failure to account

---

163. Beschlussempfehlung und Bericht des Rechtsausschusses, BT-Drucks. 16/8783, p. 57, 59.
164. Beschlussempfehlung und Bericht des Rechtsausschusses, BT-Drucks. 16/8783, p. 57 et seq.
165. Accord pour le développement et la protection des oeuvres et programmes culturels sur les nouveaux réseaux, <http://www.sacd.fr/actus/dossiers/av/docs/accord_mission_olivennes_v2.pdf>.
166. Cf. § 12(2) TMG.
167. I.e., if the rights owner requests that the identity of a customer be revealed on the basis of a user name.

for the conflict of legal obligations put on information service providers, it will be up to the courts to find a proper solution. One option lies in applying the principle of *lex posterior derogat legi priori* in the way that the new information obligations override the older § 14 TMG. Further, subsection 6 of § 140b PatG, § 24b GebrMG, §§ 19, 128, 135 MarkenG, § 101 UrhG, § 46 GeschmMG, § 37b Sortenschutzgesetz, § 9 HalblSchG as envisaged by the Government Bill should be of help: 'A person who has provided correct information without being obliged to do so […] is only liable to third parties if he/she knew that he/she was not obliged to supply the information'.

B   THE CAP ON RECOVERABLE ATTORNEY FEES FOR CEASE AND
      DESIST LETTERS

Following German case law, a rights owner sending cease and desist letters to an alleged infringer is acting as an agent of necessity because the rights owner is informing the recipient of the breach of his or her legal obligations. The recipient, who supposedly intends to live in conformity with the law, is thus enabled to cease the infringement and to avoid litigation. As a consequence, the infringer is liable to pay the injured party's attorney fees, if and insofar as the injured party was entitled to consider calling in an attorney necessary. Directive 2004/48/EC is not concerned with the matter of warning letters: Article 14 thereof solely addresses fees and costs after a judicial decision was handed down. Nonetheless, the German legislator, when implementing Directive 2004/48/EC, availed itself of the opportunity to transform case law into statute law and inserted the institution of warning letters in the draft provision of § 97a UrhG (Copyright Act). Following the Government Bill, a rights owner is supposed to send the infringer a warning letter before instituting legal proceedings in order to give the opposing party the opportunity to declare that it will in future desist from committing further infringements. Further, if the warning letter was legitimate, the recipient is liable to pay the necessary expenses (attorney fees in particular).

However, on the backdrop of developments in recent years, the government draft of § 97a UrhG also proposed a EUR 50 cap on recoverable expenses in 'straightforward cases'. The reason is the following: With the rise of the internet, rights owners and attorneys have discovered cease and desist letters as an additional means of income. There are numerous reports of attorneys sending out mass warning letters with inflated fee requests for relatively minor breaches of IP rights or competition law.[168] The courts are already trying to confine these 'warning letter floods': Following two decisions of the Federal Court of Justice in the year 2006, calling in an attorney is not 'necessary' (and thus the fee not recoverable) in straightforward instances in which the responsibility and liability for the breach of

---

168. Cf. the documentation on <www.abmahnwelle.de>. Following the report of Staatssekretär Alfred Hartenbach in Parliament, the Federal Ministry of Justice also received a high quantity of complaints.

law is obvious.[169] Instead, the injured party is held to send the warning letter itself and is unable to request compensation for its expenses.

The Government Bill sought to reinforce this case law with the proposed EUR 50 cap on recoverable attorney fees. After some debate in the Committee on Legal Affairs, where the fee cap was in particular criticized by the Liberal Democrats, there was consensus both in the Committee on Legal Affairs and in the Bundestag to retain the fee cap, but to raise it to EUR 100. § 97a (2) UrhG now reads:

> Compensation of the necessary expenses for attorney services regarding a first cease and desist letter is limited to 100 EUR in straightforward cases if the infringement was insubstantial and the infringer did not act in the course of trade.

The Committee on Legal Affairs lists the following examples in its report:[170]

– publishing a small detail of a city map on a private website without the rights owner's consent,
– publishing song lyrics on a private website without the rights owner's consent,
– publishing a photo without the rights owner's consent in an auction site listing.

C   FURTHER DEVELOPMENTS

It is now up to the Bundesrat to consider the Bill in the version enacted by the Bundestag. It is difficult to predict the outcome of those deliberations. On the one hand, the Bundestag did not follow some of the Bundesrat's proposals, most notably regarding the elimination of the requirement of a court order with respect to the processing of communications traffic data and regarding an introduction of a provision authorizing the revelation of the requested data. On the other hand, Germany is already in severe breach of its obligation to bring into force the laws necessary to comply with Directive 2004/48/EC, so the Bundesrat may decide not to prolong the process any further. At any rate, the Bundesrat does not have the power to veto the Bill, which means that even if the Bundesrat does voice its objection, the matter will be passed on to the Vermittlungsausschuss (Mediation Committee) and thus be subject to further delay, but the Act may still eventually become law in the form described herein. After the third reading of the Bill in the Bundestag, the Bundesrat (Federal Council) again deliberated upon the matter. Even though the Bundesrat reiterated its concerns regarding the transposition of Art. 8 of the Directive (supra, IV.A.), it reached the decision to abstain from a formal objection. As a result, the *Gesetz zur Verbesserung der Durchsetzung der Rechte des Geistigen Eigentums* (Act to Improve the Enforcement of Intellectual Property Rights) was adopted on 7 July 2008 and entered into force on 1 September 2008.[171]

---

169. BGH, GRUR 2007, 620 et seq.; BGH, GRUR 2007, 621 et seq. with further references.
170. Beschlussempfehlung und Bericht des Rechtsausschusses, BT-Drucks. 16/8783, p. 63.
171. Gesetz zur Verbesserung der Durchsetzung von Rechten des Geistigen Eigentums of 7 July 2008, BGBl. I, p. 1191.

Chapter 6

Conclusion

The analysis of Directive 2004/48/EU (the Directive) in this book has proceeded from point of view of examining the following: firstly, the Directive as a legal instrument of European community (EC) legislation which imposes specific obligations on Members States and secondly, the national implementation of the Directive notably as affected by principles of EC law but in particular by the substantive context of the Directive itself. That being said it is useful to place the Directive in the context of the two methods which are utilized in Community law in order to effect harmonization of national rules of procedure: on the one hand, harmonization through European Court of Justice (ECJ) case law which is decided on an ad hoc basis and which operates in the context of certain principles which circumscribe the discretion of national courts to use their own procedure: notably to the principles of effectiveness, equivalence, effective judicial protection as well as various articles of the Treaty. It was noted that certain difficulties arise from this ECJ lead harmonization which in large measure are inherent to the uncoordinated manner in which the judgments are made notably subject to references from national courts: not only an overall lack of co-ordinated purpose but a general lack of clarity as to the scope and the nature of the intervention which is required in order to ensure compliance with the aforementioned principles as they are applied to the rules of national procedure. Accordingly, harmonization through Community legislation can in principle serve to remedy certain of these difficulties notably as regards the scope and purpose of the harmonization. This is particularly the case where the legal instrument chosen, as in the instant case, is a directive where the fundamental obligation pursuant to EC Article 249 as noted is an obligation of result which is directed to the Member States, whilst the latter enjoy discretion subject to Community principles such as effective judicial protection as well as Treaty articles. However, it is submitted that in the instant case, these objectives have not been apparently fully achieved: that is assuming that the need for intervention has been demonstrated cogently through preliminary investigation notably based upon enforcement deficits caused by national procedure used in the protection of national intellectual property rights, there remains the next step: namely, the a clear definition of the reasons for scope of the Community intervention in terms of harmonization of national procedure. It is arguably at least in part, by reason of this failure to clearly define and demonstrate the need for a specific level of harmonization that the substantive obligations which are contained in certain of the articles of the Directive are not as clear as they could be: accordingly, it would seem that the uncertainty as to both the nature and the scope of the substantive obligations in Articles 4, 10, 11 and 13 of the Directive find their origin in the original failure of the Commission to have established clearly the extent to which harmonization was necessary in order to achieve the objective of effective enforcement of intellectual property rights by national procedure. Accordingly, it would seem that the primary if not definitive remedy for such uncertainty as to the determination of the scope of the substantive obligations notably in those articles is to be found in references to the ECJ pursuant to EC Article 234. Therefore, by reason of the uncertainty of the substantive scope and nature of the substantive obligation the fundamental effectiveness of the Directive as a form of legislative harmonization in contrast to the ECJ case law lead harmonization has been diminished.

A. From the point of view of an instrument of European Union (EU) legislation, it was noted that the substantive content of the Directive concerns the national rules of civil procedure as used for the enforcement of EU and national IP rights. In so far as its subject matter is in fact the harmonization or at least, partial harmonization of national procedure, the Directive can be said to be relatively exceptional given that the subject matter of most directives turns on substantive as opposed to procedural law. As noted, the purpose of the Directive is to harmonize the national rules of procedure but only to a minimum extent. Accordingly, each article of the Directive was examined in the course of the previous chapters, in conjunction with the relevant Recitals in order to ascertain as clearly as possible the nature of the substantive obligation which was thereby created. Similarly, with respect to what might be termed the ancillary obligations also created by the Directive.

Having thus established the specific substantive and ancillary obligations which the Directive creates both in terms of the actual wording of each of its articles as well as that of the various pertinent Recitals, the implementation thereof was then considered. The process of implementation both when the content of a fundamental or hard core obligation is substantive law or as in the instant case, procedural law, is subject to the same EU principles: that is the national measures which implement a directive must be clear, effective and ensure its effective legal implementation irrespective of whether substantive or procedural law constitutes the substantive obligation thereof. As is recalled, the national implementing measures must be clear particularly where rights are involved. Furthermore, in the case of the instant Directive , it was submitted that the substantive obligations create procedural rights for holders of intellectual property rights: arguably the existence of these rights is determined by the clarity with which the actual nature of the right and the class of the beneficiary thereof is defined within the various articles of the Directive in conjunction with Recitals. In particular, it was submitted that Article 4 provides for the creation of the procedural right of standing for four classes of beneficiaries as defined within subsections (a)-(d): that is, rights holders, exclusive licensees, intellectual property collective rights management societies, and professional defence societies. However, the actual nature of the rights in terms of the specific form of the procedural content is to be defined by the national rules used for implementation: that is, the Member States enjoy discretion with respect to the implementation of articles of a directive in order to ensure that the rights are indeed implemented clearly, effectively and in a manner which ensures effective legal protection all the while conforming with the actual text of the directive and ultimately Treaty principles. The significance of the existence of the rights created notably by Article 4 of the Directive is that correct implementation requires that they be implemented with particular clarity so as to ensure, among other things, that the beneficiaries of the rights understand clearly their legal entitlement in terms of scope of the protection of which they benefit. As noted earlier, ultimately the scope of this article and in particular sections (c) and (d) will no doubt need to be interpreted by the ECJ in order to ascertain whether correct implementation thereof requires the introduction of standing for the categories of defined therein notably in the national systems where such standing does not exist. As previously noted, the remedies considered within this book for the incorrect implementation or the non-implementation of articles of the Directive either entirely or individually involve the concept of interpretation in conformity and Member State liability for damages. It was felt that among other things that the remedy of direct effect was not available for the articles of the Directive by reason of their lack of legal clarity and also the restriction upon horizontal invocability of the relevant articles and Recitals thereof inherent with the concept of direct effect.

As noted earlier, Articles 10, 11 and 13 in conjunction with Article 3 of the Directive would seem to potentially pose a problem as to their scope notably in regard to implementation of English national procedure. It would seem that it in order to utilize effectively the doctrine of consistent interpretation with respect to those articles notably it may well be necessary to make a reference to the ECJ pursuant to Article 234: that is only such a reference to the ECJ will suffice in order to definitively determine whether such articles have been adequately implemented or indeed as it would appear, implementation has been inadequate thereby requiring adjustments through the application of the doctrine of consistent interpretation.

B. Furthermore, as also noted earlier, no attempt has been made within this book to analyze the implementation of the Directive in terms of national law from the comparative legal perspective. As noted in the Introduction to this book, it is felt that the comparative approach itself will not avail in order to assist in understanding the degree of harmonization which is to be achieved by or ought to be achieved by the Directive in the instant case. Arguably, the most effective approach is to analyze the implementation at least in the case of the Dutch and English procedure and the German implementation separately and individually in relation to each of the substantive and ancillary obligations as set forth in the Directive. It is only in this manner that it is possible to ascertain whether or not the Directive has been adequately implemented in accordance not only with the substantive obligations of the Directive but in conjunction with Community law principles such as effectiveness, clarity and effective legal protection. Each national implementation is effected individually and arguably is best considered therefore separately from the implementation effected by other Member States. Arguably, it is only a separate and individual consideration of each of the national implementations which will permit an identification of the problems in relation to not only the substantive and ancillary obligations of the Directive but in relation to the fundamental principles of each of the national legal systems involved. In short, it is submitted that at least in first instant a comparison of the implementations may well serve to obscure the various problems and inadequacies of the individual national implementations.

II   DUTCH IMPLEMENTATION AND ITS PROBLEMS

During the drafting of the Directive in the Netherlands doubts were uttered as to whether the effective combating of piracy and the enforcement of intellectual property rights need more procedural measures and sanctions in Dutch law than the existing domestic enforcement instruments already provide. There was also some concern about the provision which introduces the common law principle of 'pre-trial' disclosure, because 'pre-trial' disclosure makes judicial procedures, especially concerning intellectual property, too expensive and too lengthy.

Due to the late implementation of the Directive, the Dutch courts already applied Article 14 on legal costs in an anticipatory way. Article 14 differed substantially from the general practice in domestic civil cases, in which a restricted maximum amount of compensation for costs exists. Under Article 14 sometimes even full compensation for all costs was and is awarded. Article 14 of the Directive was implemented in Article 1019h Code of Civil Procedure (CCP). Up until now the Dutch courts have not acted consistently in compensating costs. The reason for this inconsistency is the double-checking which is applied to the reasonableness and the proportionality of the costs, on the one hand, and the fairness of those costs, on the other. This leaves a lot of room for the courts to determine the costs, and as a consequence legal certainty is at stake.

The Dutch legislator implemented the Directive in a new Title 15, Articles 1019-1019i CCP, in Book 3 of the CCP, entitled 'Proceedings concerning intellectual property rights'. Creating a new Title made it possible to leave the general provisions on enforcement in the CCP undisturbed. The new Title 15 in the CCP has a supplementary character with regard to all civil infringement procedures concerning intellectual property rights. The general provisions of the CCP are applicable as far as Title 15 does not determine differently. By creating a new title only for intellectual property rights, the Dutch legislator found an answer to the critical remarks aimed at the Directive's proposal, namely that the infringement of intellectual property rights is more serious than an infringement of other property rights.

Alongside Article 14, the only Directive provisions which led to practical problems concerning their implication are the Dutch articles implementing Article 7. Article 7 of the Directive which deals with provisional measures for preserving evidence was transposed in Articles 1019b-1019d CCP. This provision on the 'seizure of evidence' is completely new in Dutch civil procedure. It has also led to some uncertainty. In current legal practice a discussion is taking place about the character of the seizure for the purpose of preserving evidence, especially concerning the following question: does this seizure only mean preserving the evidence or also the right of inspection, which is considered to be too far-reaching (see subsection 3.4.4.5).

Apart from these few remarks, practice seems to be satisfied with the working of the Directive and the way in which it is implementated in the Netherlands.

III   ENGLISH IMPLEMENTATION AND ITS PROBLEMS

Generally, it may be said that the English method of implementation of the Directive involves, on the one hand, specially adopted legislation and, on the other, the use of pre-existing legislation particularly the Civil Procedure Rules (CPR) and the Supreme Court Act (SCA) (1981). Whilst in principle it would seem that legislation which is specifically adopted may implement various articles of the Directive more effectively in the sense of more clearly indicating, in particular, certain rights for the beneficiaries thereof, in reality the situation is not so obvious. Indeed, it would appear that correct and adequate implementation depends on the individual articles of the Directive and the nature of the pre-existing legislation. Furthermore, one must consider the operation of the concept of consistent interpretation, notably, in the sense of judicial implementation as applied in each particular case: the question therefore becomes the same as for specifically adopted legislation: namely, whether or not the pre-existing legislation notably when interpreted in conformity by the national courts in conformity with the Directive ensure effective implementation in the sense of legal clarity, effectiveness and effective judicial protection.[1]

As noted earlier, Article 4 (c) and (d) of the Directive may pose a problem if subsequent to an eventual reference, the ECJ decides that the obligations contained therein require the introduction of standing for the classes of beneficiaries which are described therein. As previously observed in Chapter 5, there are two possible interpretations of that article: one is that it does not require Member States to introduce a representative action for the groups described in sections (c) and (d) of Article 4. The other possible interpretation is that Article 4 (c) and (d)

---

1.   S. Prechal, *Directives in EC Law* (Oxford: OUP, 2005), op. cit., 77.

defines with sufficient clarity a rudimentary form of procedural right of standing for the category of beneficiaries which are described in both those subsections. However, by reason of their being in rudimentary form the rights can only be realized through implementation in national law which requires, among other things, the following: namely, that the Member States exercise their discretion within the confines, notably, of the text of Directive and in particular of Article 4 (c) and (d) in conjunction with principles such as effective judicial protection and eventual articles of the Treaty. Furthermore, in the event that the ECJ were to decide that the Member States were obliged to ensure that their national procedure provided for such standing, then in the instant case, it would seem that the remedial mechanism of consistent interpretation would be of no avail by reason of the absence of relevant national legislation. Accordingly, it may be necessary to consider an eventual action in damages in the following circumstances: namely, if the ECJ were to decide that those articles required introduction of such standing, failure to so to within the requisite time would correspond to the requisite principles: that is, specifically a serious breach; it would remain to establish in the particular case whether any damage were caused.

In contrast to Article 4 (c) and (d), the doctrine of interpretation in conformity would seem to apply with respect to Article 9 (1) notably as regards the requirement that the merits of the case form part of the criterion to be considered by the national court with respect to the granting of an interlocutory injunction. It would appear that the concept of interpretation in conformity could be used in this context rather more as part of what might be termed judicial implementation through the principle of conformity as opposed to actual remedial interpretation by means of the principle of conformity: that is, by reason of the fact that the possibility of using the merits of the case already exists in English case law the application of the doctrine requires, therefore, only that the national court provide an interpretation of this existing case law in conformity with the Directive in order to ensure effective and adequate implementation of Article 9 (3).

The final problem encountered in the implementation in English law concerns Articles 3 and 14 of the Directive and notably the rights involving costs of procedure, that is, access to justice and to a fair trial in terms of costs. In this regard, it was noted that the devices for funding litigation such as the conditional fee agreements which in England provide for a 100% uplift can be shifted to the losing party irrespective of whether the overall amount of costs thereby becomes disproportionate would be subject to remedial interpretation in conformity. Accordingly, it would seem that the application of this principle may require that the national court exercise its discretion pursuant to the SCA 1981 so as to ensure conformity with Articles 3 and 14 of the Directive. Therefore, it may be that such an interpretation in conformity with the Directive would lead the national court to not shift the 100% uplift to the losing party by means of the indemnity rule. In so doing, the court would specifically not apply either section 9.1 or section 11.9 of the Practice Direction for CPR 44: that is, the court would exercise its discretion pursuant to section 51 (SCA) (1981) and section 27 A (6) of the Access to Justice Act (AJA) (1999) so as not to shift the costs involving the success fee thereby avoiding the consequence of section 9.1 and the inclusion of the success fee which according to section 11.9 need not comply with the principle of proportionality. In short, it is submitted that in order to correctly implement Articles 3 and 14 of the Directive, following the principle of consistent interpretation in light of von Colson and, notably, Marleasing[2] the national court called upon to interpret national law is required to do so, as far as possible, in light of the wording and purpose of the Directive. Such an interpretation would arguably prove to be necessary in order to ensure compliance with the principle of effective protection of judicial rights and notably that of access to the courts as guaranteed by European Convention on Human Rights (ECHR) Article 6.1 as exemplified in the case of Airey.[3]

It is submitted that judicial interpretation in conformity of the relevant pre-existing legislation herein cited with the Directive would lead to the following implementation: that is, interpretation in conformity with both Articles 14 and 3 of the Directive and in particular with the principle of effective judicial protection as reflected in ECHR Article 6 as in the earlier noted case of Airey, would lead to the court exercising its discretion pursuant to section 51 of the SCA (1981) and CPR 3 (2) (m) to establish a fee cap in a manner which was not restricted by the principle established by Gage J. in Smart:[4] namely, that there will be no requirement that the jurisdiction is exercisable only where there is a real risk that the costs incurred by a litigant may bet out of hand.

Finally, it might be that some legislative modification of the CPR in the form of fixed costs may be required in order to implement Articles 3 and 14 of the Directive from the point of view of not only effectiveness but also legal certainty, clarity and perhaps above all, to ensure conformity with the principle of effective legal protection of rights as provided in such cases as Unibet[5] and Airey. As was observed previously, fixed costs represent what might be termed the potentially most restrictive method of controlling costs as opposed to mandatory maximum and or minimum fees. Nevertheless, it would seem that the advantage of the fixed costs would be the following; in Airey, the European Court of Human Rights (ECtHR) held that it was the responsibility of the State to ensure effective access to the legal system. Fulfilment of this obligation might in certain circumstances involve the provision of legal aid. However, in other circumstances, the obligation may involve the simplification of the rules of civil procedure. As noted earlier, the CPR represents the result of the attempt to simplify the rules of civil procedure in England and Wales. Accordingly, it would seem that the only method procedurally which remains available in order to control costs given that the mechanisms of budgeting and cost capping in themselves have been observed notably by Lord

---

2. *Marleasing*, Case No. C-106/ 89 (1990) ECR I 4135 op. cit.
3. *Airey v. Ireland applic*, 6289/73 (1979) ECHRR (32)305 op. cit.
4. *Smart v. East Cheshire NHS Trust* (2003) EWHC AB, Case No. SK 1700 41.
5. *Unibet* Case No. C-432/05 (2007) ECR I 2271, date of judgment 13 Mar. 2007 <www.curia.europa.eu>.

Hoffmann to be insufficient is the use of some form of fixed costs or fixed maximum costs which arguably will comply effectively with the principle of judicial protection of rights notably as illustrated in Airey. It may be that this principle of effective judicial protection expressed in the cases of Airey and recently Unibet not only justifies but may indeed require some form of fixed maximum costs given that the other methods of controlling costs such as the reform of the CPR and case management have signally failed. Accordingly, some more direct method of controlling the costs would seem to be required in order to specifically ensure that the implementation of the Directive with respect to costs as provided by Articles 3 and 14 of the Directive is not only clear and effective but most significantly ensures effective judicial protection of the rights of litigants, and notably defendants, in terms of costs. Therefore, it may possibly be that in order ensure clarity in the transposition of Articles 3 and 14 some type of fixed maximum fees at least are required which are capable of ensuring not only clarity but also conformity with the principles of proportionality as well as that of protective judicial protection as it applies to costs.

CPR 44.4 (2) provides:

> Where the amount of costs is to be assessed on the standard basis, the court will
>
> a) only allow costs which are proportionate to the matters in issue; and
> b) resolve any doubt which it may have as to whether costs were reasonably incurred or reasonable and proportionate in amount in favour of the paying party

As observed previously, it would seem that consistent interpretation of this rule with notably Article 3 (2) of the Directive which, as recalled, imposes a substantive obligation on Member States to ensure that 'Those measure, procedure and remedies shall be ... proportionate ...' will also require that CPR 44.4 (2) be effectively applied. This, however, is in the sense that overall the method used for funding litigation is proportionate to the end which is pursued, namely, the increase of access to justice.[6] It would appear that effective application of CPR 44.4 (2) in turn will require that cost capping and cost estimates provided at the allocation stage be effectively implemented by the Patent Court, as the national court, in order to ensure compliance with the wording of Article 3 (2) of the

---

6. See for example, *Suid – Hollandse*, Case No. C 174/05 (2006) ECR I 2443 at para. 28, and *Alrosa*, Case No. T-170/06, unreported judgment in date of 11 Jul. 2007 at para. 98 for a definition of proportionality; G. De Burca observes 'Proportionality in EC Law' in *Yearbook of European Law* 13 (1993): 105 at 146 concerning ECJ case law on proportionality: 'there appear to be three stages in the proportionality enquiry: ... first whether the measure was an appropriate and effective way of achieving this legitimate aim; second whether the measure was a necessary way of achieving its aim in that there was no less restrictive alternative and thirdly, whether even if the first two stages are satisfied the adverse effect on the interest or right affected was disproportionate or excessive when weighed against the aim of the measure'.

Directive as it pertains to proportionality. The judicial implementation of this article through consistent interpretation will also require that the principle of effective judicial protection be respected as noted earlier in order to ensure access to justice in terms of costs.

Finally, the remedy of action for damages against the State was considered. Arguably this remedy would only be available in the event that the doctrine of interpretation in conformity proved to be ineffective in both the interpretative and remedial sense.[7] It would appear, on the contrary, that interpretation in conformity may render the implementation of Articles 3 and 14 of the Directive effective in so far as national legislation currently exists. To the extent however, that consistent interpretation, notably, both through judicial implementation and in remedial application do not suffice to ensure effective enforcement of the aforementioned Articles 3 and 14, it would be appropriate to consider the possibility of an action in damages. Moreover it is not clear that the concept of State liability would be effective notably with respect to Articles 3 and possibly Article 14. Indeed, it is submitted that in the instant case, the wording of the Directive does not define the category of the right sufficiently clearly: that is, although the wording does provide for a right for beneficiaries that procedure 'shall not be unnecessarily costly' the Member State enjoys considerable discretion in the manner and form in which the right is to be implemented. Accordingly, it was concluded that the Directive does not define sufficiently clearly the category of the right so as to permit an action for damages. Finally, causation can only be assessed in light of the actual facts of the case albeit it would appear that it is for the ECJ to decide on the nature thereof given that causation forms one of the components of the conditions for liability of a Member State.[8]

A   MEASURES RESULTING FROM A DECISION ON THE MERITS OF THE CASE

As noted earlier it is convenient to group under this heading the measures which are provided by Articles 10, 11 and 13 of the Directive in so far as they result from the finding of a merits on the substantive cause of action for a breach of intellectual property rights. It was noted that Article 10 thereof provides: '… that appropriate measures be taken with regard to goods that they have found to be infringing an intellectual property right … ': clearly an infringement of the substantive rights must have been made.

---

7. S. Prechal, *Directives in EC Law*, 2nd edn (Oxford: OUP, 2006), op. cit., 301, see *Miret*, Case No. C-334/92 (1993) ECR I-6911, *Faccini Dori*, Case No. C-91/92 (1994) ECR I-3325, *Carbonair*, Case No. C-131/97 (1999) ECR I-1103, and *Dorsch*, Case No. C-54/96 (1997) ECR I-4961 would seem to indicate that it is only if direct effect or consistent interpretation are impossible that State liability may be considered.
8. *Brasserie du Pêcheur*, Joined Cases Nos C-46/93 and C-48/93 (1996) ECR I-1029.

Article 11 declares: ' … that where a judicial decision is taken finding an infringement of an intellectual property right …'

Article 13 establishes: ' … Member States shall ensure that the competent judicial authorities … shall order the infringer who knowingly, or with reasonable grounds to know, engaged in an infringing activity …' clearly presupposes an infringement finding.

More particularly, it was submitted that in order to ensure that the procedural rights which are involved in the aforementioned articles may be effectively implemented pursuant to Article 3 (1) and (2) of the Directive it is necessary that the court ensure that it be able to evaluate expert evidence adequately: that is, the finding of infringement is dependent upon the judge's ability to evaluate the expert evidence, particularly in the sense of understanding the scientific terminology involved with intellectual property. This is notably so in cases where the trial judge does not possess a scientific background which would facilitate comprehending and evaluating the expert evidence which may be presented before the court. Accordingly, it would appear that following in particular Recitals 3 and 17 coupled with Article 3 of the Directive, it is necessary in such cases for the court to consider using its discretion in order to appoint an assessor pursuant to CPR 35.15.[9]

As noted earlier It would seem, therefore, that the elimination of CPR 35.15 (3) and (4) may be required by application of the doctrine of consistent interpretation notably with respect to Article 3 of the Directive coupled with compliance with EU principles such as, that of legal clarity, full effect[10] and effective judicial protection of rights so as to ensure that the operation of the assessor comes squarely within the ambit of the Supreme Court Act (1981) (SCA) and the County Courts Act (1984) (CCA). Following this analysis, the restriction of CPR 35.15 to the parameters of the enabling statutes ensures, thereby, that the role of the assessor is in turn limited to one of assisting the judge to take judicial notice of the meaning of technical words. It is submitted that this restriction of the role of the assessor ensures, thereby, the incorporation of its functions into those of the tribunal. It would appear, therefore, that the assessor operating in this manner may contribute to ensuring that Articles 3, 10, 11 and 13 of the Directive are enforced and implemented in a manner which also complies with the aforementioned EU principles such as effective judicial protection, full effect and legal clarity. Similarly, in order to ensure more fully the reduction in the scope of the assessor which would result from the removal of CPR 35.15 (3) and (4), arguably, the doctrine of consistent interpretation may require an amendment of Practice Direction (PD) 7.4:[11] specifically, the words 'copies of

---

9.   Sir L. Blom-Cooper (ed.) *Experts in the Civil Courts*, Expert Witness Institute (Oxford: OUP, 2006), Ch. 8, 113-117.

10. *Commission v. Germany*, Case No. 29/84 (1985) ECR 1661 para. 18, *Commission v. UK*, Case No. 340/96 (1999) ECR I 2023.

11. L. Blom-Cooper, 'Experts and Assessors: Past Present and Future', *CJQ* 341 (2002): 352 (n. 11 *supra*) argues that the 'advice' which the assessor may provide to the judge pursuant to CPR

any report prepared by the assessor will be sent to each of the parties' would be removed in order to more effectively prevent the production of evidence by an assessor. In the event that the judge were to feel that his judgment is likely to be influenced by the advice of the assessor with respect to the meaning of particular words then it may be appropriate that he indicate to the parties the nature of this advice before judgment. This will more easily enable the parties to exercise their rights of defence in the following manner: first, they are indirectly able to respond to the assessor's advice by commenting thereupon to the judge before judgment despite the exclusion of oral cross-examination of the assessor by section 7.4 of the Practice Direction: and secondly, the parties are able to use this information given by the judge in order to assist in forming eventual grounds of appeal from the judgment. Accordingly, the rights of the defence would appear to be adequately protected by a combination of the aforementioned two provisions: namely, the possibility for the parties to respond directly although not through oral cross-examination of the assessor to the information contained in his written report prior to the entry of judgment: and additionally, the opportunity of using the judge's written comments to assist in making an appeal against the judgment where he relied upon the information provided by the assessor in making his judgment. Finally, one must note, however, that it may be necessary to make a reference to the ECJ pursuant to Article 234 in order to confirm the exact scope of the substantive rights contained within Articles 10, 11 and 13 in order to ensure that their scope indeed requires what is setforth herein as the effective form of their implementation.

B   PROBLEMS WITH LEGAL PROFESSIONAL PRIVILEGE, EXPERT WITNESS IMMUNITY, RIGHTS OF THE DEFENCE AND THE EVALUATION OF EXPERT EVIDENCE BY A JUDGE

As noted earlier, in order to ensure compliance with Article 3 (1) and (2) of the Directive implementation of Articles 10, 11 and 13 in so far as they involve taking measures which result from a decision on the merits of the case, may require the use of an assessor in certain circumstances in order to assist a judge to understand expert evidence. However, it may be that the ability of the judge to assess evidence, and notably with the assistance of an assessor, may be undermined along with possibly the rights of the defence, by a combination of a legal profession privilege and the immunity of expert witnesses in contravention of Article 3 (1) and (2) of the Directive. The eventual solution to this problem would be through the doctrine of consistent interpretation preceded by a reference to the ECJ pursuant to EC Article 234 in order to establish the exact scope and nature of the substantive obligations in Article 3 (1) and (2) in relation to those Articles 10, 11 and 13.

35.15 in fact is evidence: 'Under rule 35.15 the "advice" will qualify as evidence (35.15 (4) (b)) and Practice Direction 7.4 and to the extent that a pre-trail report from the assessor is directed by the court, the parties will have sight and the facility to make use of its contents.'

1 Disclosure of Expert Reports

As was noted earlier the CPR sought to solve various difficulties which Lord Woolf identified in both his Interim[12] and Final[13] Reports and notably those arising from the partiality of expert evidence presented in an adversarial fashion. In reality these difficulties were of two orders;[14] first, that the adversarial use of experts tended to provide partisan expert opinion favourable to the instructing and paying party rather than presenting an objective opinion with which the court could evaluate the matters in dispute; and second, that the costs involved in the pre-CPR adversarial experts were high and apparently not subject to effective control.[15] While the second problem may have been in some measure controlled by the measures introduced by the CPR whereby the extent of the use of expert evidence and its form are controlled by the judge, arguably the partisan nature of evidence presented in an adversarial manner remains. In order to more effective control and reduce the partisan element of expert evidence presented in an adversarial manner.

CPR 35.10 (3) was adopted. It is recalled that this rule provides:

(1) The expert's report must state the substance of all material instructions, whether written or oral, on the basis of which the report was written.

As was noted the Court of Appeal in Jackson[16] interpreted the expression 'all material instructions' narrowly simultaneously retaining a wide scope for Legal Professional Privilege (LPP).

Furthermore, CPR 35.10 (4) provides:

The instructions referred to in paragraph (3) shall not be privileged against disclosure but the court will not, in relation to those instructions –

a. order disclosure of any specific document; or
b. permit questioning in court, other than by a party who instructed the expert, unless it is satisfied that there are reasonable grounds to consider that statement of instructions given under paragraph (3) to be inaccurate or incomplete.

---

12. Lord Woolf, *Access to Justice, Interim Report* (1995), Expert Evidence para. 33.
13. Lord Woolf, *Access to Justice, Final Report* (1996), Expert Evidence para. 37, ibid.
14. A. Zuckerman 'Editor's Note: Disclosure of Expert Reports', *CJQ* 24 (2005): 293, D. Davies 'Current Issues: Expert Evidence: Court Appointed Experts', *CJQ* 23 (2004): 367. A. Edis QC 'Privilege and Immunity: Problems of Expert Evidence', *CJQ* 26 (2007): 40, D. Dwyer 'The effective Management of Bias in Civil Expert Evidence', *CJQ* 26 (2007): 57.
15. A. Edis, QC 'Privilege and Immunity: Problems of Expert Evidence', *CJQ* 26 (2007): 40 observes, op. cit., at 42:

    Expert evidence is a major source of difficulty in dealing justly with cases; It is expensive and causes delay in the proceedings while it is obtained and disclosed. These problems are probably inevitable and the new power to control the admissibility of expert evidence and to impose conditions on its being adduced is probably as much as can be done to address them.

16. *Jackson v. Marley Davenport Ltd* (2004) EXCA Div. 1225.

Longmore LJ then went on to interpret CPR 35. 10(4) in the following manner: namely, that communications between an expert and his instructing solicitors were protected form disclosure by LPP. The essential difficulty however with the narrow interpretation of 'all material instructions' coupled by a what might be termed a wide interpretation LPP as performed by Longmore LJ is as follows: the various exchanges between the expert and notably the party and his legal counsel arguably forms overall the evidence which is placed before the judge and eventually the assessor as well as to the opposite side. It is clear that there are two objectives and goals which must be balanced here: on the one hand LPP exists in order to ensure that a party be able to feel free to discuss his case with the expert, correct inaccuracies, change or modified theories in order to prepare his case as effectively as possible; on the other hand however, there arguably must be some proportionality in the protection granted by means of the LPP so an to ensure that the court is able to effectively evaluate if necessary with an assessor the expert opinion which is provided and that similarly the opponent be able to ensure his rights of the defence. In short, it is submitted that it is necessary for the court to be able to evaluate the expert evidence in light of the entirety of the instructions given to the expert as well as the communications which have taken place in the course of the preparation of the report which is presented to the judge as expert evidence. That is, it is not only the initial instructions which have helped the expert's opinion but also the comments which the party and his legal adviser's make on the expert's various drafts prior to the drafting of the final evidence. In short an appreciation of all of this material is required in order for the court to evaluate the evidence and for the opposite side to exercise his rights of defence. Accordingly, the narrow interpretation of the Court of Appeal in Jackson and in particular the opinion of Longmore LJ also does not enhance the ability of the CPR 35.10 (3) and (4) to reduce the potential partiality and partisanship of expert evidence arguably in violation of Article 3 (1) and (2) of the Directive: that is, it is submitted that the restrictive interpretation of CPR 35.10 (3) so as to preclude all of the communications which served to form the expert evidence may contravene the principle of effective judicial protection as in Steffensen[17] in which the ECJ established that evidential rules must comply with the requirements arising from fundamental rights such as Article 6 (1) of the ECHR. Therefore, in short, it is submitted that restricting the access of the court and the opposing party to all of the relevant communications involved in the formation of the expert evidence in favour of a wide LPP to protect one of the parties is a disproportionate as opposed to a proportionate assessment of the rules and objectives which they seek to attain: that is, the extent of the protection granted by the wide scope of LPP in Jackson is not justifiable in that its consequence is an excessive restriction of the ability of both the court and the opposing party to evaluate the quality of the expert evidence particularly with respect to partiality of the expert.

---

17. *Steffensen*, Case No. C-276/01 (2003) ECR I-3735 in particular at para. 80, see *Evans*, Case C-63/01 (2003) ECR I 14447 for an aspect of fair hearing.

However, even if the interpretation of CPR 35.10 (3) by the Court of Appeal in Jackson were found not to contravene Article 3 (1) and (2) of the Directive and in particular the principle of effective judicial protection, it is submitted that an eventual contravention may result in the following conditions: that is, where the current interpretation of CPR 35.10 (3) is considered in conjunction with the other element which characterizes expert evidence albeit not formally part of the CPR: namely, the immunity of experts. Practically speaking the immunity results in the absence of any formal method for enforcement of the duty of impartiality which the CPR seeks to enforce, that is, by reason of expert immunity. It is recalled that the objective of the immunity is apparently to ensure that expert witnesses should not be deterred from assisting the court by fear of possible consequences if any party suffers damages by reason of their opinions. It is submitted that the expert immunity when coupled with the restrictive interpretation of CPR 35.10 (3) produces a system in which of expert evidence which disproportionately undermines the ability of the court as well as the opposing party in terms of his rights of defence to deal among other things with partiality and partisan evidence. Accordingly, this combination of expert immunity and the restrictive interpretation of CPR 35.10 (3) can be said to contravene Article 3 (a) and (b) of the Directive and in particular the principle of effective judicial protection and proportionality.

In order to ensure adequate implementation of Articles 3 (a) and (b) and 10, 11 and 13, and notably the principle of effective judicial protection, it is submitted, that following the doctrine of interpretation in conformity, it will be necessary for the English court to interpret CPR 35.10 (3) and in particular the expression 'all material instructions' widely so as to include eventually all communications oral and written between the expert, the client and the legal adviser which have lead to and influenced the expert evidence tendered by the parties in litigation: that is, at least to the degree necessary to ensure that the court if necessary accompanied by the assessor and the opposing party are able to evaluate the accuracy of the evidence so as to comply with Article 3 (a) and (b) of the Directive and in particular the principles of effective judicial protection and proportionality.[18] It is clear however, that such it would be necessary to verify once again the exact scope of Articles 3 (a) and (b), 10, 11 and 13 by means of a reference to the ECJ pursuant to EC Article 234 before any definitive view could be formed on the adequacy of

---

18.   Quaere to what extent solution to the problem of impartiality of experts remains that which was proposed initially by Lord Woolf in his Interim Report at paras 20-23, namely a court appointed expert, however, with its use being extended to multitrack commercial litigation. Sir A Clarke MR observes in his Foreword to Sir L Blom-Cooper QC (ed.), *Experts in Civil Courts* (Oxford: OUP, 2006), op. cit., viii. 'The second point is that I sometimes wonder whether the adversarial process is a sensible way of putting expert evidence before the court.' A. Jolowicz 'A note on Experts', *CJQ* 23 (2004): 408 at 409 speaking of a court appointed expert observes: 'On the other hand it is suggested that the present English rules on expert evidence which attempt to get away from the adversary system without offending to much the die hard supporters of our traditional system cannot be expected to survive for ever. When the time comes for an experiment with a new system, the solution is to hand.'

implementation of these articles by the relevant national procedure and the extent
to which the concept of consistent interpretation may apply so as to effect the possible changes described herein.

IV   GERMAN IMPLEMENTATION AND ITS PROBLEMS

Up until 7 July 2008, the most significant problem with the German implementation of Directive 2004/48/EC was that no legislation had been enacted to adapt
the German law to the requirements of community law. Despite the fact that all
of the provisions of the Directive were in some way or another already reflected
in German procedural or substantive rules, it was beyond dispute that the existing
legislation was insufficient. The *Gesetz zur Verbesserung der Durchsetzung der
Rechte des Geistigen Eigentums*, which entered into force on 1 September, was
enacted subsequently to the submission of the manuscript for this book. However,
the Government Bill as discussed in Chapter 5 (with the modifications expounded
in section IV. thereof) fully reflects the eventual Act.

Before the Act entered into force, German courts were held to interpret the
existing legislation in light of Directive 2004/48/EC. There was little need for
action with respect to Art. 4, Art. 5 (regarding copyright), Art. 8 (insofar as the
information is required from an infringer), Art. 9, Art. 11, Art. 12 (which is an
optional instrument), Art. 13, Art. 14 and Art. 15 (with regard to copyright and
designs). The presumption of ownership for the owners of rights related to copyright (Art. 5) and the publication of judicial decisions with respect to intellectual
property other than copyright and designs could easily be achieved with the help
of an analogy to the existing legislation. Regarding orders for the presentation or
preservation of evidence (Art. 6, Art. 7), the German case law was in the middle
of a profound transformation, a change which was inspired by TRIPs as well as
by Directive 2004/48/EC. As both the Federal Court of Justice's decision
'Restschadstoffentfernung' and the so-called 'Düsseldorf Practice' documented,
the courts were well-aware of their responsibility to align the German law with
Community law by means of a consistent interpretation. Nonetheless, it was
extremely controversial whether an injured party possessed a right of information
against other parties than the infringer, in particular intermediaries such as internet service providers. Finally, a right to the recall and removal from the channels
of commerce was difficult to construe under the existing legislation; arguably
though, the practical need for such an instrument was relatively minor.

*The Gesetz zur Verbesserung der Durchsetzung der Rechte des Geistigen
Eigentums* tries to keep the changes initiated by the Directive to a minimum.
Insofar as the general rules of civil law or civil procedure already comply with
the requirements of the Directive, the law is left as it stands. In some instances, the
Explanatory Report to the Government Bill goes a long way to explain why the
existing or only slightly modified legislation corresponds to the provisions of
the Directive, despite a different wording and different criteria. Where the previous status quo was clearly insufficient, the new act brings about closely similar

changes to the various intellectual property acts. The legislature was very cautious not to generate any systematic changes: even in instances in which the Directive clearly prescribes a procedural measure the Act introduces substantive instruments, if equivalent measures were previously regarded as a matter of substance in German law (i.e. Art. 6, Art. 9(2) sent. 2). The prominent downside of this approach is that substantive provisions necessarily employ different criteria than procedural rules. Consequently, there is considerable room for debate whether the implementation truly effects a faithful transposition of the Directive. Finally, the Act does not rise to the challenge of introducing new rules for previously unchartered territory. This concerns the preservation of evidence according to Art. 7 of the Directive on the one hand. And it pertains to the protection of confidential information on the other hand – in this respect, the Act's silence is a particularly pity, since the envisaged 'in camera' proceedings considerably affect the fundamental right to a fair hearing as protected by Art. 103(1) of the German constitution (Grundgesetz). On the positive side, the introduction of a right to the production of documents and inspection of items (§ 140c PatG and the corresponding provisions in other IP statutes) serves to clarify the dubious legal status which resulted from the failed decision 'Druckbalken'. Finally, the transposition of the right of information (Art. 8 of the Directive) was particularly debated as regards information sought from parties other than the infringer. There is a lingering disagreement between the Bundestag and Bundesrat whether the requirement of a court order is an appropriate prerequisite in instances in which communications traffic data is processed. Moreover, the Bundestag failed to take into account the continuing conflict with data protection provisions which the cour

Appendix
Text of Directive 2004/48/EC

Corrigendum to Directive 2004/48/EC of the European Parliament and of the Council of 29 April 2004 on the enforcement of intellectual property rights

(Official Journal of the European Union L 157 of 30 April 2004)

Directive 2004/48/EC should read as follows:

**DIRECTIVE 2004/48/EC OF THE EUROPEAN PARLIAMENT AND OF THE COUNCIL
of 29 April 2004
on the enforcement of intellectual property rights**

(Text with EEA relevance)

THE EUROPEAN PARLIAMENT AND THE COUNCIL OF THE EUROPEAN UNION,

Having regard to the Treaty establishing the European Community, and in particular Article 95 thereof,

Having regard to the proposal from the Commission,

Having regard to the opinion of the European Economic and Social Committee ([1]),

After consulting the Committee of the Regions,

Acting in accordance with the procedure laid down in Article 251 of the Treaty ([2]),

Whereas:

(1) The achievement of the internal market entails eliminating restrictions on freedom of movement and distortions of competition, while creating an environment conducive to innovation and investment. In this context, the protection of intellectual property is an essential element for the success of the internal market. The protection of intellectual property is important not only for promoting

---

1.   OJ C 32, 5.2.2004, p. 15.

2.   Opinion of the European Parliament of 9 March 2004 (not yet published in the Official Journal) and Council Decision of 26 April 2004.

innovation and creativity, but also for developing employment and improving competitiveness.

(2) The protection of intellectual property should allow the inventor or creator to derive a legitimate profit from his/her invention or creation. It should also allow the widest possible dissemination of works, ideas and new knowhow. At the same time, it should not hamper freedom of expression, the free movement of information, or the protection of personal data, including on the Internet.

(3) However, without effective means of enforcing intellectual property rights, innovation and creativity are discouraged and investment diminished. It is therefore necessary to ensure that the substantive law on intellectual property, which is nowadays largely part of the *acquis communautaire*, is applied effectively in the Community. In this respect, the means of enforcing intellectual property rights are of paramount importance for the success of the internal market.

(4) At international level, all Member States, as well as the Community itself as regards matters within its competence, are bound by the Agreement on trade-related aspects of intellectual property (the TRIPS Agreement), approved, as part of the multilateral negotiations of the Uruguay Round, by Council Decision 94/800/EC (³) and concluded in the framework of the World Trade Organisation.

(5) The TRIPS Agreement contains, in particular, provisions on the means of enforcing intellectual property rights, which are common standards applicable at international level and implemented in all Member States. This Directive should not affect Member States' international obligations, including those under the TRIPS Agreement.

(6) There are also international conventions to which all Member States are parties and which also contain provisions on the means of enforcing intellectual property rights. These include, in particular, the Paris Convention for the Protection of Industrial Property, the Berne Convention for the Protection of Literary and Artistic Works, and the Rome Convention for the Protection of Performers, Producers of Phonograms and Broadcasting Organisations.

(7) It emerges from the consultations held by the Commission on this question that, in the Member States, and despite the TRIPS Agreement, there are still major disparities as regards the means of enforcing intellectual property rights. For instance, the arrangements for applying provisional measures, which are used in particular to preserve evidence, the calculation of damages, or the arrangements for applying injunctions, vary widely from one Member State to another. In some Member States, there are no measures, procedures and remedies such as the right of information and the recall, at the infringer's expense, of the infringing goods placed on the market.

(8) The disparities between the systems of the Member States as regards the means of enforcing intellectual property rights are prejudicial to the proper functioning of the Internal Market and make it impossible to ensure that intellectual property rights enjoy an equivalent level of protection throughout the Community. This situation does not promote free movement within the internal market or create an environment conducive to healthy competition.

(9) The current disparities also lead to a weakening of the substantive law on intellectual property and to a fragmentation of the internal market in this field. This causes a loss of confidence in the internal market in business circles, with a consequent reduction in investment in innovation and creation. Infringements of intellectual property rights appear to be increasingly

---

3.   OJ L 336, 23.12.1994, p. 1.

linked to organised crime. Increasing use of the Internet enables pirated products to be distributed instantly around the globe. Effective enforcement of the substantive law on intellectual property should be ensured by specific action at Community level. Approximation of the legislation of the Member States in this field is therefore an essential prerequisite for the proper functioning of the internal market.

(10) The objective of this Directive is to approximate legislative systems so as to ensure a high, equivalent and homogeneous level of protection in the internal market.

(11) This Directive does not aim to establish harmonised rules for judicial cooperation, jurisdiction, the recognition and enforcement of decisions in civil and commercial matters, or deal with applicable law. There are Community instruments which govern such matters in general terms and are, in principle, equally applicable to intellectual property.

(12) This Directive should not affect the application of the rules of competition, and in particular Articles 81 and 82 of the Treaty. The measures provided for in this Directive should not be used to restrict competition unduly in a manner contrary to the Treaty.

(13) It is necessary to define the scope of this Directive as widely as possible in order to encompass all the intellectual property rights covered by Community provisions in this field and/or by the national law of the Member State concerned. Nevertheless, that requirement does not affect the possibility, on the part of those Member States which so wish, to extend, for internal purposes, the provisions of this Directive to include acts involving unfair competition, including parasitic copies, or similar activities.

(14) The measures provided for in Articles 6(2), 8(1) and 9(2) need to be applied only in respect of acts carried out on a commercial scale. This is without prejudice to the possibility for Member States to apply those measures also in respect of other acts. Acts carried out on a commercial scale are those carried out for direct or indirect economic or commercial advantage; this would normally exclude acts carried out by end consumers acting in good faith.

(15) This Directive should not affect substantive law on intellectual property, Directive 95/46/EC of 24 October 1995 of the European Parliament and of the Council on the protection of individuals with regard to the processing of personal data and on the free movement of such data (^{4}), Directive 1999/93/EC of the European Parliament and of the Council of 13 December 1999 on a Community framework for electronic signatures (^{5}) and Directive 2000/31/EC of the European Parliament and of the Council of 8 June 2000 on certain legal aspects of information society services, in particular electronic commerce, in the internal market (^{6}).

(16) The provisions of this Directive should be without prejudice to the particular provisions for the enforcement of rights and on exceptions in the domain of copyright and related rights set out in Community instruments and notably those found in Council Directive 91/250/EEC of 14 May 1991 on the legal protection of computer programs (^{7}) or in Directive 2001/29/EC of the European Parliament and of the Council of 22 May 2001 on the harmonisation of certain aspects of copyright and related rights in the information society (^{8}).

(17) The measures, procedures and remedies provided for in this Directive should be

---

4. OJ L 281, 23.11.1995, p. 31. Directive as amended by Regulation (EC) No 1882/2003 (OJ L 284, 31.10.2003, p. 1).
5. OJ L 13, 19.1.2000, p. 12.
6. OJ L 178, 17.7.2000, p. 1.
7. OJ L 122, 17.5.1991, p. 42. Directive as amended by Directive 93/98/EEC (OJ L 290, 24.11.1993, p. 9).
8. OJ L 167, 22.6.2001, p. 10.

determined in each case in such a manner as to take due account of the specific characteristics of that case, including the specific features of each intellectual property right and, where appropriate, the intentional or unintentional character of the infringement.

(18) The persons entitled to request application of those measures, procedures and remedies should be not only the rightholders but also persons who have a direct interest and legal standing in so far as permitted by and in accordance with the applicable law, which may include professional organisations in charge of the management of those rights or for the defence of the collective and individual interests for which they are responsible.

(19) Since copyright exists from the creation of a work and does not require formal registration, it is appropriate to adopt the rule laid down in Article 15 of the Berne Convention, which establishes the presumption whereby the author of a literary or artistic work is regarded as such if his/her name appears on the work. A similar presumption should be applied to the owners of related rights since it is often the holder of a related right, such as a phonogram producer, who will seek to defend rights and engage in fighting acts of piracy.

(20) Given that evidence is an element of paramount importance for establishing the infringement of intellectual property rights, it is appropriate to ensure that effective means of presenting, obtaining and preserving evidence are available. The procedures should have regard to the rights of the defence and provide the necessary guarantees, including the protection of confidential information. For infringements committed on a commercial scale it is also important that the courts may order access, where appropriate, to banking, financial or commercial documents under the control of the alleged infringer.

(21) Other measures designed to ensure a high level of protection exist in certain Member States and should be made available in all the Member States. This is the case with the right of information, which allows precise information to be obtained on the origin of the infringing goods or services, the distribution channels and the identity of any third parties involved in the infringement.

(22) It is also essential to provide for provisional measures for the immediate termination of infringements, without awaiting a decision on the substance of the case, while observing the rights of the defence, ensuring the proportionality of the provisional measures as appropriate to the characteristics of the case in question and providing the guarantees needed to cover the costs and the injury caused to the defendant by an unjustified request. Such measures are particularly justified where any delay would cause irreparable harm to the holder of an intellectual property right.

(23) Without prejudice to any other measures, procedures and remedies available, rightholders should have the possibility of applying for an injunction against an intermediary whose services are being used by a third party to infringe the rightholder's industrial property right. The conditions and procedures relating to such injunctions should be left to the national law of the Member States. As far as infringements of copyright and related rights are concerned, a comprehensive level of harmonisation is already provided for in Directive 2001/29/EC. Article 8(3) of Directive 2001/29/EC should therefore not be affected by this Directive.

(24) Depending on the particular case, and if justified by the circumstances, the measures, procedures and remedies to be provided for should include prohibitory measures aimed at preventing further infringements of intellectual property rights. Moreover there should be corrective

measures, where appropriate at the expense of the infringer, such as the recall and definitive removal from the channels of commerce, or destruction, of the infringing goods and, in appropriate cases, of the materials and implements principally used in the creation or manufacture of these goods. These corrective measures should take account of the interests of third parties including, in particular, consumers and private parties acting in good faith.

(25) Where an infringement is committed unintentionally and without negligence and where the corrective measures or injunctions provided for by this Directive would be disproportionate, Member States should have the option of providing for the possibility, in appropriate cases, of pecuniary compensation being awarded to the injured party as an alternative measure. However, where the commercial use of counterfeit goods or the supply of services would constitute an infringement of law other than intellectual property law or would be likely to harm consumers, such use or supply should remain prohibited.

(26) With a view to compensating for the prejudice suffered as a result of an infringement committed by an infringer who engaged in an activity in the knowledge, or with reasonable grounds for knowing, that it would give rise to such an infringement, the amount of damages awarded to the rightholder should take account of all appropriate aspects, such as loss of earnings incurred by the rightholder, or unfair profits made by the infringer and, where appropriate, any moral prejudice caused to the rightholder. As an alternative, for example where it would be difficult to determine the amount of the actual prejudice suffered, the amount of the damages might be derived from elements such as the royalties or fees which would have been due if the infringer had requested authorisation to use the intellectual property right in question. The aim is not to introduce an obligation to provide for punitive damages but to allow for

compensation based on an objective criterion while taking account of the expenses incurred by the rightholder, such as the costs of identification and research.

(27) To act as a supplementary deterrent to future infringers and to contribute to the awareness of the public at large, it is useful to publicise decisions in intellectual property infringement cases.

(28) In addition to the civil and administrative measures, procedures and remedies provided for under this Directive, criminal sanctions also constitute, in appropriate cases, a means of ensuring the enforcement of intellectual property rights.

(29) Industry should take an active part in the fight against piracy and counterfeiting. The development of codes of conduct in the circles directly affected is a supplementary means of bolstering the regulatory framework. The Member States, in collaboration with the Commission, should encourage the development of codes of conduct in general. Monitoring of the manufacture of optical discs, particularly by means of an identification code embedded in discs produced in the Community, helps to limit infringements of intellectual property rights in this sector, which suffers from piracy on a large scale. However, these technical protection measures should not be misused to protect markets and prevent parallel imports.

(30) In order to facilitate the uniform application of this Directive, it is appropriate to provide for systems of cooperation and the exchange of information between Member States, on the one hand, and between the Member States and the Commission on the other, in particular by creating a network of correspondents designated by the Member States and by providing regular reports assessing the application of this Directive and the effectiveness of the measures taken by the various national bodies.

(31) Since, for the reasons already described, the objective of this Directive can best be

achieved at Community level, the Community may adopt measures, in accordance with the principle of subsidiarity as set out in Article 5 of the Treaty. In accordance with the principle of proportionality as set out in that Article, this Directive does not go beyond what is necessary in order to achieve that objective.

(32) This Directive respects the fundamental rights and observes the principles recognised in particular by the Charter of Fundamental Rights of the European Union. In particular, this Directive seeks to ensure full respect for intellectual property, in accordance with Article 17(2) of that Charter,

HAVE ADOPTED THIS DIRECTIVE:

CHAPTER I

OBJECTIVE AND SCOPE

Article 1

Subject matter

This Directive concerns the measures, procedures and remedies necessary to ensure the enforcement of intellectual property rights. For the purposes of this Directive, the term 'intellectual property rights' includes industrial property rights.

Article 2

Scope

1. Without prejudice to the means which are or may be provided for in Community or national legislation, in so far as those means may be more favourable for rightholders, the measures, procedures and remedies provided for by this Directive shall apply, in accordance with Article 3, to any infringement of intellectual property rights as provided for by Community law and/or by the national law of the Member State concerned.

2. This Directive shall be without prejudice to the specific provisions on the enforcement of

rights and on exceptions contained in Community legislation concerning copyright and rights related to copyright, notably those found in Directive 91/250/EEC and, in particular, Article 7 thereof or in Directive 2001/29/EC and, in particular, Articles 2 to 6 and Article 8 thereof.

3. This Directive shall not affect:

(a) the Community provisions governing the substantive law on intellectual property, Directive 95/46/EC, Directive 1999/93/EC or Directive 2000/31/EC, in general, and Articles 12 to 15 of Directive 2000/31/EC in particular;

(b) Member States' international obligations and notably the TRIPS Agreement, including those relating to criminal procedures and penalties;

(c) any national provisions in Member States relating to criminal procedures or penalties in respect of infringement of intellectual property rights.

CHAPTER II

MEASURES, PROCEDURES AND REMEDIES

Section 1

General provisions

Article 3

General obligation

1. Member States shall provide for the measures, procedures and remedies necessary to ensure the enforcement of the intellectual property rights covered by this Directive. Those measures, procedures and remedies shall be fair and equitable and shall not be unnecessarily complicated or costly, or entail unreasonable time-limits or unwarranted delays.

2. Those measures, procedures and remedies shall also be effective, proportionate and dissuasive and shall be applied in such a manner as to avoid the creation of barriers to legitimate trade and to provide for safeguards against their abuse.

Article 4

Persons entitled to apply for the application of the measures, procedures and remedies

Member States shall recognise as persons entitled to seek application of the measures, procedures and remedies referred to in this chapter:

(a) the holders of intellectual property rights, in accordance with the provisions of the applicable law;

(b) all other persons authorised to use those rights, in particular licensees, in so far as permitted by and in accordance with the provisions of the applicable law;

(c) intellectual property collective rights-management bodies which are regularly recognised as having a right to represent holders of intellectual property rights, in so far as permitted by and in accordance with the provisions of the applicable law;

(d) professional defence bodies which are regularly recognised as having a right to represent holders of intellectual property rights, in so far as permitted by and in accordance with the provisions of the applicable law.

Article 5

Presumption of authorship or ownership

For the purposes of applying the measures, procedures and remedies provided for in this Directive,

(a) for the author of a literary or artistic work, in the absence of proof to the contrary, to be regarded as such, and consequently to be entitled to institute infringement proceedings, it shall be sufficient for his/her name to appear on the work in the usual manner;

(b) the provision under (a) shall apply *mutatis mutandis* to the holders of rights related to copyright with regard to their protected subject matter.

Section 2

Evidence

Article 6

Evidence

1. Member States shall ensure that, on application by a party which has presented reasonably available evidence sufficient to support its claims, and has, in substantiating those claims, specified evidence which lies in the control of the opposing party, the competent judicial authorities may order that such evidence be presented by the opposing party, subject to the protection of confidential information. For the purposes of this paragraph, Member States may provide that a reasonable sample of a substantial number of copies of a work or any other protected object be considered by the competent judicial authorities to constitute reasonable evidence.

2. Under the same conditions, in the case of an infringement committed on a commercial scale Member States shall take such measures as are necessary to enable the competent judicial authorities to order, where appropriate, on application by a party, the communication of banking, financial or commercial documents under the control of the opposing party, subject to the protection of confidential information.

Article 7

Measures for preserving evidence

1. Member States shall ensure that, even before the commencement of proceedings on the merits of the case, the competent judicial authorities may, on application by a party who has presented reasonably available evidence to support his/her claims that his/her intellectual property right has been infringed or is about to be infringed, order prompt and effective provisional measures to preserve relevant evidence in respect of the alleged infringement, subject to the protection of confidential information. Such measures may include the detailed description, with or without the taking of samples, or the physical seizure of the infringing goods, and, in

appropriate cases, the materials and implements used in the production and/or distribution of these goods and the documents relating thereto. Those measures shall be taken, if necessary without the other party having been heard, in particular where any delay is likely to cause irreparable harm to the rightholder or where there is a demonstrable risk of evidence being destroyed.

Where measures to preserve evidence are adopted without the other party having been heard, the parties affected shall be given notice, without delay after the execution of the measures at the latest. A review, including a right to be heard, shall take place upon request of the parties affected with a view to deciding, within a reasonable period after the notification of the measures, whether the measures shall be modified, revoked or confirmed.

2. Member States shall ensure that the measures to preserve evidence may be subject to the lodging by the applicant of adequate security or an equivalent assurance intended to ensure compensation for any prejudice suffered by the defendant as provided for in paragraph 4.

3. Member States shall ensure that the measures to preserve evidence are revoked or otherwise cease to have effect, upon request of the defendant, without prejudice to the damages which may be claimed, if the applicant does not institute, within a reasonable period, proceedings leading to a decision on the merits of the case before the competent judicial authority, the period to be determined by the judicial authority ordering the measures where the law of a Member State so permits or, in the absence of such determination, within a period not exceeding 20 working days or 31 calendar days, whichever is the longer.

4. Where the measures to preserve evidence are revoked, or where they lapse due to any act or omission by the applicant, or where it is subsequently found that there has been no infringement or threat of infringement of an intellectual property right, the judicial authorities shall have the authority to order the applicant, upon request of the defendant, to provide the defendant appropriate compensation for any injury caused by those measures.

5. Member States may take measures to protect witnesses' identity.

Section 3

Right of information

Article 8

Right of information

1. Member States shall ensure that, in the context of proceedings concerning an infringement of an intellectual property right and in response to a justified and proportionate request of the claimant, the competent judicial authorities may order that information on the origin and distribution networks of the goods or services which infringe an intellectual property right be provided by the infringer and/or any other person who:

(a) was found in possession of the infringing goods on a commercial scale;

(b) was found to be using the infringing services on a commercial scale;

(c) was found to be providing on a commercial scale services used in infringing activities; or

(d) was indicated by the person referred to in point (a), (b) or (c) as being involved in the production, manufacture or distribution of the goods or the provision of the services.

2. The information referred to in paragraph 1 shall, as appropriate, comprise:

(a) the names and addresses of the producers, manufacturers, distributors, suppliers and other previous holders of the goods or services, as well as the intended wholesalers and retailers;

(b) information on the quantities produced, manufactured, delivered, received or ordered, as well as the price obtained for the goods or services in question.

3. Paragraphs 1 and 2 shall apply without prejudice to other statutory provisions which:

(a) grant the rightholder rights to receive fuller information;

(b) govern the use in civil or criminal proceedings of the information communicated pursuant to this Article;

(c) govern responsibility for misuse of the right of information;

or

(d) afford an opportunity for refusing to provide information which would force the person referred to in paragraph 1 to admit to his/her own participation or that of his/her close relatives in an infringement of an intellectual property right;

or

(e) govern the protection of confidentiality of information sources or the processing of personal data.

Section 4

Provisional and precautionary measures

Article 9

Provisional and precautionary measures

1. Member States shall ensure that the judicial authorities may, at the request of the applicant:

(a) issue against the alleged infringer an interlocutory injunction intended to prevent any imminent infringement of an intellectual property right, or to forbid, on a provisional basis and subject, where appropriate, to a recurring penalty payment where provided for by national law, the continuation of the alleged infringements of that right, or to make such continuation subject to the lodging of guarantees intended to ensure the compensation of the rightholder; an interlocutory injunction may also be issued, under the same conditions, against an intermediary whose services are being used by a third party to infringe an intellectual property

right; injunctions against intermediaries whose services are used by a third party to infringe a copyright or a related right are covered by Directive 2001/29/EC;

(b) order the seizure or delivery up of the goods suspected of infringing an intellectual property right so as to prevent their entry into or movement within the channels of commerce.

2. In the case of an infringement committed on a commercial scale, the Member States shall ensure that, if the injured party demonstrates circumstances likely to endanger the recovery of damages, the judicial authorities may order the precautionary seizure of the movable and immovable property of the alleged infringer, including the blocking of his/her bank accounts and other assets. To that end, the competent authorities may order the communication of bank, financial or commercial documents, or appropriate access to the relevant information.

3. The judicial authorities shall, in respect of the measures referred to in paragraphs 1 and 2, have the authority to require the applicant to provide any reasonably available evidence in order to satisfy themselves with a sufficient degree of certainty that the applicant is the rightholder and that the applicant's right is being infringed, or that such infringement is imminent.

4. Member States shall ensure that the provisional measures referred to in paragraphs 1 and 2 may, in appropriate cases, be taken without the defendant having been heard, in particular where any delay would cause irreparable harm to the rightholder. In that event, the parties shall be so informed without delay after the execution of the measures at the latest.

A review, including a right to be heard, shall take place upon request of the defendant with a view to deciding, within a reasonable time after notification of the measures, whether those measures shall be modified, revoked or confirmed.

5. Member States shall ensure that the provisional measures referred to in paragraphs 1 and 2 are revoked or otherwise cease to have effect,

upon request of the defendant, if the applicant does not institute, within a reasonable period, proceedings leading to a decision on the merits of the case before the competent judicial authority, the period to be determined by the judicial authority ordering the measures where the law of a Member State so permits or, in the absence of such determination, within a period not exceeding 20 working days or 31 calendar days, whichever is the longer.

6. The competent judicial authorities may make the provisional measures referred to in paragraphs 1 and 2 subject to the lodging by the applicant of adequate security or an equivalent assurance intended to ensure compensation for any prejudice suffered by the defendant as provided for in paragraph 7.

7. Where the provisional measures are revoked or where they lapse due to any act or omission by the applicant, or where it is subsequently found that there has been no infringement or threat of infringement of an intellectual property right, the judicial authorities shall have the authority to order the applicant, upon request of the defendant, to provide the defendant appropriate compensation for any injury caused by those measures.

Section 5

Measures resulting from a decision on the merits of the case

Article 10

Corrective measures

1. Without prejudice to any damages due to the rightholder by reason of the infringement, and without compensation of any sort, Member States shall ensure that the competent judicial authorities may order, at the request of the applicant, that appropriate measures be taken with regard to goods that they have found to be infringing an intellectual property right and, in appropriate cases, with regard to materials and implements principally used in the creation or manufacture of those goods. Such measures shall include:

(a) recall from the channels of commerce;

(b) definitive removal from the channels of commerce;

or

(c) destruction.

2. The judicial authorities shall order that those measures be carried out at the expense of the infringer, unless particular reasons are invoked for not doing so.

3. In considering a request for corrective measures, the need for proportionality between the seriousness of the infringement and the remedies ordered as well as the interests of third parties shall be taken into account.

Article 11

Injunctions

Member States shall ensure that, where a judicial decision is taken finding an infringement of an intellectual property right, the judicial authorities may issue against the infringer an injunction aimed at prohibiting the continuation of the infringement. Where provided for by national law, non-compliance with an injunction shall, where appropriate, be subject to a recurring penalty payment, with a view to ensuring compliance. Member States shall also ensure that rightholders are in a position to apply for an injunction against intermediaries whose services are used by a third party to infringe an intellectual property right, without prejudice to Article 8(3) of Directive 2001/29/EC.

Article 12

Alternative measures

Member States may provide that, in appropriate cases and at the request of the person liable to be subject to the measures provided for in this section, the competent judicial authorities may order pecuniary compensation to be paid to the injured party instead of applying the measures provided for in this section if that person acted unintentionally and without negligence, if execution of the measures in question would cause him/her disproportionate harm and if pecuniary compensation to the injured party appears reasonably satisfactory.

Section 6

Damages and legal costs

Article 13

Damages

1. Member States shall ensure that the competent judicial authorities, on application of the injured party, order the infringer who knowingly, or with reasonable grounds to know, engaged in an infringing activity, to pay the rightholder damages appropriate to the actual prejudice suffered by him/her as a result of the infringement.

When the judicial authorities set the damages:

(a) they shall take into account all appropriate aspects, such as the negative economic consequences, including lost profits, which the injured party has suffered, any unfair profits made by the infringer and, in appropriate cases, elements other than economic factors, such as the moral prejudice caused to the rightholder by the infringement;

or

(b) as an alternative to (a), they may, in appropriate cases, set the damages as a lump sum on the basis of elements such as at least the amount of royalties or fees which would have been due if the infringer had requested authorisation to use the intellectual property right in question.

2. Where the infringer did not knowingly, or with reasonable grounds know, engage in infringing activity, Member States may lay down that the judicial authorities may order the recovery of profits or the payment of damages, which may be pre-established.

Article 14

Legal costs

Member States shall ensure that reasonable and proportionate legal costs and other expenses incurred by the successful party shall, as a general rule, be borne by the unsuccessful party, unless equity does not allow this.

Section 7

Publicity measures

Article 15

Publication of judicial decisions

Member States shall ensure that, in legal proceedings instituted for infringement of an intellectual property right, the judicial authorities may order, at the request of the applicant and at the expense of the infringer, appropriate measures for the dissemination of the information concerning the decision, including displaying the decision and publishing it in full or in part. Member States may provide for other additional publicity measures which are appropriate to the particular circumstances, including prominent advertising.

CHAPTER III

SANCTIONS BY MEMBER STATES

Article 16

Sanctions by Member States

Without prejudice to the civil and administrative measures, procedures and remedies laid down by this Directive, Member States may apply other appropriate sanctions in cases where intellectual property rights have been infringed.

CHAPTER IV

CODES OF CONDUCT AND ADMINISTRATIVE COOPERATION

Article 17

Codes of conduct

Member States shall encourage:

(a) the development by trade or professional associations or organisations of codes of conduct at Community level aimed at contributing towards the enforcement of the intellectual property rights, particularly by recommending the use on optical discs of a code enabling the identification of the origin of their manufacture;

(b) the submission to the Commission of draft codes of conduct at national and Community level and of any evaluations of the application of these codes of conduct.

Article 18

Assessment

1. Three years after the date laid down in Article 20(1), each Member State shall submit to the Commission a report on the implementation of this Directive.

On the basis of those reports, the Commission shall draw up a report on the application of this Directive, including an assessment of the effectiveness of the measures taken, as well as an evaluation of its impact on innovation and the development of the information society. That report shall then be transmitted to the European Parliament, the Council and the European Economic and Social Committee. It shall be accompanied, if necessary and in the light of developments in the Community legal order, by proposals for amendments to this Directive.

2. Member States shall provide the Commission with all the aid and assistance it may need when drawing up the report referred to in the second subparagraph of paragraph 1.

Article 19

Exchange of information and correspondents

For the purpose of promoting cooperation, including the exchange of information, among Member States and between Member States and the Commission, each Member State shall designate one or more national correspondents for any question relating to the implementation of the measures provided for by this Directive. It shall communicate the details of the national correspondent(s) to the other Member States and to the Commission.

CHAPTER V
FINAL PROVISIONS

Article 20

Implementation

1. Member States shall bring into force the laws, regulations and administrative provisions necessary to comply with this Directive by 29 April 2006. They shall forthwith inform the Commission thereof.

When Member States adopt these measures, they shall contain a reference to this Directive or shall be accompanied by such reference on the occasion of their official publication. The methods of making such reference shall be laid down by Member States.

2. Member States shall communicate to the Commission the texts of the provisions of national law which they adopt in the field governed by this Directive.

Article 21

Entry into force

This Directive shall enter into force on the 20th day following that of its publication in the *Official Journal of the European Union*.

Article 22

Addressees

This Directive is addressed to the Member States.

Done at Strasbourg, 29 April 2004.

For the European Parliament   *For the Council*
The President   *The President*
P. COX   *M. McDOWELL*

Bibliography

Ahrens, H.-J., 'Gesetzgebungsvorschlag zur Beweisermittlung bei Verletzung von Rechten des geistigen Eigentums', [2005] *Gewerblicher Rechtsschutz und Urheberrecht*, 837-840.

The Annual Enforcement Report <http://www.patent.gov.uk/enforcereport2005. pdf>.

Arnull, A. & Dashwood, A., (eds) *Wyatt and Dashwood's European Union Law*, (Oxford: Oxford University Press, 2004).

Ashurst Report, Waelbroeck, D., Slater, D, & Even-Shoshan, G., *Study on the Conditions of Claims for Damages: Comparative Report*, prepared for the European Commission, August 2004.

Auer-Reinsdorff, A., 'Der Besichtigungsanspruch bei Rechtsverletzungen an Computerprogrammen', [2006] *Der IT-Rechts-Berater*, 82-86.

Baumbach, A., W. Lauterbach, J. Albers & P. Hartmann, *Zivilprozessordnung* (66th edn, C.H. Beck, München, 2008).

Berlit, W., 'Auswirkungen des Gesetzes zur Verbesserung der Durchsetzung von Rechten des geistigen Eigentums im Patentrecht', [2007] *Wettbewerb in Recht und Praxis*, 732-738.

Beyerlein, T., 'Ergänzender Leistungsschutz gemäß § 4 Nr 9 UWG als "geistiges Eigentum" nach der Enforcement-Richtlinie (2004/48/EG), [2005] *Wettbewerb in Recht und Praxis*, 1354-1358.

Blom-Cooper, L. QC (ed), *Experts in the Civil Courts, Expert Witness Institute* (Oxford: OUP, 2006).

Bornkamm, J., 'Der Schutz vertraulicher Informationen im Gesetz zur Durchsetzung von Rechten des geistigen Eigentums – In-camera-Verfahren im Zivilprozess?' in *Festschrift für Eike Ullmann*, H-J. Ahrens, J. Bornkamm and H-P. Kunz-Hallstein (eds) (Saarbrücken, juris, 2006), pp. 893-912.

Boulouis, J., *Le droit institutionnel des Communautés européennes*, 2nd edn (Paris: Montchrestien, 1990).

Bowman, Sir J., *Review of the Court of Appeal (Civil Division)* September 1997 <www.dca.gov.uk/civil/report>

CCBE Economic Submission to the Commission Profess Report on Competition in Professional Services (2006) p. 1: <www. ccbe.org/doc/En/ccbe_economic_ submission_310306_en.pdf> 1 September 2007.

Civil Justice Court , Improving Access to Justice Through Collective Actions: A Series of Recommendations to the Lord Chancellor 05.08.2008 <www. civiljusticecouncil.gov.uk>, 10 August 2008.

Copenhagen Economics, 'The Legal Profession: Competition and Liberalisation' (Copenhagen, January 2006).

Cornish, W. & D. Llewelyn, *Intellectual Property: Patents, Copyright, Trade Marks and Allied Rights*, 5th edn (London: Sweet & Maxwell, 2003).

Czychowski, C., 'Auskunftsansprüche gegenüber Internetzugangsprovidern "vor" dem 2. Korb und "nach" der Enforcement-Richtlinie der EU', [2004] *Multimedia und Recht*, 514-519.

Deutsche Vereinigung für gewerblichen Rechtsschutz und Urheberrecht (GRUR), 'Gemeinsame Stellungnahme der Ausschüsse für Patent-und Gebrauchsmusterrecht, Geschmacksmusterrecht und Urheberrecht zum Referentenentwurf für ein "Gesetz zur Verbesserung der Durchsetzung von Rechten des geistigen Eigentums"', [2006] *Gewerblicher Rechtsschutz und Urheberrecht*, 393-395.

Deutsche Vereinigung für gewerblichen Rechtsschutz und Urheberrecht (GRUR), 'Stellungnahme zum Vorschlag der Kommission für eine Richtlinie über die Maßnahmen und Verfahren zum Schutz der Rechte am geistigen Eigentum', [2003] *Gewerblicher Rechtsschutz und Urheberrecht*, 682-685.

Dougan, M., *National remedies before the Court of Justice: Issues of harmonisation*, (Oxford: Hart Publishing, 2004).

Dreier, T., 'Ausgleich, Abschreckung und andere Rechtsfolgen von Urheberrechtsverletzungen: Erste Gedanken zur EU-Richtlinie über die Maßnahmen und Verfahren zum Schutze der Recht an geistigem Eigentum', [2004] *Gewerblicher Rechtsschutz und Urheberrecht, Internationaler Teil*, 706-712.

Drexl, J., R. Hilty and A. Kur, 'Vorschlag für eine Richtlinie über die Maßnahmen und Verfahren zum Schutz der Rechte am geistigen Eigentum – eine erste Würdigung', [2003] *Gewerblicher Rechtsschutz und Urheberrecht, Internationaler Teil*, 605-608.

European Commission, Green Paper, *Combatting Counterfeiting and Piracy in the Single Market* , COM (98) 0596 FINAL, 22.10.1998 <www.ec.europa.eu> 13 April 2008

European Commission, *Final Report on the Responses to the European Commission Green Paper on Counterfeiting and Piracy*, 7.6.1999, <www.ec.europa.eu> 13 April 2008

European Commission, *Communication from the Commission to the Council, the European Parliament and Economic and Social Committee: Follow-up to the*

Green Paper on Combatting Counterfeiting and Piracy in the Single Market COM 2000/0789 Final, 17 April 2000 <www.ohim.eu.int>

European Commission: *Proposal for a Directive of the European Parliament and of the Council on Measures and Procedures to Ensure the Enforcement of Intellectual Property Rights*: COM (2003) 46 FINAL, 30 January 2003 <www.ec.europa.eu>, 1 April 2008

European Commission: Directorate General Single Market, Centre for Economics and Business Research, *Final Report: Counting Counterfeits: Report Presenting a Method to Collect, Analyse and Compare Date on Counterfeiting and Piracy in the Single Market* 15 July 2002, <www.ec.europa.eu>, 13 April 2008.

Eisenkolb, J., 'Die Enforcement-Richtlinie und ihre Wirkung', [2007] *Gewerblicher Rechtsschutz und Urheberrecht*, 387-393.

European Commission, Commission Report on Competition in Professional Services COM (2004) 83 9 Feburary 2004. <www.ec.europa.eu> 13 April 2008

European Commission, *Commission Staff Working Paper on Damages Actions for Breach of > EC Anti-Tust Rules* SEC (2008) 4040, <www.ec.europa.eu> 13 April 2008

European Commission, Commission Staff Working *Paper:Annex to the Green Paper, Damages Actions for Breach of the EU Anti Trust Rules*, SEC (2005) 1732<eur-lex.europe.eu> 1 September 2007

European Commission, *External Impact Study: Making Anti-Trust Damages Actions More Effective in the EU: Welfare Impact and Potential Scenarios*: Final Report, CEPS, EUR and LUISS: Contract DG COMP (2006) A3/012 <www.ec.europa.eu> 13 April 2008

European Commission, *Green Paper: Damages Actions for Breach of the EC Anti-Trust Rules* COM (2005) 672, Final, <eur-lex.europe.eu > 1 September 2007

European Commission, *Impact Assessment Report, Staff Working Document*, SEC (2008) 405, <www.ec.europa.eu> 13 April 2008

European Commission, *Proposal for measures and procedures to ensure the enforcement of intellectual property rights*, COM (2003) 46 final <eur-lex. europa.eu> 1 March 2008

European Commission, *White Paper: Damages Actions for Breach of the EC Anti-Trust Rules* COM (2008) 125, <www.ec. europa.eu> 13 April 2008

European Economic and Social Committee: Document on the 'Proposal *for a Directive of the European Parliament and of the Council on* Measures and Procedures to Ensure the Enforcmeent of Intellectual Property Rights' (COM (2003) 46 Final 203/0024 (COD)) <www.ec.europa.eu> 13 April 2008

European Parliament, *Report on the proposal for a directive of the European Parliament and of the Council on measures and procedures to ensure the enforcement of intellectual property rights* (Rapporteur J. Fourtou), A5-0468/2003, <www.europarl.europa.eu>, 1 March 2008

Frank, C. and N. Wiegand, 'Der Besichtigungsanspruch im Urheberrecht de lege ferenda', [2007] *Computer und Recht*, 481-487.

Freudenthal, M. in: *La Armonización del Derecho de Obligaciones en Europe*, ed. F. Badosa Coll and E. Arroyo i Amayuelas, (Valencia, Tirant Lo Blanch, 2006).

Fezer K-H., *Markenrecht* (3rd edn, München, C.H. Beck, 2001).

Frey, D. and M. Rudolph, 'EU-Richtlinie zur Durchsetzung der Rechte des geistigen Eigentums', [2004] *Zeitschrift für Urheber- und Medienrecht*, 522-529.

Grünberger, M., 'Die Urhebervermutung und die Inhabervermutung für die Leistungsschutzberechtigten', [2006] *Gewerblicher Rechtsschutz und Urheberrecht*, 894-903.

Harte-Bavendamm, H., 'Der Richtlinienvorschlag zur Durchsetzung der Rechte des geistigen Eigentums', in *Festschrift für Winfried Tilmann*, E. Keller, C. Plassmann and A. v.Falck (eds) (Köln, Heymanns, 2003), pp. 793-805.

Hartley, T., *The Foundations of European Community Law* 5th edn, (Oxford: Oxford Unviersity Press, 2003).

Hodges, C., *Multi-Party Actions* (OUP, Oxford 2001)

H. M. Treasury, *Gowers Review of Intellectual Property* (Dec 2006) <www.hm-treasury.gov.uk/medi/583/91/pbr06_gowers_report_755.pdf>, October 1 2007.

Hoeren, T., 'High-noon im europäisch.en Immaterialgüterrecht', [2003] *Multimedia und Recht*, 299-303.

Hommerich, C., H. Prütting et. al., *Rechtstatsächliche Untersuchung zu den Auswirkungen der Reform des Zivilprozessrechts auf die gerichtliche Praxis – Evaluation ZPO-Reform*, <www.bmj.bund.de/media/archive/1216.pdf>, 1 March 2008.

House of Commons Library, *The Treaty of Lisbon: Amendments to the Treaty Establishing the Euroepan Union*, Research Paper 07/86 6.12.07, <www.parliament.uk/commons/lib/research/rpintro.htm>

House of Commons, *Trade and Industry Committee Publications:* 8th Report, Session 1998-99

12.6.1999 <www.parliament.the-stationery-office.co.uk>

House of Lords Select Committee on European Union, *The Future Status of the Charter of Fundamental Rights*, HL Paper 48, Session 2002-03, <www.publications.parliament.uk>

Institut für Höhere Studien, 'Economic Impact of Regulation in the field of Liberal Profession in different Member State for the European Commission DG Competition' (Wien, January 2003).

Jaeschke, J., 'Produktpiraten sollen Schiffbruch erleiden', [2004] *JurPC*, Web-Dok. 258/2004.

Jans, J. R. de Lange, S. Prechal and R. Widdershoven, *Europeanisation of Public Law* (Groningen, Europa Publishing, 2007).

Jolowicz, A., *On Civil Litigation* (Cambridge University Press, Cambridge, 2000)

Knaak, R., 'Die EG-Richtlinie zur Durchsetzung der Rechte des geistigen Eigentums und ihr Umsetzungsbedarf im deutschen Recht', [2004] *Gewerblicher Rechtsschutz und Urheberrecht, Internationaler Teil*, 745-750.

Koch, F., 'Die Enforcement-Richtlinie: Vereinheitlichung der Durchsetzung der Rechte des geistigen Eigentums in der EU, [2006] *Der IT-Rechts-Berater*, 42.

Kühnen, T., 'Die Besichtigung im Patentrecht' [2005] *Gewerblicher Rechtsschutz und Urheberrecht*, 185-196

LECG, *Competition in the Professions: a Report prepared for the Director General of Fair Trading*: Office of Fair Trading (238) March 2001, <www.oft. gov.uk/shared_oft/reports/professional_bodies/oft 238>, September 30 2007.

Leible, S., 'Zu den Problemen der Geltendmachung von Rechtsverletzung des geistigen Eigentums', [2007] *Kommentierte BGH-Rechtsprechung Lindenmaier-Möhring*, 208363.

Lenaerts, K., I. Maselis & R. Bray (eds) *Procedural Law of the Euroepan Union* (2nd edn. London, Sweet & Maxwell, 2006)

Lenaerts, K. P. van Nuffel & R. Bray (eds) *Constitutional Law of the European Union* (2nd edn, London, Sweet & Maxwell, 2006)

Lonbay, J. and A. Biondi, (eds) *Remedies for Breach of EC Law* (Chichester, John Wiley & Sons, 1997).

Lüpke, T. and R. Müller, '"Pre-Trial Discover of Documents" und § 142 ZPO – ein trojanisches Pferd im neuen Zivilprozessrecht?', [2002] *Neue Zeitschrift für Insolvenzrecht*, 588-589.

Matthews, P., and H. M. Malek, QC, *Disclosure* (London, Sweet & Maxwell, 2001).

McGuire, M-R., 'Beweismittelvorlage und Auskunftsanspruch nach der Richtlinie 2004/48/EG zur Durchsetzung der Rechte des Geistigen Eigentums', [2005] *Gewerblicher Rechtsschutz und Urheberrecht, Internationaler Teil*, 15-22.

McGuire, M-R., 'Die richtlinienkonforme Auslegung des § 142 ZPO: Anmerkung zu BGH 1.8.2006 - X ZR 114/03 – Restschadstoffverwertung', [2007] *Zeitschrift für Gemeinschaftsprivatrecht*, 34-38.

Mes, P., *Patentgesetz, Gebrauchsmustergesetz* (2nd edn, München, C.H. Beck, 2005).

Metzger, A. and W. Wurmnest, 'Auf dem Weg zu einem Europäischen Sanktionenrecht des geistigen Eigentums?', [2003] *Zeitschrift für Urheber- und Medienrecht*, 922-933.

Meyer, H-P. and O. Linnenborn, 'Kein sicherer Hafen: Bekämpfung der Produktpiraterie in der Europäischen Union', [2003] *Kommunikation & Recht*, 313-322.

Middleteon, Sir P., *Report on Civil Justice and Legal Aid Reforms* September 1997 <www.dca;gov.uk.civil.report>

Musielak, H-J. (ed.), *Kommentar zur Zivilprozessordnung mit Gerichtsverfassungsgesetz* (5th edn, München, Franz Vahlen, 2007).

Nägele, T. and C. Nitsche, 'Gesetzentwurf der Bundesregierung zur Verbesserung der Durchsetzung von Rechten des geistigen Eigentums' [2007] *Wettbewerb in Recht und Praxis*, 1047-1058.

Nicolini, K. and H. Ahlberg (eds), *Möhring/Nicolini, Urheberrechtsgesetz* (2nd edn, München, Franz Vahlen, 2000).

Office of Fair Trading, *Private Actions in Competition Law: Effective Redress for Consumers and Business – Recommendations*, 26 November 2005 <www.oft. gov.uk> 15 April 2008

Office of Fair Trading, *The Deterrent Effect of Competition Enforcement by the OFT: a Report Prepared for the OFT by Deloitte:* OFT 962, November 2007 <www.oft.gov.uk> 15 April 2008

Pahlow, L., 'Anspruchskonkurrenzen bei Verletzung lizenzierter Schutzrechte unter Berücksichtigung der Richtlinie 2004/48/EG', [2007] *Gewerblicher Rechtsschutz und Urheberrecht*, 1001-1007.

Patnaik, D., 'Enthält das deutsche Recht effektive Mittel zur Bekämpfung von Nachahmungen und Produktpiraterie?' [2004] *Gewerblicher Rechtsschutz und Urheberrecht*, 191-198.

Peukert A. and A. Kur, 'Stellungnahme des Max-Planck-Instituts für Geistiges Eigentum, Wettbewerbs- und Steuerrecht zur Umsetzung der Richtlinie 2004/48/EG zur Durchsetzung der Rechte des geistigen Eigentums in deutsches Recht' [2006] *Gewerblicher Rechtsschutz und Urheberrecht*, Internationaler Teil, 292-303

Peysner, J. and M. Seneviratne, 'The Management of Civil Cases': DCA Research Series 9/05 (London, Nov.2005) <www.dca.gov.uk/research/2005/9_2005.htm>, 15 September 2007.

Peysner, J. and M. Seneviratne, 'The Management of Civil Cases : the Courts and the Post – Woolf Landscape' (London, Dec 2005) <www.dca.gov.uk/research/2005/9_2005.htm> , September 15, 2007.

Prechal, S., *Directives in EC Law* (2nd edn, Oxford, Oxford University Press, 2005).

Raabe, F., 'Der Auskunftsanspruch nach dem Referentenentwurf zur Verbesserung der Durchsetzung von Rechten des geistigen Eigentums', [2006] *Zeitschrift für Urheber- und Medienrecht*, 439-443.

Rand Corporation, Institute for Civil Justice, *Just, Speedy and Inexpensive: An Evaluation of Judicial Case Management Under the Civil Justice Reform* Act (1996) <www.rand.org/pubs/monograph_report/MR800>, September 15, 2007.

RBB Economics, *Economic Impact of Regulation in Liberal Professions, A critique of the IHS report.* (9 September2003) <www.ccbe.org/doc/En/rbb_ihs_critique_en>, 1 October 2007.

Robert, P. and A.A. S. Zuckerman, *Criminal Evidence* (Oxford University Press, Oxford, 2004).

Rose, R., S. Sime, and D. French, *Blackstone's Civil Practise* (Oxford University Press, Oxford, 2004).

Rosenberg, L., K. H. Schwab and P. Gottwald, *Zivilprozessrecht* (16th ed, C.H. Beck, München 2004).

Santos Gil, A.B.E. dos, in: Molengrafica 1996, *Europees Privaatrecht, Opstellen over Internationale transacties in Intellectuele eigendom*, (Lelystad, Koninklijke Vermande, 1996).

Schermers, H. and D. Waelbroeck, *Judicial Protection in the European Union* (The Hague, Kluwer Law International, 2002).

Schlosser, P., 'Wirtschaftsprüfervorbehalt und prozessuales Vertraulichkeitsinteresse der nicht primär beweisbelasteten Prozeßpartei' in

Festschrift für Bernhard Großfeld, U. Hübner and W. Ebke (eds) (Recht und Wirtschaft, Heidelberg, 1999), pp. 997-1016.

Seichter D., 'Der Auskunftsanspruch nach Artikel 8 der Richtlinie zur Durchsetzung der Rechte des geistigen Eigentums' in *Festschrift für Eike Ullmann*, H-J. Ahrens, J. Bornkamm and H-P. Kunz-Hallstein (eds) (Saarbrücken, juris, 2006), pp. 983-998

Seichter, D., 'Die Umsetzung der Richtlinie zur Durchsetzung der Rechte des geistigen Eigentums, [2006] *Wettbewerb in Recht und Praxis*, 391-400.

Seichter, D., 'Die Verfolgung von Verletzungen geistiger Eigentumsrechte durch Verbraucher im Internet', [2007] *Verbraucher und Recht*, 291-297.

Sime, S., *A Practical Approach to Civil Procedure* (5th edn, Oxford, OUP, 2002).

Simon, D., *La Directive européenne* (Paris, Dalloz, 1997).

Spoor, J.H., D.W.F. Verkade and D.J.G. Visser, *Auteursrecht*, third ed., (Deventer, Kluwer, 2005).

Storme, M. (ed) Rapprochement du Droit Judiciaire de l'Union Européenne - Approximation of Judicary Law in the European Union, (Amseterdam, Martinus Nijhoff, 1994)

Spindler, G. and J. Dorschel, 'Vereinbarkeit der geplanten Auskunftsansprüche gegen Internet-Provider mit EU-Recht', [2006] *Computer und Recht*, 341-347.

Spindler, G. and M-P Weber, 'Der Geheimnisschutz nach Art. 7 der Enforcement-Richtlinie' [2006] *Multimedia und Recht*, 711-714

Spindler, G., and M-P. Weber, 'Die Umsetzung der Enforcement-Richtlinie nach dem Regierungsentwurf für ein Gesetz zur Verbesserung der Durchsetzung von Rechten des geistigen Eigentums', [2007] *Zeitschrift für Urheber- und Medienrecht*, 257-266.

Tilmann, W., 'Beweissicherung nach Art. 7 der Richtlinie zur Durchsetzung der Rechte des geistigen Eigentums', [2005] *Gewerblicher Rechtsschutz und Urheberrecht*, 737-740.

Tilmann, W., 'Beweissicherung nach europäischem und deutschem Recht' in *Festschrift für Eike Ullmann*, H-J. Ahrens, J. Bornkamm and H-P. Kunz-Hallstein (eds) (Saarbrücken, juris, 2006), pp. 1013-1023.

Tilmann, W. and M. Schreibauer, 'Die neueste BGH-Rechtsprechung zum Besichtigungsanspruch nach § 809 BGB', [2002] *Gewerblicher Rechtsschutz und Urheberrecht*, 1015-1022.

Van der Bergh, R. and Y. Motagnie, *Theory and Evidence in the Regulation of the Latin Notary Profession*, ECRI Report 0604, June 2006; <www. mediaseor. neon.estrate.nl/publications/theory-and-evidence-regulation-latin-profes.pdf, 1 October 2007.

v.Hartz, N., 'Beweissicherungsmöglichkeiten im Urheberrecht nach der Enforcement-Richtlinie im deutschen Recht', [2005] *Zeitschrift für Urheber- und Medienrecht*, 376-383.

Van Mierlo, A.I.M and F.M. Bart, *Parlementaire Geschiedenis, Herziening van het burgerlijk procesrecht*, (Deventer, Kluwer, 2002).

Waller, L.J. (ed.) White Book Service (2007) Vol 1: (London, Sweet & Maxwell, 2007).

Wandtke, A-A. and W. Bullinger (eds), *Urheberrecht* (2nd edn, München, C.H. Beck, 2006).

Wesseling-van Gent, E.M., in: *Het verzamelen van feiten en bewijs: begrenzing versus verruiming, een kruisbestuiving tussen civiel procesrecht en ondernemingsprocesrecht*, (Den Haag, Boom Juridische Uitgevers, 2006).

Wichers Hoeth, L., *Kort begrip van het intellectuele eigendomsrecht*, eds. Ch. Gielen and N. Hagemans, A.O. (Zwolle, W.E.J. Tjeenk Willink, 8th ed., 2000).

Woolf Lord Interim Report Access to Justice (1995) <www.dca.gov. uk/civil/ interim/chap25.htm>.

Woolf Lord *Final Report on Access to Civil Justice* (1996) <www.dca.gov.uk/ civil/report>.

Yearbook of European Law (Oxford, Clarendon Press, 2006)

Geimer, R., R. Greger et al., *Zöller, Zivilprozessordnung* (26th edn, Köln, Otto Schmidt, 2007).

Zonlyski, C., *Méthode de transposition des directives communautaires : étude à partir de l'exemple du droit d'auteur et des droits voisins*. Doctoral Thesis in Private Law, Université Panthéon-Assas, Paris,. (Date of thesis defence: 9 December 2005).

Zuckerman, A.A.S., *Civil Procedure* (2nd edn, Lexis Nexis, London, 2003).

Zuckerman, A.A.S., S. Chiarlori & P. Gottwald, *Civil Justice in Crisis: Comparative Perpectives of Civil Procedure* (Oxford, OUP, 1999)

Zuckerman , A.A.S., *Principles of Criminal Evidence* (Oxford University Press, Oxford, 1989).

Selected Websites

Bundesgerichtshof (Germany): <www.bundesgerichtshof.de> for case law of the Federal Court of Justice

Bundesjustizministerium (Germany): <www.bmj.bund.de>

Case law: <www.rechtspraak.nl>: site for Dutch caselaw

Civil Justice Council (UK)<www.civiljusticecouncil.gov.uk>, 1 October 2007

Competition Appeal Tribunal (UK) <www.cattribunal.gov.uk>, 1 October 2007

Court Services – High Court and Court of Appeal Judgments – England <www.courtservice.gov.uk>, 1 October 2007

Deutsches Patent-und Markenamt (Germany): <www.dpma.de>

Department of Constitutional Affairs (UK) <www.dca.gov.uk>, 1 October 2007

Dokumentations- und Informationssystem für Parlamentarische Vorgänge (DIP, Germany): <dip21.bundestag.de>

Electronic Journal of Comparative Law <www.ejcl.com>, 1 October 2007

European Commission <www.eu.int>, 1 October 2007

European Court of Justice <www.curia.europa.eu>, 1 October 2007

House of Commons: Hansard Daily Debates <www.publications.parliament.uk>

House of Lords, Select Committee on European Union <www.publications.parliament.uk>

Intellectual Property Office (UK) <www.ipo.gov.uk>, 1 October 2007

Office of Fair Trading (UK) <www.oft.gov.u> 16 April 2008

Patents County Court (UK) <www.hmcourts-service.gov.uk>, 1 October 2007

Parliamentary Publications (UK) House of Lords Judgments <www.publications.parliament.uk>, 1 October 2007

Rand Corporation <www.rand.org>, 1 October 2007

World Intellectual Property Organization (WIPO) <www.wipo.int>, 1 April 2008.

Index